Ethical
Practice
in the
Human
Services

We dedicate this book to those who have modeled and given shape to our own sense of "being ethical." To our parents who raised us in households where ethics were lived; to Ginny and John, our patient and supportive partners; and to all those in the helping professions who not only practice ethically but make the concerted effort to "be ethical."

SAGE was founded in 1965 by Sara Miller McCune to support the dissemination of usable knowledge by publishing innovative and high-quality research and teaching content. Today, we publish over 900 journals, including those of more than 400 learned societies, more than 800 new books per year, and a growing range of library products including archives, data, case studies, reports, and video. SAGE remains majority-owned by our founder, and after Sara's lifetime will become owned by a charitable trust that secures our continued independence.

Los Angeles | London | New Delhi | Singapore | Washington DC | Melbourne

Ethical Practice
in the
Human Services

From Knowing to Being

Richard D. Parsons | Karen L. Dickinson

West Chester University of Pennsylvania

Los Angeles | London | New Delhi
Singapore | Washington DC | Melbourne

FOR INFORMATION:

SAGE Publications, Inc.
2455 Teller Road
Thousand Oaks, California 91320
E-mail: order@sagepub.com

SAGE Publications Ltd.
1 Oliver's Yard
55 City Road
London, EC1Y 1SP
United Kingdom

SAGE Publications India Pvt. Ltd.
B 1/I 1 Mohan Cooperative Industrial Area
Mathura Road, New Delhi 110 044
India

SAGE Publications Asia-Pacific Pte. Ltd.
3 Church Street
#10–04 Samsung Hub
Singapore 049483

Acquisitions Editor: Nathan Davidson
Editorial Assistant: Heidi Dreiling
Development Editor: Abbie Rickard
eLearning Editor: Gabrielle Piccininni
Production Editor: Bennie Clark Allen
Copy Editor: Karin Rathert
Typesetter: Hurix Systems Pvt. Ltd.
Proofreader: Ellen Brink
Indexer: Wendy Allex
Cover Designer: Michelle Kenny
Marketing Manager: Shari Countryman

Printed in the United States of America

Library of Congress Cataloging-in-Publication Data

ISBN: 978-1-5063-3291-8

This book is printed on acid-free paper.

MIX
Paper from
responsible sources
FSC® C014174

16 17 18 19 20 10 9 8 7 6 5 4 3 2 1

BRIEF CONTENTS

DETAILED CONTENTS

PREFACE

For those working in the helping profession, the power of the helping relationship and the helping dynamic, be it as a counselor, psychotherapist, social worker or consultant, is more than evident. Equally evident is the fact that engaging in a helping relationship as a professional carries a very powerful and awesome set of responsibilities. Sadly, by omission or commission, not all those serving as professional helpers respect the power of the helping dynamic and as a result, fail to protect the welfare of their clients.

As helpers, we are given the responsibility to care for individuals who, by definition of needing help, are often those who are most vulnerable to manipulation. And while premeditated and blatant abuses of client welfare are the exception within human services, they do occur and demonstrate the power of the helping relationship, even when the "helper" chooses to do harm. Equally deleterious to client welfare are those instances when ignorance of ethical standards and codes of conduct mitigate client help or cause harm. In these situations, helpers may appear to be acting on behalf of the client, but their ignorance of or their failure to embody the established codes of conduct and standards of practice impeded the progress of both client and profession.

STANDARDS OF PRACTICE ●

Professional help-givers need standards of practice and guidelines for making the many complex ethical decisions encountered in the practice and performance of their duties. The recognition of the need for education in standards and codes of ethics is commonplace across the human services profession. To this end, numerous texts have been created to describe, explain, and illustrate the specific ethical principles guiding the practice of various human service providers.

This book, while addressing ethical issues and principles in human service professions, including social work, counseling, psychology, and marriage and family therapy, moves beyond mere explanation and illustration to highlighting the underlying moral principles and values that serve as foundation for these codes and attempts to facilitate the reader's ownership of these principles and the resulting specific ethical codes.

● TO BE ETHICAL

This is not the first text to discuss the unique challenges and needs for ethical professional practice. As with many of the other texts, this books cites the latest ethical standards as explicated by professional organizations such as the American Counseling Association (ACA), the American Association for Marriage and Family Therapy (AAMFT), the American Psychological Association (APA), the American School Counselor's Association (ASCA), the International Association for Group Psychotherapy and Group Processes (IAGP), and the National Association of Social Workers (NASW) (Appendix A). Throughout the book, the principles advanced by these organizations are defined and illustrated with fictional case illustrations. Knowing one's professional codes of ethics is essential. However, knowledge alone is insufficient.

There is abundant evidence, both research and anecdotal, that illustrates that while the understanding of the codes of conduct is core to professional training, understanding/comprehension alone is insufficient to guarantee these principles will be lived out in practice. Frequency of ethical violation highlights the fact that knowledge sometimes fails to take form in actual practice decisions. It is this gap between "knowing" and "doing" or, if you will, between understanding the ethics of one's profession and "being" the embodiment of those ethics that serves as the raison d'etre for this text. The unique and primary focus of the text is in helping the reader go beyond comprehending their profession's codes of ethics to assimilating, owning, and personally valuing these standards of ethical practice. The text, while providing a review of the ethical principles which frame practice, is focused less on knowing ethics . . . and more on being ethical.

● TEXT FORMAT AND CHAPTER STRUCTURE

Research suggests that procedural knowledge is acquired as the result of practice accompanied by feedback. Practice and feedback will be central to this text. Case illustrations and directed practice activities will be employed as teaching tools throughout the text. Each chapter, with the exception of the preface, will provide a blending of theory, practice, and guided personalized application. The chapters will include the following:

- A listing of chapter objectives
- Explanation of the constructs presented with the chapter, along with the supportive research
- Explanation of specific, core elements of one's professional code of ethics
- Case illustrations demonstrating the constructs/concepts presented within the chapter
- Guided practice exercises, in order for the readers to "experience" the constructs and concepts under discussion
- A concluding case illustration
- A cooperative learning exercise
- A list of web-based and literature-based resources of additional material

As a teaching tool, the text not only highlights the cognitive domain facilitating the readers comprehension of the what and why of their profession's code of ethics but also the affective domain as well. Throughout the text, guided exercises are provided and designed to engage the reader's awareness of their own valuing processes. The purpose of the exercises is twofold. First, it is hoped that the exercise will help to clarify the points under discussion. Second and more importantly, it is hoped that the exercises will help the reader personalize the materials presented and assimilate values, which are in line with professional ethics, into his or her practice.

CHAPTER OVERVIEW ●

As noted above, the focus of each chapter is on helping the reader not only **understand** the what and why of each component of one's professional code of conduct but more importantly to see and **own the value** of adhering to the ethical principle at a personal and professional level. The resounding theme is the calling to "BE" ethical, and LIVE one's ethics . . . not merely employing them as a professional duty.

Each chapter will include extensive case illustrations along with guided exercises to assist the reader to move from comprehension to application and valuing.

● A FINAL THOUGHT

This book, like most other texts, can be an impersonal compendium of information. Hopefully, the case illustrations and the exercises will help to make it less impersonal. The real key, however, is you, the reader. As you read this book, make the material personal. Invest yourself in the exercises: The more of you placed into your reading, the more the material will be able to stimulate your growth as an ethical helper.

This preface ends with a reminder that ethics is not simply a thing to be memorized. The principles, and standards of ethical practice go beyond a demand for comprehension and a demonstration of that comprehension by performance on a pencil and paper test. Ethical principles in and of themselves are valueless. It is in the embodiment of those principles in **being ethical** that life is given to these principles and our desires to be effective human service providers can be fulfilled.

Richard D. Parsons
Karen L. Dickinson

Calling All Instructors!

SAGE's password-protected companion website includes the following text-specific instructor resources:

- Test banks provide a diverse range of pre-written options as well as the opportunity to edit any question and/or insert personalized questions to effectively assess students' progress and understanding.
- Editable, chapter-specific PowerPoint® slides offer complete flexibility for creating a multimedia presentation for the course.

Please sign in at **http://study.sagepub.com/parsonsethics.**

ACKNOWLEDGMENTS

As with any text, while the names on the cover identify the authors, the credit for the book's creation extends well beyond those so identified. From those whose research is cited within to the many who have helped take our ideas and help craft them into the words you are about to read, we truly are appreciative.

We particularly would like to acknowledge the encouragement and direction provided by those who reviewed the materials in their initial stages. Special thanks go out to Gary Schilmoeller, University of Maine; Keith M. Wismar, Dillard University; and Marie K. (Mickey) Crothers, University of Wisconsin-Eau Claire. Their candid feedback made this text better than it would have been without their insights.

We would like to acknowledge the support and guidance provided by the wonderful people at SAGE. To our friend and one time editor at SAGE Publishing, Kassie Graves, your vision has been inspiring and we thank you. To Abbie Rickard, Carrie Montoya, Bennie Clark Allen, and Karin Rathert, your professional expertise and guidance has provided the scaffolding we needed to produce this work.

Additionally, we thank Emily DeVivo, our graduate assistant who helped us with hours of updating codes. Finally and most heartfelt, we would like to acknowledge the tireless assistance provided by our graduate assistant Jennifer Toby. Her competence in checking our research, investigating resources, and simply keeping us gently on task was key to the creation of this final product. Thank you, Jen, we'll miss you.

SAGE Publishing gratefully acknowledges the following reviewers:

Judith Beechler, *Midwestern State University*

Ellen Behrens, *Westminster College*

Steven Berman, *University of Central Florida*

Kananur Chandras, *Fort Valley State University*

Kathleen Curran, *NHTI-Concord's Community College*

Steven Farmer, *Northern Arizona University*

Perry Francis, *Eastern Michigan University*

Charles Kelly, *Northwestern Connecticut Community College*

Julie Koch, *Oklahoma State University*

Candace McLain, *Tait Colorado Christian University*

Emeka Nwadiora, *Temple University*

Lisa Ray, *University of Central Arkansas*

Sharon Sisti, *Hilbert College*

Anna Viviani, *Indiana State University*

Ginger Welch, *Oklahoma State University*

Christine Wilkey, *Saint Mary-of-the-Woods College*

Shannon Wolf, *Dallas Baptist University*

Kathleen Woods, *Chadron State College*

ABOUT THE AUTHORS

Richard D. Parsons, PhD, is a full professor in the Counselor Education Department at West Chester University. Dr. Parsons has over 40 years of university teaching experience in counselor preparation programs. Prior to his university teaching, Dr. Parsons spent nine years as a school counselor in an inner city high school. Dr. Parsons has had a private clinical practice for over 30 years and serves as a consultant to educational institutions and mental health service organizations throughout the tri-state area of Pennsylvania, New Jersey, and Delaware, and he has been the recipient of many awards and honors, including the Pennsylvania Counselor of the Year award.

Dr. Parsons has authored or coauthored over 80 professional articles and books. His most recent books include the series of four training texts for school counselors *Transforming Theory Into Practice* (Corwin Press); and individual texts including *Becoming a Skilled Counselor, Field Experience and Counseling Theory* (Sage), and *Counseling Strategies That Work! Evidenced-Based for School Counselors* (Allyn & Bacon*)*.

Karen L. Dickinson, PhD, is an associate professor in the Counselor Education Department at West Chester University of Pennsylvania and coordinator of the School Counseling Certification program. Dr. Dickinson has over 10 years of experience teaching at the university level in counseling preparation programs. Dr. Dickinson spent over three decades in the K–12 educational system, supporting students as a general education and special education teacher and school counselor. In addition to her numerous state, regional, and national presentations, and articles addressing the needs of college students with disabilities, she is a contributing author for the text: *Working with Students with Disabilities: Preparing School Counselors* (Sage).

PART I

Helping: The Role and Influence of the Helper

CHAPTER 1

Ethics: Core to Professional Helping

Maria: Hi. Are you Ms. Wicks? I'm Maria. Mr. Brady told me that I had to come talk with you.

The opening exchange between Maria and Ms. Wicks, while on the surface appearing quite typical of many exchanged within a school social counselor's office, belies the fact that the relationship that will unfold and the dynamics of their exchanges will be challenging and fraught with ethical challenge.

While the process of helping can appear so natural and most of the time relatively easy, when viewed from the perspective of those in the human service professions, it is in truth complex and filled with challenges for both the helper and the client. Those within the human service professions understand that helping another person cope with a problem or facilitating that person's movement toward a specific outcome is a very responsible process. It is a process that is done with intention and reflection and demands training and professional competence. It is also true that this helping process is not and cannot be formulaic. One cannot simply follow a step-by-step recipe in progressing toward the desired goals.

Within any helping encounter, the professional helper is called upon to make numerous decisions, decisions that call to question his or her own personal values as well as his or her professional codes of conduct and ethics.

The unique role and influence of the helper within the developing ethical helping relationship is the focus of the current chapter.

● OBJECTIVES

The chapter will present the role that the helper's beliefs, values, and ethics play in shaping the decision-making that occurs within the helping dynamic. After reading this chapter, you should be able to do the following:

- Define helping as a dynamic process, reflecting both an artistry and a science.
- Describe the unique ethical responsibilities and roles of the professional helper within a helping relationship.
- Identify the salient characteristics of the effective helper and the degree to which you currently possess these characteristics.
- Identify the reciprocal roles and responsibilities of both the client and the helper in an ethical helping relationship.

● THE HELPING PROCESS: A BLENDING OF ART AND SCIENCE

The effective helper understands and appreciates the fact that helping is not simply the sterile application of techniques or procedures. While a helper's understanding of what to do may be grounded in theory and research, the when and how to do it require a sensitivity that extends well beyond theoretical knowledge and technical efficiency. Consider the many options and decision points afforded the helper working with Kim and the way that the helper's personal and professional ethics can influence the choices made and the direction taken (See Case Illustration 1.1).

Case Illustration 1.1

Kim

Kim is a college freshman. During her first week of school, she came to speak to a counselor in the University Counseling Center. On entering the office, she stated that she had a "minor issue" and then continued with, "I know school has just started, and I am just a naive little helpless

---

freshman, but, I (looks down to the floor), well, I . . . (voice becomes soft and quiet) have a kind of . . . well a . . . I guess you could call it a small, but not real small problem, with my roommate. Look, I don't want to seem like a complainer, I'm not . . . am I? But (fidgeting a little), geez, this is kind of embarrassing to talk about, I mean you're a guy (giggles), of course you know that, but . . . oh, HELL, I'm just gonna say it. I think my roommate . . . is . . . well, she, let's say is nothing like me. No, what I mean to say is . . . I really like guys (smiles flirtatiously) even though I haven't had a chance to meet anyone here, except the freshman boys, but anyway . . . I don't think she does, if you know what I mean. Well anyway, you get the idea. Don't you? I just need another room!"

In reviewing Kim's complaint, did you feel that the roommate was the problem, or was something else on Kim's mind? Was there a problem? While Kim was verbally expressive, what did you notice about her behavior? Her style of communicating? Should the counselor have stopped Kim and asked a question at any point? Should the counselor have confronted Kim? How might Kim's style of sharing or even the type of issues and values she is expressing interact with the counselor's values? So many questions, all without simple, clear answers—questions that target not only the steps to be taken by the counselor but also the underlying values, beliefs, and ethics guiding those steps.

As previously suggested, helping is a process for which there is no one tried and true sequence of steps to be applied. Helping is not an automatic, cold, and distant process of problem solving. It is truly an awesome encounter, one engaging clients' and helpers' feelings and values as well as their minds. The complexity and dynamic nature of the helping process is infused with subjectivity, intuition, and often confusion, rendering its facilitation as much of an art as a science. It is important to realize that as with any art, the product reflects not only the subject, in this case the client, but also the artist. Each participant mobilizes his or her values, beliefs, needs, and even dreams to make the very best of an increasingly intimate relationship.

As a contributor to this product and process, what might the counselor depicted in Case Illustration 1.1 have contributed to the dynamic with Kim? What did the counselor feel? What needs and concerns did the counselor bring to this interaction? What feelings, thoughts, and behaviors were stimulated or elicited by Kim? The uniqueness of the helper tints the process and outcome of the helping relationship. Two different counselors working with Kim may have attended to different pieces of her story or her style and may have moved toward different outcomes or the same outcome through different paths. Exercise 1.1 provides an opportunity to identify the way the personal uniqueness of each helper can influence the very nature and outcome of the helping encounter.

Exercise 1.1

You as Helper—You as Artist

Directions: Return to Kim's case. As you read the descriptions and review Kim's presentation, try to develop a complete image of the interaction. Imagine you are the counselor. What does Kim look like? Where are you standing? What might you have been doing prior to her coming to see you? What else is on your things to do list? After developing a real sense of the scenario, with you as counselor, respond to the following questions:

- What meaning did you make of all of the varied verbal and nonverbal (e.g., looking down, flirting, etc.) communications?

- How do you interpret the para-linguistic (i.e., intonation in her voice, volume, etc.) messages?

- What elements of her style or her message did you pay attention to?

- How did you "feel" about Kim?

- What did you want to do?

- What are your feelings about the possibility of working with Kim?

Compare your observations and conclusions with a colleague's or classmate's: Did he or she focus on other data? Have other feelings? How might one's focus be influenced by personal values, beliefs, prejudices, or ethics? What role might the "person" of the helper play in defining the nature and direction of this helping relationship?

While the person of the helper will come into play in shaping the process of helping, it is important that as professionals we employ a standard of service, a guide to performance, one that helps to place a governor on the influence that our own personal values and subjectivity can exert within the relationship. That governor is found within each of the human service profession's codes of ethics. It is a governor that moves our helping from personal to professional.

THE HELPING PROCESS: ●
THE MEETING OF CLIENT AND HELPER

Albeit a very unique and special relationship, the helping relationship is *first and foremost* exactly that, a relationship. It is important to note that too often in our eagerness to be of assistance, we rush in with our answers, our directions, and our solutions, trying desperately to do something to "solve the problem." We must remember that helping is a process that not only assists clients in their goal attainment but also positions them to be better able to cope in the future. It is a process that is *realized* in the context of a helping relationship (Parsons & Zhang, 2014). The quality of the relationship is therefore the keystone to the helping process and thus needs to be of primary concern to all seeking to develop their helping skills.

Helping: A Special Kind of Interpersonal Process and Response

Social encounters and social relationships are not unfamiliar. The normal chitchat nature of these encounters is more or less familiar and comfortable for all of us. The helping relationship, however, is quite different from these typical social encounters. It is a relationship with singular focus on the needs of the client and one in which the role and functioning of the helper is guided by professional standards and ethics of service rather than personal wants or needs.

Helping is a process by which one person, the helper, interacts with another in a way to facilitate this other's (the client's) involvement and movement toward specific outcomes. Unlike most social exchanges, *primacy is given to one member,* the client. It is the client's needs, concerns, and goals that are the focus of the encounter. It is the client's welfare that is the focus of the relationship and the driving force behind the ethical helper's decision-making. Consider the exchange provided in Case Illustration 1.2.

Like other social encounters, this one is marked by verbal exchanges and sharing of information. While it is certainly an interaction, it differs from the more typical social exchange, not just in the content of the interaction but also in the fundamental nature of that content. In this and all helping exchanges, the nature and substance is the matter of the client. As with other social encounters, there is a goal implied, but this again reflects the need and current

---

Case Illustration 1.2

Telephone Crisis Worker

Crisis: Intervention Worker: Yes, ma'am. I can hear that you are very upset.

I know it seems scary. Yes, ma'am, I am here, I am listening. Could you describe what is happening?

Client: (Voice on the Phone Screaming): My baby is turning blue . . . oh, my God . . . my baby . . . my baby!

Helper: (Interrupting): Ma'am! Ma'am!

Client: (Trying to Catch her Breath): Yes?

Helper: It is important for you to try to focus on what I am telling you. Can you hear me?

Client: Yes . . . but my . . .

Helper: (Interrupting): I know it's hard for you to keep listening to my voice, but you must try. Roll your baby over on her stomach, place your left hand under her belly, and lift her stomach off the floor. Now with your right hand give her a gentle yet firm slap in the middle of the back, between her shoulder blades. Go ahead, you do that and tell me what's happening. I can hear you.

(The helper continues talking as she listens to the mother.) Good . . . I can hear the baby now, the baby is crying, that's good. Open the baby's mouth, put your finger in, and clear out anything that may be inside her mouth.

Great . . . her cries are clear and strong.

Client: (Sobbing): She . . . she is looking better; she coughed up a plastic grape.

Thank you, thank you . . . you saved her life.

---

state of the client, not the helper, and emphasizes the utilization of the client's resources and movement toward a specific outcome (Parsons & Zhang, 2014). While the helper in this situation may have been about to take a coffee break or may have felt anxious and wished she could have simply handed the phone to another, it was not her needs that were central to this encounter.

As a result of this "focus on one," the purpose and outcome of the interaction reflect the needs and goals of that one, and these are specified and terminal. Unlike other social encounters that may be open-ended, with both parties remaining engaged as long as their individual needs are being met, the helping relationship is designed to achieve some specific goal, in service of the client, and then terminate with the achievement of that goal. Once the goal is attained, the need for the helping relationship no longer exists. This outcome-specific and terminal nature of helping cannot be forgotten. Nor can the helper forget that it is the needs, concerns, and goals of the client which are primary to the shaping and development of the helping relationship and not their own. This point is highlighted across our various codes of ethics (see Table 1.1).

Table 1.1   Ethical Principles Promoting the Welfare of the Client(s)

Professional Organization	Ethical Principle
American Counseling Association (2014)	A.1. Client welfare a. Primary responsibility. The primary responsibility of counselors is to respect the dignity and to promote the welfare of clients.
American Psychological Association (2010)	Principle E. Respect for people's rights and dignity Psychologists respect the dignity and worth of all people, and the rights of individuals to privacy, confidentiality, and self-determination.
National Association of Social Workers (2008)	1.01. Commitment to clients Social workers' primary responsibility is to promote the well being of clients. In general, clients' interests are primary.
American Association for Marriage and Family Therapy (2015)	1. Responsibility to clients Marriage and family therapists advance the welfare of families and individuals.
American School Counselor Association (2010)	A.1. Responsibility to students School counselors (a) have a primary obligation to the students, who are to be treated with dignity and respect as unique individuals. B.1. Responsibilities to parents/guardians School counselors (b) respect the rights and responsibilities of custodial and noncustodial parents/guardians and, as appropriate, establish a collaborative relationship with parents/guardians to facilitate students' maximum development.

When the needs, wants, and concerns of the helper take center stage at the expense of the client, we have the potential for unethical behavior and a less than helping exchange. Exercise 1.2 should help to clarify this important distinction between a helping encounter and other social interactions.

Exercise 1.2

Helping as a Unique Social Encounter

Directions: Complete the exercise and then share your responses with a colleague or classmate to see how individual differences can impact the responses and the potential for the helping process.

Part I: Below you will find three different types of social encounters in which you may be currently engaged or may be seeking to develop. Select one of these encounters and write your responses to the questions that follow.

Relationships:

- A relationship with a person to whom you are attracted

- A relationship with a person of authority who evaluates your performance (e.g., professor, supervisor, boss, etc.)

- An encounter with a possible employer.

Questions:

- What is your primary goal for this encounter? What would you like to achieve or gain through this relationship?

- Assuming that your goal is achieved, what need(s) within you would be met?

- How might your need and your desire to achieve this specific goal impact your style of interacting? What would you share or not share? How would you share it? How would you behave? As you interact with this other person, what thoughts and concerns might you experience?

Using your written responses regarding your goal, needs, and interactional style, how might these factors affect the nature of a helping relationship should you, the helper, bring them to this exchange? Why is it important for you to reflect on these factors now and as you grow professionally?

THE ROLE OF THE CLIENT IN THE PROCESS OF CHANGE ●

On a surface level, the roles and functions of the participants in this formal helping process are clear. The client brings concerns to a trained helper and expects the helper to help formulate appropriate goals and to employ effective strategies that will realize those goals. What could be simpler? But helping, as noted, is a relationship in which the unique roles and responsibilities of the participants are not always simple or clear.

Some helpers, in their eagerness to be of assistance, deprive the client of the opportunity to take an active role within the helping process. These helpers often relegate the clients to the role of a "victimized party" in need of the helper's assistance and thus place the brunt of the responsibility of the process of change on the helper's shoulders.

The perspective taken here is that helping is a collaborative process, with both the helper and the client having responsibilities and roles to be played within the process. Such collaboration is evidence of the helpers valuing and respecting the autonomy of the client, a position articulated throughout our various professional codes of ethics (e.g., American Association for Marriage and Family Therapy [AAMFT], American Counseling Association [ACA], American Psychological Association [APA], American School Counselor Association [ASCA], National Association of Social Workers [NASW]).

While there is a unique role to be played by the helper, the client also has both a role and responsibility within the relationship. For example, clients can be expected to not only set and keep appointments and pay fees agreed upon but also to help plan goals, follow through with agreed upon goals, and keep the helper informed about progress toward those goals. And it is the ethical responsibility of the helper to assist the client to understand and enact his or her role.

Freedom and Responsibility to Choose Wisely

If we revisit the client-helper exchange that opened this chapter, we might question both the "freedom" and the "choice" afforded Maria, the client. It is clear, at least from her initial presentation, that her perspective was that she *"had to come to talk with"* Ms. Wicks.

While absolute freedom may not be afforded clients under certain conditions (such as those who are involuntarily committed), even these clients have the freedom and responsibility to choose wisely within the more narrowed range of choice provided (see Chapter 8). Through open communication with the helper, the client will develop a realistic expectation about treatment and treatment outcome. With this knowledge, the client can decide if and to what degree he or she wants to be engaged in this helping relationship. Even Maria has the freedom to choose to come, to stay, or to even talk. The helper, Ms. Wicks, can assist Maria to understand these options, along with the possible consequence for each. It is then Maria's role, as client, to decide what she wants from the helping process and what she is willing to do to achieve this goal.

Assume Control of Their Participation in the Helping Process

Helping is not something one does to another; it is a process that one does with another. Helping works best when clients enter into the process voluntarily and assume some control over it. Even when a client is required, forced, or coerced to come for help, progress will be facilitated by assisting the client to affirm the relevance of the helping and to develop a willingness to participate in the process. This is true even if the only control clients wish to exert is to terminate the relationship, which is their right. As noted by one organization's code of ethics, counselors respect the right of the client to even "refuse service" (ACA, 2014, A.2.e).

It is incumbent on the ethical helper to assist the client to see the potential benefit of this helping relationship while affirming his or her right to assume control over his or her participation. Case Illustration 1.3 reveals how a helper who believes that the client has the right and responsibility to assume control can facilitate the development of a helping relationship in which control and direction is shared.

Case Illustration 1.3

Maria Assumes Control

The following exchange occurred shortly after Ms. Wicks greeted Maria and invited her to take a seat.

Maria: I don't want to be here, I didn't do anything.

Ms. Wicks: You sound like you don't want to be here, but you are. Would you like to return to class?

Maria: No way! He is a jerk!

Ms. Wicks: Well, we have 20 minutes before the next change of class. If you would like, maybe you could tell me what happened?

	Maybe in talking about it we could come up with a plan to make it better.
Maria:	I don't like talking.
Ms. Wicks:	Well, you don't have to, and if you would rather, you could spend the rest of the period in the career center or reviewing college brochures. But you do look and sound upset and I would like to help if I could.
Maria:	Let me just take a minute. Can I get a drink of water? I'll be right back and I'll tell you what happened.

Imagine the impact on this helping relationship and the possibility of providing Maria help if Ms. Wicks, the helper, took a rigid, authoritative stance, stating "Sit down young lady! If Mr. Brady sent you here, you will stay here!"

The specific details over what falls within the realm of control of the client and what belongs to the helper are not predefined. Early in the development of each helping relationship, roles and boundaries need to be established (see Chapter 8). The specifics will vary according to the nature of the problem at hand, the therapeutic approach employed, and the specific orientation and values of the participants.

Make Use of the Information Provided?

It is hoped that the client will assume a role that shows both an interest in understanding the nature of the current situation and a desire to develop either a different coping style or a different life position. It is, however, a role that they have a right not to embrace. A helper may make recommendations and suggestions that if accepted by the client may facilitate the achievement of his or her goal. The client, however, is under no obligation to follow the specific recommendations or suggestions of the helper. The client can and will decide how he or she will employ the information provided.

The fact that a client can decide to use or not use the advice, the information, or the insight gained by working with a helper may appear obvious. Yet it is not unusual for a helper who has extended himself or herself to a client to feel disappointed, perhaps even angry, at a client who appears to be less than compliant. This point may become a bit clearer after completing Exercise 1.3.

Exercise 1.3

A Client Chooses to Reject Help

Directions: The following is a brief exchange between Alice (the client) and Tim (the social worker). Tim has been working with Alice in a program geared to help single mothers find employment. This is the sixth time they have met.

As you read the vignette, try to place yourself in the shoes of the helper. After reading the case illustration, respond to the following questions. As with previous exercises, it may prove beneficial for you to share your responses with a colleague.

Alice: (the client): Hi. Sorry I'm late, but I got a phone call from an old friend just as I was going out the door.

Tim: (the helper): Well, Alice, we have approximately 20 minutes left in your appointment. How about we use the remainder of the session to discuss how well you did with your telephone calls?

Alice: I know I agreed to attempt to call at least three jobs for possible interviews, but this was a busy week. Plus I had a friend in town and we wanted to hang out a little. So I just kinda figured we could do it another time.

Tim: Okay, but in addition to making the calls, you also agreed to complete the interest inventory I gave you. Maybe we could review your profile. Do you have that?

Alice: Oh, the inventory . . . you know what, I remember you giving it to me, but I think I must have misplaced it or something. Do you have another one? I could try to complete it for next time.

Tim: Alice, I am a bit confused. We have been meeting for six weeks, and even though you stated that you really want to work on identifying a possible career path and to get back to work, you seem to have some difficulty following through on the things we discuss. Each time we have decided on some type of "homework," such as looking at ads from the paper or social network sites, going to speak with a nurse's aide about her experiences in that career, or the interest inventory, you have had difficulty completing the tasks.

Alice: Well, I'm sorry, but a lot of the things you suggest seem dumb. And other things are just not convenient for me to do! So what should I do now?

Now that you have read the scenario, respond to the following questions. You may want to share your ideas with a colleague:

- If you were the helper in this scenario, how might you be feeling about Alice?

- How might your feelings about Alice be manifested in your interchange? How may they impact your desire to work with Alice?

- How would you respond to Alice's comment that "a lot of the things you suggest seem dumb"?

- At this point, how easy is it for you to remember that the client has a right to choose the degree to which he or she will follow your recommendations?

- If the client called and wanted your assistance with another problem, would you be willing to help?

When a helper has invested time, energy, and part of the self into supporting a client, it may be hard for him or her to accept the client freedom to use or not use the help provided. And yet, that is the client's right, and as professional helpers, we need to guard against the loss of our objectivity and the making of our needs as primary, two conditions that can result in our violation of professional boundaries (See Chapters 10 and 14). Respecting the right of the client to choose can place the professional in personal and sometimes legal pressure points and thus is not always easy to enact. This is more dramatically brought home in situations in which the client's choice is to ignore the helper's recommendations and advice results in the client's loss of life (see Case Illustration 1.4).

Case Illustration 1.4

A Client Chooses Death

Roberto is a 67-year-old widower with two adult children. At the age of 60, Roberto was diagnosed with ALS (amyotrophic lateral sclerosis). Over the course of the last year, Roberto has experienced a rapid decline in his health and has become depressed. Dr. Sebring, a pastoral

(Continued)

(Continued)

counselor, has been working with Roberto for his depression. Dr. Sebring has been employing a number of cognitive techniques to help Roberto reframe his life condition in such a way as to reestablish meaning, even with his disease. Roberto has been very engaged in his counseling and employed the various techniques and strategies suggested by Dr. Sebring. As a result of his involvement in counseling, Roberto has found relief from his depression.

Roberto's disease has been progressing, and within the last week, he has lost his ability to swallow. Roberto's physician wants to insert a feeding tube, but Roberto has refused this procedure. Dr. Sebring has continued to work with Roberto, encouraging him to embrace life and to follow his physician's recommendation. Roberto, however, is clear and determined that he does not want to be admitted to a hospital, nor does he want to have the feeding tube inserted. Roberto refuses to accept the recommendations of either his physician or Dr. Sebring, knowing full well that his refusal will result in his starvation and death.

While it may be hard for any helper to accept a client's refusal to accept and follow a recommendation designed to maintain life, the fact remains that the decision, even this life and death decision, rests with the client. It is the client who will ultimately decide if and how to use the information and the assistance provided, even when not following such assistance results in his or her death.

● THE ROLE OF THE HELPER IN THE PROCESS OF CHANGE

As noted throughout the previous section, the helping process is clearly a joint venture, with significant roles to be played by both the client and helper. But even with the assumptions about client responsibilities, one cannot forget that the client comes to the helping relationship often confused, anxious, and most certainly vulnerable. Helping is a relationship of power: The helper is entrusted to use that power wisely and ethically (see Chapter 10), with the client's welfare being central. This concern for client welfare serves as the organizing principle behind the various roles assumed and practices employed by those within the human service professions. Most standards (see Table 1.1.) include statements such as that presented by the ACA, "The primary responsibility of counselors is to respect the dignity and promote the welfare of clients" (ACA, 2014, Principle A.1.a).

Although the specific way this obligation and role of the helper is manifested will be influenced by the theoretical approach, the nature of the problem, the unique characteristics of the client, and the context within which the help is provided, there are a number of responsibilities that universally fall to the helper in a helping relationship. Helpers are generally responsible for the following: (a) defining and maintaining a helping relationship; (b) facilitating a helping alliance; and (c) facilitating the client's movement toward some specific outcome.

Defining and Maintaining a Helping Relationship

The helping relationship is oftentimes very intense and almost always intimate. Clients are invited to disclose the very personal details of their lives and their situations. A helping relationship is characterized by a power differential that leaves the client vulnerable to the helper's actions. Therefore, it is the helper who has the ethical responsibility for the nature and direction of the relationship (Parsons & Zhang, 2014). The helper is ethically responsible for creating and maintaining the boundaries that keep the client safe during these vulnerable times (see Chapter 8) and competently providing service that has a reasonable chance of assisting the client (see Chapter 11).

Unlike other relationships in which the goal is to respond to and care for each other's needs, in helping it is the helper's responsibility to address the client's needs and NOT the other way around. The helper is responsible for defining and maintaining some control over the types of information being discussed and the nature of the relationship as appropriate to the client. Relationships in which the helper is using the interaction with the client to meet his or her own needs threaten this principle of professional contact. Returning, for example, to the *ACA Code of Ethics* (ACA, 2014), we see the mandates to not only avoid sexual and romantic relationships (ACA, 2014, A.5.a) but to also be aware to be cautious anytime extending the boundaries outside of the confines of the professional interaction (ACA, 2014, A.6.b) "to ensure that judgment is not impaired and no harm occurs." Consider the following case illustration (Case Illustration 1.5) as it elucidates this point.

Case Illustration 1.5 highlights the danger when the helper's needs take center stage at the cost of the client. For a human service provider to maintain focus on the client and client welfare, they must be aware of their own unmet needs and the possibility that these may impact their objectivity and ability to provide ethical, effective service. This issue is further developed in the upcoming chapters, especially Chapter 10 (Boundaries and the Ethical Use of Power) and Chapter 14 (Competence and the Ethics of Self-Care).

Case Illustration 1.5

A Helper Who Needs to Be Needed

Aneesha is a school counselor in a public middle school. She has been working for the past month with Leonard, a seventh-grade student. His homeroom teacher referred him to the school counselor. The teacher expressed her concern that Leonard was very shy and somewhat vulnerable to being manipulated by his peers. The teacher thought that Leonard could use some assertiveness training.

Aneesha has recently divorced. She has found herself feeling lonely and has tried to compensate by spending more time at work. Aneesha comes early to school and stays late. She has begun to contact students with whom she had previously worked, checking on their status and asking if they would like to come in to talk with her.

In the month Aneesha has worked with Leonard, his homeroom teacher has noted a change in Leonard. He appears more verbally expressive, both in class and with peers. Further, Leonard has made it very clear to his teacher that he would like to discontinue counseling. Leonard explained to his teacher that he had asked Aneesha if he could stop coming for a while, and she said that it wasn't time yet. Leonard asked if the teacher would talk to the counselor.

The teacher shared her observations with the counselor along with Leonard's request. However, the counselor responded in no uncertain terms that she was the professional and "knew when it was right to stop."

However, prior to moving to these later chapters and their in-depth discussion of this issue, we invite you to consider the following exercise (Exercise 1.4), as it raises your own awareness of the potential for such intrusion of personal needs and violations of professional boundaries.

Recognizing the potential negative impact that one's unmet needs and concerns may have on the helping relationship is an essential step, yet not sufficient. In addition to recognizing these unmet needs, the ethical helper needs to be able to maintain his or her professional role and emotional objectivity throughout the helping encounter. One strategy employed by many helpers in establishing and maintaining the helping relationship is to formally define the nature and boundaries of the relationship in terms of a helping contract. Such a contract provides the client with the information necessary for him or her to provide consent for service (see Chapter 8) and can serve as a means for clarifying the nature, limits, responsibilities,

Exercise 1.4

Recognizing a Helper's Unmet Needs

Directions: Along with a classmate or colleague, review the following case description. Then read the descriptions of the five helpers listed below.

The case situation and client description: The client is a 45-year-old mother of four. She came to a marriage counselor, complaining that her husband was insensitive to her needs as a woman and as a person. In her sessions, she described her husband as traditional and somewhat chauvinistic. She stated that while he was a good provider, he was not willing to allow her to go back to school and develop a career of her own. When discussing their sexual relationship, the woman complained that her husband had a low sex drive while she was very sexual and would like to experiment with creative sexual activities.

Five potential therapists:

- A female therapist who divorced her husband, returned to school, and just completed her degree

- A male therapist who comes from a traditional family and who himself has a stay-at-home wife and three children

- A male therapist who is married and is currently having financial difficulties

- A therapist who came from a broken home in which the divorce process was very drawn out and painful

- A therapist who has been without an intimate partner for over two years

Next:

- Identify each helper's possible unmet needs.

- Discuss the ways that the various helper characteristics and potential unmet needs may negatively impact the helping relationship.

and rights of the helping relationship. In developing a contract, the helper encourages the client to specify goals and expectations as well as to affirm the boundaries of the relationship. While there are no hard and fast rules about the elements of a helping contract, items that seem to be essential to the informing nature of contracts have been identified by Bennett, Bryant, VandenBos, & Greenwood (1990) and are presented in Table 1.2.

Even though not all helpers endorse the value of a formal contract, all of our codes of conduct and ethical practice direct us to share information within the capacity of the client to understand that information and do so in language appropriate to the client's level of comprehension (see Chapter 8).

Facilitating the Development of a Helping Alliance

A second responsibility of a helper is to facilitate the development of a working relationship with the client. It is important for the helper to attempt to reduce the client's initial anxiety by providing the facilitative conditions for helping. Creating a warm and workable relationship in an atmosphere of understanding and acceptance is primary to the helping process.

Table 1.2   Elements of a Written Contract

While we are not suggesting the use of a contract as a risk management technique, one should consult local laws that govern contracting, especially in terms of consumer rights. If a contract is employed, the following are some of the elements to be considered for inclusion:

- Name of helper and client

- A preliminary schedule of sessions

- A date when sessions will begin

- A statement of goals

- A description of the model, techniques, and strategies to be used

- A description of potential negative effects of treatment

- A description of alternative techniques that might be employed, along with a willingness to assist the client to find these alternatives

- Fee structure and payment schedule

- Statement regarding fee policy for missed appointments, telephone contacts, and so forth

- A statement regarding the limits of confidentiality

- A statement of "no guarantee" of success and invitation regarding freedom to renegotiate the terms of the contract at any time

- Signatures that identify client understanding and acceptance

Source: Bennett, B. E., Bryant B. K., VandenBos, G. R., & Greenwood, A. (1990). *Professional liability and risk management.* Washington, DC: American Psychological Association. Reprinted with Permission.

Therefore, in addition to increasing our self-awareness of the limiting and potentially negative impact our biases may have on the helping process, it is also clear that we, as helpers, need to develop a number of values and attitudes that assist the client to begin to share his or her story.

The effective, ethical helper will demonstrate qualities of acceptance, warmth, and genuineness (Parsons & Zhang, 2014; Principe, Marci, Glick, & Ablon, 2006). While these conditions may not be sufficient for positive outcomes in every case, it does appear that they are key to the helping alliance and contribute in a facilitative way to the positive outcomes of helping. Just as it may be assumed that ethical helpers are knowledgeable and skilled, they must also be people who can demonstrate these facilitative qualities of acceptance, warmth, and genuineness.

As will be discussed in detail in Chapter 14 (Competence and the Ethics of Self-Care), the demonstration of these qualities can be eroded because of conditions such as burnout and compassion fatigue. The very nature of our work makes us vulnerable to physical, emotional, social, and spiritual exhaustion. As such, it is the ethical responsibility of all human service providers to (a) know the signs of burnout and compassion fatigue, (b) engage in strategies that prevent or reduce the possibility of encountering these conditions, and (c) if needed, take steps to protect themselves and their clients if in the grips of either burnout or compassion fatigue.

Facilitating the Client's Movement Toward Some Specific Outcome

In addition to providing the structure and conditions of a helping relationship, the helper is expected to bring special knowledge and skill to the interaction, which, when applied within the helping process, will assist the client to more effectively cope with the issue at hand. A fundamental principle to which all professional groups subscribe is that a helper must be aware of the limitations of her professional competencies and not exceed those limitations in the delivery of her services.

When operating alone in our offices with no faculty member or supervisor looking over our shoulder, our real desire to help the client before us may seduce us into trying new techniques or approaches or even attempting to help with problems that are beyond our training and our experience. Knowing the limits of our competence; being willing to seek ongoing training, supervision, and consultation; or making a referral to another helper when the situations calls for knowledge and skills outside our competency are all characteristic of an ethical helper, a point that will be discussed in greater detail in the upcoming chapters.

● CONCLUDING CASE ILLUSTRATION

We began the chapter with a brief introduction to Maria, a client seeking the assistance of the school counselor, Ms. Wicks. We will continue to follow the development of the helping encounter between Maria and Ms. Wicks throughout the upcoming chapters.

As you read the expanded case illustration, try to identify the presence of the various concepts and important terms described within the chapter. Further, as you read the case, place yourself in the role of the helper and begin to identify the various concerns and areas of ethical consideration you might experience in that role.

Maria: Hi. Are you Ms. Wicks? I'm Maria. Mr. Brady told me that I had to come talk with you.

Ms. Wicks: Hi. Yes, I am Ms. Wicks (getting up to shake Maria's hand). Why don't you come in and have a seat? (Ms. Wicks makes a mental note about Maria's appearance. Maria, while appearing annoyed, is a very attractive girl. She looks you in the eye as she speaks and appears self-confident. Maria's manner of dress is somewhat seductive. Her skirt is very short and tight and her sweater has a very low neckline.)

Maria: I don't want to be here. I didn't do anything.

Ms. Wicks: You sound like you don't want to be here, but you are here. Would you like to return to class?

Maria: No way! He's a jerk!

Ms. Wicks: You certainly sound angry. Maria, I know you said you don't want to be here, but since you are I would love to hear what happened and see if I could be of some help? We have 20 minutes before the next change of class. If you would like, maybe you could tell me what happened? Maybe in talking about it we could come up with a plan to make it better.

Maria: I don't like talking.

Ms. Wicks: Well you don't have to. It really is your choice. If you prefer you could spend the rest of the period in the career center or reviewing college brochures? But you do look and sound upset and I would like to help if I could.

Maria: Let me just take a minute. Can I get a drink of water? I'll be right back and I'll tell you what happened.

Ms. Wicks: (after Maria comes back): Well, how was that? Better? You know I really do understand it is a bit strange to talk to someone you don't know. But I've been able to meet and talk with a lot of the people here at school, and it has been my experience that sometimes this has been very helpful. You may or may not know, but I am a school counselor, and I have been trained to help people problem solve. Do you have any questions about what I do here or what a school counselor is?

Maria: No, not really. You spoke with one of my friends who was having problems with his mom and dad. Did you see Jose Ramirez?

Ms. Wicks: You know Maria, one of the things I think is very important when I work with people is that I respect their privacy. In fact, when you and I talk about some things, I will keep them in confidence. I mean, I won't tell anyone about what we talk about without your permission. Now there are some exceptions to that, like if you tell me you are going to hurt yourself or try to hurt someone else, then I can't keep that secret. Your life is too important to me, so I would want to get as many people as possible to help me keep you safe.

Maria: Yeah, I know about confidentiality. I've gone to a shrink before.

Ms. Wicks: Since we have a few more minutes, maybe we could talk about getting together later today so that you could tell me what happened, and maybe together we could decide if you and I could work on it? What do you think?

Maria: Yeah, that's cool. I have a report to give in my next class, but then I have study hall after that. Could I come back then?

Ms. Wicks: (looking at her calendar): Yes, I'm free. That's my lunchtime. How about if we share a sandwich here in the office and get to know each other a bit better?

Maria: Okay.

Ms. Wicks: (reaching in her desk): Here is a pass. So I'll see you at 12:15. There's the bell. Get back to your class, and give a great report! See you in a bit!

Reflections

1. Did you see any evidence of the creation of boundaries to this relationship?
2. Did Maria enact the role and responsibilities of a client, which were discussed within the chapter?

3. If you were the helper in this situation, how might Maria's appearance, style, or story impact your objectivity or ability to be an effective, ethical helper?

4. What do you think Ms. Wicks needs to consider as she prepares to continue to enact her role as an ethical helper, meeting with Maria at 12:15?

● COOPERATIVE LEARNING EXERCISE

The purpose of this chapter was not only to introduce you to the nature of the helping process, the roles to be played by both the client and the helper, and the unique ethical challenges to be confronted within this role of helper but also to have the you think about your own self in the role of helping. Being in touch with what you bring to the helping encounter is an essential first step to becoming an ethical and effective helper. Therefore, before proceeding to the next chapter, reflect on the following and discuss your reflections with a supervisor, colleague, or classmate.

- Review your responses to this chapter's exercises. Were you honest? Did you invest energy in responding? If not, why not? What might this suggest about your investment in becoming an effective, ethical helper?
- What did you learn about yourself as a helper? What specific elements of helping as presented within this chapter excite you or concern you?
- Which particular characteristics of the effective, ethical helper do you feel you possess most strongly, and which do you feel you need to focus on developing?
- How might you approach the reading, the exercises, and the reflections in the next chapter to maximize your development as a more self-aware, ethical helper?

● SUMMARY

- The complexity and dynamic nature of the helping process is infused with subjectivity, intuition, and confusion, rendering its facilitation as much an art as a science.
- While a foundation of theory and research serves as the base for effective helping, the dynamic process is highly influenced by the personal application and artistry of the helper as he or she adapts technology and research findings to the unique characteristics of individual clients.

- Unlike other social encounters, helping is a process that places focus, emphasis, and value on the needs of one member, the client.
- The role of the helper is first and foremost to attend to the welfare of the client.
- It is important for the ethical helper to inform the client of the nature and limits of the helping relationship.
- It is essential that the ethical helper be aware of and take steps to assure that his personal needs do not intrude and affect the helping dynamic.
- For a human service provider to maintain focus on the client and client welfare, they must be aware of their own unmet needs and the possibility that these may impact their objectivity and ability to provide ethical, effective service.

IMPORTANT TERMS ●

boundaries

burnout

compassion fatigue

competence

defining and maintaining a
   helping relationship

emotional objectivity

promoting the welfare of the
   client

right to refuse

unmet needs

ADDITIONAL RESOURCES ●

Print

Fairbum, C. G., & Cooper, Z. (2011). Therapist competence, therapy quality, and therapist training. *Behavior Research and Therapy, 49*(6–7), 373–378. Retrieved from http://www.ncbi.nlm.nih.gov/pmc/articles/PMC3112491/

Landy, N. (2010). *Counselor Supervision*. New York: Routledge.

Parsons, R. D., & Zhang, N. (2014). *Becoming a Skilled Counselor*. Thousand Oaks, CA: Sage.

Web-Based

ACA's Taskforce on Counselor Wellness and Impairment. www.counseling.org/wellness_taskforce/index.tm

Williams, R. (2011). The importance of self-care. ASCA School Counselor. Retrieved from https://www.schoolcounselor.org/magazine/blogs/january-february-2011/the-importance-of-self-care

● REFERENCES

American Association for Marriage and Family Therapy. (2015). *Code of ethics.* Retrieved from http://www.aamft.org/iMIS15/AAMFT/Content/Legal_Ethics/Code_of_Ethics.aspx

American Counseling Association. (2014). *Code of ethics.* Retrieved from http://www.counseling.org/resources/aca-code-of-ethics.pdf

American Psychological Association. (2010). *Ethical principles of psychologists and code of conduct.* Retrieved from http://www.apa.org/ethics/code/index.aspx

American School Counselor Association. (2016). *ASCA ethical standards for school counselors.* Retrieved from https://www.schoolcounselor.org/school-counselors-members/legal-ethical

Bennett, B. E., Bryant B. K., VandenBos, G. R., & Greenwood, A. (1990). *Professional liability and risk management.* Washington, DC: American Psychological Association.

National Association of Social Workers. (2008). *Code of ethics.* Retrieved from http://socialworkers.org/pubs/code/default.asp

Parsons, R. D., & Zhang, N. (2014). *Becoming a skilled counselor.* Thousand Oaks, CA: Sage.

Principe, J. M., Marci, C. D., Glick, D. M., & Ablon, J. S. (2006). The relationship among patient contemplation, early alliance and continuation in psychotherapy. *Psychotherapy: Theory, Research, Practice, Training, 43,* 238–242.

CHAPTER 2

Helper Variables:
What the Helper Brings to
the Helping Relationship

Ms. Wicks: Maria, let me see if I understand what you are saying. You are sexually active and you don't care that you are engaged in unprotected sex. The possibility of becoming pregnant or contracting a sexually transmitted disease, even AIDS, doesn't concern you. Is that what you are saying?

Ms. Wicks, the counselor in our sample case, appears to be actively listening and accurately reflecting Maria's explicit message. However, one must wonder about the manner in which she reflects that message. As a trained professional, Ms. Wicks is most likely attempting to remain objective as she continues her work with her client, Maria. But objectivity does not mean emotionally detached or without one's own values and beliefs.

Ms. Wicks has feelings, expectations, biases, and values regarding adolescents engaging in unprotected sex, and while she is attempting to maintain a professional objectivity, to assume she can remain value free is naive at best and when viewed from the perspective of professional ethics, can be dangerous. Does Ms. Wicks's tone of voice, inflection, or even body language reveal her own biases and beliefs regarding unprotected adolescent sexual behavior?

The complexity of a helping process as a problem-solving venture, along with the potential for intense emotional reactions to be experienced by all involved, makes the helping process highly vulnerable to the influence of the needs, interests, beliefs, and expectations of both helper and client. We enter a helping relationship as we enter all relationships, full of personal expectations, biases, and values. Further, as with any of our encounters, these expectations, biases, and values cannot help but influence the nature of our exchange and the fundamental dynamic of the helping relationship, often in profound ways.

As suggested in Chapter 1, the ethical helper needs to be aware of her or his values, biases, and expectations, along with circumstances wherein these personal values, biases, and expectations may interfere with the effective helping of another. It is these affective and subjective factors that the helper brings to the relationship, along with the ethical challenges that can result, that serve as the focal point for the current chapter.

● OBJECTIVES

Extending the discussion started in Chapter 1, which illustrated the role of the helper in the process of change, the current chapter will discuss the role that a helper's values, biases, and professional models and orientation play in giving shape to the helping process and this process of change. After reading this chapter, you should be able to do the following:

- Explain the need for helpers to increase self-awareness of personal values, beliefs, and expectations.
- Describe the ethical steps to be taken when helper-client values conflict.
- Discuss the value of a helper having a theoretical model along with the ethical challenges that can arise if such a model is "imposed" without awareness of "best practice" procedures.
- Define what is meant by "helper competence."

● HELPER VALUES

As human service providers, we are directed to care for those within our charge or, as noted by one organization, the American Counseling Association (ACA), our primary responsibility is "to respect the dignity and promote the welfare of clients" (2014, Principle A.1.a). This directive to promote the welfare of the client leads us to attend to the client's needs, values, and desires as these give shape to the goals of the helping encounter and the nature of each helping interaction. This client focus is most likely obvious. As professionals, we understand that our helping is a dynamic process that takes place within the context of social interaction and as such, all members involved, including the professional helper, contribute to the focus and processes encountered. While our ethics direct us to attend to the needs of our clients, what may not be obvious or expected is the role that the helper's values, needs, beliefs, and interests play in coloring the helping process. Consider the following case illustration as it demonstrates the potential influence that the helper's personal values, needs, beliefs, and interests may exert within the helping process (Case Illustration 2.1).

Case Illustration 2.1

Michele: Maintaining Objectivity

Michele is a social worker for the Department of Human Services in a large metropolitan city. From all accounts, she is a consummate professional, respected by her peers and supervisors and truly embraced by all her clients. Because of her own competence, Michele is often given some of the hardest cases to handle.

Michele and her husband of five years have, for the past two years, unsuccessfully tried to have a child. Michele has just found out that she is unable to get pregnant because of scar tissue lining her fallopian tube. This news has been very upsetting to Michele, and she is currently in counseling.

Michele has continued to go to work and has been able to maintain an active professional calendar. Michele has just been assigned a new case. Judy is an 18-year-old single woman who is currently living in a halfway house for people progressing through a drug treatment program. The following is part of the intake interview between Michele and Judy.

Michele: Hi, Judy. Please come in and have a seat. Thanks for coming.

Judy: No problem.

Michele: As you know, I am a social worker for the Department of Human Services, and I will be your caseworker while

(Continued)

(Continued)

	you are at Hansen House (*the halfway house*). I will help you coordinate your work and therapy schedules and work with you in trying to develop a career development plan.
Judy:	Yeah, I kind of know what you do. I've done this before.
Michele:	You have?
Judy:	Well, not the halfway house. The drug thing. But I had a social worker when I was 11 and another time, like at 13 or 14, living in Detroit.
Michele:	So you worked with a social worker before. Could you tell me what that was like?
Judy:	It was okay. I had to go 'cause I was living on the street and I got pregnant a couple of times and tried to abort it myself.
Michele:	You were pregnant?
Judy:	Duh, yeah.
Michele:	But you were just a kid! Just 11!
Judy:	Yeah, so? I was having sex when I was like 9 or 10. I must have gotten pregnant like four times, with two abortions and two "whatevers."
Michele:	Whatever? Judy, you are talking about human life here.
Judy:	Whoa, cool it . . . that was then. I thought you were supposed to be helping me with this career thing? I don't need another person preaching at me!

Clearly, Michele's personal interest in childbearing and current experience of sadness and grief around her inability to conceive is making it difficult for her to remain emotionally detached as she listens to Judy's story. Keeping her focus on the client and what is best for that client appears to be difficult for this provider. While professional boundaries are essential for ethical helping, the concept of helper detachment and total objectivity is truly a myth, one that if gone unchallenged can prove detrimental to the helping relationship.

Helpers: Detached and Objective

The fact that helpers' biases, expectations, or values are active in the helping process may run contrary to your own belief that helpers must be totally objective, totally value free. It is neither possible nor desirable to be "scrupulously neutral with respect to values in the counseling relationship" (Corey, Corey, & Callanan, 1988, p. 67). While the idea of *value neutrality* is unrealistic, *value imposition* is possible and as noted throughout professional codes of ethicsm must be guarded against. For example, the American School Counselor Association code of ethics states that school counselors "respect students' values, beliefs, sexual orientation, gender identification/expression and cultural background and exercise great care to avoid imposing personal beliefs or values rooted in one's religion, culture or ethnicity (ASCA, 2016, Standard A.1.f). A similar statement can be found in the *ACA Code of Ethics* (ACA, 2014), which notes: "Counselors are aware of their own values, attitudes, beliefs and behaviors and avoid imposing values that are inconsistent with counseling goals and respect for the diversity of client" (Standard A.4.b).

The ethical and effective helper understands that his practice decisions and interactions are not value neutral. The ethical and effective helper, while recognizing the influence of his or her own values, continues to strive to assist the client in finding the direction that is most congruent with the client's own values, needs, and goals. This is not always easy. Consider the delicate situation a practitioner may find himself or herself in when working with a client who has gone through a decision-making process and without coercion from others has decided to end his life because of extreme suffering involved with a terminal illness. Balancing the ethical value of protecting a client's right to autonomy and self-determination with organizational policies, legal statute, and the practitioners own beliefs and values can be quite daunting. The potential influence of the helpers' values, needs, beliefs, and interest within the helping relationship is a point of concern and interest for all professional organizations (Table 2.1).

While professional organizations cannot police personal values, their codes of ethics clearly highlight the ethical mandate to recognize the existence of these values and to monitor the potential role they play in guiding a provider's decisions. While our professional organizations have codified set of values to guide professional practice, one cannot simply compartmentalize the ethics of the professional helper versus the virtue, value, and ethics of the person of the helper.

As the title of this book suggests, ethical practice demands more than knowing ethics. Ethical practice demands the development of the practitioner as an ethical person. It is imperative for all ethical helpers to increase awareness of their own personal values, beliefs, and expectations, along with an understanding of the degree to which these can and do give shape to their professional identity and the decisions and behavior they enact within the helping encounter.

Table 2.1   Ethical Principles Regarding Objectivity

Professional Organization	*Statement on Ethical Principles Regarding Objectivity*
American Association for Marriage and Family Therapy (2015)	3.2. Marriage and family therapists pursue appropriate consultation and training to ensure adequate knowledge of and adherence to applicable laws, ethics, and professional standards.
American Counseling Association (2014)	A.4.b. Counselors are aware of—and avoid imposing—their own values, attitudes, beliefs, and behaviors. Counselors respect the diversity of clients, trainees, and research participants and seek training in areas in which they are at risk of imposing their values onto clients, especially when the counselor's values are inconsistent with the client's goals or are discriminatory in nature.
American Psychological Association (2010)	2.06. Personal problems and conflicts a. Psychologists refrain from initiating an activity when they know or should know that there is substantial likelihood that their personal problems will prevent them from performing their work-related activities in a competent manner. b. When psychologists become aware of personal problems that may interfere with their performing work-related duties adequately, they take appropriate measures, such as obtaining professional consultation or assistance, and determine whether they should limit, suspend, or terminate their work-related duties.
National Association of Social Workers (2008)	1.06. Social workers should be alert to and avoid conflicts of interest that interfere with the exercise of professional discretion and impartial judgment. Social workers should inform clients when a real or potential conflict of interest arises and take reasonable steps to resolve the issue in a manner that makes the clients' interests primary and protects clients' interests to the greatest extent possible. In some cases, protecting clients' interests may require termination of the professional relationship with the proper referral of the client.

Helper Values and Expectations: Shaping the Helping Relationship

Many professional helpers (e.g., counselors, psychotherapists, psychologists, and social workers) present themselves as totally objective, totally value free. As noted above, total objectivity is not possible. It is possible that the feelings experienced in the helping encounter or the values and expectations with which the helper enters the relationship can distort the helpers' objectivity and interfere with the effective utilization of an appropriate helping process. These feelings can oftentimes be quite subtle in their development and thus can go unrecognized until they have done their damage, a point highlighted in our previous case of Michele (see Case Illustration 2.1).

Helpers cannot always keep their own values out of the helping process. Helper value systems can influence the helper's view of goals, strategies, and even topics discussed. However, while it is unrealistic to assume one can leave personal values outside the office doors, it is essential for the ethical practitioner to be aware of her personal motivations, values, worldviews, and biases, especially as these may impact her professional decisions and actions (Collins, Arthur, Wong-Wylie, 2010). And as much as possible, the ethical practitioner will understand how his personal values can conflict with a client's needs and in those situations, take steps to reduce that possibility. Exercise 2.1 will help illustrate the potential conflict that can exist between helper values and client needs.

Exercise 2.1

Identifying Areas of Helper Value Conflict

Directions: Part 1: Review the characteristics and experiences of each of the following helpers and assume that his or her unique experience may cause biases in a particular direction. Next, identify a type of client problem for which the helper will have very strong feelings (for or against) and thus may have difficulty remaining non-judgmental and objective.

Discuss with your colleagues or classmates the impact such biases may have on the helping process.

Counselor A: A female professional who had to pay for her own college and post baccalaureate education, even as her family objected that a place for women is in the home

(Continued)

(Continued)

Counselor B: A divorced professional who experienced and continues to experience a bitter dispute over child custody

Counselor C: A person who was raised in a very strict, Bible-oriented religious family and who identifies herself as a Christian fundamentalist

Counselor D: An overachieving, highly successful, somewhat driven helper who has been accused of being a workaholic by his coworkers

Part 2: For each of the following clients, identify one of the counselors (listed above) who may have difficulty in remaining objective and non-judgmental:

Client A: A person considering an abortion

Client B: A person considering suicide

Client C: A child abuser

Client D: A person having an extramarital affair

Client E: A person wishing to break away and become independent of her parents

As may be evident in the illustrations provided in Exercise 2.1, helper values and biases can interfere with effective helping and ethical practice. Our codes of ethics direct us to establish professional boundaries, to monitor and assess progress, and to engage with supervision, all as ways to reduce bias and value imposition and support ethical behavior. But even with these ethical practices, it may be necessary, when a professional's personal values are so strong, to share those values and their potential influence with the client. A client has a right to know where the helper stands on various issues presented within in the helping process. To do less is to deprive the client of the respect due and prevents conditions necessary for the expression of client autonomy and self-determination, all values undergirding ethical practice.

Because of the potential influence that a helper's personal values have for affecting the counseling relationship, it is important for all ethical helpers to identify and understand the role their personal values may play in their enactment of the role as helper and to do so prior to engaging in a helping relationship. Through such heightened self-awareness, a helper may be more able to monitor the potential influence that his or her values and expectations may have in the helping relationship and even know if and when a client should be referred to another professional more capable of supporting his needs.

While you are in the early stages of your professional formation, it may be hard to determine how your values may help or hinder your effectiveness as a human service provider. Exercise 2.2 is designed to increase self-awareness of values and bias. As with each of the exercises, it is suggested that responses are shared and discussed with your colleagues or classmates.

Exercise 2.2

Areas of Personal Bias

Directions: Part 1: For each of the following, identify your belief, your attitude, or your value about the issue presented. Along with a classmate or colleague, discuss the potential impact your position on each of these issues may have as you engage in the helping process.

  Equality of genders

  Fidelity in marriage

  Children's rights

  The recreational use of drugs

  Date rape and the responsibility of the person raped

  Cheating in school

  The viewpoint that one should be able to pull himself or herself up by the bootstraps

  The sanctity of marriage

  A women's right to choose an abortion

  Alternative lifestyles

Part 2: Through personal reflection and discussion of your responses to Part I, identify those items in Part I for which you have strong opinions, attitudes, or values. Identify the type of client problems in which these values may interfere with your ability to remain objective and non-judgmental.

The challenge for the ethical helper is to use personal values to enhance the helping process without abusing the power of the relationship or the vulnerability of the client. While it is clear that the ethical helper will resist the temptation to become a missionary for a particular value, she or he will also attempt to be a model of health and well-being and when appropriate give voice to how his or her values serve that state of wellness.

When Values Conflict

The mutual nature of the helping process almost ensures that there will be times when the individual values, beliefs, and needs of the helper and client may conflict. While respecting the client and accepting the client's right to choose his or her own values, a helper may not agree with or embrace those values. Consider the Case Illustration 2.2.

Case Illustration 2.2

Conflicting Values

Howard is a clinical psychologist who is married with three children, ages 9, 14, and 18. Howard married at the age of 20 and worked full-time as he finished his senior year in college and continued as a graduate student. When his wife, Lisa, became pregnant, the couple mutually decided that Lisa would stop working and would be a stay-at-home mom, at least until their children were in high school. Both Lisa and Howard value the importance of children having a full-time parent at home, especially during what Howard calls the formative years.

Howard has just received a call from a new client, Tangelique. In a brief telephone intake, Howard learns that Tangelique is 31 years old, a member of a major law firm, and on track to become a partner. Tangelique's husband, Ralph, is a physician completing his surgical residency. Tangelique is three months pregnant and, according to Tangelique, she and Ralph are fighting a lot and having "serious marital conflict." The conflict centers on the issue of child care following delivery. Tangelique wants to return to work as soon as possible and feels that the baby can do very well receiving "good professional child care." Ralph strongly believes that it is essential for a parent to be at home, especially during these early years. Ralph stated he would be willing to stay at home if he had completed his residency, but he has

---

a year and a half to finish. He wants Tangelique to stay home for the next two years and then they can decide what to do. Tangelique is willing to cut back on her 60 hours a week to 30 or 40, but this is totally unacceptable to Ralph.

As Howard listens to the presenting concern, he becomes very aware of his strong feelings of agreement with Ralph, even prior to meeting the couple. Tangelique stated that she and her husband agree that professional counseling is important at this point in their relationship, and they would like to schedule an appointment.

Under these conditions, the ethical helper will expose those values in conflict and then along with the client, review these areas of value conflict in order to decide how they may impact the decisions made in the helping process. When the conflict is such that it interferes with the helper's ability to effectively assist the client, the ethical helper will prepare the client for referral to another helper who is more able to serve that client's needs (see Chapter 11). The direction to refer is not only good practice, it is ethical practice and responsive to clear mandates made within our various codes of ethics (see Table 2.2).

Helper Orientation: A Theoretical Agenda for Helping

In addition to having our practice decisions influenced by personal values and expectations, our view of the "reality" of the helping encounter will be shaped by the model of helping we have embraced and employ. The information presented by each client often appears somewhat disjointed and disconnected. Each helper needs to weave a thread of consistency or find a theme within the information so that she or he can understand what is "really" going on and how best to approach this situation. Most helpers find that making sense out of the information provided by the client is aided by the use of a theoretical model or framework (Parsons & Zhang, 2014a).

Theories of helping—such as behavioral theory, psychoanalytic theory, cognitive theory, systems theory, and the like—provide frameworks for understanding the meaning of a person's actions as well as offer prescriptions for how to help the person move to a more fully functioning life. However, just as these theoretical models help us to "make sense" of the information provided by the client, we must be sensitive to the possibility that such a model can impose "sense" on the data offered (see Case Illustration 2.3) and

Table 2.2 The Ethics of Referral

Professional Organization	Statement on Ethical Principles Regarding Objectivity
American Association for Marriage and Family Therapy (2015)	1.10. Referrals Marriage and family therapists respectfully assist persons in obtaining appropriate therapeutic services if the therapist is unable or unwilling to provide professional help.
American Counseling Association (2014)	A.11.b. Inability to assist clients If counselors determine an inability to be of professional assistance to clients, they avoid entering or continuing counseling relationships. Counselors are knowledgeable about culturally and clinically appropriate referral resources and suggest these alternatives. If clients decline the suggested referrals, counselors should discontinue the relationship.
American Psychological Association (2010)	10.10. Terminating therapy a. Psychologists terminate therapy when it becomes reasonably clear that the client/patient no longer needs the service, is not likely to benefit, or is being harmed by continued service.
American Mental Health Counselors Association (2010)	5.d. If mental health counselors determine that services are not beneficial to the client, they avoid entering or terminate immediately the counseling relationship. In such situations, appropriate referrals are made. If clients decline the suggested referral, mental health counselors discontinue the relationship.
American School Counselor Association (2016)	A.6.d. Develop a plan for the transitioning of primary counseling services with minimal interruption of services.
National Association of Social Workers (2008)	1.06. In some cases, protecting clients' interests may require termination of the professional relationship with the proper referral of the client.

in fact be limited in validity and usefulness, especially when employed with those with diverse worldviews (See Chapter 4).

While it is possible that Jimmy, the client in our case illustration (Case Illustration 2.3), is having difficulty resolving issues around his own sexuality, his father-son relationship, and so on, and as a result acts silly in class because he is anxious, it is just as likely that Tom is simply making him

---

Case Illustration 2.3

Finding or Imposing Meaning?

Peggy is a recent graduate with a master's degree in counseling. Peggy has always wanted to be a counselor and has been very taken by the psychodynamic view of helping. Peggy intends to go on for additional training and someday become a psychoanalyst.

Peggy is currently employed as a middle-school counselor. She is currently meeting with Jimmy, age 11. Jimmy was sent to her office by his health-science teacher, who is very concerned with Jimmy's tendency to giggle and "act silly" during health class. When asked about his behavior in class, Jimmy describes the following:

"I sit next to Tom. He's my best friend. But he is a goof. He is always making funny noises or saying things about what we are talking about in class, and I can't help it, I just start to laugh. I always get caught and Tom gets away with it."

Peggy asks Jimmy to tell her what they are studying and what types of things Tom may say.

Jimmy responds, "I don't know . . . something to do with becoming a man and a woman, puberty or something like that, I don't know."

At this point, Peggy starts to challenge Jimmy and ask for other information about his relationship with his parents.

"Jimmy, you keep saying you don't know. Is it that you don't know or that you find it difficult to talk about these types of things?

"Jimmy, it would be helpful to me if you could tell me a little about your family and your relationship with you parents, especially your dad."

---

laugh. Peggy's interest in a psychoanalytic theory as well as her own limited training may be directing her to see meaning where none exists.

The ethical practitioner needs to be competent and grounded within the theory and research supporting the helping process (see Chapter 11). Beyond being able to identify the model from which one approaches the helping process, it is also imperative that as an ethical helper, one remembers that theories and models provide only tentative frameworks, not absolute directives, and our decisions, our actions, and our plans need to be tested for validity and utility in each situation. Table 2.3 provides a number of questions that can be used in reviewing the models one employs for both utility and validity for use with any one client or within any one helping relationship.

Table 2.3 Guidelines for Reflections on Operating Model

Our theoretical, operative models help give shape to how we see our clients, their problems, prognoses, goals, and pathways to those goals. It is important to check the utility and validity of our models for each of our clients and helping encounters. Questions to consider in reflecting on our operational models of helping:

- Can I explain the major assumptions and tenets of my model to a colleague?

- Is it employed by others within the field?

- Is there support (clinical, anecdotal, empirical) for this model?

- Can I demonstrate its utility and validity for understanding this current case? What are the limitations and inherent biases built into this model?

- Are there specific clients or client problems for which this model will not be effective?

Reflecting and Validating Interpretations

Theoretical models can assist a helper to gather data, connect the information provided, and draw hypotheses and tentative conclusions about the meaning of those data. The ethical helper will keep focused on the "hypothesis testing" nature of this process (Parsons & Zhang, 2014b). As data are provided, the effective helper needs to hazard tentative guesses about meanings and connections to previous data. Once these hypotheses have been established, the helper needs to go about the process of finding more information to validate his or her hypotheses or revise these hypotheses as new information is revealed.

The ethical helper will not only continue to identify and articulate his or her model of helping but will remain vigilant in his or her evaluation and testing of the validity of that model.

● HELPER COMPETENCE: BEYOND KNOWLEDGE AND SKILL

The ethical helper is a competent helper. While competence implies the possession of the knowledge and skill required to practice (see Chapter 11), it also implies the ability to implement and apply that knowledge and skill. Competence goes beyond simply knowing, it requires doing. As such, helpers need to be self-aware and self-caring (see Chapter 14) so as to provide the best care they can.

Care of the Helper: Essential to Maintaining Competence

As will be discussed in greater detail in Chapter 14, working as a human service provider positions us to experience both physical and emotional exhaustion and depletion. Walking with clients who themselves share stories of trauma, emotional exhaustion, and stress-filled lives can result in our vicarious experience of these issues. With mounting stress, a helper's ability to care about and care for the client can be threatened and the possibility of providing ethical, competent practice reduced. In recognition of this possible impact on helper competence, our professional organizations developed codes of ethics that address this issue of practitioner impairment (see Table 2.4)

As noted with the statements found in Table 2.4, maintaining one's health and well-being is not just a good idea but also an ethical responsibility. It is important for all practitioners to monitor their health and well-being and engage in practices that reduce the possibility of impairment as a result of work-related stress (Zhang & Parsons, 2016; Bennett, Bryant, VandenBos, & Greenwood, 1990). There are a number of steps that all ethical helpers can do in attempting to reduce the potential negative effects of helper stress. In fact, rather than simply focusing on the identification of impairment and the introduction of effective remedial programs, the ethical helper will attempt to employ preventive steps, such as continued education, personal therapy, supervision, and peer interaction. Specific steps that may help to reduce the potential impact of stress on the functioning of the helper include

- *Set realistic expectations*. Ethical helpers recognize that they are not omnipotent. The healthy, ethical helper sets realistic expectations for him or herself, the client, and the outcome of any one helping relationship.
- *Take care of self.* It is important for helpers to eat properly, rest, and exercise. Helping is an energy-draining activity, and the ethical, healthy helper will take steps needed to ensure her or his own health is maintained.
- *Organize and manage*. Boundaries need to be established that not only organize your professional day but also help to distinguish the professional from the personal aspects of your life. The ethical, healthy helper will schedule variations into the day, including sufficient breaks to take care of paperwork, personal needs, or even to take a moment's breather.
- *Keep perspective*. Helpers need to remember that helping is part of their life, not all of their life. The effective helper will also establish mechanisms for ongoing professional support (e.g., supervision,

personal counseling, peer involvement, continuing education) to maintain objectivity and professional distance, especially when working with particularly difficult cases.

Table 2.4 Selected Statements on Professional Impairment

Professional Organization	Statement on Professional Impairment
American Counseling Association (2014)	C.2.g. Counselors monitor themselves for signs of impairment from their own physical, mental, or emotional problems and refrain from offering or providing professional services when impaired. They seek assistance for problems that reach the level of professional impairment, and, if necessary, they limit, suspend, or terminate their professional responsibilities until it is determined that they may safely resume their work. Counselors assist colleagues or supervisors in recognizing their own professional impairment and provide consultation and assistance when warranted with colleagues or supervisors showing signs of impairment and intervene as appropriate to prevent imminent harm to clients.
American Psychological Association (2010)	2.06. Personal problems and conflicts a. Psychologists refrain from initiating an activity when they know or should know that there is a substantial likelihood that their personal problems will prevent them from performing their work-related activities in a competent manner. b. When psychologists become aware of personal problems that may interfere with their performing work-related duties adequately, they take appropriate measure such as obtaining professional consultation or assistance and determine whether they should limit, suspend, or terminate their work-related duties.
National Association of Social Workers (2008)	4.05.b. Social workers whose personal problems, psychosocial distress, legal problems, substance abuse, or mental health difficulties interfere with their professional judgment and performance should immediately seek consultation and take appropriate remedial action by seeking professional help, making adjustments in workload, terminating practice, or taking any other steps necessary to protect clients and others.
American Association for Marriage and Family Therapy (2015)	3.3. Seek assistance Marriage and family therapists seek appropriate professional assistance for issues that may impair work performance or clinical judgment.

THE ETHICS OF THERAPEUTIC CHOICE ●

Licensed and certified mental health providers are required to not only provide clients with care that an ordinary, average person should exercise under such circumstances but to provide services that compare to that of their professional peers. A mental health professional who fails to meet the relevant standard of care, when compared with that of other professionals in the same community with comparable training and experience, is not only performing unethically but may also be found to be negligent in his or her duty to provide care. The evidence for such negligence will rest on the clinical correctness and efficacy of the treatment that was given, along with the practitioner's judgment in choosing it (Bennett et al., 1990).

Ethically and legally, a practitioner needs to not only be competent and skillful in the application of her or his helping skills but needs to employ those skills and approaches that have generally been accepted within the profession as appropriate and customary. One professional organization directs its members to "use techniques/procedures/modalities that are grounded in theory and/or have an empirical or scientific foundation" (ACA, 2014, Principle C.7.a). This point is also echoed in the Ethical Principles of Psychologists and Code of Conduct that directs their members to employ strategies that are "based upon established scientific and professional knowledge of the discipline" (APA, 2010, Standard 2.04). Professionals who employ "innovative strategies" not only run the risk of malpractice based on the principle of negligence but at minimum, run the risk of failing their ethical responsibility to provide the best care possible to their client. When a practitioner engages in the use of an innovative technique, she would be wise to follow the directive offered by the ACA to "explain the potential risks, benefits, and ethical considerations of using such techniques/procedures/modalities. Counselors work to minimize any potential risks or harm when using these techniques/procedures/modalities" (ACA, 2014, Principle C.7.b).

Selecting the Appropriate Treatment

Practice decisions, including those involving methods and strategies for treatment, need to be made as reflections of those values that underpin our ethical principles, that is, *beneficence,* our desire to promote the health and well-being of our clients, and *nonmaleficence,* the mandate to "do no harm." The American Mental Health Counselors Association, for example, directs its members as part of its code of ethics to employ "individual counseling plans that offer reasonable promise of success" (AMHCA, 2010, Principle B.1.a). Similar directives can be seen across our various professional codes of conduct.

For some practitioners, their choice of treatment approach stems from a personal intuition, "gut feeling," or simply the practitioner's liking. The use of intuition or gut feeling as criteria for choosing and employing a treatment regimen opens the practitioner to not only poor decision-making and ineffective intervention but also to ethical violation. For the ethical practitioner, practice decision, including choice of treatment strategies, needs to reflect customary and accepted practice and reflect the practitioner's critical understanding of the current state of the research guiding practice.

It is not only an ethical imperative but also a legal reality that practitioners must employ those strategies demonstrated to be best practice in each given situation. When techniques have some general acceptance and are not used, the practitioner runs the risk of not only performing unethically, but he or she may also be held legally accountable and found to be negligent in the professional duty to provide care. In areas for which there is not solid research to direct best practice or for which the standard of the profession is not clearly articulated, the ethical practitioner will employ those techniques for which there is a theoretical rationale and evidence that at least the local community and the ordinary, average practitioner would employ as customary practice. Awareness of the standards of practice defining accepted intervention strategies as well as familiarizing oneself with customary modes of service is essential for ethical practice. Exercise 2.3 has been designed to assist you in this process.

Exercise 2.3

Customary and Accepted Practice

Directions: For each of the presenting problems listed do the following:

- Contact a human service professional in your community and inquire into his or her general approach or strategy employed in this situation.

- Review the research in the past five years pointing to the efficacy and outcome for specific interventions when employed with this type of problem.

- Identify your own approach to this situation and include your rationale.

Problem Area	Human Service Professional	Research	Personal Approach
Depression	Dr. Wicks: Employs cognitive behavior therapy (CBT) (Beck, Rush, Shaw, & Emery, 1979)	NIMH studies demonstrating effectiveness of CBT (Elkin et al., 1989)	I would use CBT plus referral for medication if warranted. Supported by research and local practice professionals.
An 11-year-old child diagnosed with ADHD			
A 35-year-old woman diagnosed with agoraphobia			
A 42-year-old man arrested with Driving Under the Influence; he has a longstanding history of alcoholism			
A child (6 years old) who appears to have been burned (burn marks) and may continue to be abused			
A hostile 28-year-old male reporting a desire to "severely hurt his boss"			

● PROFESSIONALIZATION, PROFESSIONAL ETHICS, AND PERSONAL RESPONSE

Professionalization is "the process by which an occupation, usually on the basis of a claim to special competence and a concern for the quality of its work and benefits to society, obtains the exclusive right to perform a particular kind of work, to control training criteria and access to the profession, and to determine and evaluate the way the work is to be performed" (Chalk, Frankel, & Chafer, 1980, p. 3). Once professionalized, an occupation develops professional associations or societies that promote the profession, safeguard the rights of their members, and facilitate the exchange of information. In professional fields, such as helping, national professional organizations develop rules for appropriate conduct for their memberships (e.g., American Counseling Association, American Psychological Association, National Association of Social Workers, American Association for Marriage and Family Therapy). These codes become the standards for these groups and provide practitioners with a guide to making ethical decisions.

Codes of Ethics

These professional associations and societies also develop codes and standards of practice that are created to enhance the quality of the professional work performed by their members. In the previous sections of this chapter, we have made reference to some of these specific standards, and it is these standards, these codes of ethics, as applied to the practice of helping that will serve as the basis for the remainder of this text.

Our codes of ethics not only serve as guides to professional decision-making and professional practice but also function as a covenant to those we serve (Ponton & Duba, 2009). Our ethical codes exist primarily to protect the public from unethical or incompetent professionals and to protect the profession from unethical practices by any of its members. As discussed in Chapters 3 and 7, these standards by themselves do not always provide clear direction for helpers to follow in order to avoid conflict or to make the best decisions for all involved and maintain freedom from legal entanglement. Our codes are not recipes or step-by-step directions to follow, but rather they are guidelines that require the helper's best personal and professional judgment in selection, reflection, and application to individual situations.

Moving Beyond Professional
Standards to Personal Response

As mental health and human service providers, we need to have a clear understanding of professional standards along with knowledge of local, state, and federal policies that impact professional practice. Beyond this understanding and knowledge, however, the ethical practitioner needs to work to move knowledge to action by making these principles personal values and guided moral responses.

Sadly, for many practitioners, the ethics and practice guidelines that they were taught in school lose definition and impetus as they become absorbed within the experience of daily practice. The pressures of everyday life may lead practitioners to view these codes of ethics as abstract concepts that they think about only when they hear or read about an ethics violation by a colleague. Some practitioners view ethics either as rules designed to hinder practice decisions or to serve as a lever to remove colleagues who may not be as concerned about themselves, their clients, or the profession as we might be (Bennett et al., 1990, p. 7).

We need to move beyond simply seeing codes of ethics as abstract concepts, leverages, or hindrances and begin to view them as personal ethical imperatives. This is the reason for this book. It is hoped that as you proceed through the text, engaging with the case illustrations and guided exercises, you will move from simply knowing and understanding ethical principles to being ethical. Evidence of that transition from knowing to being takes form in your decisions and behaviors that (a) respect and support client autonomy; (b) extend and manifest a desire to place the welfare of the client above all else; and (c) ensure you do no harm while treating all your clients, regardless of presenting complaint or personal characteristics with justice and fidelity (Zhang & Parsons, 2016).

CONCLUDING CASE ILLUSTRATION ●

Returning to our ongoing case of Ms. Wicks and Maria, we can see that Ms. Wicks has identified a number of values or beliefs that are currently giving shape to Maria's decision-making. As you continue to read the case, place yourself in the role of the helper and consider your position and reactions as they parallel or contrast with those exhibited by Ms. Wicks. After reading the interaction, consider the points raised in the section entitled Reflections. How might your personal reactions guide your interaction and decision-making in regard to Maria's situation?

Ms. Wicks: Maria, let me see if I understand what you are saying. You are sexually active and you don't care that you are engaged in unprotected sex. The possibility of becoming pregnant or contracting a sexually transmitted disease, even AIDS, doesn't concern you. Is that what you are saying?

Maria: Well, the way you are saying it . . . it sounds like I'm stupid.

Ms. Wicks: No, I apologize if that is how it sounded. I guess when I heard you say that you were engaging in unprotected sex and I assumed you were at risk of contracting AIDS, it upset me. Maybe that's what you heard in my tone?

Maria: Not that it is any of your business, but I am sexually active. And becoming pregnant, I would like that. I would like to have his child of love!

Ms. Wicks: So you feel relatively certain that both you and your boyfriend are free of any sexually transmitted diseases and that as long as you stay monogamous that shouldn't be a problem?

Maria: Yeah, we've even talked about it!

Ms. Wicks: But, I don't quite understand your view of becoming pregnant. You seem to want that?

Maria: Hey, I'm a woman and my guy is a real man. A baby would be proof of our love, a gift from God!

Reflections

1. What is your current level of competence in regard to working with adolescent, Latina females? How might this impact your ability to work with Maria? What specifically might you have difficulty with?
2. Ms. Wicks has accepted that her own values and beliefs may have influenced the tone of her response. In an attempt to share her own perspective while valuing the position of the client, she offers the clarification regarding her tone of voice. How would you have responded to Maria's challenge that you thought she was stupid? The same as Ms. Wicks? More strongly? Not at all?
3. Maria is introducing a number of value-laden issues (e.g., adolescent premarital sex, out-of-wedlock pregnancy, children as evidence of maturity, gifts from God, etc.). How is your perspective

similar? Different? How might your perspective give shape to your response?

4. What goal would you have for this encounter? How has that goal been influenced by your own values, family experience, and culture?

COOPERATIVE LEARNING EXERCISE ●

The purpose of the chapter was to familiarize you with the role that specific helper variables—such as values, theoretical orientation, competence, and cultural sensitivity—play in the formation of a helping process and to have you begin to increase your awareness of your helper variables as they may inform your professional decision-making.

Part I: Identify your own values as they impact your opinion on each of the following:

- Divorce
- Abortion
- Extramarital sexual affairs
- Spanking
- Marijuana
- Sexual orientation
- Children's rights
- Importance of schedules and planning
- Importance of success and achievement
- Spirituality

Part 2: For each of the following, identify a goal and a treatment strategy that you may employ. After identifying your own goals and strategies, share these with a supervisor, colleague, or classmate and attempt to identify alternative goals and strategies that would be appropriate and helpful. Finally, identify how your own opinions, biases, values, and culture experiences may have influenced your selection of goals and treatment strategies for each of the following:

- A woman, age 38, who has been married for 11 years, has over the course of the past 8 months had an affair with her husband's business partner. The affair has resulted in her becoming pregnant. She is stressed and is asking for direction as to what she should do.
- A 12-year-old has been referred to you by his parents who found "drug stuff" in his room. The child disclosed to you that he has been smoking marijuana since the beginning of the school year (last three months) and

has found that it makes him feel less stressed and depressed. Further, he disclosed that he is upset because he knows he is gay and doesn't know if his parents will accept that. He has asked you NOT to tell his parents.

● You are working with a senior in high school who has been referred by his teacher. The student, while having a documented IQ of 148, is currently barely passing his classes. When confronted, he explains that he is simply placing more value and importance in getting in touch with his spiritual side and his "connectedness to all living things" and that he has decided to learn and attend to things that have personal relevance regardless of grades and class rankings.

● SUMMARY

● It is neither possible nor desirable to be neutral with respect to values in the counseling relationship, and to assume such could be ethically dangerous.

● Ethical helpers increase awareness of their own personal values, beliefs, and expectations and the role they play in giving shape to their professional identity and behavior within their role as a counselor.

● Establishing professional boundaries and maintaining professional detachment and objectivity in service of the client, while never absolute, remains a goal of ethical helping.

● When client and helper values conflict, the ethical helper will expose those values in conflict and then, along with the client, review these areas of value conflict in order to decide how they may impact the decisions made in the helping process.

● When the conflict is such that it interferes with the helper's ability to effectively assist the client, the ethical helper will prepare the client for referral to another helper who is more in line with the client's needs and values.

● A helper's theoretical orientation and model not only provide a framework for understanding the information provided by the client but can also impose meaning on the data offered.

● The ethical helper will not only continue to identify and articulate her or his model of helping but will remain vigilant in her or his evaluation and testing of the validity of that model.

● The ethical helper is a competent helper. Competence goes beyond simply knowing; it requires doing. As such, helpers need to be self-aware and self-caring so as to provide the best care they can.

- As professionals, we not only provide clients with care that an ordinary, average person should exercise under such circumstances, but also our service reflects our professions standard of care.
- As professional helpers, we are called to operate within a framework of ethics as defined by our specific professional organizations.
- Codes of ethics are reflections of our commitment to our clients and to one another to provide for the welfare of the clients.
- Knowing one's code of ethics is insufficient. Being ethical, embracing those codes as personal, professional values, is necessary.

IMPORTANT TERMS ●

burnout	professionalization
codes of ethics	professional boundaries
competence	professional objectivity
cultural sensitivity	self-determination
customary practice	standard of care
decision-making strategy	theoretical model
hypothesis testing	value free
practitioner impairment	

ADDITIONAL RESOURCES ●

Print

Consoli, A. J., Kim, B. S. K., & Meyer, D. M. (2008). Counselor's values profile: Implications for counseling ethnic minority clients. *Counseling and Values, 52*, 181–197.

Granello, D. H., & Yong, M. E. (2012). *Counseling today: Foundations of professional identity.* Upper Saddle River, NJ: Pearson.

Rogers, C. (1980). *A way of being.* Boston: Houghton Mifflin.

Sheperis, D. S., Henning, S. L., & Kocet, M. M. (2015). *Ethical decision making for the 21st century counselor.* Thousand Oaks, CA: Sage.

Web-Based

Dobrin, A. (2012). Am I right? How to live ethically. Retrieved from http://www.scu
.edu/ethics/practicing/decision/thinking.html

Josephson, M. (2014). *The six pillars of character.* Retrieved from http://josephson-
institute.org/MED/MED-2sixpillars.html

Shallcross, L. (2010). Putting clients ahead of personal values. *Counseling Today.*
Retrieved from http://ct.counselin.org/2010/11/putting-clients-ahead-of-personal-
values

● REFERENCES

American Association for Marriage and Family Therapy. (2015). *Code of ethics.*
Retrieved from https://www.aamft.org/iMIS15/AAMFT/Content/Legal_Ethics/
Code_of_Ethics.aspx

American Counseling Association. (2014). *Code of ethics.* Retrieved from http://
www.counseling.org/resources/aca-code-of-ethics.pdf

American Mental Health Counselors Association. (2010). *American Mental Health
Counselors Association code of ethics.* Retrieved from http://www.amhca.org/
assets/content/AMHCA_Code_of_Ethics_11_30_09b1.pdf

American Psychological Association. (2010). *Ethical principles of psychologists and
code of conduct.* Retrieved from: http://www.apa.org/ethics/code/principles.pdf

American School Counselor Association. (2016). ASCA *ethical standards for
school counselors.* Retrieved from: http://www.schoolcounselor.org/
school-counselors-members/legal-ethical

Beck, A. T., Rush, A. J., Shaw, B. F., & Emery, G. (1979). *Cognitive therapy of depression.*
New York: Guilford Press.

Chalk, R., Frankel, M. D., & Chafer, S. B. (1980). *AAAS professional ethics project.*
Washington, DC: American Association for the Advancement of Science.

Collins, S., Arthur, N., & Wong-Wylie, G. (2010). Enhancing reflective practice
through multicultural counseling in cultural auditing. *Journal of Counseling &
Development, 88,* 340–347.

Corey, G., Corey, M. S., & Callanan, P. (1988). *Issues and ethics in the helping professions* (3rd ed.). Pacific Grove, CA: Brooks/Cole.

Elkin, I., Shea, M. T., Watkins, J. T., Imbers, S. D., Sotsky, S. M., Collins, . . . Paroloff,
M. D. (1989). National Institute Health treatment of depression collaborative
research program: General effectiveness of treatment. Reprinted from the
Archives of *General Psychiatry, 46,* 971–983.

National Association of Social Workers (2008). *Code of ethics of the National
Association of Social Workers.* Retrieved from https://www.socialworkers.org/
pubs/code/code.asp

Parsons, R. D., & Zhang, N. (2014a). *Counseling theory.* Thousand Oaks, CA: Sage.

Parsons, R. D., & Zhang, N. (2014b). *Becoming a skilled counselor.* Thousand Oaks, CA: Sage.

Ponton, R. F., & Duba, J. D. (2009). The ACA code of ethics: Articulating counseling's professional covenant. *Journal of Counseling & Development, 87,* 117–121.

VandenBos, G. R., & Greenwood, A. (1990). *Professional liability and risk management.* Washington, DC: American Psychological Association.

Zhang, N., & Parsons, R. D. (2016). *Field experience: Transitioning from student to professional.* Thousand Oaks, CA: Sage.

CHAPTER 3

Ethical Standards: Guidelines for Helping Others

Maria: Gee, being a counselor is a great job!

Ms. Wicks: Yes, it is, Maria, I enjoy it very much.

Maria: I mean you get to sit in this office and just listen to people complain, you know—chat AND get paid for it!

It is not that unusual to find individuals who believe that "helping" is simply a process of social chatting and that helpers—be they counselors, psychologists, social workers, and so on—are at best nice people and at worse frauds. Contrary to this view, those in the helping profession know and appreciate that as a formal process and a profession, helping is a powerful, awesome process that carries with it equally powerful and significant responsibilities.

Sadly, it is all too easy to find examples of helpers who have abused this power and responsibility. One need only to turn on a television talk show to find examples of unethical therapists who have sexually abused their clients, counselors who have ignored their clients' suicidal pleas for help, or even medical and social service workers who have personally gained from the misfortune of others. As helpers, we are given the responsibility to care for individuals, who by definition of needing help are often those who are most vulnerable to manipulation. Given the potential vulnerability of their clients and the power of the helping dynamic, helpers need guidelines for professional decision-making that not only protect but care for those seeking their help. Professional ethics and codes of conduct provide those guidelines.

● OBJECTIVES

The decision-making of the professional counselors, psychologists, social workers, and marriage and family therapists is formed through training and acquired knowledge and skills and guided by their professional codes of conduct and ethics. The chapter will introduce you to the ethical guidelines employed by these professionals. While the uniqueness of each of these professions is reflected within their own ethical principles and codes of conduct, each shares common concern for the welfare of the client. The current chapter discusses the need for these ethical principles and highlights the commonality of ethical principles shared across these professions.

After reading this chapter you should be able to do the following:

- Describe common values and points of concern evidenced in various professional codes of ethical practice.
- Describe what is meant by autonomy, beneficence, and nonmaleficence.
- Describe what is meant by informed consent, competence, confidentiality, and professional boundaries.

● FORMAL ETHICAL STANDARDS: THE EVOLUTION OF A PROFESSION

Ethics, including professional ethics, are at their core a set of values and beliefs that have been articulated as a guide to sound, moral decision-making. In the most recent revision of the *American Counseling Association Code of Ethics*, for example, the committee charged with the revisions delineated specific professional values that are meant to inform all counselors' practices, teaching, supervision and research (Meyers, 2014). The values highlighted within the preamble of the *ACA Code of Ethics* (2014) include the following:

- enhancing human development throughout the life span;
- honoring diversity and embracing a multicultural approach in support of the worth, dignity, potential, and uniqueness of people within their social and cultural contexts;
- promoting social justice;
- safeguarding the integrity of the counselor–client relationship; and
- practicing in a competent and ethical manner.

Neither the values underlying our professional codes of conduct nor the codes themselves bloom in a vacuum. They reflect the meaningful experiences and discussions of the members of a profession. And just as our professions develop over time, in response to expanded knowledge, changing demands and client needs, our ethical codes evolve. They are truly living documents. Documents that are intended to educate all members of the profession and those whom they serve as to the specific responsibilities and expectations of the profession and those operating within the role of professional. And while each of the helping professions shares concerns for the welfare of those whom they serve, the form that concern and service takes is shaped by the unique history, composition and professional values of each profession. For example, the 2014 ACA Code of Ethics makes it clear that "The American Counseling Association (ACA) is an educational, scientific, and professional organization whose members work in a variety of settings and serve in multiple capacities. Counseling is a professional relationship that empowers diverse individuals, families, and groups to accomplish mental health, wellness, education, and career goals" (ACA, 2014, p. 3). Whereas the unique identity and responsibilities of those working within the field of social work is presented within the preamble to their professional code of ethics as, "The primary mission of the social work profession is to enhance human well-being and help meet the basic human needs of all people, with particular attention to the needs and empowerment of people who are vulnerable, oppressed, and living in poverty. Social workers promote social justice and social change with and on behalf of clients" (National Association of Social Workers [NASW], 2008).

Our codes of ethics are more than public pronouncements of our professional identity. They are also guidelines for practice. Our codes serve as a standard, accepted by the members of our profession, against which practice decisions and actions can be judged. Thus, when confronted with choices, a practitioner can decide as to the rightness and wrongness of each option, using the code of conduct and ethical principles for that profession as the guideline (see Case Illustration 3.1).

Case Illustration 3.1

Making an Ethical Decision

Dr. Louise Thompson is a licensed clinical social worker in private practice. She has been working with Alfonso, a 52-year-old construction worker who was self-referred for depression. Dr. Thompson has been working with Alfonso for approximately eight sessions. In the course of her work, she has identified a primary contributor to Alfonso's depression. Alfonso is currently on physical disability from his job and now that his physical condition appears to be healing, he has many self-doubts about his ability to return to work. As Alfonso stated, he wishes that he could stay on disability forever.

Dr. Thompson has just received a certified letter from the disability insurance company asking her (a) to assess and report on her client's ability to return to work and (b) to send all of her records for its review. Dr. Thompson is concerned that, while Alfonso's physical condition is on the mend, his depression impairs his ability to problem solve, which may be a problem and potential danger given his line of work. Further, Dr. Thompson has recorded in her notes some of Alfonso's quotes regarding his disdain for his foreman at work, his desire to stay on disability, and his fantasies about damaging the current construction project. She is worried about how these will be interpreted by the company's insurance firm.

Dr. Thompson is not sure if she should even respond to these requests, especially not being completely sure of her competence to judge capability to return to work. Also, in terms of her clinical notes, she wonders if she should edit her notes or refuse to send some file information. It appears that in some ways what is best for the client may be not to honor the request or to do so after carefully filtering the information. But her concern is whether this is legal. Is it ethical? Dr. Thompson wants to do what is best for her client, while practicing within the standards and codes of conduct for her profession. But the standard is not clear, at least to her, so she is unsure what to do. Luckily, Dr. Thompson belongs to the National Association of Social Workers. She contacted the association and its legal/ethical consultants and in dialogue with them, has decided on a plan of action. Without her awareness of the complexity of these requests or her ability to refer to her professional association, Dr. Thompson might have made decisions that not only would harm her client but legally and ethically jeopardize her ability to practice.

In addition to serving as guidelines for practice, our codes serve as guidelines, from which our professions can govern ethical practice. Behind each profession's code of ethics is a mechanism of governance that gives substance to the ethical principles. Through the use of articulated educational requirements, members of a profession are guided in the development and enactment of their professional roles. Further, when these members fail to perform or practice within the established standard, procedures for disciplining and sanctioning can be enacted (see Case Illustration 3.2).

Case Illustration 3.2

Sanctioning a Member

While it is rare, any single incident of sexual misconduct is one too many for a profession that operates on the implicit trust of its clients. The following reflects one case (significant details have been modified in order to ensure anonymity) in which the sexual misconduct of one practitioner came to the attention of a second.

Dr. L., a clinical psychologist, was working with a new client who presented herself as depressed and anxious. In ascertaining some background material, Dr. L. discovered that the client had been in therapy for the past four years with a certified marriage and family therapist. Additional data gleaned over the course of the next five sessions revealed that this therapist had seen the client and her husband for marriage counselling but in the course of the counseling referred the husband to another therapist and began treating this client for her "sexual dysfunctions."

As revealed by the client, the previous therapist started a sexual affair with her that continued for one year, while she was still under his professional care. The client said that she had become increasingly depressed in the past few months as a direct result of her previous therapist terminating both the sexual contact and the therapeutic relationship. The explanation he provided was simply that she was too needy and too dependent for him to help her. To make matters worse, she works in the same organization as the therapist and rumor has it that he is currently having an affair with another client.

The client expressed her anger and disgust as well as guilt over the affair. Dr. L. worked on helping her understand that maintaining appropriate boundaries was not her responsibility but that of the therapist. As a result of their sessions together, the client, while not seeking or desiring any legal recourse, shared her concern that this man had access to

(Continued)

(Continued)

other vulnerable female clients and that she would not feel good unless she could stop that. Together, she and Dr. L. contacted the American Association for Marriage and Family Therapy (AAMFT), which was the professional association of the previous therapist. After an exhausting fact-finding period, the AAMFT Board concluded that not only was this claim valid but that a history of such behavior existed. The board revoked his certification, provided him with a treatment and mentoring plan, and forwarded its decision to the local state board of licensing. The therapist, in addition to holding a certificate as a marriage and family therapist, also was licensed to practice within his state. As a result of AAMFT's action, his license was revoked.

Thus, these codes of conduct and these ethical principles exist not simply as statements of aspiration but are in fact mandates and standards of professional practice: standards that reflect the knowledge and general consensus of a profession at any given time. However, just as our professions continue to develop in response to new opportunities, demands, knowledge, and technology, so to do our codes of ethics evolve and develop. For example, most codes of conduct prior to the 1990s didn't provide for increased sensitivity toward (a) diversity and multicultural issues, (b) responding to clients with HIV/AIDS, or (c) nonprofessional relationships between helpers and clients. The ongoing awareness among professionals about the importance of these and other emerging issues has been given voice within the latest editions of these evolving codes of ethics. Because the codes are evolving, it is important that practitioners maintain participation within their professional associations and remain informed about the latest research and literature regarding the ethics of practice.

● ACROSS THE PROFESSIONS: A REVIEW OF ETHICAL STANDARDS OF PRACTICE

Typically, practitioners within a profession also hold membership within the associations representing that profession (see Appendix A). Most counselors, for example, belong to the American Counseling Association (ACA); psychologists, to the American Psychological Association (APA); marriage and family therapists, to the American Association for Marriage and Family

Therapy (AAMFT); and social workers, to the National Association of Social Workers (NASW). These professional organizations provide their members with specific statements of guidelines for ethical practice (see Appendix B) and help give clarification to the uniqueness of the role and function of that profession. The ethical principles and codes of conduct included within this text (see Appendix B) reflect the latest versions of these standards. It is important for the practitioner to not only know these standards but to review association news and updates regarding ethics and codes of conduct.

COMMON CONCERNS AND SHARED VALUES ACROSS THE PROFESSIONS ●

The specific codes of conduct as articulated by each professional organization (see Appendix B) constitute the mandatory ethics of that profession, reflecting the unique demands and responsibilities of those within that profession. However, cutting across and through the unique principles found within in each profession's code of ethics are four core values (i.e., autonomy, beneficence, nonmaleficence and justice) that serve as the conceptual basis for the specific ethical principles (see Table 3.1).

Thus, while each specialty in the helping field may emphasize one or another ethical principle of practice, it is clear that primary to each of these codes is the concern for and consideration of the welfare and well-being of those with whom these professionals work (see Exercise 3.1).

It is commonly held, across the professions, that the helping relationship exists for the clients' benefit, for their care and NOT for the personal needs or benefits of the helper. The codes of ethics are structured to highlight that focus and guide practice in such a way as to service the needs of the client and protect his welfare. The helper who uses the helping relationship to make herself or himself feel powerful, important, or needed is placing her or his needs before those of the client and is being unethical. It is in placing the rights and needs of the client as primary that an ethical helper begins to establish the general framework for ethical practice. The ethical helper—regardless of the specific helping profession—demonstrates this primacy of the rights and needs of the client by providing the client with informed consent, establishing confidentiality, and creating boundaries that maintain a professional, competent relationship. While each of these concepts will be explored in depth in subsequent chapters, they are introduced here.

Table 3.1 Fundamental Principles Underlying Professional Codes of Conduct

Professional Organization	Autonomy/ Self-Determination	Beneficence/ Promote Good	Nonmaleficence/ Avoid Harm	Justice/Equal Treatment
American Psychological Association (2010)	Principle E. Respect for people's rights and dignity Psychologists respect the dignity and worth of all people, and the rights of individuals' privacy, confidentiality, and self-determination. Psychologists are aware that special safeguards may be necessary to protect the rights and welfare of persons or communities whose vulnerabilities impair autonomous decision-making. Psychologists are aware of and respect cultural, individual, and role differences . . . Psychologists try to eliminate the effect on their work of biases based on those factors, and they do not knowingly participate in	Principle A. Beneficence and nonmaleficence Psychologists strive to benefit those with whom they work and take care to do no harm. In their professional actions, psychologists seek to safeguard the welfare and rights of those with whom they interact professionally and other affected persons, and the welfare of animal subjects of research. When conflicts occur among psychologists' obligations or concerns, they attempt to resolve these conflicts in a responsible fashion that avoids or minimizes harm. Because psychologists' scientific and professional judgements and actions may affect the lives of others, they are alert to and guard against personal, financial, social, organizational, or	3.04. Avoiding harm Psychologists take reasonable steps to avoid harming their clients/patients students, supervisees, research participants, organizational clients, and others with whom they work, and to minimize harm where it is foreseeable and unavoidable.	3.01. Unfair discrimination In their work-related activities, psychologists do not engage in unfair discrimination based on age, gender, gender identity, race, ethnicity, culture, national origin, religion, sexual orientation, disability, socioeconomic status, or any basis proscribed by law.

Professional Organization	Autonomy/ Self-Determination	Beneficence/ Promote Good	Nonmaleficence/ Avoid Harm	Justice/Equal Treatment
	or condone activities of others based upon such prejudices.	political factors that might lead to misuse of their influence. Psychologists strive to be aware of the possible effect of their own physical and mental health on their ability to help those with whom they work.		
American Counseling Association (2014)	Introduction Counselors encourage client growth and development in ways that foster the interest and welfare of clients and promote formation of healthy relationships. Trust is the cornerstone of the counseling relationship, and counselors have the responsibility to respect and safeguard the client's right to privacy and confidentiality.	A.1.a. The primary responsibility of counselors is to respect the dignity and promote the welfare of clients.	C.6.d. Exploitation of others. Counselors do not exploit others in their professional relationships.	A.10.c. In establishing fees for professional counseling services, counselors consider the financial status of clients and locality. If a counselor's usual fees create undue hardship for the client, the counselor may adjust fees, when legally permissible, or assist the client in locating comparable, affordable services.

(Continued)

Table 3.1 (Continued)

Professional Organization	Autonomy/ Self-Determination	Beneficence/ Promote Good	Nonmaleficence/ Avoid Harm	Justice/Equal Treatment
National Association of Social Workers (2008)	1.02. Self-determination Social workers respect and promote the right of clients to self-determination and assist clients in their efforts to identify and clarify their goals. Social workers may limit clients' rights to self-determination when, in the social worker's professional judgment, clients' actions or potential actions pose a serious, foreseeable, and imminent risk to themselves or others.	1.01. Commitment to clients Social workers' primary responsibility is to promote the well-being of clients. In general, clients' interests are primary. However, social workers' responsibility to the larger society or specific legal obligations may on limited occasions supersede the loyalty owed clients, and the clients should be so advised.	1.06. Conflicts of interest b. Social workers should not take unfair advantage of any professional relationship or exploit others to further their personal, religious, political, or business interests.	4.02. Discrimination Social workers should not practice, condone, facilitate, or collaborate with any form of discrimination on the basis of race, ethnicity, national origin, color, sex, sexual orientation, gender identity or expression, age, marital status, political belief, religion, immigration status, or mental or physical disability. 4.04. Dishonesty, fraud, and deception Social workers should not participate in, condone, or be associated with dishonesty, fraud, or deception.

Exercise 3.1

Identifying Core Values of Ethical Conduct

Directions: For each of the following identify the core value (i.e., autonomy, beneficence, nonmaleficence, justice) being demonstrated and whether the helper's actions are in support (s) or in violation (v) of that core value.

Illustration	*Core Value*	*Support? "S"*	*Violation? "V"*
The helper directs the client in terms of what needs to be done and what goals will be set for each session.			
The helper cancels an appointment with a client because she pays on a sliding scale and he has the opportunity to schedule a full-pay client in that time slot.			
The helper explains to the client that the types of things the client wishes to discuss and the goals he, the client, wishes to achieve require techniques for which the helper is not trained and therefore a referral might be in order.			
The client called in crisis. The client was feeling very hopeless and, while apologetic about calling the counselor, expressed her fear that she may hurt herself. Even though the helper was in the middle of a family celebration, she spent the time needed to assess the level of crisis and to ensure that the client felt safe and was with someone who could continue to monitor her, and she offered to set up an immediate appointment for the following day.			

Informed Consent

The ethical helper will demonstrate a respect for the rights of the client to be fully informed. Clients need to be provided with information that enables them to make informed choices. Clearly, this can pose a challenge in that the helper needs to attain a balance of providing the information needed for informed decision-making at a time and in a manner that the client can understand and successfully use that information. Too much information, too soon, can prove overwhelming, anxiety provoking, and even destructive to the helping process. The goal of informed consent is to promote cooperation and participation of the client in the helping process. The specifics of such an informing process, in terms of what to present and how to present it, often create delicate situations and ethical dilemmas as presented in Exercise 3.2. These will be more fully explored in Chapter 8.

Exercise 3.2

An Issue of Informed Consent

Directions: Below you will find a number of scenarios involving a helper and a client for whom informed consent is an issue. As you read the scenarios, identify what, if anything, you would tell the client.

Scenario 1: Allison has been directed by her employer to go to counseling at their Employee Assistance Program (EAP) because of her "attitude at work." The EAP has been directed to evaluate Allison for drug use and to make a report to the employer. What, if anything, should the EAP counselor tell the client?

Scenario 2: Timothy walks into his high school counselor's office. Timothy says that he is thinking about running away from home. Further, he states that if he is unable to get away from his parents, he will "kill himself." What information should the counselor convey to this client?

Scenario 3: A child psychiatrist is working with an 8-year-old child with severe attention deficit with hyperactivity. The child's parent told him that this was an "allergy doctor" who may give him some "allergy" medicine. What do you feel the psychiatrist should tell the client?

Confidentiality

For helping to be effective, the client must feel free to disclose and share private concerns. For such a sense of freedom to exist, the client needs to feel that the interaction is one that is confidential. As with other areas of practice, confidentiality is not absolute, nor are decisions to hold in confidence always black and white (see Exercise 3.3). The use of confidentiality requires professional judgment, which at times can be very challenging. Chapter 9 provides a detailed look at the issue of confidentiality, its limitations, and special challenges.

Exercise 3.3

Confidentiality?

Directions: Along with a classmate or colleague, read each of the following client scenarios. Identify those in which you feel confidentiality should be maintained and those, if any, in which information needs to be disclosed. After reading Chapter 7, review your initial responses to this exercise and see if they change.

- A 13-year-old tells a school counselor that she is going to have sex with an older boy.

- A husband, in marriage counseling with his wife, calls the counselor and informs the counselor that he is currently having an affair with a man but does not want that disclosed in their joint sessions.

- An irate worker informs a counselor that "if I don't get a raise I'm going to kill Harold" (the worker's boss).

- A young woman informs her therapist that she has herpes and refuses to tell the man she is about to marry.

- A 14-year-old student tells his counselor that he is gay and is interested in experiencing a homosexual relationship.

- A depressed elderly man tells the nursing home social worker that he has been saving his medications and intends to overdose on them.

Appropriate Boundaries for Professional Relationships

Finally, it is generally agreed that the client has a right to enter a professional relationship with the helper. Relationships in which the helper is using the interaction with the client to meet his or her own personal needs or situations in which there exists a dual relationship between the helper and the client—such as may be the case when the helper and client have social and personal relationships—threaten this principle of professional contact. As with all of the ethical guidelines, it is not a simple, cut-and-dried matter. Clearly, there are times and situations when one may be a friend and yet be able to gain the professional objectivity to assist the client. Under these situations, it is important for the helper to attempt to define and maintain some control or boundaries on the types of information being discussed or on the nature of the relationship as it may be appropriate to each of the varied roles (e.g., friend or helper) (see Case Illustration 3.3). The issues of boundaries and the ethical use of power are discussed in detail in Chapter 10.

Case Illustration 3.3

Maintaining Boundaries and Clarifying Roles

Alex is a school counselor working at Mt. Helena High School. Alex was asked to work with a female student, Nguyen, who was new to the school and about whom the teacher, Mr. E., had some "serious concerns." Alex liked to consult with teachers whenever possible, so before meeting with the student, he went to talk with Mr. E. In conversation with Mr. E., he discovered that Mr. E. was concerned that this girl "looked just like his girlfriend Kim," and he just recently discovered that his girlfriend "was a liar and cheat." When asked directly as to the relevance, Mr. E. became very upset, started to cry, and said, "It's not Nguyen who needs the help, it's me—I can't get over her, I can't believe she was cheating on me. I feel like such an idiot."

Alex asked Mr. E. to come down to his office. Alex felt that he needed to reach out to his colleague in crisis and attempt to assist him in calming down and maybe make a plan for dealing with his own emotional upset. The following dialogue ensued:

Alex: It is clear that what has happened with you and Kim has been very upsetting to you. It even seems to be carrying over into your work.

Mr. E: (crying): It is. I can't sleep. I haven't eaten in the last two days. I don't care anymore.

Alex: It can certainly feel crushing when you lose someone you cared about.

Mr. E: (gaining some composure): Alex, I feel like such a fool; she and I were talking about getting married. But apparently she thought there was something wrong with me sexually or I couldn't . . .

Alex: (interrupting): Joe, it sounds like you have a lot of questions that need to be answered. Questions about your relationships, maybe even questions about yourself and the types of relationships you find yourself in . . . I know this is a painful time, but sometimes these are the times when, with the help of another; we really can gain some insight and grow.

Mr. E: I know, it just hurts so much! You said, with the help of another. Would you work with me?

Alex: First of all, Joe, I'm honored you've asked. But you and I are colleagues. We need to work together all of the time, plus I am trained as a school counselor and really not able to provide you the counseling that would be best for you. I do know people who are excellent for these kinds of experiences and I could give you their names and maybe even help you make a connection, if you would like.

Mr. E: Yeah . . . think I really need to do this. Thanks, Alex. I would appreciate those names. And (smiling) you don't have to call Nguyen down, she'll be fine.

Helper Competence

A final ethical principle shared across the various helping professions is that a helper must be aware of the limitations of his or her own professional competence and not exceed those limitations in the delivery of his or her service. It is all too easy for a helper to find himself or herself alone in an office or in the field of practice without teachers, mentors, or supervisors looking over her or his shoulder and assume that she or he can try this or that new technique or approach or deal with any and all problems or situations presented. Such is not the case. New techniques and new approaches need to be learned and practiced under the appropriate supervision. Similarly, we cannot be everything to everybody (see Case Illustration 3.4).

Case Illustration 3.4

Knowing Limits of Competence

Lewis is a marriage and family therapist certified through AAMFT. Lewis has been in private practice for two years and has already developed a reputation as an ethical, effective helper. A couple called and asked to make an appointment because they were having a lot of problems "communicating." During the intake interview, Lewis discovered that the wife had been sexually abused by both her father and her uncle from the age of 4 through to the age of 17. The woman revealed that, while she had never had counseling or therapy for this issue of abuse, she felt that she had resolved this issue and no longer had any problem with it.

As the interview continued, it became clear to Lewis that Elsa (the wife) was severely depressed and gave evidence of problems much deeper than the marital communications problem originally presented. Since Lewis didn't feel competent to diagnose the level of her problems or the possible existence of a personality disorder, he felt that proceeding as the couple requested to investigate communication issues might be a disservice to the couple and might even cause harm to the wife, should it engage her in painful memories. Lewis explained his concerns to the couple and helped them understand the value of the referral he was making.

Through careful, sensitive dialogue with this couple and an awareness of the limits of his own competence, Lewis was able to help this couple, and more specifically Elsa, get the assistance that they needed.

Knowing the limits to our competence, being willing to seek ongoing training and supervision, and knowing when to seek consultation from a colleague or make a referral to another helper are all characteristics of an ethical helper and are all discussed in detail in Chapters 11, 13, and 14.

● BEYOND KNOWING: A CALL TO BEING ETHICAL

It is clear that to be an ethical practitioner one must be fully aware and knowledgeable about the specific codes of conduct governing one's profession. However, as suggested previously, these codes of ethics reflect the ever-changing demands and needs of the members of that profession and the experiences of competing rights and responsibilities arising in the course of professional practice. As such, the codes are continually reviewed and revised. The ethical helper needs to keep current on his or her understanding of the literature reflecting the issues involved in ethical practice. Further, ethical practitioners need to consult with knowledgeable colleagues or members of their associations' boards of ethics anytime they have a concern about the ethical conflict of their practice decisions. This level of awareness and level of knowledge is the minimum for the ethical practitioner.

However, as noted, the focus of this text and the goal of each professional is not simply to know the ethical principles of one's profession. The call is for each professional to assimilate and incorporate these principles into his or her decision-making process (see Chapter 7). An organization's code of conduct and articulated ethical principles represent the collective concern and values of the members of that organization. However, until they are assimilated and personally valued by the practitioner, they remain only nice ideas and wishful guidelines. As each helper develops within his or her professional practice, he or she will not only gain increased knowledge and skill but will also begin to formulate internal values and standards of practice. The ethical helper must be willing to reflect on the guidelines provided by his or her profession as well as relevant dialogue with colleagues and then continue to formulate his or her own values that will then direct his or her helping interactions. In this way, the codes of ethics move from nice ideas or even meaningful statements to becoming embodied ways of practicing.

The goal is not simply to "know" ethics but rather to be ethical. The remainder of the book is devoted to help you in the process of moving from knowing ethics to being ethical.

CONCLUDING CASE ILLUSTRATION ●

Returning to our ongoing case of Ms. Wicks and Maria, Ms. Wicks has identified a number of values or beliefs that are currently giving shape to Maria's decision-making and to the helping relationship that is beginning to take significant shape.

As you read the exchange below, begin to identify explicit or implicit areas of potential ethical conflict. While no specific violations of ethics may have occurred to this point, a number of issues are revealed for which an understanding of the code of professional ethics would be essential as a guide for Ms. Wick's decision-making. The questions at the end of the exchange are provided to guide you in your reflections.

Maria: You know I just realized that you got me talking about stuff . . . like sex and stuff that I don't tell nobody.

Ms. Wicks: I truly appreciate your willingness to share things about yourself, it really . . .

Maria: (interrupting): Yeah . . . but you are not going to tell anyone. I mean like you know my aunt.

Ms. Wicks: Your aunt?

Maria: Yeah, Gloria Enrique. She was a teacher in Elsewhere High, where you used to work. Anyway, she told me you guys are like a priest and you can't say anything to anybody about what I tell you. Like, now this is just a for instance, but, what if I tell you I'm going to run away and go live with my boyfriend because he's dying of AIDS. You can't tell my mom or my aunt?

Ms. Wicks: Your boyfriend has . . .

Maria: (again, interrupting): Yeah, we talked about it and stuff . . . but this happened before he met me . . . so like I'm the only one who knows and I want to be with him and take care of him.

Reflections

1. Does the fact that Ms. Wicks previously worked with Maria's aunt violate any professional values? Create a possible boundary conflict?
2. Maria sees the mental health practitioner as protecting her confidentiality the same way a priest may regard material shared in the confessional. What are your feelings about this? What do you think Ms. Wicks should say? Do?
3. What should Ms. Wicks do about this new information regarding Maria's intent to run away? Is that something she should hold in confidence? How about the information about the boyfriend having AIDS? Should she disclose this information? If so, to whom? If not, why not?
4. Of all the information, both explicit and implied, that Ms. Wicks has gained to this point, what, if anything, should be documented and recorded?

● COOPERATIVE LEARNING EXERCISE

The purpose of this chapter was to introduce you to the role and function of professional ethics. But beyond this cognitive purpose, the hope was also to stimulate you to begin to value the need for a professional code of ethics and a desire to embrace it for your profession. The following is intended to assist you in this valuing process.

As with all of these cooperative exercises, the benefit that comes from the guided personal reflection is augmented by the sharing of this perspective with others.

Directions: Read each of the following scenarios. Identify areas of ethical concern in which issues of autonomy, beneficence, nonmaleficence, and justice may be operative:

- In the case illustration, the client, Maria, shared the possibility that she was having unprotected sex with a boyfriend whom she identified as having AIDS. Since AIDS is a medical condition and sexual activity is a personal decision, should either of these issues be of ethical concern for Ms. Wicks?
- Given your current level of training and the ethical concern for practicing within one's level of competence, what type of helping or for what type of client or problem do you currently feel competent to assist? What else will you need to do to increase your level of competence to be an ethical professional?
- If codes of ethics are commonly shared guidelines to be employed by each member of a specific profession, what role and level of responsibility does a member have in monitoring that his or her colleagues practice ethically?
- Identify two forms of unethical practice that you feel deserve maximum sanctioning by one's profession. What form should the sanctioning take?

SUMMARY

- Professional codes of ethics serve to educate the public and the members of that profession as to the specific responsibilities and expectations of that role and thus provide a mechanism for monitoring professional accountability and providing for improvement of practice.
- Each professional organization provides its members with specific guidelines for ethical practice and helps give clarification to the uniqueness of the role and function of that profession.
- While codes of ethics are unique to each profession, the following principles cut across the varied codes: (a) autonomy or the value of self-determination; (b) beneficence or the promotion of good for others; (c) nonmaleficence, meaning to do no harm; and (d) justice.

- The goal for ethical practice demands more than simply knowing the ethical principles of one's profession. The call is for each professional to assimilate and to incorporate these principles into his or her decision-making process.
- Ethical helpers must be willing to reflect on the guidelines provided by their profession, dialogue with colleagues about the guidelines, and then continue to formulate and reformulate their own values, which will then direct their helping interactions.

● IMPORTANT TERMS

American Association for
  Marriage and Family Therapy
  (AAMFT)

American Counseling
  Association

American Psychological
  Association (APA)

autonomy

beneficence

boundaries

codes of conduct

competent

confidentiality

decision-making process

ethics

informed consent

justice

marriage and family therapist

National Association of Social
  Workers (NASW)

nonmaleficence

power

professional relationship

sanction

● ADDITIONAL RESOURCES

Print

Bashe, A., Anderson, S. K., Handelsman, M. M., & Klevansky, R. (2007). An acculturation model for ethics training: The ethics autobiography and beyond. *Professional Psychology: Research and Practice, 38*(1), 60–67.

Jennings, L., Sovereign, A., Bottoroff, N., Mussell, M., & Vey, C. (2005). Nine ethical values of master therapists. *Journal of Mental Health Counseling, 27*(1), 32–47.

Kitchener, K. S. (1984). Intuition, critical evaluation and ethical principles: The foundation for ethical decisions in counseling psychology. *Counseling Psychologist, 12*(3), 43–55.

Sheperis, D. S., Henning, S. L., & Kocet, M. M. (2016). *Ethical decision making for the 21st century counselor.* Thousand Oaks, CA: Sage.

Sisti, D. A., Caplan A. L., & Rimon-Greenspan, H. (2013). *Applied ethics in mental health care: An interdisciplinary reader.* Cambridge, MA: MIT Press.

Web-Based

American Association for Marriage and Family Therapy. (AAMFT) (2015). *Codes of ethics.* Retrieved from http://www.aamft.org/imis15/content/legal_ethics/code_of_ethics.aspx

American Counseling Association. (2014). *Code of ethics.* Retrieved from http://www.counseling.org/resources/aca-code-of-ethics.pdf

American Mental Health Counselors Association. (2010). *Code of ethics.* Retrieved from http://c.ymcdn.com/sites/www.amhca.org/resource/resmgr/Docs/AMHCA_Code_of_Ethics_2010_up.pdf

American Psychological Association. (2010). *Ethical principles of psychologists and code of conduct.* Retrieved from http://www.apa.org/ethics/code/principles.pdf

National Association of Social Workers. (2008). *Code of ethics* (Rev. ed.). Retrieved from http://www.socialworkers.org/pubs/code/code.asp

REFERENCES ●

American Counseling Association. (2014). *Code of ethics.* Retrieved from http://www.counseling.org/resources/aca-code-of-ethics.pdf

American Psychological Association. (2010). *Ethical principles of psychologists and code of conduct.* Retrieved from http://www.apa.org/ethics/code/principles.pdf

Meyers, L. (2014). A living document of ethical guidance. *Counseling Today.* Retrieved from http://ct.counseling.org/2014/05/a-living-document-of-ethical-guidance/

National Association of Social Workers. (2008). *Code of ethics* (Rev. ed). Retrieved from: http://www.socialworkers.org/pubs/code/code.asp

CHAPTER 4

Ethical Practice in an Increasingly Diverse World

A serious moral vacuum exists in the delivery of cross-cultural counseling and therapy services because the values of a dominant culture have been imposed on the culturally different consumer.
(Pedersen & Marsella, 1982, p. 498)

The Pedersen and Marsella (1982) quote with which we opened the chapter is certainly both a warning against and a condemnation of unethical professional practice. Granted, the observation was made over 30 years ago, and we can take some comfort in the fact that our professions' attention to multiculturalism has become so widespread and intense that it has been called a "fourth force" (Pedersen, 1999). In addition, professional organizations (e.g. AAMFT, ACA, AMHCA, APA, NASW) have realized and have continued to discuss the implications of multiculturalism on the ethics of practice, which in turn have resulted in the extensive revisions of the codes governing ethical practice (see Table 4.1).

Human service professions have made clarion calls for practitioners to become multiculturally competent, warning of the possibilities that our own cultural values and biases can override those of our clients (ACA, 2005). Even though most professionals recognize the ethical responsibility

Table 4.1 Calling for Cultural Competence

Professional Organization	Statement on
American Association for Marriage and Family Therapy (2015)	1.1. Marriage and family therapists provide professional assistance to persons without discrimination on the basis of race, age, ethnicity, socioeconomic status, disability, gender, health status, religion, national origin, sexual orientation, gender identity or relationship status.
American Counseling Association (2014)	Page 4. "Counselors actively attempt to understand the diverse cultural backgrounds of the clients they serve . . ."
American Mental Health Counselors Association (2010)	C.1.g. Recognize the important need to be competent in regard to cultural diversity and are sensitive to the diversity of varying populations as well as to changes in cultural expectations and values over time.
National Association of Social Workers (2008)	1.05.c. Social workers should obtain education about and seek to understand the nature of social diversity and oppression with respect to race, ethnicity, national origin, color, sex, sexual orientation, gender identity or expression, age, marital status, political belief, religion, immigration status, and mental or physical disability.
American Psychological Association (2010)	Principle E. Psychologists are aware of and respect cultural, individual, and role differences, including those based on age, gender, gender identity, race, ethnicity, culture, national origin, religion, sexual orientation, disability, language, and socioeconomic status, and consider these factors when working with members of such groups.

to practice in a multiculturally sensitive manner (Lee, 2003), the reality is that in practice the avoidance of the negative effect of internalized bias and narrow worldviews is not an easy, nor is it a "one-time" task. Undoing our internalized prejudicial attitudes and bias requires an ongoing process of learning and unlearning in order to become and remain an ethical, multiculturally competent practitioner (Duan & Brown, 2016).

The current chapter is but one source and stimulant for that learning and unlearning. The chapter highlights the need for each practitioner to increase his or her awareness of both personal and professional biases; biases that can color his or her view of clients and even the approaches employed to assist them in their time of need. The chapter invites the reader to not only understand the codes of ethics that specifically address issues of diversity but, more importantly, to develop a perspective that allows him or her to engage in all practice decisions with multicultural sensitivity.

OBJECTIVES ●

As such the current chapter will help you to do the following:

- Increase your awareness of your own "worldview" and its potential impact on your practice decisions.
- Understand those ethical standards specifically addressing issues of diversity and the need to develop multicultural competence.
- Value the need to employ a lens of multicultural competence to review and reconsider (a) elements guiding the therapeutic relationship, (b) the processes of assessment and diagnosis and, (c) the formulation and implementation of a treatment plan.

PREJUDICE: PERVASIVE IN AND THROUGHOUT ● THE HELPING PROFESSION

Human behavior, human problems, and the process of helping occur within a social and cultural context. For a human service professional to view individual concerns or a person's problems as separate from that person's social, cultural context is to misunderstand them. There was a time when we in human services worked with clients of similar ethno-cultural backgrounds. However, the "flattening" of our world has increased the diversity of the populations we serve. No longer are we simply working with those who may differ from us in terms of social class or education, but we now engage with clients who differ from us in terms their fundamental worldviews, beliefs, and values. Our professions are truly multicultural in the populations we serve, with both the helper and client bringing unique cultural values and social roles to the interaction.

It is generally agreed among human service providers that appropriate treatment necessitates awareness of critical differences between ourselves and our clients in our beliefs and sensitivities as related to mental health, including such things as the presentation or expression of symptoms and even possible treatment preferences (Snowden, 2003). In fact, it could be argued that human service providers who do not integrate cross-cultural factors (e.g., gender, sexual orientation, ethnicity, race, age, social class) into their practice infringe on the client's cultural autonomy and basic human rights and thus lessen the chances for the development of an effective therapeutic relationship and process. Clearly, these conditions would serve as fodder for unethical practice. Increasing one's competence in providing ethical and effective service to an increasingly diverse client base begins with an increased awareness of the potential of both personal and professional bias and restricted worldviews.

Increasing Awareness of Personal Worldview

As indicated above (see Table 4.1), our professional codes of practice are clear in their directives regarding the need for ethical practitioners to increase awareness, sensitivity, and competence in working with a diverse client population. Our own cultural conditioning and the values and beliefs, or if you will, "worldview" that have been created can be identified as an "invisible veil," which not only operates outside of our consciousness but colors our assumptions about the nature of reality, ideal health and pathology, and approaches to helping (Sue, 2004). Our educational programs have incorporated multicultural counseling training throughout their curricula, and it is most likely that you have been or most certainly will be challenged to review your own worldview in order to increase your awareness of how that worldview may taint your assumptions and your expectations regarding your client and the service you will provide.

To be effective, ethical helpers, we must be sensitive to (a) our own cultural framework and the way it biases our attitudes, values, behaviors, and approaches to helping, and (b) the client's cultural makeup and the role this plays in the creation and resolution of the problem presented. The requirement is NOT that one becomes expert and master of all cultural nuance. The goal is to be aware of one's own worldview as it serves to filter and color client information and the dynamic of the helping relationship. Consider Case Illustration 4.1, which not only demonstrates one school counselor's desire to be helpful but also the negative effects that her somewhat limited and prejudicial worldview has on the helping relationship and dynamic.

Case Illustration 4.1

School Counselor: Filtering Client Information

Ms. Thompson is a senior high school counselor working with college placement. She has been recognized as extremely competent and quite successful at assisting her students to gain entrance to the colleges of their choice. Ms. Thompson also prides herself on being able to help her students gain entrance to the "best colleges."

Ms. Thompson is about to meet with Lida Alvarez, a transfer student who has shown an aptitude for mathematics. Lida's family recently moved to this district, having lived in a neighboring district for the past six years. Lida's family originally came from Argentina. Her family (Lida, an older brother, mother, father, and paternal grandparents) moved to the United States when Lida was 10 years old.

Ms. T: Hi, Lida. I'm Ms. Thompson, your college counselor. I see from your records that you are and have been a very good student. You appear to have a real knack for mathematics. I am interested in knowing what colleges you have begun to consider.

Lida: I am not thinking about going to college, at least not right after I graduate from high school.

Ms. T: Lida, if it is a financial issue there are a number of scholarships for which you would be a great candidate. I have a lot of success getting money for students.

Lida: No, it's not the money. I will be going to work with my siblings and dad in our family restaurant.

Ms. T: That is nice, Lida. However, don't you think that a person with your abilities should consider doing something beyond restaurant work?

Lida: It's not just restaurant work; it is our family's restaurant. It was originally my grandfather's and has been in our family for fifty

(Continued)

(Continued)

        years. They started it in Argentina, which my uncle's family continues to run, and we have had this one in the United States for six years now. This has been my grandfather's dream to bring his restaurant to the United States.

Ms. T: I didn't mean to suggest it is not a good restaurant. I just thought you may find it more stimulating and challenging to go on to college, maybe before you work in the restaurant.

Lida: Ms. Thompson, I am sure you mean well, but this really isn't about college, the restaurant, money, or any of that . . . it is about family, and for now my family needs me to work in the restaurant, and I want to be part of the tradition my grandfather started. There may be time later when I will want to consider something else, including college, but for now I am looking forward to graduating and helping out with my family. But, thanks for your help.

Potential Bias: Beyond the Personal to the Profession

While it is clear that this one counselor, Ms. Thompson, failed to grasp the value that family has for this one student and thus was pushing her "college agenda," it is not just our personal worldviews that can limit our understanding of our clients and the best means of providing them with ethical, effective service. The focus on elevating our awareness of personal bias and limited worldviews is essential. What may be missed in our training or our experience is the realization of the very subtle yet insidious effects of ingrained bias in our Western model of mental health and human service delivery. It is possible that the theories and paradigm employed to guide our processes of case conceptualization and treatment planning, having their roots in Western Psychology, are in fact prejudicial and limiting in our collective perspective. As such, it is essential that we not only increase our awareness of and sensitivity to our own personal bias but also those biases ingrained within our professional models of service delivery.

The European American worldview has been the basis for development of counseling as a profession, and the White middle class values have set the tone, the limit, the scope, and the process for counseling practices (Duan & Brown, 2016). Our theories have generally emerged from a philosophy that

(a) separates mind and body, (b) attempts to reduce experiences to a singular cause and, (c) sees the world in a deterministic (cause-effect) relationship (Kimura et al., 2005).

The effect of these assumptions and perspectives is that human service providers with a Western bias tend to focus on rational more than relational, logic more than emotion, competition more than cooperation, independence more than interdependence, and an individualistic rather than a collectivistic interest (Duan & Brown, 2016). It has been suggested that such an ethnocentric perspective of traditional mental health services has resulted in the underutilization of counseling services by ethnic and racial minorities (Ponterotto, Casas, Suzuki, & Alexander, 2001) and the overdiagnosis of various mental disorders of the culturally diverse (Schwartz & Feisthamel, 2009).

Our codes contain the ethical mandate to understand the cultural backgrounds of diverse clients; however, our practice is most often colored by a strong valuing of autonomy and individuality, elements that most clearly reflect the culture, norms, and values of Western society (Atkinson, 2004) and may demonstrate an insensitivity to our clients' diverse worldviews, where the valuing is on acceptance of rather than control over that which is uncontrollable or where the focus is on family and community rather than individual achievement and autonomy (Laurent & Dong, 2015).

Consider the following brief illustration of a young Chinese American woman, Changchang (Case Illustration 4.2).

Case Illustration 4.2

Changchang

Changchang is a 28-year-old MBA graduate student who has moved back in with her parents as a way of saving money during her years in graduate school. Changchang is single and like many in her program of study, deeply engaged in her graduate work. Changchang came to the counseling center with concerns about her stress level and the impact it is having on her physically (being unable to sleep, losing weight, frequent headaches) as well as her ability to concentrate on her studies. The initially identified source of the stress was the conflict she was experiencing with her parents. She described her parents as people who highly value academic achievement, to the exclusion of all other

(Continued)

(Continued)

activities. It is this exclusive focus on her academic tasks and performance and her parental "prohibitions" about her engaging with other students in a social context that have resulted in her feeling "devalued," "almost infantile," and most certainly "trapped." Changchang loves her parents and is truly grateful for their financial support during her attendance at graduate school. She shared her intense feelings of guilt about being "ungrateful" but noted that she was not sure that she could continue to endure their "old world values."

For many practitioners presented with a client such as Changchang (see Case Illustration 4.2), the focus of intervention may be on assisting her to challenge her guilt as being both irrational and dysfunctional in nature. The clinician may assist the client to reframe her perspective so as to allow for her acceptance of her own autonomy and right of self-determination. While such a focus would seem supported by our core values emphasizing client autonomy and be congruent with a cognitive approach to therapy, some (see Laurent & Dong, 2015) have suggested that these feelings of guilt may be of value within an Asian culture, in that they perpetuate an interdependent, harmonious, and peaceful family relationship and thus are neither irrational nor dysfunctional. Without one's developed multicultural competence, this value and perspective may be missed.

An illustration such as this is not presented as a directive to abandon our valuing of autonomy or the cognitive perspective but rather to encourage all human service providers to be aware of the subtle bias that may be operating in our practices and to be open to alternative worldviews presented by our clients.

While individual practitioners and our professions, as a whole, have made vast improvement in challenging this ethnocentric perspective, more research with expansive and representative samples will need to continue in order to increase the validity of our assessment procedures, diagnoses, and treatment protocols. In the meantime, it is essential that each of us, as ethical and effective practitioners, be mindful of our own personal limited worldviews and the limitations and potential bias ingrained in the professions in which we are engaged. Such increased awareness and acceptance of the myriad of worldviews is not only good practice but reflective of our ethical standards (see Table 4.1). Exercise 4.1 now invites you to consider potential values, assumptions, and biases ingrained in our Western-Psychology approach to helping.

Exercise 4.1

Examining Values, Assumptions, and Biases

Directions: Below you will find a table listing common targets or issues encountered by those in human services. Your task is to consider how the characteristics and culture of the client invite the clinician to revisit the issue through an alternative cultural lens. The exercise may require some research and in a couple of cases, you have been provided "hints" as to what to consider.

Issue	Mainstream Human Service Position	Client Description	Multicultural Consideration
(example) Establishing as a goal of counseling to increase the client's assertiveness	Human services value autonomy and the right to self-determination, thus this would, could be a legitimate goal.	A 43-year-old female from South Asia	The culture emphasizes finding meaning in group solidarity and relationship, de-emphasizing individualism and individual uniqueness.
Use of "smacking" and spanking in child rearing		A Dominican single mother who values the development of *respeto* in her 8-year-old child	
Physical contact (hugging) between a clinician and a client		A 61-year-old Arab male	

(Continued)

(Continued)

Issue	Mainstream Human Service Position	Client Description	Multicultural Consideration
Eye contact between therapist and client		A 23-year-old female from China, currently enrolled in a clinical psychology graduate program and receiving supervision in her internship	
Hallucinogen Intoxication		A 27-year-old member of a Native American Church	
Dependent-attachment behaviors		A 31-year-old Japanese female expressing a need for intense interpersonal attachment (hint: check the concept of *amae*)	
Bibliotherapy		A school counselor working with a second-grade Puerto Rican male having difficulty controlling aggressive impulses (hint: the value of *cuentos*)	
Concept of "time"		A 25-year-old Latino male with a weekly appointment with a clinical psychologist	

RESPONDING TO THE CHALLENGE ●

Over the course of the past 30 years, the human service professions have become increasingly aware of the role of culture and the potential of cultural bias in our theory and practice. As a result, there have been significant changes in the operational assumptions that undergird our approaches to service delivery (Ivey, Ivey, & Simek-Morgan, 1997). Some of the assumptions that have been challenged include (a) our very concept of normality, (b) the professions' emphasis on the individual (versus family or community), (c) the valuing of a goal of client growth in independence, (d) the universality of linear thinking, and (e) the reliance on verbal communications (Sue & Sue, 1999).

As evident in our evolving and evolved professional codes of ethics human service providers value the need to integrate cultural awareness and sensitivity into all aspects of our work. And as noted by Duan & Brown (2016), to provide service to culturally diverse clients, in the absence of such awareness and competency, is unethical.

The Ethical Practitioner Is AWARE

While increasing one's awareness and knowledge of alternative worldviews is necessary, we are in agreement with Sue et al. (2006) that competency goes beyond knowledge and skill and needs to be reflected in the very values, orientation, and "person" of the therapist. The challenge for all ethical practitioners is to increase awareness of her own assumptions, values, and biases as they undergird practice decisions. Such awareness is foundational to ethical practice, as noted by both the American Counseling Association (ACA, 2015, C.2.a) and the American Mental Health Counselors Association. (AMHCA, 2010, C.1.1)

> Whereas multicultural counseling competency is required across all counseling specialties, counselors gain knowledge, personal awareness, sensitivity, dispositions, and skills pertinent to being a culturally competent counselor in working with a diverse client population (ACA, 2015, C.2.a).

> Will actively attempt to understand the diverse cultural backgrounds of the clients with whom they work. This includes learning how the mental health counselor's own cultural/ethical/racial/religious identity impacts his or her own values and beliefs about the counseling process. (AMHCA, 2010 C.1.l)

The ethical counselor not only has an increased awareness of his personal worldview as it intersects with other/alternative worldviews but also values the dynamic influence that one's cultural, values, and beliefs have on practice decisions. See Exercise 4.2.

Exercise 4.2

Personal Worldview

Directions: Below you will find a number of "issues" and client "descriptors" that may elicit a strong personal reaction, reflecting a specific value, attitude, belief, or even bias. We invite you to reflect on each as they may influence your attitude and approach to a client with this characteristic or type of problem. It may help to discuss your reactions with a colleague, peer, or supervisor.

Client Characteristic:

- An overly indulged and pampered teen

- A strong, somewhat rigid, ethnocentric individual

- An unmarried, pregnant woman

- A veteran living on the street

- A 90-year-old showing signs of failing cognition

- A victim of a fire with massive total body scarring

- An abused spouse

Presenting Complaints/Issues:

- Heroin addiction

- Pedophilia

- Personality disorder—borderline

- Oppositional defiant disorder

- Hoarder

- Conflict with sexual orientation

- Multiple suicide attempts

Culture, Worldview, and the Nature of Professional Relationship

We now understand that much of what we took as *standard practice* when establishing a therapeutic relationship needs to be revisited with an eye toward our client's alternative culture and worldview. For example, while we in the West have generally embraced the value of counseling and mental health services, such is not the case in much of South Asia. For many South Asians who are experiencing psychological and development challenges, the preferred method of intervention is to seek support and assistance from an authority figure or extended family member. In many ways, this reflects their perspective that significant decision-making is the prerogative of the head of the household and targets that which is best, not so much for the individual as for the family (Chandras, 1997). In the rare circumstances where a South Asian client presents to an outsider for help, it would not be unusual to encounter familial demands to be consulted and or included in the therapy sessions, since issues and concerns are viewed as family business and not just that of the individual (Das & Kemp, 1997).

The ethical practitioner working with such a client would approach the establishment of informed consent, the setting of limits to confidentiality and boundaries, and even the valuing of client autonomy with an awareness of and sensitivity to this worldview, a point that is highlighted by our ethical codes of conduct (see Table 4.2).

Table 4.2 Ethical Practice: Manifesting Cultural Awareness and Sensitivity

Practice Focus	Organization	Code
Informed Consent	American Counseling Association (2014)	Standard A.2.c. The informed consent process and awareness of the role that language differences can play in the counseling relationship
Confidentiality	American Counseling Association (2014)	Standard B.1.a. Confidentiality and privacy from a cultural perspective
Diagnosis/ Assessment	American Counseling Association (2014)	Standards E.5.b, E.5.c, & E.8. Cultural sensitivity in the process of diagnosis and assessment

Autonomy

One of the fundamental principles that serves as a foundation to our ethical codes is the valuing of self-determination (i.e., autonomy). This valuing of the client as an autonomous agent gives direction to clinical decisions ranging from gaining informed consent, through goal setting, to termination.

Most practitioners understand that this principle of autonomy requires that protection be given to potentially vulnerable populations, such as children, the elderly, the mentally ill, or prisoners for whom autonomy of decision-making may be restricted. However, a question may arise as to the balancing of the clinician's valuing of autonomy with a client's valuing of a collective cultural worldview.

The very nature of this valuing of autonomy dictates that the clinician provides clients with the opportunity to choose what shall or shall not happen to them. But as suggested above, under some conditions (e.g., working with a client from South Asia) an alternative worldview may shift this power of decision-making to a source outside that of the client.

Informed Consent

In support of the value of autonomy, human service providers understand the need to provide all clients with that information that positions them to be able to make an informed decision regarding engagement in treatment. Informed consent is essential to our professional practice. It is not only in support of our core ethical value of autonomy but also is an expression of our valuing of the moral principle of beneficence.

Our codes of ethics and professional practice emphasize the need for clinicians to provide information in a way that is understandable to the client. For example, the American Counseling Association notes, "Counselors communicate information in ways that are both developmentally and culturally appropriate . . ." (ACA, 2014, Standard A.2.c). A similar directive is found in the American Psychological Association's code, where psychologists are directed to "obtain the informed consent of the individual or individuals using language that is reasonably understandable to that person or persons" (APA, 2010, Principle 3.10), and the National Association of Social Workers code, which highlights the need to provide clients with essential information in clear and understandable language: "Social workers should use clear and understandable language to inform clients of the purpose of the services, risks related to the services, limits to services because of the requirements of a third-party payer, relevant costs, reasonable alternatives, clients' right to refuse or withdraw consent, and the time frame covered by the consent" (NASW, 2008, Principle 1.03).

The ethical, multiculturally competent counselor is not only concerned with the specific language employed when seeking informed consent but is also sensitive to the very impact that the process of gaining informed consent can have on some clients from diverse cultural backgrounds. By establishing conditions where our clients can make an informed decision to engage or not to engage, human service providers facilitate a sense of empowerment. This practice of seeking informed consent, while appearing somewhat commonplace, can be a transformational experience for those clients whose culture may have limited their sense of personal power. Consider how the client feels in Case Illustration 4.3.

Case Illustration 4.3

I Can Choose?

Louisa is a 38-year-old Latina woman who has come to see Dr. Lane, a psychologist, at the urging of her pastor. Louisa has been very sad since her mother's death a few months ago. Her children are all in school during the day, and she has never had a job outside the home, as she feels she must follow her husband's wishes to stay home and take care of the family. She expressed extreme loneliness to her pastor one day after church, and although she doesn't think her husband would approve, she took the pastor's advice and made an appointment with Dr. Lane. The following is the first encounter between Dr. Lane and Louisa.

Dr. Lane: Hello, Louisa, it is very nice to meet you.

Louisa: Hello, Dr. . . . I'm not sure what you can do, but my pastor told me to come, and I'll do whatever you suggest if it'll make me feel better.

Dr. Lane: Well, I'm very glad you decided to come. We can talk about what you would like to talk about, and we can certainly see if there are things that you would like to change.

Louisa: You mean, you aren't just going to tell me what to do?

Dr. Lane: No, we can talk about those things together. But first, I'd like to go over what these sessions will do and what they won't do. Then you can decide if you think you would like to continue having these sessions with me.

Louisa: You mean, I can choose what to talk about? I could go somewhere else? I can choose?!

As you can tell from Louisa's response in Case Illustration 4.3, she was surprised that she was given a choice to make decisions on her own. For some clients, the respect, autonomy, and empowerment experienced within a therapeutic relationship may be received with a real sense of joy, awakening, and personal growth. However, not all clients will have such a positive response. It is possible that a client could experience stress and anxiety as a result of being placed in a position of such empowerment and decision-making, as it conflicts with ingrained cultural values. As such, it is important for all practitioners to be sensitive to the potential of such value conflicts and, as directed by one code of ethics, to "consider cultural implications of informed consent procedures and, where possible, counselors adjust their practices accordingly" (ACA, 2015, Standard A.2.c).

Confidentiality

Our codes of ethics and practice are clear in their support of treating a client's disclosure, when possible, as confidential. While the directive is clear, what may be less obvious is that this respect for client privacy as embodied in our codes of confidentiality may fail to consider the unique challenges to this principle when working with a client from another culture and/or worldview.

Consider a situation of a school counselor who finds herself in between school policy and cultural values (see Case Illustration 4.4).

Being ethical demands not only an understanding of our codes but also the application of those codes in conjunction with a respecting of a client's values and worldview. This point has been clearly articulated in the *ACA Code of Ethics*, which states, "Counselors maintain awareness and sensitivity regarding cultural meanings of confidentiality and privacy. Counselors respect differing views toward disclosure of information. Counselors hold ongoing discussions with clients as to how, when, and with whom information is shared" (ACA, 2014, Standard B.1.a).

As such, the counselor in our case illustration (Case Illustration 4.4) could neither simply follow the dictate of the organization in which she worked nor guarantee absolute confidentiality. Resolution of this ethical dilemma is not simple or clear cut. To resolve what is a culturally complex situation in a way that reflects the codes of professional practice and organizational policy while at the same time honors the client's worldview will require the counselor's reflection, sensitivity, consultation (with supervisors) and collaboration with the client.

Case Illustration 4.4

Please Don't Tell My Parents

Dr. Alonzo, the school counselor at S. J. H. High School, found herself in a bit of a quandary when approached by a 16-year-old student seeking counseling. The student presented as angry, anxious, and mildly depressed over the fact that her parents refuse to allow her to date, and as such she had been denied the opportunity to go to the prom with a boy from her class.

Given the presenting concern and the fact that the student's grades had been dropping, the counselor agreed to work with the student and in line with school policy informed the client of the need to obtain parental permission for continued contact. To the counselor's surprise, the statement that parental permission would be needed elicited a strong and unexpected reaction from the student. The student pleaded with the counselor to maintain confidence.

Dr. Alonzo was aware that the student's parents were immigrants from India and that the student's engagement in personal counseling may be creating a values conflict. While supporting the student's healthy development and unfolding sense of autonomy and empowerment, Dr. Alonzo was aware of the family and cultural values that empower parents and even extended family members to decide when and with whom dating, courting, and even marriage will take place. In addition, while accepting the school policy requiring parental consent for all "personal" counseling, she understood that the very fact this student had disclosed such personal and familial information to a family "outsider" would be seen by her parents as a violation of family values and a source of shame for the family. It was this concern that served as the source of the student's strong emotional response regarding the need to seek parental permission.

Not only was the student now in crisis, but also the counselor found that she was stuck between two cultures: those of the student's family and the school in which she worked.

Boundaries

While all codes of ethics caution against engaging in multiple relationships with clients, professional and personal, the strict adherence to such boundary controls may not be relevant or even realistic for those working in multicultural settings. Further, it is possible that sometimes it is more harmful to adhere to strict boundaries than it is to interact in a genuine, culturally congruent manner.

In some settings, it is by participating in community activities, such as graduation parties, community celebrations, or even sporting events, that one can gain the trust of clients. When these events are extensions of family celebrations, the human service provider, while being aware of the need to be cautious and considerate in what she does or says, must also be sensitive to cultural rules of hospitality so as not to be insulting or rude while attempting to maintain a semblance of appropriate boundaries. Such cultural sensitivity and awareness would extend to issues such as nonsexual physical contact, the sharing of personal information, and even the reception of gifts.

Consider the situation in which a therapist is attending the college graduation party of a client with whom he did both career and personal counseling. At the party, he is presented a gift as a token of appreciation for all that he (and the client) had achieved. Many human service providers, whose codes of ethics caution against the "potential danger" of accepting gifts from a client, might find the situation one that not only makes them feel uncomfortable but also signals a violation of professional boundaries. This is especially true if the worth of the gift is significant and where the possibility of exploitation may exist (AAMFT, 2015). However, while our standards of practice caution the potential danger of accepting gifts from clients, they also invite us to "attend to cultural norms when considering whether to accept gifts from or give gifts to clients (AAMFT, 2015, Standard 3.9) and "recognize that in some cultures, small gifts are a token of respect and gratitude" (ACA, 2015, Standard A.10.f) and that rejection could be an insult and potentially damaging.

Thus, human service providers need to aware of the cultural meaning of gift giving and the possibility that rejection could signal disrespect. This might be especially true for those clients who come from a culture that stresses hospitality, reciprocity, or the importance of gift-giving rituals (Barnett & Bivings, 2002).

Defining and Assessing a Presenting Concern

In defining mental health and diagnosing pathology, human service providers often employ a set of behaviors that have collectively been accepted as evidence of normality and ideal mental health (Sue, Sue, & Sue, 2006). The problem with such a paradigm is that it is possible that certain specific cultural behaviors could be viewed as pathological when assessed through a culturally narrow lens. One example offered by Duan and Brown (2016) is that of an Asian American woman who is perceived as weak in ego strength and low in self-esteem, given her tendency to be highly compromising and tolerant of spousal anger. A lack of cultural awareness on the part of mental health providers and the tendency to employ diagnostic categories and criteria in another culture without ensuring their validity can result in inappropriate diagnoses. Codes of ethics, such as that of the American Counseling Association, caution against such a monocultural perspective: "Counselors recognize that culture affects the manner in which clients' problems are defined and experienced. Clients' socioeconomic and cultural experiences are considered when diagnosing mental disorders" (ACA, 2014, Standard E.5.b).

When engaging in clinical assessment, all mental health providers are ethically directed to employ approaches and instruments with proven validity and reliability. For example, "mental health counselors are directed to choose assessment methods that are reliable, valid and appropriate based on the age, gender, race, ability and other client characteristics. If tests must be used in the absence of information regarding the aforementioned factors, the limitations of generalizability should be duly noted" (AMHCA, 2010, D.1.a).

While it is obvious that current standardized "Western" instruments demand a level of linguistic competence, the risk to validity and utility goes beyond the client's language capabilities. It is essential that the multiculturally competent and ethical practitioner not only ensure that procedures account for language difference but also employ concepts that are familiar and similar across cultures and normative standards that reflect the culture and uniqueness of the client. Psychologists, for example, have been directed by their code of ethics to employ those instruments where the psychometric properties have been established for the population being assessed (APA, 2010, Sections 9.02b, 9.02c) and interpret results from the perspective and language of the client (APA, 2010, Section 9.06).

A similar stance is articulated in the *ACA Code of Ethics*, stating "counselors select and use with caution assessment techniques normed on populations other than those of the client. Counselors recognize the effects of age, color, culture, disability, ethnic group, gender, race, language preference, religion, spirituality, sexual orientation, and socioeconomic status on test administration and interpretation, and they place test results in proper perspective with other relevant factors" (ACA, 2014, Standard E.8).

Without these measures, one can commit errors not just in diagnosis and classification but treatment planning and implementation. Again, as noted in one profession's code of ethics, "Mental health counselors consider multicultural factors (including but not limited to gender, race, religion, age, ability, culture, class, ethnicity, sexual orientation) in test interpretation, in diagnosis, and in the formulation of prognosis and treatment recommendations" (AMHCA, 2010 D.2.c).

As such, it is imperative that when engaging in assessment, practitioners consider the degree to which they (a) know the range of normal behavior for this client's group; (b) know the patterns of disorder for this client's group; (c) know what the client's group considers the cause of disorder to be; and (d) know what treatment preferences the client may have and whether alternatives are available (Marsella, 2011).

Establishing and Implementing a Treatment Plan

When we speak of cultural competence in the provision of our services, we target more than the practitioner's knowledge of another culture. In developing culture competence, service providers need to embrace and value the need to be able to adapt interventions to meet the culturally unique needs of their clients (Whaley & Davis, 2007). In responding to the ethno-cultural uniqueness of our clients, we must come to respect the potential pernicious effects of myopically viewing standards of normality and treatment approaches through Western assumptions and practices. A point which is reflected in our professional codes of practice is illustrated by the statement found in the code of the American Mental Health Counselors Association, as was noted earlier.

Being sensitive and responsive to a client's cultural values and background in developing intervention goals and processes is essential if one is to be an ethical practitioner. As noted by the American Mental Health Counselors Association (2010), the ethical multiculturally competent practitioner will work to devise "integrated, individual counseling plans that offer reasonable promise of success and are consistent with the abilities, ethnic, social, cultural, and values backgrounds, and circumstances of the clients" (AMHCA, 2010, B.1.a). Consider the case of Valentina V. (see Case Illustration 4.5).

For many service providers, working with a client such as Valentina (Case Illustration 4.5), the valuing of client "autonomy" may give shape to treatment goals (e.g., increasing personal empowerment and self-determination) and even treatment strategies (e.g., use of cognitive interventions). While a counselor's focus on self-determination and empowerment as goals for counseling might be viewed as developmentally appropriate, they may

---

Case Illustration 4.5

Valentina V.

Valentina, an 18-year-old high school senior, entered the counseling center presenting as both anxious and depressed. Valentina is a Hispanic American whose grandfather left Mexico 30 years ago. The family—both grandparents, mom, dad and Valentina's two older siblings—work in a small family owned farm and restaurant.

Valentina has demonstrated a gift for mathematics and has shared her interest in pursuing a degree in mathematics in hopes of becoming an actuary. Valentina, while excited about the possibilities that lay ahead, including the real possibility of receiving numerous scholarship offers, is also aware of the family tradition and expectation for all members of the family to engage in the family farming and restaurant business.

While there has been no direct prohibition presented by her family, the discussion within the family is about Valentina taking over all the bookkeeping responsibilities from her mom, living at home, and eventually marrying from within her community. The family expectations, when contrasted to the excitement and hope shared by her college-bound friends, has made Valentina feel torn between two worlds and has resulted in her increased stress, anxiety, and depression. The conflict is affecting Valentina's ability to concentrate, and as a result, her grades have fallen dramatically. When asked about her school performance, Valentina's comment is "why bother?"

---

also fail to reflect sensitivity and an awareness of the cultural context in which the client has been raised and the resultant values ingrained. It is essential to ethical and effective practice that we not only have clarity about our own values and biases but also respect alternative worldviews and the power of the ingrained cultural values. With such an awareness and sensitivity, the counselor in this case may be able to facilitate Valentina's identification of all the issues involved and the depth to which she is experiencing a personal values conflict in which she is moved to accomplish both things— that is, to embody familial and cultural expectations as well as to experience new challenges and directions in her own life.

In addition to processing therapeutic goals through a multicultural lens, the ethical practitioner will also be sensitive to the need to modify intervention approaches so that they are sensitive and responsive to a client's unique cultural orientation. While such modification may result in the inclusion of more "native" approaches and/or collaboration with elders of the community or identified healers, it also may direct the human service provider to actually ensuring that there is a community-based network of support. If these services are not present, the ethical professional should attempt to develop them by working with community leaders (Marsella, 2011).

● CONCLUDING CASE ILLUSTRATION

As you continue your engagement with Maria, it is important to attempt to view Ms. Wicks's interaction and interventions as they may or may not reflect her awareness of and sensitivity to multicultural issues. In Chapter 2, you were asked to reflect on your own competence in working with adolescents and Latina females. We now want to expand our view of this interaction through a multiculturally sensitive lens.

As previously suggested, it may be helpful to place yourself in the role of counselor, contrasting your reactions to those exhibited by Ms. Wicks. Finally, after reading and reflecting upon the interaction, consider the points raised in the section entitled Reflections.

Ms. Wicks: I can appreciate that you have in fact reached sexual maturity and feel like a women rather than a child and that you feel that becoming pregnant at this point in your life would be a sign of God's blessing. Could you help me to understand how this fits with your Catholic beliefs in the importance of marriage prior to having a baby?

Maria: I go to church and my God is a God of love, and He wouldn't let anything happen unless it was right.

Ms. Wicks: Clearly you have strong beliefs and opinions, and I guess my question was seen as a challenge to those beliefs, but I was just trying to clarify my own understanding. Also, I wonder if you have any experience with young couples who had a baby where it was not really good for the parents, the couple, or the baby?

Maria: Yeah, there are plenty of sluts in our community that pop out babies. But this is different—they are not born out of love. Just sex!

Ms. Wicks: Have you and your boyfriend talked about how a baby in your life may change your life? You know, things like your ability to go out socially, or the financial impact, or . . .

Maria: Not yet . . . he doesn't want to discuss these things. . . . He just says, "We'll work it out."

Ms. Wicks: How do you feel about his response?

Maria: Honestly, it is frustrating. My cousin had a baby when she was 16 and had to drop out of school and is now living with my grandmother and is really having a tough time. I don't want that to happen to me.

Reflections

1. Most human service providers with a Western bias tend to focus on rational more than relational, logic more than emotion, competition more than cooperation, independence more than interdependence, and an individualistic rather than a collectivistic interest (Duan & Brown, 2016). Is there any evidence that Ms. Wicks may be operating from such a Western-biased perspective? If so, what impact, if any, does it have on the relationship and process of working with Maria?

2. At one point, Ms. Wicks appeared to be confronting Maria's position that a baby would be evident of God's approval of the relationship. How did you feel about that part of the interaction? Were there any ethical issues that may have been revealed?

3. From your perspective, does the revelation of Maria's participation in unprotected sex, along with her apparent valuing of the possibility of becoming pregnant, raise any concerns on your part regarding confidentiality?

4. As you see the unfolding of this interaction, what goal would you have for moving into the next session? How does this goal reflect your sensitivity to and valuing of the multicultural factors, including, gender, race, religion, age, ability, culture, class, ethnicity, and so forth?

COOPERATIVE LEARNING EXERCISE ●

Throughout this chapter, emphasis was placed on the subtle and pernicious effects that one's personal values and biases can have on professional practice. Further, it was noted that given the "Western-Psychology" bias found within our models and theories of practice, human service providers are potentially at risk of failing to "respect" and account for alternative worldviews while establishing goals and treatment plans. The final exercise (Exercise 4.3) is offered as an opportunity to increase both awareness and sensitivity to bias, both personal and professional, and their potential impact on service delivery.

Exercise 4.3

Value Conflicts: Personal and/or Professional

Part 1: Part I invites you to review the brief description of each case and identify a specific goal and treatment approach or strategy that you would employ. After identifying your own goals and strategies, share these with a classmate, colleague, or supervisor. Is there any commonality? What do you feel is the source of the commonality, should such exist? If there are significant differences in the goals and strategies established, discuss the possible source of such diversity of opinion.

- The client is a 27-year-old single woman experiencing anxiety about the man whom she has been dating for 15 months and who she believes is about to ask her to marry him.

- The client, a 34-year-old male, was "mandated" to attend counseling after being stopped for a traffic violation and discovered to have an ounce of marijuana in the car.

- A 52-year-old female came to counseling because of anxiety and concerns about taking a job promotion, which would require relocation to another state.

Part 2: In Part 2, we have provided some additional information about the clients. As an ethical practitioner, would you, based on this information, modify your original goal and/or approach? If so, how and why?

- The client is a refugee from Somalia and a victim of the practice of genital mutilation as a child. Additionally, the gentleman, while Muslim, is from Saudi Arabia and not Somalia.

- The client is from Nepal and is one of eight graduate students attending the local university here in the United States. As he explained, the traffic violation (i.e., "rolling" through a stop sign) occurred when he was on his way to meet up with the members of his community to celebrate the festival of Holi. Further, he explained that the marijuana was *bhang*, the leaves and tops of the plant that would be consumed at the festival.

- The client is a very successful PhD biochemist who has rapidly advanced in a major pharmaceutical company. She is an only child of Chinese parents and recently had her mother (father is deceased) move from China to live with her, because of her mother's failing health. Her mother is just beginning to feel comfortable with her team of health care providers, and with the client finally accepting the new position, the thought of relocating with her daughter has caused her mother extreme anxiety.

Part 3: Along with your classmate, colleague, or supervisor, discuss the potential influence of personal or professional bias that may have been revealed by this exercise.

SUMMARY ●

- It is generally agreed among human service providers that appropriate treatment necessitates awareness of critical differences between minority individuals and others in beliefs and sensitivities related to mental health, including expression of symptoms, and in treatment preferences (Snowden, 2003).
- Our own cultural conditioning and the resultant values and beliefs color our assumptions about the nature of reality, ideal health and pathology, and approaches to helping (Sue, 2004).
- Some of the assumptions that have been challenged include (a) our very concept of normality, (b) the professions' emphasis on the individual (versus family or community), (c) the valuing of a goal of client growth in independence, (d) the universality of linear thinking, and (e) the reliance on verbal communications (Sue & Sue, 1999).
- The European American worldview has been the basis for development of counseling as a profession, and the White, middle class values have set the tone, the limit, the scope, and the process for counseling practices (Duan & Brown, 2016).
- Our theories have generally emerged from a philosophy that (a) separates mind and body, (b) attempts to reduce experiences to a singular cause and, (c) sees the world in a deterministic (cause-effect) relationship (Kimura, et al., 2005).
- When assessing clients, multiculturally competent and ethical practitioners not only ensure that procedures account for language difference but also employ concepts that are familiar and similar across cultures and normative standards that reflect the culture and uniqueness of the client.

- In working with clients of diverse backgrounds, it is imperative that one (a) knows the range of normal behavior for this client's group; (b) knows the patterns of disorder for this client's group; (c) knows what the client's group considers the cause of disorder to be; and (d) knows what treatment preferences the client may have and whether alternatives are available (Marsella, 2011).

● IMPORTANT TERMS

assessment	informed consent
autonomy	interventions
awareness	multiculturalism as "fourth force"
boundaries	
confidentiality	multiculturally competent
deterministic view	personal worldview
diagnosis	Western Psychology

● ADDITIONAL RESOURCES

Print

Abdullah, T., & Brown, T. L. (2011). Mental illness stigma and ethnocultural beliefs, values and norms: An integrative review. *Clinical Psychology Review, 31,* 934–948.

Duan, C., & Brown, C. (2016). *Becoming a multiculturally competent counselor.* Thousand Oaks, CA: Sage.

McAuliffe, G. (2009). *Culturally alert counseling: An introduction.* Thousand Oaks, CA; Sage.

Sue, D. W., & Sue, D. (2013). *Counseling the culturally diverse: Theory and practice* (6th ed.). Hoboken, NJ: John Wiley.

Web-Based

Association for Multicultural Counseling and Development. Providing global leadership, research, training and development for multicultural counseling professionals with a focus on racial and ethnic issues. http://multiculturalcounseling.org/

Multicultural Counseling and Social Justice Competencies. Websites linked to this site are (a) general websites regarding the study of social justice, culture, and race- or culture-specific information; and (b) psychology and counseling websites, especially those related to cultural competence and social justice or advocacy. http://toporek.org/websites.html

Nigatu, H. (2013, December 9). 21 racial microaggressions you hear on a daily basis. *Buzzfeed*, retrieved from http://www.buzzfeed.com/hnigatu/racial-microaggressions-you-hear-on-a-daily-basis

Video Clip of "Gua Sha/The Treatment" portrays the different cultural values between Western society (i.e., the legal and social welfare services in the United States) and a Chinese American family. http://www.youtube.com/watch?v=gMq9FDq_A0s Race: The Power of an Illusion: http://www.pbs.org/race/000_General/000_00- Home.htm

REFERENCES ●

American Association for Marriage and Family Therapy. (2015). *Code of ethics.* Retrieved from https://www.aamft.org/iMIS15/AAMFT/Content/Legal_Ethics/Code_of_Ethics.aspx

American Counseling Association. (2005). *Code of ethics.* Alexandria, VA: Author.

American Counseling Association. (2014). *Code of ethics.* Retrieved from http://www.counseling.org/resources/aca-code-of-ethics.pdf

American Mental Health Counselors Association. (2010). *Code of ethics.* Retrieved from http://c.ymcdn.com/sites/www.amhca.org/resource/resmgr/Docs/AMHCA_Code_of_Ethics_2010_up.pdf

American Psychological Association. (2010). *Ethical principles of psychologists and code of conduct.* Retrieved from http://www.apa.org/ethics/code/principles.pdf

Atkinson, D. R. (2004). *Counseling American minorities* (6th ed.). Boston: McGraw Hill.

Barnett, J. E., & Bivings, N. D. (2002). *Culturally sensitive treatment and ethical practice. The Maryland Psychologist, 48*(2), 8, 25.

Chandras, K. V. (1997). Training multiculturally competent counselors to work with Asian, Indian Americans. *Counselor Education and Supervision, 37,* 50-59.

Das, A. K., & Kemp, S. F. (1997). Between worlds: Counseling South Asian Americans. *Journal of Multicultural Counseling and Development, 25,* 23-33.

Duan, C. & Brown, C. (2016). *Becoming a multiculturally competent counselor.* Thousand Oaks, CA: Sage.

Ivey, A. E., Ivey, M. B., & Simek-Morgan, L. (1997). *Counseling and psychotherapy.* Needham Heights, MA: Allyn & Bacon.

Kimura, H., Nagao, F., Tanaka, Y., Sakai, S. Ohnishi, S. T., & Okumura, K. (2005). Beneficial effects of the Nishino breathing method on the immune activity and stress level. *Journal of Alternative Complementary Medicine, 11,* 285-291.

Laurent, M. G., & Dong, S. (2015). East meets West. In R. Parsons and N. Zhang, *Counseling theory: Guiding reflective practice* (pp. 443–465). Thousand Oaks, CA: Sage.

Lee, C. C. (2003). *Multicultural issues in counseling: New approaches to diversity* (3rd ed.). Alexandria, VA: American Counseling Association.

Marsella, A. J. (2011). *Twelve critical issues for mental health professionals working with ethno-culturally diverse populations.* Retrieved from http://www.apa.org/international/pi/2011/10/critical-issues.aspx

National Association of Social Workers. (2008). *Code of ethics* (Rev. ed.). Retrieved from http://www.socialworkers.org/pubs/code/code.asp

Pedersen, P. (1999). *Multiculturalism as a fourth force.* Washington, DC: Brunner/Mazel.

Pedersen, P. B., & Marsella, A. J. (1982). The ethical crisis for cross-cultural counseling and therapy. *Professional Psychology, 13,* 492–500.

Ponterotto, J. G., Casas, J. M., Suzuki, L. A., & Alexander, C. M. (Eds.). (2001). *Handbook of multicultural counseling* (2nd ed.). Thousand Oaks, CA: Sage.

Schwartz, R. E., & Feisthamel, K. P. (2009). Disproportionate diagnosis of mental disorders among African American versus European American clients: Implications for counseling theory, research and practice. *Journal of Counseling and Development, 87*(3), 295–301.

Snowden, L. R. (2003, February). Bias in mental health assessment and intervention: Theory and evidence. *American Journal of Public Health. 93*(2), 239–243. Retrieved from http://www.ncbi.nlm.nih.gov/pmc/articles/PMC1447723/

Sue, D. (2004). Whiteness and ethnocentric monoculturalism: Making the "invisible" visible. *American Psychologist, 59*(8), 761–769. doi:10.1037/0003-066X.59.8.761

Sue, D., Sue, D., & Sue, S. (2006). *Understanding abnormal behavior* (8th ed.). Boston, MA: Houghton Mifflin.

Sue, D. W., & Sue, D. (1999). *Counseling the culturally different: Theory and practice* (3rd ed.). New York, NY: Wiley.

Sue, D. W., Arredondo P., & McDavis, R. (1992). Multicultural counseling competencies and standards: A call to the profession. *Journal of Counseling and Development, 70,* 477–486.

Whaley, A. L., & Davis, K. E. (2007). Cultural competence and evidence-based practice in mental health services: A complementary perspective. *American Psychologist, 62*(6), 563–574.

PART II

Ethics and Standards of Practice: The Professions' Response

CHAPTER **5**

Ethics and the Law

Mr. Harolds: Hi, Michelle. What's up?

Ms. Wicks: Tom, could I talk to you about some legal concerns?

Mr. Harolds: Legal concerns? Certainly, but I'm not a lawyer.

Ms. Wicks: No, I know that—but you seem to stay current with laws and regulations regarding counseling and to tell you the truth, I'm not sure if it is a problem or not.

Mr. Harolds: Well, you certainly sound concerned. What's up?

Most mental health practitioners enter the profession intending to employ their knowledge and skills to assist those in need—not concerning themselves about the legal complications of the issues and the people with whom they work. The reality is that, just as there are ethical principles and guidelines that need to be considered when making professional decisions, there are also legal mandates and implications of which the ethical practitioner must be fully aware.

Laws, including legislation, court decisions, and regulations, have grown both in presence and importance in the practice of human service. Many federal statutes, such as those requiring the reporting of suspected abuse or the protection of confidential records and HIPAA laws as well as case law, have impacted practitioners' ethical judgments involving informed consent, conflicts of interest, dual relationships, practitioner competence, and termination of services (Reamer, 2013). Issues defining the rights of clients, the rights of the practitioner, the way in which services are selected and provided, and the nature of the relationship between the practitioner and client are all being shaped by the professional codes of conduct and now by extension of those codes into law. Some complain that law has made practitioners more concerned for personal liability than client welfare. Bergantino (1996), for example, states: "In our current psycholitigious world . . . we only have left brains, and . . . only what is 'appropriate' is thought to constitute therapy. Forget 'excellence' . . . Our profession is now defined by those who want to make the world safe for mediocrity!" (p. 31).

The sad truth is that practitioners are vulnerable to legal action, and many have opted to play it safe at the expense of providing the best service for their clients. While litigation is a reality that now must be placed within the mix of professional decision-making, laws are not meant to make practitioners feel threatened. Quite often the law parallels and further codifies sound ethical practice and as such, need not induce anxiety or concern within the ethical practitioner. But there are times when the relationship between ethics and legality is not clear or in fact may appear in conflict. At those times, the question becomes, what's the ethical helper to do?

The current chapter focuses upon the unique and ever-evolving relationship between professional codes of conduct and the law, in hopes of helping practitioners find an answer to this question.

● OBJECTIVES

The relationship of professional ethics and the laws governing professional practice is the focus of the current chapter. After reading this chapter, you should be able to do the following:

- Describe the obligations incurred by a helper who has established a "special relationship" with a client.
- Explain what is meant by "duty to care" and what defines that obligation.
- Describe how licensure and/or certification may lend legal power to the professional codes of conduct.
- Provide examples of ethical practice that may be illegal and the legal requirements that may violate professional codes of ethics.
- Describe one model for identifying and resolving conflict between ethics and legality.

THE HELPING PROCESS AS A LEGAL CONTRACT ●

As a result of malpractice suits and legal actions, it is generally recognized that a professional relationship or even the perception that the relationship is a professional one constitutes the basis of the existence of legal duty to provide appropriate care for a client. The professional help giver, by the very nature of holding himself or herself out in practice, implies that he or she will conduct himself or herself in a skillful and responsible manner and will follow the dictates of that profession's code of ethics.

The issue of whether helping is contractual and thus a minimum duty of care is established rests with the courts' decision as to whether a "special relationship" existed that would be sufficient to create a "duty of care." Such a special relationship can certainly be created with the use of formal treatment contracts in which the "duties" of each party are specified (see Exercise 5.1). However, the establishment of a formal contract articulating the relationship between client and practitioner or the rendering of a bill and exchange of money for services is not necessary in order to provide evidence of a special relationship and a duty to care.

A special relationship between helper and client can be established as a result of implicit acts. Courts, for example, may determine that a special relationship and thus a duty to care was established by the helper's action of taking notes, scheduling formal appointments, and even advertising as one who can provide unique, helping services. These actions can be interpreted as reflecting an intent to render service and thus constitute a basis of establishing the intent to form a special relationship and thus a contract to provide the care. As with many areas of law and ethics, there is no singular court case or clear directive that determines what actions, beyond a formal contract, can be used to demonstrate an intent to form a special relationship and thus a duty to provide care.

While there has not been a single court definition and ruling that provides a universal standard regarding implicit contract or duty to care, numerous state rulings have begun to give shape to this contract of professional service. In what now stands as a classic case, the Supreme Court of Wisconsin (*Bogust v. Iverson*, 1960) ruled against the parents of a student,

Jane Dunn filed suit against the director of student personnel services at Stout State College. The parents alleged there was negligence, because the director failed to provide proper guidance or protection for the student, who committed suicide. In the ruling against the parents, the Wisconsin Supreme Court referred to the defendant as a teacher and not a counselor and as such reported no special relationship had been established. "To hold that a teacher who has no training, education, or experience in medical

Exercise 5.1

The Use of Contracts: Formal and Informal

Many mental health practitioners, as a reflection of their concern to assist clients to be fully informed, have begun to provide clients with "contracts" of service. These contracts can be more or less formalized, ranging from simple information sheets with identified fees, cancellation policies, and so forth, to a formal statement requiring signatures and witnesses from all parties involved.

Directions: Contact each of the following: (a) a residential treatment program or hospital, (b) a free clinic, (c) a private practitioner, (d) a university counseling center, (e) an elementary or high school counseling center, and (f) a local church or religious organization. For each of these service providers identify each of the following:

- Do they employ some form of agreement or contract when providing services (counseling, mental health) to their clients? If so, why, and what is included? If not, why not?

- Do they provide informational brochures or materials? Do these describe any special services that are offered and any requirements or responsibilities of the clients?

- When they see a client, do they maintain records? Collect a fee? Schedule appointments (versus simply walk-in service)?

- Do they feel that their clients perceive that the services they offer are professional in nature, even if no fees are collected?

Share your data with your colleagues or classmates. Discuss which of the service providers appear to employ contracts or actions that would characterize them as establishing "special relationships" with their clients and therefore incurring a duty to care.

fields is required to recognize in a student a condition the diagnosis of which is in a specialized and technical medical field, would require a duty beyond reason" (*Bogust v. Iverson*, 1960). A later ruling that suggested specialized training and credentialing were needed prior to the establishment of a special helping relationship and the duty to care was *Nally v. Grace Community Church*. In *Nally v. Grace Community Church* (1988), the parents of a 24-year-old, Kenneth Nally, sued the Grace Community Church and its pastors for negligence when their son committed suicide after receiving several years of informal counseling. Kenneth also saw secular psychologists and psychiatrists during these years, and following an unsuccessful attempt at suicide in 1979, his parents rejected the recommendations of a psychiatrist to have him committed. This recommendation was also made by one of the pastors of the church and similarly rejected. The California Supreme Court ruled in favor of the church and its pastors because it found that there was no duty of care that was breached by them and no special relationship that would create such duty. In this case, the California court made a distinction between non-therapists, counselors, and professional therapists—such as psychiatrists or certified psychologists and counselors. Since the pastors were non-therapists without the requisite special relationship, the court did not find or impose the duty of care. These two rulings appear to point to the essential need to be recognized as a professional helper as defined by one's credentials, such as licensure, as the basis for a special relationship and to identify that duty to care has been established. However, in *Eisel v. Board of Education of Montgomery County* (1991) new legal precedent was set.

As noted, previously the courts did not find a duty of care in situations in which a non-professional attempted to provide help to a client. This was true even in situations in which an outpatient client who may have been suicidal was seen by a school counselor. However in the *Eisel* case, the court noted a special relationship sufficient to create a duty of care when an adolescent in a school setting expresses an intention to commit suicide and the counselor becomes aware of such intention. In *Eisel*, the court noted that the school, as a result of standing in loco parentis, does have a special duty to exercise reasonable care to protect a pupil from harm. Further, the relationship of school counselor and pupil is not devoid of therapeutic overtones, as suggested by the counselor's job description. Thus in addition to pointing to special training, licensing, and certification, the existence of a special relationship and the duty to care can be established based simply on the job definition from which one provides service. *Eisel* (1991) strengthened counselors' legal obligation to students by satisfying for the first time the first element of negligence and declaring that school counselors have a special relationship with students and owe a duty to try to prevent a student's suicide (Stone, 2003).

Another approach to the definition of a special relationship between helper and client bases it on the principle of fiduciary responsibility. Anytime an individual places his or her trust in a party who has the potential to influence his or her action, a fiduciary relationship exists (Black, 1991). In the case of mental health provision, the counselor or therapist becomes a "fiduciary," in that the helping relationship requires that the client have confidence and trust in the recommendations that are being made by the practitioner (Simon & Shuman, 2007).

When a fiduciary relationship exists, a practitioner has these obligations (a) to act with good faith and loyalty toward a client (*McInerney v. MacDonald*, 1992); (b) to not abuse the power imbalance by exploiting the client (*Norberg v. Wynrib*, 1992); and (c) to act in the best interest of the client (*Hodgkinson v. Simms*, 1994).

While the anxiety surrounding the possibility of litigation may serve as a motive for practitioners to be more fully aware of the law applicable to their practice, knowledge and awareness of the law is a professional responsibility regardless of anxiety. Professional codes of conduct direct practitioners to know and practice in ways consistent with the law. For example, "psychologists' fee practices are consistent law" (APA, 2010, 6.04.b).

● THE LEGAL FOUNDATION OF ETHICAL PRACTICE

The process and relationship between health and human service professionals and their clients is increasingly shaped by law. Issues such as informed consent, confidentiality, and competency as well as mandates, such as the mandated reporting of child abuse and duty to warn, are significant influences on the practice of human service (see Case Illustration 5.1). In addition, courts of law can employ regulatory and ethical standards for health and human services professionals as ways of identifying negligence, malpractice, and liability.

Case Illustration 5.1

The Changing Face of School Counseling

The following was the result of an interview with Mr. L., an elementary school counselor. Legal precedents relative to Mr. L.'s comments have been inserted.

Well, I've been an elementary school counselor now for over 23 years, and I can tell you my job and my strategies in working with children have changed dramatically as a result of litigation. I mean, there was a time when I first started that if a kid was acting out or causing a real disruption in a classroom, we could simply have him removed, suspended, as a way of providing a "wake up call." Try that now and you will find yourself sued. Everything requires DUE PROCESS now.

In 1975, the Supreme Court ruled in *Goss v. Lopez*: "Due process requires, in connection with a suspension of 10 days or less, that the student be given oral or written notice of the charges against him and, if he denies them, an explanation of the evidence the authorities have and an opportunity to present his side of the story" (p. 581). This even gets to the point that you start to worry about using "time out" procedures, because it may be argued that you are excluding a child from his right to have an education. I don't know, I feel like I should have become a lawyer rather than a counselor.

Goss v. Lopez (1975) focused on exclusion from an education, and while it did not define or give examples of de minimis punishments that would not require due process, they probably would include practices like after school detentions or "time outs" or even temporary exclusion from extracurricular activities.

And another area that you have to be super cautious about is record keeping. I mean, it used to be that my records were confidential, and no one had access. Now I feel like any one can waltz in and see my files, since they are school files. Where's the privacy? A lot of the counselors in our district simply keep special files or school-only files that parents don't have access to.

The Family Educational Rights and Privacy Act (FERPA) provides parents and students 18 and older with certain rights with regard to the inspection and dissemination of "education records." As a federal law, it applies to school districts and schools that receive federal financial assistance through the U.S. Department of Education. FERPA makes clear that all education records, no matter where they are stored or how they are identified (i.e., "school only") must be made available. However, not all information obtained by a counselor need be disclosed. The legislative history of FERPA clarifies that education records do not include the "personal files of psychologists, counselors, or professors if these files are entirely private and not available to other individuals" (120 Cong. Rec. 27, 36533 (1974).

Codes of ethics provide guidelines for practice decisions; however, they are not binding unless they are otherwise codified or incorporated into law. Granted, professional associations have the power to sanction their members for unethical practice, via admonishment, suspension or expulsion. But the extent of the sanctions is limited, and such sanctioning does not automatically imply legal action. The professions' codes of conduct, however, do often provide the basis or at a minimum a standard for developing laws and regulations that govern the practice of that profession. In most states, the ethical principles and standards of practice have been incorporated into laws or regulations that not only govern requirements for certification or licensure but serve as consumer laws governing the practice of mental health services (Bennett, Bryant, VandenBos, & Greenwood, 1990). While this may vary state by state, it is important for all engaging in mental health services to understand the relationship of ethical code to legal mandate (see Exercise 5.2).

Exercise 5.2

State Laws Codifying Professional Ethics

Directions: Licensed psychologists, in some states, will find that a violation of their code of ethics places them at risk not only of facing sanction of the board, but also of prosecution by the state in which they practice.

Contact the department of state, the attorney general's office, or the department of license and measurements for your state and do the following:

- Inquire if your state licenses mental health professionals. If so, which professions?

- What does the law say about the practice of those within that profession who are not licensed or about those from other professions who practice within that state?

- Request a copy of the licensing law within your state.

- Inquire if the code of ethics for your profession has the force of law within your state.

While the professional codes of conduct have been incorporated into laws, in some cases, the reverse has been true; that is, the legal system has stimulated mental health professions to develop and enhance their ethical standards. Mental health professionals employ sensitive and careful ethical practices to ensure that clients will not hurt themselves or others. The steps taken to warn and protect potential victims of dangerous clients are clearly integrated into all professional standards of conduct and were stimulated by the landmark decision surrounding the *Tarasoff v. The Regents of the University of California* (1976) court case (see Chapter 9). An illustration of how case law has given shape to ethical principles of practice can be found in Case Illustration 5.2.

Case Illustration 5.2

The Issue of Duty to Warn

Jonathan was referred to Dr. Ranklin, a licensed psychologist who provided services to employees of Company L. as part of its Employment Assistance Program. In the initial session, Dr. Ranklin explained his role and the fact that he was contracted by Company L. to provide employees with brief, solution-focused counseling and referral. Dr. Ranklin also described the conditions of confidentiality and provided Jonathan with an information sheet about the services available.

During the initial session, Jonathan revealed his intent to "get even with Alex" (his immediate supervisor). When asked what "get even" meant, Jonathan stated, "Alex has been on my case ever since he became a supervisor. He thinks he's hot stuff, better than the rest of us. He keeps calling me lazy and asks if I've seen the shrink yet; he told me he made the referral to you. Anyway, he does this stuff in front of the other guys and I have had it. I'm just going to wait for him one night this winter, when it's dark, and get him out in the parking lot."

When asked if he could provide more information about what it was he was planning, Jonathan went into great detail: "I know where he parks and he always leaves just around 5:45, after most of the guys have cleared out of the lot. I'm going to be waiting for him. I'll just hide in the dark and when he goes to get into the car, I will whip him terribly. I've got an ax handle with his name all over it. I'll crack that dumb head of his and then we'll see who's crazy. If he dies, that's his problem."

Throughout the session, Dr. Ranklin attempted to gain a guarantee that Jonathan really wouldn't do what he was saying, but each time Jonathan insisted that he would and that Alex deserved it. When reminded of the "limits of confidentiality" that Dr. Ranklin explained and that were listed in the handout, Jonathan said, "I don't care. You can tell him or anyone. He deserves it and I'm going to give it to him."

Since all attempts to persuade Jonathan to commit to not harming Alex were unsuccessful, Dr. Ranklin felt duty bound to protect his client (Jonathan) from legal action and his identified victim (Alex) from potential harm. Thus, he made an appointment to meet with Alex to disclose this information.

(Continued)

(Continued)

Dr. Ranklin's actions were stimulated by the now famous *Tarasoff* (1976) case and subsequent state case laws in Nebraska where he practiced. Dr. Ranklin knew that while confidentiality was an ethical directive, in Nebraska, therapists are required to initiate whatever precautions are necessary to protect the potential victims of the patient (*Lipari v. Sears, Roebuck & Co.,* 1980).

Many of the ethical principles to be discussed and illustrated within the upcoming chapters have strong legal foundations. Thus, in addition to providing a review of the principles, some of the laws and court decisions that tint or give further shape to the application of these principles will be discussed. Table 5.1 provides a thumbnail view of a couple of these legal decisions and their impact on professional practice.

Ethical Does Not Always Equal Legal

While codes of ethics most often overlap with legal requirements, they are distinct from them and in some cases, may be in conflict. The potential for conflict has been recognized within the American Psychological Association code of ethics (2010), which states:

Table 5.1 Examples of Laws as Foundation for Ethical Practice

Ethical Issue	Legal Rulings
Boundary Violations	A number of rulings (e.g., *Mazza v. Huffaker*, 300 S.E. 2d 833, [1983]; *Horak v. Biris*, 474 N. E. 2d 13 [1985]) argue that due to the power differentials within the relationship and the potential for abuse of power, sexual relationships between client and practitioner are actionable as malpractice.
Competence	The foundation for negligence is based, in part, on the failure to use knowledge, skill, and care ordinarily exercised in similar localities (*Carlton v. Quint*, 77 Cal. App. 4th 690, 699 (2000) [91 Cal. Rptr. 2d 844]).
Confidentiality	Duty to break confidence in service of the duty to warn was established in *Tarasoff v. The Regents of the University of California* 551 P.2d 334 (Cal. Sup. Ct., 1976).

If psychologists' ethical responsibilities conflict with law, regulations, or other governing legal authority, psychologists clarify the nature of the conflict, make known their commitment to the Ethics Code, and take reasonable steps to resolve the conflict consistent with the General Principles and Ethical Standards of the Ethics Code. Under no circumstances may this standard be used to justify or defend violating human rights. (APA, 2010, Principle 1.02)

Unethical, Yet Legal

Conflict can occur when a practitioner's decisions are unethical and yet remain legal. For example, in most states it is not legally mandated that a practitioner inform a client of the limitations to confidentiality or how confidential information may be used, but many professional codes of ethics require that such limitations be clearly described to the client (see Table 5.2).

Ethical, Yet Illegal

There are times when a practitioner's actions may be considered illegal yet fall within the codes of ethical conduct. Consider the situation in which a client with AIDS refuses to inform an identified sexual partner about the AIDS or take steps to protect that partner. Although disclosure of a client's status as having AIDS or being HIV positive without that client's permission is illegal, in many states, the ethical duty to protect third parties from harm may direct the practitioner to disclose this information to the current sexual partner.

Table 5.2 Notification of Limits to Confidentiality

Professional Ethical Standards	Statement of Notification
American Psychological Association (2010)	4.02.a. Psychologists discuss . . . (1) the relevant limits of confidentiality and (2) the foreseeable uses of the information generated through their psychological activities. b. Unless it is not feasible or is contradicted, the discussion of confidentiality occurs at the outset of the relationship and thereafter as new circumstances may warrant.

(Continued)

Table 5.2 (Continued)

Professional Ethical Standards	Statement of Notification
National Association of Social Workers (2008)	1.07 Privacy and confidentiality d. Social workers should inform clients, to the extent possible, about disclosure of confidential information and the potential consequences, when feasible before the disclosure is made. This applies whether social workers disclose confidential information on the basis of a legal requirement or client consent. e. Social workers should discuss with clients and other interested parties the nature of confidentiality and the limitations of clients' right of confidentiality. Social workers should review with clients circumstances where confidential information may be requested and where disclosure of confidential information may be legally required. This discussion should occur as soon as possible in the social worker–client relationship and as needed throughout the course of the relationship.
American Counseling Association (2014)	A.2.b. Types of information needed Counselors explicitly explain to clients the nature of all services provided. They inform clients about issues such as, but not limited to, the following: the purposes, goals, techniques, procedures, limitations, potential risks, and benefits of services; the counselor's qualifications, credentials, relevant experience, and approach to counseling; continuation of services upon the incapacitation or death of the counselor; the role of technology; and pertinent information. Counselors take steps to ensure that clients understand the implications of diagnosis and intended use of tests and reports. Additionally, counselors inform clients about fees and billing arrangements, including procedures for nonpayment of fees. Clients have the right to confidentiality and to be provided with an explanation of its limits, including how supervisors and/or treatment or interdisciplinary team professionals are involved, to obtain clear information about their records, to participate in the ongoing counseling plans, and to refuse any services or modality changes and to be advised of the consequences of such refusal. A.2.d. Inability to give consent When counseling minors, incapacitated adults, or other persons unable to give voluntary consent, counselors seek the assent of clients to services and include them in decision making as appropriate. Counselors recognize the need to balance the ethical rights of clients to make choices, their capacity to give consent or assent to receive services, and parental or familial legal rights and responsibilities to protect these clients and make decisions on their behalf.

Professional Ethical Standards	*Limitations to Confidentiality*
American Psychological Association (2010)	4.05.b. Psychologists disclose confidential information without the consent of the individual only as mandated by law, or where permitted by law for a valid purpose, such as to (1) provide needed professional services; (2) obtain appropriate professional consultations; (3) protect the client/patient, psychologist, or others from harm; or (4) obtain payment for services from a client/patient, in which instance disclosure is limited to the minimum that is necessary to achieve that purpose.
National Association of Social Workers (2008)	1.07. Privacy and confidentiality c. Social workers should protect the confidentiality of all information obtained in the course of professional service, except for compelling professional reasons. The general expectation that social workers will keep information confidential does not apply when disclosure is necessary to prevent serious, foreseeable, and imminent harm to a client or other identifiable person. In all instances, social workers should disclose the least amount of confidential information necessary to achieve the desired purpose; only information that is directly relevant to the purpose for which the disclosure is made should be revealed.
American Counseling Association (2014)	B.2. Exceptions The general requirement that counselors keep information confidential does not apply when disclosure is required to protect clients or identified others from serious and foreseeable harm or when legal requirements demand that confidential information must be revealed. Counselors consult with other professionals when in doubt as to the validity of an exception. Additional considerations apply when addressing end-of-life issues.
American Association for Marriage and Family Therapy (2015)	2.2. Written authorization to release client information Marriage and family therapists do not disclose client confidences except by written authorization or waiver, or where mandated or permitted by law. Verbal authorization will not be sufficient except in emergency situations, unless prohibited by law. When providing couple, family, or group treatment, the therapist does not disclose information outside the treatment context without written authorization from each individual competent to execute such a waiver. In the context of couple, family, or group treatment, the therapist may not reveal any individuals' confidences to others in the client unit without the prior written permission of that individual.

It is clear that the relationship between law and ethics is not always clear-cut. In the most desirable state, our professional ethics and the law are in concert, as is the case when maintaining confidentiality is protected under the law. And while it is clear that actions that are both illegal and unethical must be avoided, clarity is blurred in situations where one's ethical directive runs contrary to a legal mandate, as might be the case where a professional feels it is essential to a client's welfare to maintain confidentiality even when confronted with a court order.

Ethical and legal standards are by their very nature broad in spirit and language, thus open to situational interpretation. As a result, practitioners must remain informed about the legal interpretations of the applications and misapplication of the ethics of practice and practice decisions as they continue to unfold through legislation and court decisions.

● WHEN ETHICS AND LEGALITIES COLLIDE

When ethics and law collide, the practitioner will need to use his or her own sense of judgment about the issues and directions to be taken. Such judgment should be formed on accurate understanding of the specific ethical principles involved and the laws governing practice decisions. As noted previously, psychologists confronted by such a conflict are directed to "clarify the nature of the conflict, make known their commitment to the Ethics Code, and take reasonable steps to resolve the conflict consistent with the General Principles and Ethical Standards of the Ethics Code" (APA, 2010, Principle 1.02). While the mental health practitioner is not called upon to be a legal expert, it is important that the practitioner have some knowledge of court rulings (local, state, and federal), since such rulings provide the precedents for future actions by the courts. Clearly, the better informed a practitioner is, the more likely conflicts between legal and ethical principles can be resolved.

It is generally believed that mental health professions have an obligation to abide by the legal requirements of the situation. This obligation is most often considered as prima facie, meaning that the legal obligation needs to be considered in every case and only set aside when ethical and/or legal reasons of greater importance compel such action. However, the uniqueness of each situation and the characteristics of each client complicate the decision to be made.

There may be situations in which, even with the greatest understanding of both the law and the ethical principles, a clear path resolving the conflict cannot be found. It is possible that the action mandated by law may not appear to be in the best ethical interest of the client. Such a conflict places the mental health practitioner in quite a moral and professional dilemma. This would certainly be the case for the counsellor attempting to protect confidentiality of her client with HIV/AIDS while at the same time being sensitive to her duty to warn a third party of potential harm (Alghazo, Upton, & Cioe, 2011). Under these situations, it is the responsibility of the professional to review all of the pertinent information, discerning which avenue both upholds the intent of the law and essence of the professions ethics while providing the maximum benefit to the client. It will be essential for the mental health practitioner confronted by such dilemmas to employ a well-developed decision-making model. While this topic of ethical decision-making and models that serve that purpose is presented in Chapter 7, it is worthwhile to review one somewhat classic approach as offered by Remley (1996).

Remley (1996, p. 288) provides four steps for counselors to take when confronted by an apparent conflict between ethics and the law. These steps have been adapted and are listed below:

1. The practitioner should identify all of the forces that are impacting issues regarding the professional decision and behavior. While the conflict may certainly be the result of an ethical principle or a legal mandate, other forces, such as policies and procedures within a specific workplace, accreditation rules or requirements, and even parameters for funding, may be the source of the conflict rather than the law.

2. When the question is one of law, legal advice should be obtained. Quite often the state or national associations may provide legal consultants who are trained in both the mental health field and the legal profession. Another source of legal advice may be obtained through one's liability insurance company.

3. If there is a problem in applying an ethical standard or in understanding the requirements of an ethical standard, the practitioner should consult with a colleague and those perceived as experts within the field. Again, it is also useful to contact the local, state, or national associations and speak to members of the ethics board.

4. If a force other than law or ethics (for example, employment requirements) is suggesting that a practitioner take some action he or she perceives as illegal, the counselor should obtain legal advice to determine whether such action is indeed illegal and what form of recourse or protection is available should the counselor refuse to follow the directive to perform this illegal act (see Chapter 6).

The need for ethical practitioners to remain informed as evolving ethics receive the force of the law through court decisions and/or evolving law gives new shape to codes of conduct cannot be overemphasized. Fortunately, practitioners are not alone in their concern and their quest. State and national associations, along with liability insurance companies, provide continuing education programs to update the practitioner's knowledge and may even provide consultation services in case of conflict. The final exercise (Exercise 5.3) is provided to help increase your awareness of the supports available to assist you in becoming both an ethical and legal practitioner.

Exercise 5.3

Resources in Support of the Ethical-Legal Practitioner

Directions: It is essential to remain informed about the changing face of law and codes of professional conduct as you continue to develop and practice as a helper. Ongoing information and continuing education programs are often provided by state and national associations along with the various companies providing liability insurance for your profession. Similarly, these same resources oftentimes provide "hotline" consultation for their members who may feel conflicted about a practice decision.

- Contact your state organization and inquire about its website or ways that you can be informed about state legal decisions that may impact your own professional practice. Ask if you can be placed on a mailing list or list-serve announcing continuing education programs geared to updating practitioners on relevant law and ethical principles of practice.

- Contact your national organization and inquire about its website or ways that you can be informed about recent legal decisions impacting your practice and continuing education programs geared to updating practitioners on relevant laws and ethical principles of practice.

- Contact your liability insurance carrier and inquire whether it provides continuing education programs on issues of ethics and legality and if it provides a discount for those who attend.

- Contact each of the above and inquire about the availability of legal assistance or ethical-legal consultation should you have a question or conflict. Identify the process for connecting with this service as well as any fees that may be involved.

CONCLUDING CASE ILLUSTRATION ●

Returning to the scene with which we opened the chapter, we find Ms. Wicks (Maria's counselor) sharing concerns with a colleague. As you read the exchange, look for issues of an ethical nature, issues or concerns that may, in your opinion, have legal foundation and/or implications, and the existence of conflict between Ms. Wicks's ethical standards and the law.

Mr. Harolds: Hi, Michelle. What's up?

Ms. Wicks: Tom, could I talk to you about some legal concerns?

Mr. Harolds: Legal concerns? Certainly, but I'm not a lawyer.

Ms. Wicks: No, I know that, but you seem to stay current with laws and regulations regarding counseling, and to tell you the truth, I'm not sure if it is a problem or not.

Mr. Harolds: Well, you certainly sound concerned. What's up?

Ms. Wicks: Well, I'm not sure actually. I've been counseling a student who shared with me that she is currently dating and having unprotected sex with a boy whom she reports as having AIDS. She's 18, and the information was revealed to me in my role of counselor. I am not sure if I am legally responsible to report this.

Mr. Harolds: Did you share your concern with your client?

Ms. Wicks: Yes, and she simply states that she doesn't care. You know, this is love, and God wouldn't punish her by letting her get AIDS.

Mr. Harolds: Wow, that's sad. Michelle, when you first met with her, what instructions did you give her regarding the limits to confidentiality?

Ms. Wicks: Tom, I know I explained about disclosing information if she informed me of her intent to harm her herself, but I'm not sure how this fits.

Mr. Harolds: This is tough. After all, she's your client, not the boy. I know individuals with AIDS have a right to privacy, but she is placing herself in harm's way. I don't really know. Why don't we call the state board and ask to speak to one of their ethical-legal consultants? Remember, I told you I wasn't a lawyer!

Ms. Wicks: Tom, I just appreciate you hearing me out and confirming for me that this is not so clear-cut. I agree that calling may be the thing to do.

Reflections

1. Do you feel that Ms. Wicks should have gotten Maria's consent to speak with Tom?
2. Do you feel that the specific information shared with Tom was a violation of Maria's right to confidentiality?
3. Do you feel that the potential for conflict between law and ethics exists in this case? If so, where? If not, why not?
4. How do you feel about the fact that Ms. Wicks contacted a colleague in a situation like this? Is there anything else she should have done instead or in addition?

● COOPERATIVE LEARNING EXERCISE

The purpose of the chapter was to familiarize you with the unique and sometimes conflicting relationship between law and professional codes of ethics. Because they are broadly stated, both ethical and legal standards are open to situational interpretation. The remaining chapters provide more detailed information about specific, ethical principles and laws applying to those guidelines.

Below you will find three scenarios. Along with your colleagues, read each scenario and identify whether you feel they present issues that are free of conflict or represent a conflict of law and ethics. Where conflict exists, identify the nature of the conflict. Is it legal and unethical, illegal and ethical, or unethical and illegal? Next, contact a professional practitioner in your area and ask him or her for an opinion about the nature of the situation. Finally, as you read more about specific ethical principles in the upcoming chapters, return to these scenarios to see if your initial opinions change.

Scenario 1: A girl, age 13, comes to a school counselor and asks for advice and direction on where and how to go about securing an abortion. The school counselor gives her the names and numbers of a number of agencies that counsel women seeking an abortion. The school counselor also promises the student not to inform her parents. Was the decision a conflict of law and ethics? If so, what was the nature of the conflict? Which part of the counselor's behaviors or decisions were conflictual?

Scenario 2: A Vietnam War veteran voluntarily contracted for counseling with a licensed social worker for what was determined to be post-traumatic stress disorder. In the process of therapy the vet reported his intention to kill some college students who, according to the vet, prolonged the war through their protests. When asked to identify the specific students, the client simply said, "It doesn't matter as long as they are in college." The therapist did not take steps to inform anyone about this threat. Should he? Is there a conflict of law with ethics? If so, what is the nature of that conflict?

Scenario 3: Dr. Ortez works in the counseling center at a local university. Dr. Ortez had provided career counseling for a graduate student named Liz. It has been a year since Liz has graduated and over 15 months since her last session with Dr. Ortez. Dr. Ortez calls Liz to inquire how she is doing and, while on the phone, asks her on a date. Did Dr. Ortez violate any ethical principles? Any laws?

SUMMARY ●

- In performing one's practice, the helper provides implicit agreement of his or her duty to the client.
- The issue of whether helping is contractual and thus a minimum duty of care is established rests with the court's decision as to whether a "special relationship" existed that would be sufficient to create a duty of care.
- Anytime an individual places his or her trust in a party who has the potential to influence his or her action, a fiduciary relationship exists (Black, 1991).
- Given this definition, it could be reasonably argued that all professional helping relationships have this fiduciary responsibility.
- In most states, the ethical principles and standards of practice have been incorporated into laws or regulations that not only govern requirements for certification or licensure but also serve as consumer laws governing the practice of mental health services.
- While codes of ethics most often overlap with legal requirements, they are distinct from them and in some cases may be in conflict.
- When ethics and law collide, the practitioner will need to use a good decision-making model to guide decisions and directions.
- Remley (1996) provided four steps that counselors should take when confronted by an apparent conflict between ethics and the law: (1) Identify the forces that are at issue, (2) obtain legal advice, (3) consult with colleagues or experts in the field of professional ethics, and (4) seek legal advice, when forces other than law and ethics are at the core, in order to understand available options.

● IMPORTANT TERMS

Bogust v. Iverson	implicit acts
contractual	legal precedent
duty beyond reason	*Nally v. Grace Community Church*
duty to care	prima facie
Eisel v. Board of Education	principle of fiduciary responsibility
ethical, yet illegal	unethical, yet legal

● ADDITIONAL RESOURCES

Print

Corey, G., Corey, M., Corey, C., & Callanan, P. (2015). *Issues and ethics in the helping professions with ACA 2014 Codes* (9th ed.). Stamford, CT: Cengage Learning.

Fischer, L., & Sorenson-Paulus, O. (1996). School law for counselors, psychologists and social workers (3rd ed.). White Plains, NY: Longman Publishers.

Pope, K. S., & Vasquez, M. J. T. (2016). *Ethics in psychotherapy and counseling: A practical guide* (5th ed.). John Wiley & Sons.

Stone, C. (2013). *School counseling principles: Ethics and law* (3rd ed.). Alexandria, VA: American School Counselors Association (ASCA).

Swenson, L. C. (1997). Psychology and law for the helping professions. Pacific Grove, CA: Brooks/Cole.

Woody, R. H. (1997). Legally safe mental health practice: Psycholegal questions and answers. Madison, CT: Psychosocial Press.

Web-Based

American Counseling Association. (n.d.). NEW ACA 2014 *code of ethics*: A 6-part webinar series. Retrieved from https://www.counseling.org/continuing-education/webinars/new-aca-2014-code-of-ethics-a-6-part-webinar-series

American School Counselor Association. (n.d.). Legal and ethical specialist training. Retrieved from http://www.schoolcounselor.org/school-counselors-members/professional-development/asca-u/legal-specialist-training

Counseling Today. (2015). *Tag archives: Ethical and legal issues.* Retrieved from http://ct.counseling.org/tag/ethics-legal-issues/

Social Work Ethics and Law Institute. (n.d.). http://socialworkers.org/sweli/default.asp

Stone, C. B., & Zirkel, P. A. (2010). *School counselor advocacy: When law and ethics may collide, 13*(4), 244–247. Retrieved from: http://www.jstor.org/stable/42732954

REFERENCES ●

Alghazo, R., Upton, T. D., & Cioe, N. (2011). Duty to warn verses duty to protect confidentiality: Ethical and legal considerations relative to individuals with AIDS/HIV. *Journal of Applied Rehabilitation Counseling, 42*(1), 43–49. Retrieved from http://search.proquest.com/docview/859615858?accountid=34899

American Psychological Association. (2010). *Ethical principles of psychologists and code of conduct*. Retrieved from http://www.apa.org/ethics/code/principles.pdf

Bennett, B. E., Bryant, B. K., VandenBos, G. R., & Greenwood, A. (1990). *Professional liability and risk management*. Washington, DC: American Psychological Association.

Bergantino, L. (1996, Fall). For the defense: Psychotherapy and the law. *Voices*, 29–33.

Black, H. C. (1991). *Black's law dictionary* (Abridged, 6th ed.). St. Paul, MN: West Publishing.

Bogust v. Iverson, 102 N.W.2d 288 (Wis. 1960).

Carlton v. Quint, 77 Cal.App.4th 690, 699 (2000) [91 Cal.Rptr.2d 844].

Eisel v. Board of Education of Montgomery County, 68, 130,135.

Goss v. Lopez, 419 U.S. >565 (1975).

Hodgkinson v. Simms, 117 DLR (4th) 161 (1994).

Horak v. Biris, 474 N. E. 2d 13 (1985).

Mazza v. Huffaker, 300 S.E. 2d 833 (1983).

McInerney v. MacDonald, 93 DLR (4th) 415 (1992).

Nally v. Grace Community Church, 47 Cal.3d 378 (1988).

Norberg v. Wynrib, 92 DLR (4th) 449 (1992).

Reamer, F. G. (2013). Eye on ethics: Essential law in social work ethics. *Social Work Today*. Retrieved from http://www.socialworktoday.com/news/eoe_101813.shtml

Remley, T. P., Jr. (1996). The relationship between law and ethics. In B. Herlihy & G. Corey (Eds.), *ACA ethical standards casebook* (5th ed., pp. 285–292). Alexandria, VA: American Counseling Association.

Simon, R. I., & Shuman, D. W. (2007). *Clinical manual of psychiatry and law*. Washington, DC: American Psychiatric Publishing.

Stone, C. (2003). Suicide: A duty owed. *ASCA School Counselor*. Retrieved from https://www.schoolcounselor.org/magazine/blogs/march-april-2003/suicide-a-duty-owed

Tarasoff v. The Regents of the University of California, 551 P.2d 334 (Cal. Sup. Ct., 1976).

CHAPTER 6

Conflict: The Reality of "Being Ethical" Within the Real World

Ms. Wicks: Hi, Tom it is me again.

Mr. Harolds: Hey, how are you? Did you get that information from the state association?

Ms. Wicks: Not yet. They are supposed to call me. But, things are getting more confusing . . .

Mr. Harolds: Really?

Ms. Wicks: Ms. Armstrong, the principal at the school, informed me that it is understood in the district that we are not to counsel students regarding sexual issues. She said it is not a formal policy, just something that "we" all know not to do. So, I'm not sure if I broke a law or violated a code of ethics or may have stepped over the line in terms of my job definition. I am so confused!

When working with a client, a helper needs to be aware of and sensitive to the many individual issues and concerns presented by the client. In addition, the helper also needs to be fully cognizant of the ethical and legal implications of his or her own professional decisions in relationship to these client concerns. Now, to complicate matters even more for those practitioners working within an organization or a system, be it a school, a hospital, an agency, or a company, individual practice decisions must also reflect and be congruent with policies, procedures, and informal standards and values operating within that system.

The current chapter looks at the ethical culture of social systems and the influence it exerts on the practice decisions of those helpers working within that system. The chapter will discuss the impact of working for and within an organization. Further, in this chapter we will look at situations in which conflicts arise when what the professionals feel is best for the individual client falls outside of or even runs contrary to policies, procedures, or values of the organization. Under these conditions, what's a practitioner to do?

● OBJECTIVES

The chapter will review the process and implications of making ethical practice decisions within an organizational or system context. Attempting to balance the needs of the individual client with the requirements of the employing organization and other interested parties (e.g., managed care organizations) is not an easy or clear-cut process. After reading this chapter you should be able to do the following:

- Define what is meant by "system culture."
- Discuss the impact of system culture on ethical decision-making.
- Identify possible points of ethical conflict when working in a managed care environment.
- Identify possible points of ethical conflict when working with third-party payees.

● SERVING THE INDIVIDUAL WITHIN A SYSTEM

Professional practice does not occur within a vacuum. At a minimum, professional practice occurs within the social context of a client and a helper. But for those working within an organization, professional practice and ethical decision-making occurs not only within this dyadic system but also within the context of the larger system or organization in which the helper works. Ethical problems in professional practice are often the result of the confluence of context, setting, and standards of practice. Practitioners who work in schools, clinics, or hospitals, and/or those who serve as providers for managed care can find themselves in conflict with these competing client systems (see Case Illustration 6.1).

Case Illustration 6.1

A Diagnostic Dilemma

Linda Alfreds is a new school psychologist, the first ever employed by the Hallstead School District. Linda's job involves performing all psycho-educational assessments, especially those required for special education placement. Linda was informed, however, that with the exception of a few "slower" children, the district really didn't have children with special needs, which according to the superintendent was a blessing, since they have very limited monies for providing such services.

Linda was asked to see Marquis, a transfer student, who was reported as having difficulty keeping up with the work in a number of his classes. The test data presented Marquis as an impulsive child, with a significant receptive language problem. From her work at a previous school district, Linda knew that Marquis would benefit from placement in a resource room with a special education teacher trained in learning disabilities and language disorders.

Linda discussed the situation with her department chairperson and was told that the district did not have resource room personnel. However, the other middle school in the district did provide a classroom for "slow learners." The chairperson directed Linda to record Marquis as being retarded rather than as having a language disability, since this would at least get him some special services. It was clear to Linda that the data would not support this diagnosis, but identifying the child with a language disability might fail to provide any special teaming assistance to Marquis.

Certainly the school psychologist presented in Case Illustration 6.1 is confronted with a serious ethical and potentially legal dilemma. As in this case, practice decisions must clearly reflect not only the needs of the client as well as the characteristics and orientation of the helper but also the unique characteristics and demands of the context or organization in which the helping occurs. Balancing all of these unique needs is not always easy or clear-cut. The ethical practitioner needs to be aware of the system and the subtle and oftentimes not so subtle influences that a system can exert. Such an awareness begins with an understanding of the nature of systems.

As used here, a system is "an entity made up of interconnected parts with recognizable relationships that are systematically arranged to serve a perceived purpose" (Kurpius, 1985, p. 369). As one of the interconnected parts within a work setting, the human service provider needs to fully understand the roles enacted, the relationship that exist, the values and assumptions that support these relationships, and the degree to which all of these exert pressure on the performance of one's duties. One cannot be an ethical-effective provider of service without full awareness of the system and system dynamics in which he works

It is not unexpected that when working in a system with multiple constituents that conflict in performance of one's duties may emerge. This may occur in a situation of a school counselor who feels that what is best for the student may be contrary to the policy or procedures of the school, for whom they work. Or it is possible that one working in an employee assistance program (EAP) might experience the pressure of a divided loyalty. When under contract to provide employees services, one might feel a strain between the desire to maintain employee confidentiality while understanding that the contract exists with the employee's place of business, and there may be a legitimate need to know on the part of that employee's manager. Under these conditions, information regarding the client's treatment as related to job performance may be within the need to know and thus conflicts with the client's right of privacy and confidentiality. The practitioner, while respecting the confidentiality of the information gathered, needs to be sensitive to the obligations agreed to in contracts with the organization. The EAP counselor described in Case Illustration 6.2 appears to have developed a plan for balancing the needs of the organization with the rights of the client.

Case Illustration 6.2

**Balancing the Needs of the System and the Client:
A Case of Confidentiality**

Hanna Johannsen was a private practicing mental health counselor who was certified as an EAP counselor. In addition to seeing clients for a fee, Hanna provided EAP services to the members of a local school district. In this EAP capacity, Hanna received a contracted fee and was to provide three to five sessions free of charge to any school district employee who desired such counseling. In addition, should additional counseling be desired or required, Hanna would make a referral to another provider, and the employee would then be responsible to continue on a fee-for-service basis.

As part of the contract with the school superintendent, the EAP counselor was to provide monthly reports that included (a) the number of people seen, (b) the specific school in which the employee worked, (c) the job class (i.e., teacher, administrator, staff, etc.), (d) the type of problem presented, (e) the number of sessions utilized, and (f) and evaluation of the outcome. While the specific names of clients and any details of the nature of the problem presented were not to be disclosed, Hanna felt that the information requested was such that it could jeopardize the confidentiality of those who utilized this EAP service.

Hanna worked out a compromise with school administration so that all first sessions could be made completely confidential. In that first session, as part of setting the boundaries of confidentiality, Hanna explained to each client the types of data she would reveal to the superintendent and asked the client for their informed consent before making additional appointments. If the client would not give that consent, Hanna would provide a referral list and share no information about the contact with the central office.

ETHICAL CULTURE OF SOCIAL SYSTEMS ●

Organizations—or for that matter, any social system (e.g., families)—develop their own values or standards that guide decision-making and practice within that system. These values, which may take form explicitly in an organization's value statement or implicitly as behavior guiding day-to-day decisions, serve as a core to what has been described as systems culture (Schein, 2010). Schein described system culture as a "pattern of shared basic assumptions that the group learned as it solved its problems of external adaptation and internal integration, that has worked well enough to be considered valid and, therefore, to be taught to new members as the correct way you perceive, think, and feel in relation to those problems" (Schein, 2010, p. 18). The assumptions that serve as the base for the development and maintenance of a system's culture form the unquestioned, non-debatable truths and reality of people within the system. These develop when a solution or procedure works repeatedly. As a result, those involved begin to take it for granted to the point where what was once only a hunch or possibility starts to get viewed and treated as a reality. These basic assumptions then serve as the foundation from which the system defines structures and processes to guide its operations. This is an important concept for the ethical practitioner to grasp, because when members of an organization embrace these assumptions, they in turn shape what the members value and the form these values take (see Exercise 6.1).

The cultural values of a system become enacted in the way members prioritize and function-shaping policies, decision-making, and other operations. Practice decisions, therefore, may begin to reflect institutional values and organizational ethics more than they represent "best practice" or codes of professional conduct. While it is possible that organizational ethics can parallel those of the profession, in view of the fact that the purpose of an organization may be different than the purpose of any one helping relationship, the organizational ethics may not only be conflictual but may act to undermine the values and ethics of the practitioner (see Exercise 6.2).

While it is clear that the ethical practitioner must be aware of the oftentimes subtle influence of a system's culture on his or her practice decision,

---

Exercise 6.1

Making Culturally Compatible Choices

Directions: Below is a table that provides a social context, a focus for a practitioner, and two practice decision options. Along with a colleague, select the options that you feel would most likely be encouraged and/or supported by that particular social context and provide your rationale for your selection.

Social-Organizational Cultural Context	Focus for Practice Decision	Practice Decision Options	Selection and Rationale
(sample) Catholic High School	Increased evidence of student pregnancy	1. Guidance unit on sexual behavior, safe sex, and sexually transmitted diseases 2. Guidance unit on self-esteem and value of abstinence	Option 2, given the school's belief that sex outside of marriage is unacceptable and immoral

Social-Organizational Cultural Context	Focus for Practice Decision	Practice Decision Options	Selection and Rationale
A free-standing clinic that is funded primarily through managed care contracts	A client diagnosed as depressed, with the possibility of having an early history of sexual abuse	1. Referral for anti-depressant medication 2. Contract for long term, "recovered memories" therapy	
A military industrial complex, making "sensitive" technical equipment	A personnel director who is approached by an upper level manager experiencing extreme financial pressures and who has had fantasies of "selling technology" to other governments	1. Respect the confidentiality of the relationship and work with the employee on stress reduction 2. Report the fantasies to his supervisor	
A public school, with limited special education facilities and funding	A school psychologist who believes a student is in serious need of ongoing individual psychotherapy	1. Recommend therapy to his family as part of an Individual Education Program 2. Suggest that his family may find it useful to contact an outside therapist	

Exercise 6.2

Goals: Values and Decisions

Directions: As noted within the chapter, decisions are made that not only reflect the values held, but the goals desired. Below you will find a scenario, system and practitioner goals, and decision options. Your task is to identify the decisions preferred by the system along with those preferred by the practitioner. Next identify the situations in which these are parallel or in conflict.

Scenario	System Goals	Practitioner Goal	Decision Preferred by System	Decision Preferred by Practitioner	Parallel or Conflict
1. (sample) Star football player has a very bad sprained ankle.	Win the big game	Rest the ankle	Allow the student to play	Sideline the student for one game	Conflict
2. The top salesman for a corporation has embraced his alcoholism and is committed to a treatment program.	Maintain sales	Maintain salesman's health	Adjust sales region to allow salesman to attend meetings while continuing sales	Encourage and support in attending meetings	
3. A social worker noted that a fifth grade teacher who is approaching retirement has a number of physical problems, has been falling asleep in class, and often verbally abuses the children for making noise.	Educate children in fulfillment of the schools mission	Protect children from verbal abuse and show concern for an aging teacher with ill health	Try not to make too public for the remainder of the semester and then provide the teacher with an early retirement package	Work with the teacher in developing some cooperative learning units while providing supportive counseling around the benefits of retirement	

Scenario	System Goals	Practitioner Goal	Decision Preferred by System	Decision Preferred by Practitioner	Parallel or Conflict
4. A residential setting for individuals with severe emotional problems	To provide therapy while at the same time reducing patient disruption	To provide therapy geared at empowering individuals to take responsibility for their own actions	Reliance on medication including sedatives	Using the minimum amount of medication in order to support the client's development of cognitive/behavioral methods of control	

the question remains: "If enculturated, how does one identify the operating assumptions, values, and culture?" It has been suggested that the use of interpretation of the artifacts and values reveals basic assumptions (Schein, 2010). Artifacts would include the visible, tangible, or concrete manifestations, be they the physical surroundings and their appointments, the stories or oral histories still shared, and even the rituals and ceremonies practiced, whereas a system's values are revealed in what the system views as important in terms of goals, activities, relationships, and feelings (Schein, 2010)). By reviewing the way those within the system traditionally and continually address specific problems posed by the situations they face in common, the ethical practitioner can begin to understand the system's values.

WHO IS THE CLIENT? ●

One seminal question that needs to be addressed when working within an organization is "Who is the client?" While this at first may appear to be a simple question to answer, balancing a practitioner's responsibility to the employing organization while at the same time servicing the individual helper seeker is not always that clear-cut or easy. The various professional organizations are aware of this potential confusion and area of conflict and have attempted to provide practitioners with guidelines for their practice decisions (see Table 6.1).

Table 6.1 Ethics of Practice Serving Client and Organization

Professional Ethical Standards	Statement on Serving Client and Organization
American Counseling Association (2014)	C.2.g. Counselors monitor themselves for signs of impairment from their own physical, mental, or emotional problems and refrain from offering or providing professional services when impaired. They seek assistance for problems that reach the level of professional impairment, and, if necessary, they limit, suspend, or terminate their professional responsibilities until it is determined that they may safely resume their work. Counselors assist colleagues or supervisors in recognizing their own professional impairment and provide consultation and assistance when warranted with colleagues or supervisors showing signs of impairment and intervene as appropriate to prevent imminent harm to clients.
American Psychological Association (2010)	1.03. If the demands of an organization with which psychologists are affiliated or for whom they are working are in conflict with this Ethics Code, psychologists clarify the nature of the conflict, make known their commitment to the Ethics Code, and take reasonable steps to resolve the conflict with the General Principles and Ethical Standards of the Ethics Code. Under no circumstances may this standard be used to justify or defend violating human rights.
National Association of Social Workers (2008)	3.09.a. Social workers generally should adhere to commitments made to employers and employing organizations. 3.09.b. Social workers should work to improve employing agencies' policies and procedures and the efficiency and effectiveness of their services. 3.09.c. Social workers should take reasonable steps to ensure that employers are aware of social workers' ethical obligations as set forth in the *NASW Code of Ethics* and of the implications of those obligations for social work practice. 3.09.d. Social workers should not allow an employing organization's policies, procedures, regulations or administrative orders to interfere with their ethical practice of social work. Social workers should take reasonable steps to ensure that their employing organizations' practices are consistent with the *NASW Code of Ethics*.

Although the various professional organizations address the issue of serving individuals and organizations, it is still for the individual practitioner to resolve questions such as, does the ethical practitioner, when working with individual members of an organization, make decisions that are best suited for the goals and objectives of the institution, even if not in the best interest of the individual care seeker? Or does the individual and the individual's well-being take primacy? (See Case Illustration 6.3.)

Case Illustration 6.3

Who Is the Client?

Col. R. J. Wipps was a clinical psychologist working in service of the U.S. Army's Special Service Division. Col. Wipps provided testing and individual counseling to those involved with Special Services.

Col. Wipps was approached by D. L. Kingsley, an officer in charge of a highly sensitive military project. D. L. came to Col. Wipps because of what he reported to be extreme stress as a result of financial difficulties that he was currently experiencing. D. L. noted that he was concerned that his wife would leave him if something didn't happen soon to improve their lifestyle. When asked what he was attempting to do to resolve the financial problems, D. L. was quick to note that "nothing short of something illegal" could help. When confronted directly about whether he had considered illegal activities, D. L. stated: "Of course not . . . but I've been drinking a lot lately and God only knows what I could do if I get drunk!"

Col. Wipps recommended that D. L. take a medical leave while he went into a treatment program for the alcohol and also received some individual and marital counseling. D. L. said he would think about it but really did not feel that was necessary. D. L. asked if he would be able to see Col. Wipps for some counseling during this really stressful time. D. L. also wanted to be sure that the relationship would be confidential.

For Col. Wipps (see Case Illustration 6.3), questions existed about whether individual confidentiality should be respected or whether this individual posed a significant security risk and thus should be identified to appropriate personnel. In part, the answer to this question rested on whom Col. Wipps identified as his client, D. L. Kingsley or the U.S. Army. Most guidelines, like that of the American Counseling Association (ACA) (see

Table 6.1) indicate that the client is the primary concern for the ethical helper and the institution secondary. But it could be argued that accepting a position within an organization is a tacit agreement to serve as its agent and to embrace its values and standards of practice. In fact, the *ACA Code of Ethics* (2014) advised that acceptance of employment is essentially an agreement with the principles and policies of the institution, and that "counselors strive to reach agreement with employers regarding acceptable standards of client care and professional conduct . . . " (ACA, 2014, Principle D.1.g).

It would appear, therefore, that the ethical practitioner needs to be accountable and responsive to both the system of employment and the individual clients served within that system. As such, it is essential that the practitioner not only understand but also commit to the mission of the organization as well as the specific values underlying that mission and the ways it becomes manifested in the procedures, policies, and decision-making processes. This does not mean to suggest a blind allegiance to the organization at the cost of the individual. In fact, it can be argued that the ethical helper will attempt to change organizational policies and procedures that are not healthy for those within the system. For example, the *ACA Code of Ethics* states: "Counselors alert their employers of inappropriate policies and practices. They attempt to effect changes in such policies through constructive action within the organization. When such polices are potentially disruptive or damaging to clients or may limit the effectiveness of services provided and change cannot be affected, counselors take appropriate further action" (ACA, 2014, D.l.h). In a similar vein the American Psychological Association (APA) directs its members that "if the demands of an organization with which psychologists are affiliated or for whom they are working are in conflict with this Ethics Code, psychologists clarify the nature of the conflict, make known their commitment to the Ethics Code, and take reasonable steps to resolve the conflict with the General Principles and Ethical Standards of the Ethics Code. Under no circumstances may this standard be used to justify or defend violating human rights" (APA, 2010). The significance of this responsibility to confront organizational policies and practices that are deemed damaging to clients or in some way forcing practitioner unethical behavior is highlighted by the ACA directive that if there is an irreconcilable conflict between the institution's practices and those standards established by the code, resignation from employment should be considered (ACA, 2014, Principle D.1.h).

Thus, while some practitioners find themselves feeling responsible for championing the client's right to confidentiality in the face of the organization's rules and regulations, in some situations, this is neither legal nor ethical. For example, in the military, confidentiality is guided by federal statutes, Department of Defense regulations, and the specific service (i.e., Army, Navy, Air Force) regulations, a point that needs to be considered by Col. Wipps (see Case Illustration 6.3). While supporting respect for the privacy of the individuals, these directives also mandate access to confidential materials by federal employees on a "need to know" basis (Neuhauser, 2011).

An ethical practitioner attempts to resolve conflicts between organizational need and individual need in a way that not only reflects the desire of the practitioner to be supportive of his or her organization but also upholds the professional code of ethics. Thus, when confronted by the desire to protect the care seeker's privacy while abiding by the rules and regulations of the organization in which one is employed, the use of advanced warning on the limits of confidentiality would be essential as a means of serving both the organization of employment and the care seeker.

When There Are Multiple Masters

Ethical practitioners will not only know the mission, objectives, and values of the organizations within which they work, but will also make known to their employers the nature of their own professional ethical commitments. Beyond this, it appears that an ethical practitioner will also share with his or her clients the obligations of fidelity and conditions of employment and how these may flavor the helping relationships and the practitioner's decisions. This is especially important when an organization's disclosure policy places additional limits on the confidentiality between client and helper (see Case Illustration 6.2).

Recently, the issue of multiple clients or conflicts between the needs of an employing organization with those of the client has taken on a new dimension with the introduction of managed care. Managed care is a term applied to a widespread set of attempts to contain health care costs. The term has been used to describe "any type of intervention in the delivery and financing of health care that is intended to eliminate unnecessary and inappropriate care and to reduce costs" (Langwell, 1992, p. 22). Under managed care, third-party payers review requests for the initial delivery of services, determine the volume of services to be provided, and review any subsequent requests for service. Given the level of involvement in the professional decision process, it could be argued in managed care situations the practitioner has in fact two clients, the primary client being the person seeking assistance and the secondary client being the managed care company. The potential for conflict can arise in that the needs and goals of these two clients may not always be congruent.

Managed care is essentially an economic strategy designed to provide care of or better quality for less money. While the concept of cost containment is noble, the reality is that the goals of managed care can be in conflict with those of the practitioner (Meyers, 1999). Metzl (2012), for example, argues that managed care's desire to create a homogenous cost effective product or template for treatment planning, while perhaps working with the administration of EKGs to patients with chest pain are not applicable to the nonhomogenous client base presenting with depression, personality disorders, or other form of mental health conditions.

Under these conditions, the question that can arise is, at what point does the cost containment interfere with the client's needs and the helper's ethical practice?

Managed care may challenge the practitioner's ability to provide ethical practice. Managed care stresses time-limited interventions, cost-effective treatment, toward preventive rather than remedial processes (Metzl, 2012). Professional literature raises several concerns about the impact of managed care on the effectiveness of treatment provided (Roberts & Hurley, 2012). As noted by these authors (Roberts & Hurley, 2012), managed care could result in clients receiving undertreatment, in that they may go underdiagnosed, experience restricted referral, and have insufficient follow-up. Thus, the policies of managed care may conflict with the practitioner, especially when utilization review decisions are contrary to professional judgment or when short-term or limited interventions are inadequate forms of treatments. Ethical rules and standards are often incongruent with the realities of treatment situations. In a managed care environment with restrictions to the number of sessions allowed, adhering to professional guidelines for risk management and standard of care service may simply be unrealistic.

In addition to potentially restricting treatment choice, the third party review can also compromise client privacy. Given these potential areas of conflict, what is the ethical practitioner to do?

At a minimum, the ethical practitioner needs to inform clients how their delivery of services may be influenced by managed care policies and restrictions. Our professional codes have addressed this concern by directing clinicians to provide clients information needed to understand the potential conflict and the limits imposed on practice. For example, APA directs its members as follows:

> When psychologists agree to provide services to a person or entity at the request of a third party, psychologists attempt to clarify at the outset of the service the nature of the relationship with all individuals or organizations involved. This clarification includes the role of the psychologist (e.g., therapist, consultant, diagnostician, or expert witness), an identification of who is the client, the probable uses of the services provided or the information obtained, and the fact that there may be limits to confidentiality. (APA, 2010, Principle 3.07)

A point echoed in the codes of ethics presented by the American Association for Marriage and Family Therapy (AAMFT, 2015, Principle 1.13), beyond informing clients of the third-party relationship, practitioners are directed to gain client permission prior to any disclosure to that third party (e.g., ACA, 2014, B.3.d; AMHCA, 2010, 2.q; NASW, 2008, 1.07.h).

Another concern that can arise when working within a managed system is that of balancing the requirements of managed care's cost containment principle with the ethical concern of providing quality of care, when such care requires extending services beyond that sanctioned by the managed care agency. How it is accomplished is truly the dilemma faced by all managed care providers. Do therapists continue pro bono? Do they challenge the managed care gatekeepers about artificial limits to needed care?

While the limitations to the number of sessions to be paid by insurance may make good economic and business sense for the insuring body, the question remains: What happens to the client once these limits are reached? Should the client continue to need care, the helper is ethically bound not to abandon him or her. The helper could refer the client needing additional treatment or provide pro bono services. Both strategies invite complication. How does one refer if referral sources are limited? How does one provide pro bono services to so many and survive financially? The answer may lie in the decisions an ethical practitioner makes before engaging in managed care service. Haas and Cummings (1995) advise therapists to consider the question of how to provide service to the client and how to avoid abandoning clients without going bankrupt before one joins a managed care plan. Understanding the nature of the managed care contract and resolving areas of professional standards of practice and care with those of economic necessity is a must for the ethical helper (see Exercise 6.3).

Exercise 6.3

Serving Clients in a Managed Care Environment

Directions: Contact two private practitioners who provide clinical services and are part of a managed care organization. Ask the practitioners each of the following questions:

- What are the limits to the types and/or length of services you can provide to your managed care clients?

- Are there are any unique limitations to the confidentiality of your records when working with managed care clients?

(Continued)

(Continued)

- What, if any, avenues of appeal do you have regarding the decisions made by the managed care utilization review boards?

- How do you inform your clients of the special conditions regarding type and length of service, utilization review, confidentiality, and so forth, that may exist by the nature of providing managed care services?

- Have you turned down any opportunities to join a particular managed care group because you found it too restrictive?

- Have you been able to change any policies, procedures, or requirements in the managed care organization of which you are a part as a way of better servicing your clients?

- As a provider in managed care, what do you find to be the most challenging factor to your ability to provide ethical, professional care for your clients?

● BEYOND PROFESSIONAL STANDARDS: A PERSONAL MORAL RESPONSE

While it is easy to grasp and comprehend the dilemmas one may face as the varying demands, needs, and responsibilities of client, profession, and system of employment converge on a practitioner, positioning oneself to make the ethical decision may be quite another story. The existence and potential impact of these forces is not a simple intellectual or academic issue. It is a real-life dilemma that has the potential to impact the client, the practitioner, and the therapeutic relationship. Restrictions of modes and duration of treatment not only have the potential to undermine effectiveness but also can erode the professional's personal and professional values. The limited autonomy on professional decision-making may increase the stress experienced in practice and contribute to conditions of burnout and empathy fatigue (See Chapter 14). Confronted with these conditions, the ethical practitioner may find herself confronted by a conflict between the institution's practices and the standards established by her professional code. Such conflicts will require ethical practitioners to clarify and resolve these conflicts in a way that maximizes adherence to ethical dictates of their profession. This can be facilitated by establishing a preplan of resolving potential conflicts between organization and professional ethics and values, including adjusting contracts and contract demands so that they are in line with system goals AND professional standards. When this is not possible, then it is the contention of these authors that the ethical practitioner should consider resignation. Exercise 6.4 is provided as a stimulus for your own development of such a preplan.

Exercise 6.4

Recontracting or Resigning

Directions: Part 1: Below you will find a number of organizational policies or procedures that a practitioner would need to follow. Identify those you find objectionable. How would you attempt to rework these policies/procedures before you would resign your post?

Organizational Directive (Policies/ Procedures)	Rework or Recontract	Resign?
All clinical records, including notes, are open to inspection by anyone identified as an executive administrator within the organization.	Attempt to specify the specific types of data open for review and tie each level of data to a specific administrator with a "need to know." Further, all clients would be informed as to the access to records.	Yes, if not modified
Allowed only to utilize a brief therapy form of service. Therapy restricted to eight sessions maximum.		

(Continued)

(Continued)

Organizational Directive (Policies/ Procedures)	Rework or Recontract	Resign?
Prior to providing service, all intake information must be shared with a review board in order to achieve permission to continue. Further, a specific treatment plan and progress reports must be completed after every four sessions.		
As an employee, you are required to provide service, in-house, for all the clients you see, regardless of their needs and your level of training.		
You are required to acquire a minimum of 30 continuing education credits in your professional field every 2 years.		

Part 2: Ask an individual care provider who is a member of a managed care program to show you his or her contract and statement of responsibilities, policies, and procedures governing service delivery. Review this contract and identify areas that you feel may potentially compromise your ability to provide ethical practice.

CONCLUDING CASE ILLUSTRATION ●

Returning to the scene with which we opened the chapter, we find Ms. Wicks (Maria's counselor) expressing her felt conflict among the informal values and rules of conduct held within the system in which she works, her concern for her client, and her understanding of her professional code of ethics. As you read the continuing dialogue, try to identify some of the values and/or underlying assumptions existing within that school's culture and begin to identify where and how these may conflict with this particular counselor's understanding of her professional code of conduct. The questions in the reflection section that follows the exchange should help you in this process.

Ms. Wicks: Hi, Tom, it is me again.

Mr. Harolds: Hey, how are you? Did you get that information from the state association?

Ms. Wicks: Not yet, they are supposed to call me. But, things are getting more confusing . . .

Mr. Harolds: Really?

Ms. Wicks: Ms. Armstrong, the principal at the school, informed me that it is understood in the district that we are not to counsel students regarding sexual issues. She said it is not a formal policy, just something that "we" all know not to do. So now I'm not sure if I broke a law, or violated a code of ethics, or may have stepped over the line in terms of my job definition. I am so confused!

Mr. Harolds: Well, Michelle, this is a very conservative community, and the truth is that with so many of our students having Latino backgrounds, we really don't want to impose mainstream cultural values where they don't belong.

Ms. Wicks: But, Tom, it is not like I'm going to promote a particular position here. I am just very concerned that she is making some decisions that could prove harmful and even potentially lethal to her.

Mr. Harolds: It is clear you are concerned about your client, but you need to understand something. In the past, we attempted to help the students make what we thought were value decisions. In fact, in health class we used to have a unit on sexuality and sexually transmitted diseases. Well, 5 years ago a parent group took the health teacher, the principal, and the school superintendent all to court for supposedly "imposing moral values" on their children. As a result, we removed health from our curriculum, replaced it with something on career choices, and created a parent supervisor board for the school that reviews curriculum decisions. So the superintendent is likely to be extremely sensitive about anything that may be interpreted as promoting a set of values or beliefs. I guess Ms. Armstrong is simply trying to avoid pressure from the central office. No sense rocking the boat.

Reflections

1. Assuming that Mr. Harolds's depiction of the way the system operates is accurate, what would be the primary value or motive driving decisions around controversial topics?
2. When it comes to decision-making, which of the following would you suspect takes primacy in the culture of that school: Do what's expedient? Avoid conflict at all costs? Be politically correct? Do what is best for the students?
3. Could you identify an artifact that reflects the operating values and assumptions within that school?
4. What do you feel Ms. Wicks should do? In relationship to her client? Future clients? Her principal? Her job definition and contract?

● COOPERATIVE LEARNING EXERCISE

Directions: With a colleague, review each of the following scenarios and

- Identify potential areas of conflict
- Decide if the behavior of the practitioner is ethical
- Identify decision options available for the practitioner
- Discuss possible preplan options that could have been implemented to reduce the potential of conflict.

Scenario 1: High School Counselor

A high school counselor has been working with a student athlete who was self-referred, because of his concern about his tendency to attend underage drinking parties on the weekends and become intoxicated. The student expressed genuine concern over these tendencies and appeared willing to work with the counselor in order to curtail both the desires and the actions. He is particularly concerned with changing his behaviors, as the basketball season has just begun and he is the starting center for the team. There is a zero-tolerance policy for student athletes engaging in illegal activities, such as underage drinking. The counselor feels that he should warn the basketball coach about the student's tendencies toward attending parties and drinking on the weekends.

Scenario 2: An Employee Assistance Provider (EAP)

Dr. Livingston is a licensed social worker working in private practice. Dr. Livingston also provides short-term counseling to employees of a local manufacturing plant. In this capacity as an employee assistance counselor, she has agreed to provide short-term (maximum of five visits) counseling to all employees and offers referral services for those needing more extended care. Further, her contract calls for her to consult with managers in order to increase their effectiveness when working with their employees.

In working with Helen, Dr. Livingston discovered that Helen and her coworkers have been punching in and out for one another and, as a result, have developed a system where they can cut approximately 8 hours a week off their actual work while recording and receiving pay for a full 40-hour week. Helen is a little troubled by this procedure but reports this is what everybody does. Dr. Livingston feels that she should report this information to Mr. Hansen, the owner of the company, since it is he with whom she has a contract.

SUMMARY ●

- Practice decisions made must reflect not only the needs of the client and characteristics and orientation of the helper but also the unique characteristics and demands of the context or organization in which the helping occurs.
- A professional role as well as the expectations of professional behavior is shaped in response to the organization's expectations and needs; therefore, these expectations are incorporated as standards and guides for practice decisions.
- System culture is a pattern of basic assumptions invented, discovered, or developed by a given group as it learns to cope with its problems of external adaptation and internal integration. The pattern has worked well enough to be considered valid and is taught to new members as

the correct way to perceive, think, and feel, in relationship to those problems.

- Once enculturated within a system, it is easy for the cultural values to become enacted in the way members prioritize and function—shaping policies, decision-making, and other operations. As such, practice decisions may begin to reflect institutional values and organizational ethics more than they represent "best practice" or codes of professional conduct.

- Most guidelines, like that of the ACA, indicate that the client is the primary concern for the ethical helper and the institution secondary. But it could be argued that accepting a position within an organization is a tacit agreement to serve as its agent and to embrace its values and standards of practice.

- The ethical practitioner needs to be accountable and responsive to both the system of employment and the individual clients served within that system.

- Ethical practitioners will share with their clients the obligations of fidelity, conditions of employment, and how these may flavor the helping relationships and the practitioners' decisions. One special situation in which it is clear there may be more than one client is in the case of managed care.

- Managed care is essentially an economic strategy designed to provide care of equal or better quality for less money. The policies of managed care may conflict with the decisions of an ethical practitioner, especially when utilization review decisions are contrary to professional judgment or when short-term or limited interventions are inadequate forms of treatments.

- Understanding the nature of the managed care contract and resolving areas of professional standards of practice and care with those of economic necessity is a must for the ethical helper.

- Acceptance of employment is essentially an agreement with the principles and policies of the institution. When conflict exists between the institution's practices and the standards established by the code, the ethical practitioner needs to clarify and resolve conflicts in a way that maximizes adherences to ethical dictates of his or her profession. This can be facilitated by establishing a preplan of resolving potential conflicts between organization and professional ethics and values, including adjusting contracts and contract demands so that they are in line with system goals AND professional standards. When this is not possible, then it is the contention of these authors that the ethical practitioner will consider resignation.

IMPORTANT TERMS ●

artifacts

basic assumptions

client

cultural values

ethical culture of social systems

limits of confidentiality

managed care

need to know

organizational ethics

preplan

system

utilization review

ADDITIONAL RESOURCES ●

Print

Houser, R., Wilczenski, F. L., & Ham, M. (2006). *Culturally relevant ethical decision-making in counseling*. Thousand Oaks, CA: Sage.

Sperry, L. (2007). *The ethical and professional practice of counseling and psychotherapy*. New York, NY: Pearson.

Thompson, R. (2012). *Professional school counseling: Best practices for working in the schools*. New York, NY: Taylor & Francis.

Web-Based

Daniels, J. A. (2001). Managed care, ethics, and counseling. *Journal of Counseling and Development, 79*, 119–122. doi: 10.1002/j.1556-6676.2001.tb01950.x

Glosoff, H. L., & Pate, R. H., Jr. (2002). Privacy and confidentiality in school counseling. *Professional School Counseling, 6*(1), 20–27.

Kremer, T. G., & Gesten, E. L. (1998). Confidentiality limits of managed care and clients' willingness to self-disclose. *Professional Psychology: Research and Practice, 29*(6), 553–558. Retrieved from http://dx.doi.org/10.1037/0735-7028.29.6.553

Mappes, D. C., Robb. G. P., & Engels, D. W. (1985). Conflicts in ethics and law in counseling and psychotherapy, *Journal of Counseling and Development, 64*(4), 246–252. Retrieved from http://onlinelibrary.wiley.com/doi/10.1002/j.1556-6676.1985.tb01094.x/abstract

Reamer, F. G. (2008). When ethics and the law collide, *Social Work Today, 8*(5). Retrieved from http://www.socialworktoday.com/archive/EoESepOct08.shtml

Stone, C. (2006, January). Confidentiality and the need to know. *ASCA school-counselor*. Retrieved from http://schoolcounselor.org/magazine/blogs/january-february-2006/confidentiality-and-the-need-to-know

● REFERENCES

American Association for Marriage and Family Therapy. (2015). *Code of ethics.* Retrieved from https://www.aamft.org/iMIS15/AAMFT/Content/Legal_Ethics/Code_of_Ethics.aspx

American Counseling Association. (2014). Code of ethics. Retrieved from http://www.counseling.org/resources/aca-code-of-ethics.pdf

American Mental Health Counselors Association. (2010). *Code of ethics.* Retrieved from http://c.ymcdn.com/sites/www.amhca.org/resource/resmgr/Docs/AMHCA_Code_of_Ethics_2010_up.pdf

American Psychological Association. (2010). *Ethical principles of psychologists and code of conduct.* Retrieved from http://www.apa.org/ethics/code/principles.pdf

Haas, L. J., & Cummings, N. A. (1995). Managed outpatient mental health plans: Clinical, ethical and practical guidelines for participation. In D. N. Bersoff (Ed.), *Ethical conflicts in psychology.* Washington, DC: American Psychological Association.

Kurusu, D. J. (1985). Consultation interventions: Successes, failures and proposals. *The Counseling Psychologists, 13,* 368–389.

Langwell, K. M. (1992). The effects of managed care on use and costs of health services. (Staff memorandum). Washington, DC: Congressional Budget Office.

Metzl, J. M. (2012). Managed mental health care: An oxymoron of ethics? *Jefferson Journal of Psychiatry,* 35–42.

Meyers, C. (1999). Managed care and ethical conflicts: Anything new? *Journal of Medical Ethics, 25*(5), 382–387.

National Association of Social Workers (Rev. ed., 2008). *Code of ethics.* Retrieved from http://www.socialworkers.org/pubs/code/code.asp

Neuhauser, J. A. (2011). Lives of quiet desperation: The conflict between military necessity and confidentiality. *Creighton Law Review, 44,* 1003–1044.

Roberts, M. C., & Hurley, L. K. (2012). Managing managed care. New York, NY: Springer.

Schein, E. (2010). *Organizational culture and leadership* (4th ed.). San Francisco, CA: Jossey-Bass.

CHAPTER 7

Ethical Decision-Making

Ms. Wicks: You know, this job seemed easier when I was in school. All the case examples used in class were so clear-cut. It was easy to understand what was ethical and what was not.

Mr. Harolds: You would think there would be clear-cut answers to what you are supposed to do, and when you are supposed to do it.

Ms. Wicks: That's certainly not the case in my fieldwork! Professional practice in real life is not always that clear.

The student's reflection of how real life differs from the somewhat "artificial" life of the textbook or academic setting highlights the fact that ethics and ethical practice are not as simple or as clear-cut as may be assumed or certainly desired. As one in the early stage of your professional life, the thought of committing a violation against your professional ethics may seem foreign and remote. Sadly, violations or at least behavior approaching ethical violations are neither foreign nor remote. As reported by one organization, nearly 5,000 ethical inquiries regarding counselor decisions and practices were made in 2011 (ACA, 2012).

Our professional codes are "guidelines," neither recipes nor clear directives. While it is essential to understand and embrace our ethical codes, it is equally important for each professional and professional-in-training to understand, embrace, and employ a process that will facilitate the application of these codes, especially in those situations where clear, ethical pathways are less than evident.

● OBJECTIVES

The current chapter will review models for ethical decision-making and provide an integrated model that helps clinicians move from the recognition and assessment of an ethical dilemma through planning, implementing, and evaluating the impact of their practice decisions. Case illustrations and guided exercises are provided to not only add to the clarity of understanding but to facilitate, your valuing of the need for an ethical decision-making process to guide your own practice decisions.

After reading this chapter you should be able to do the following:

- Not only understand but also value the need and importance of employing ethical decision-making models to guide practice decisions;
- describe a number of step-wise and value-based models of ethical decision-making;
- identify and explain common elements that can be crafted into a more generic, integrated model for ethical decision-making; and
- apply an integrated model of ethical decision-making to illustrated cases.

● CODES OF ETHICS: GUIDES NOT PRESCRIPTIONS

A set of rules and directives that would result in efficient and ethical professional practice would be something clearly welcomed by student and professional alike. However, as should be clear by now, such prescriptions or recipes for professional practice do not exist, nor does every client and every professional condition provide clear-cut avenues for progress.

Professional practice is both complex and complicated. The issues presented are often confounded and conflicting. The process of making sense of the options available and engaging in the path that leads to effective, ethical practice cannot be preprogrammed but rather needs to be fluid, flexible, and responsive to the uniqueness of the client and the context of helping. The very dynamic and fluid nature of our work with clients prohibits the use of rigid, formulaic prescriptions or directions. Never is this so obvious as when first confronted with an ethical dilemma.

Consider the subtle challenges to practice decisions presented in Case Illustration 7.1. The case reflects a decision regarding the release of information and the potential breach of confidentiality. The element confounding the decision, as you will see, is that the client was deceased and it was the executrix of the estate providing permission to release the information to a third party.

As noted, the main question to be considered in this case is, does confidentiality extend into the grave and if not, under what conditions can

---

Case Illustration 7.1

Conditions for Maintaining Confidentiality

While all clinicians have been schooled in the issue of confidentiality and the various conditions under which confidentiality must be breached (e.g., prevention of harm to self or another), the conditions of maintenance of confidentiality can be somewhat blurred when the material under consideration is that of a client who is now deceased. Consider the case of Dr. Martin Orne, MD, PhD.

Dr. Orne was a psychotherapist who worked with Anne Sexton, a Pulitzer Prize winner. Following the death of Ms. Sexton, an author, Ms. Middlebrook, set out to write her biography. In doing her research, Ms. Middlebrook discovered that Dr. Orne had tape-recorded a number of sessions with Ms. Sexton in order to allow her to review the sessions, and he had not destroyed the tapes following her death.

Ms. Middlebrook approached Linda Gray Sexton, the daughter of the client and the executrix of the estate, seeking permission to access these tapes of the confidential therapy sessions as an aid to her writing. The daughter granted permission for release of the therapeutic tapes.

A number of questions could be raised around this case, including the ethics of tape-recording or the ethics of maintenance of the tapes following the death of the client. However, the most pressing issue involves the conditions under which confidentiality should be maintained. The challenge here is, should Dr. Orne release the tapes in response to the daughter's granting of permission, or does his client have the right to confidentiality even beyond the grave?

(should) it be violated? You may find it informative to discuss that question with your classmates or colleagues, and to aid in that discussion, you may want to consult the following website for additional information on the case (http://www.dianemiddlebrook.com/sexton/tpg12-91.html).

While our standards and professional codes of practice can help us in resolving questions, such as that found in Case Illustration 7.1, they do not (nor do they purport to) provide clear direction and solution in any and all situations. Even principles such as *informed consent*, *confidentiality*, and *boundaries*, while appearing clear and easily applied, can be challenging to enact in professional practice. Consider these principles in light of some challenging practice conditions (see Table 7.1).

Clearly, as a human service provider, you will encounter situations in which you are confronted by an ethical dilemma. The situation may include if and when

Table 7.1 Challenges to Clarity

Issue/Code	Challenge	Real Life Challenge: Case Scenario	Direction? Decision?
Confidentiality Keep information confidential unless legal requirements demand that confidential information be revealed or a breach is required to prevent serious and foreseeable harm to the student. (ASCA, 2016, A.2.e)	To act or not to act requires the counselor to interpret the meaning of *serious and foreseeable harm* and judge a client's/ student's behavior as serious enough to break confidentiality.	A 17-year-old high school senior discloses the fact that she is trying to "secretly" get pregnant as a way of making her boyfriend make a commitment to her. A 12-year-old middle school student has shared that she is actively engaging in sexual activity, including intercourse, with one of her eighth-grade peers.	How might you apply the concept of "prevent serious and foreseeable harm to the student"? Could a case be made in either illustration for breaking confidentiality? How about maintaining confidentiality?
Boundaries A psychologist refrains from entering into a multiple relationship if the multiple relationship could reasonably be expected to impair the psychologist's objectivity, competence, or effectiveness in performing his or her functions as a psychologist, or otherwise risks exploitation or harm to the person with whom the professional relationship exists. APA, 2010, 3.05)	The challenge is to define those conditions where the multiple relationships could be expected to impair one's objectivity, competence, or effectiveness. While some situations are clear, as in having a romantic relationship with a current client, others may fall in those shades of gray.	A clinical psychologist in private practice is invited to serve as head coach for the high school girls' soccer team. To her surprise, she arrived at the first team meeting to discover that the team's star player is also her client. While participating in a single-parents group at her local church, a practicing psychologist is approached by a previous client who "invites" her out for a drink following one of the meetings.	Can the clinician engage in both roles—as coach and therapist? Is "socializing" with this previous client allowable?

Issue/Code	Challenge	Real Life Challenge: Case Scenario	Direction? Decision?
Informed Consent Clients have the freedom to choose whether to enter into or remain in a counseling relationship and need adequate information about the counseling process and the counselor. (ACA, 2014, A.2.a)	Challenges could include the following: Are there conditions that inhibit a client's ability to provide informed consent? Do all clients have the ethical right of freedom to choose or are there conditions (e.g., age, diagnosis, court mandate, etc.) that limit that freedom?	The client, who is 26 years old, came to the session having been driven by his father. During the initial intake, it became clear to the counselor that the client had some form of neurological impairment not previously disclosed. The client is an 8-year-old, third-grade student who was referred by his teacher because of what she felt was unusually aggressive drawings and stories in his journal.	How might this issue of neurological damage influence the clinician's approach to "informed consent"? Does age, issue, or context (i.e., school) affect the client's right of freedom to choose?

to disclose confidential information without a client's consent (e.g., a suicidal client) or the ethics of limiting a client's right to self-determination (e.g., when involuntary hospitalization is required) or even the appropriateness of engaging in nonprofessional relationships with a former client. These ethical dilemmas are difficult to resolve, because by one definition, that of Kitchener as cited in Shiles (2009), an ethical dilemma occurs when "there are good but contradictory ethical reasons to take conflicting and incompatible courses of action" (p. 43). As such, the ethical dilemmas we encounter are by definition often subtle and always, by definition, without a singular clear path to resolution. Consider the findings of one study assessing 450 members of the American Psychological Association's Division 29 (Psychotherapy) by Pope, Tabachnick, & Keith-Spiegel (1987). Of the 83 separate behaviors the members were asked to rate according to ethicality, very few—for example, having sex with a client or breaking confidentiality if clients are suicidal or homicidal—were clear-cut. Most of the 83 fell in what the authors termed "gray areas" between being ethical and unethical. Such data highlights the difficulty one experiences when faced with an ethical dilemma and the need for a sound model of ethical decision-making.

● ETHICAL DECISION-MAKING: A RANGE OF MODELS

Life—at least our professional lives—would be easier if all practice decisions and ethical dilemmas were black or white. As should now be evident, the ethical nature of our practice decisions are most often colored in many shades of gray, and thus the path to follow is not always clear.

For some, the goal is to follow the ethical codes from a mandatory perspective and thus be true to the letter of the law. While this is a basic level of ethical functioning and may serve to protect the human service provider to avoid legal trouble, this should not be the main focus of our ethical choices. We are called to embrace our ethics on an aspirational level. For one embracing aspirational ethics, the goal is not self-protection but rather client welfare. While it is our duty, our responsibility, to understand and embrace our codes of ethics (i.e., *mandatory ethics*), the execution of these codes in practice demands that we engage in self-reflection and the employment of a decision-making process that results in what is best for each of our clients (i.e., *aspirational ethics*). Reliance on one's "gut-feelings" or intuition, in the absence of reflection on that which is both mandatory and aspirational, presents an ethical problem in itself, given the greater risk to the public (Welfel, 2010).

In complex situations, the American Counseling Association's (ACA) Ethics Committee, for example, recommends that counselors explore professionally accepted decision-making models and choose the model most applicable to their situation (Kocet, 2006). This position has even been codified in the *ACA Code of Ethics* where it is noted: "When counselors are faced with an ethical dilemma, they use and document, as appropriate, an ethical decision making model . . . " (ACA, 2014, Code I.1.b).

While there is no one specific ethical decision-making model that has been identified as most effective and globally embraced, it is important, as noted by the ACA (2014, p. 3), for practitioners to be familiar with a credible model of decision-making. To this end, numerous authors have offered models for ethical decision-making, a sampling of which is offered in the next section. Each model offers a unique perspective or lens through which to view practice decisions and ethical dilemmas and as such are worthwhile, considering as each may reflect your style of practice and/or the context in which you work.

Ethical Justification Model

Kitchener (1984) has provided what some feel is the foundation for ethical decision-making (see Sheperis, Henning, & Kocet, [2016]). In fact, many of the ethical decision models use Kitchener's virtues as a springboard for their development (Urofsky, Engels, & Engerbretson, 2008).

Kitchener (1984) was aware of the then existing limitations to ethical codes and thus directed psychologists to consider the fundamental ethical principles that not only serve as the foundation for professional codes but provide a conceptual vocabulary for analyzing ethical issues when direction is less than clear. Kitchener invited practitioners to employ the values of autonomy, nonmaleficence, beneficence, fidelity, and justice (see Chapter 3) as reference points when making ethical decisions. From this perspective, clinicians would ensure that their decisions not only treated each client equally given equal circumstances (justice) but also supported client freedom to choose (autonomy). Further, based on these principles, a practitioner's ethical decisions would be made in a way that not only avoided harming the client (nonmaleficence) but promoted help and health (beneficence).

For example, while having a sexual relationship with a client is clearly unethical, the question of ethics when applied to other nonsexual, multiple-role relationships with former clients may be less obvious (Anderson & Kitchener, 1998). In these situations, the codes may not be clear and directive. Kitchener (1984) would suggest that clinicians allow their concern about not undoing therapeutic gains (i.e., nonmaleficence) along with their desire to refrain from affecting client self-determination (i.e., autonomy) to guide their decision to engage or not to engage in these nonsexual, multirole relationships. To further clarify this perspective, we invite you to engage in Exercise 7.1, applying foundational values.

When exploring an ethical dilemma, reflection on these moral values or principles may offer insight into the path best chosen. However, it has been suggested (e.g., Forester-Miller and Davis, 1996) that in complicated cases the employment of a step-wise decision-making model may be useful.

Step-Wise Approach

Forester-Miller and Davis (1996) detailed one step-wise approach that was presented in the ACA document "A Practitioner's Guide to Ethical Decision Making" (http://counseling.org/docs/ethics/practitioners_guide .pdf?sfvrsn=2). The authors presented a practical, seven-step process for ethical decision-making. The steps included the following:

Step 1: Identify the problem articulating the ethical concern. During this step, the practitioner needs to gather information that sheds light on the depth and breadth of the situation. The authors suggest that the practitioner consider questions such as, is this an ethical, legal, professional, or clinical problem or perhaps some combination? Is the issue a reflection of me, the client, others in the client's life, and/or the system in which I work? Answering these questions helps focus the targets for resolution.

Exercise 7.1

Applying Foundational Values

Directions: The task is to review the following situations confronting a therapist. Your task is to first decide what you would do. Next—and this may be best done in consult with a classmate, colleague, or professor—view your decision through the values of autonomy, nonmaleficence, beneficence, fidelity, and justice. Would this process alter your initial decision?

Situation	Your Decision	Autonomy	Nonmaleficence	Beneficence	Fidelity	Justice
An 8-year-old, third-grade student attempts to hug the school counselor upon entering the office.						
In a group session, which is working on social skills, a client diagnosed with autism offers a hug to the therapist.						
The client, a 74-year-old religious sister (nun) brings a hand-knit scarf as a gift to the therapist.						

Situation	Your Decision	Autonomy	Nonmaleficence	Beneficence	Fidelity	Justice
At a fund raising dinner, the chair of the event introduces himself to the guest speaker, a psycho-therapist within the community. He then asks how his brother is progressing in his therapy, noting that his brother is under his care and it is he who is paying for the therapy.						

Step 2: Apply the ACA Code of Ethics. While developed for use by counselors and thus the reference to *ACA Code of Ethics*, this decision-making process could be employed by all mental health professionals by making reference to the appropriate professional standard and code at this step in the process. It is important to review the codes in order to identify all standards that may apply to the situation. If the codes do not provide clear and direct insight into the path of resolution, additional steps of the decision-making process will be necessary.

Step 3: Determine the nature and dimensions of the dilemma, noting the scope of the issue engaging the current professional literature, colleagues, and even professional associations to ensure the most current perspective on this type of problem is incorporated.

Step 4: Generate a possible course of action that could result in resolution. During this step, be creative; brainstorm in order to develop the widest possible selection of options.

Step 5: Consider the potential consequences of all options. It is important to identify all possible implications of each course of actions as it may impact the client, others, and even yourself. Identify the option or combination of options that best serve the situation.

Step 6: Evaluate the selected course of action. At this step, it is especially important to be sure that the path selected will not create additional ethical concerns.

Step 7: Implement the course of action. Once the pathway has been selected and implemented, it is important to assess to ensure that the desired impact or outcomes were achieved.

The employment of such a step-wise approach DOES NOT ensure that each practitioner, in similar situations, would arrive at the same path or outcome. However, the use of this or similar systematic models allows each clinician to not only give evidence of their valuing of ethics and ethical decision-making but to be able to articulate and explain their deliberations and reflections in the selection of a course of action.

Case Illustration 7.2 highlights the use of this approach and Exercise 7.2 invites you to employ the model on simulated case dilemma.

Case Illustration 7.2

Confidentiality Violation?

The client, Mr. E., left a message on Dr. Ellis's voicemail asking that the therapist send a bill summarizing all contact over the past year. As noted on the voicemail, Mr. E. was going to submit the summary to his insurance for possible reimbursement. Mr. E. left no further instructions.

In order to expedite the process Dr. Ellis decided to send the summary to his client's office fax machine. While the cover sheet accompanying the bill had a large, very clear statement of confidentiality, it also included the doctor's name, practice name, and address at the bottom. After faxing the summary, Dr. Ellis began to be concerned, because he was unclear as to whether the fax machine was in a public place or available only to this client. As such, he attempted to call the client to inform him of the sent fax only to find that he was out sick.

Step 1: Identify the problem articulating the ethical concern. Clearly, while the client directed him to assemble a summary statement, the manner and medium for delivery could cause concern for the client. The summary not only contained specific dates of the individual sessions but also included codes indicating the diagnosis as well as codes indicating the form of treatment (i.e., individual psychotherapy). The private and sensitive nature of this material was not for public consumption, and the doctor questioned whether the cover sheet noting the information was confidential was sufficient to protect the client's privacy.

Step 2: Apply the code of ethics. Dr. Ellis was a licensed professional counselor and member of the ACA, so he consulted the *ACA 2014 Code of Ethics*. In reviewing the code, he became concerned that he may have violated the following:

A.1.a. Primary responsibility. The primary responsibility of counselors is to respect the dignity and promote the welfare of clients.

B.1.c. Respect for confidentiality. Counselors protect the confidential information of prospective and current clients. Counselors disclose information only with appropriate consent or with sound legal or ethical justification.

B.2.e. Minimal disclosure. To the extent possible, clients are informed before confidential information is disclosed and are involved in the disclosure decision-making process. When circumstances require the disclosure of confidential information, only essential information is revealed.

B.6.b. Confidentiality of records and documentation. Counselors ensure that records and documentation kept in any medium are secure and that only authorized persons have access to them.

B.6.f. Assistance with records. When clients request access to their records, counselors provide assistance and consultation in interpreting counseling records.

Step 3: Determine the nature and dimensions of the dilemma. Dr. Ellis consulted with a colleague and attempted to research information on the use of electronic media and faxes in mental health practice. It became clear that while the use of fax transmissions is always dangerous, it should clearly be used only when the intended party has sole access to the fax or is standing by the machine and ready to retrieve it, a point that would require verification via telephone. Further, in considering ACA ethics, Dr. Ellis realized

(Continued)

(Continued)

that he should have consulted with the client, clearly identifying potential risks and costs to faxing this information and then gained written permission for the client. The other issue raised by way of his consulting was the possibility that sending billing information could be a violation of the client's company policy regarding use of company fax or even a possible violation of debt collection laws, since an outstanding balance was listed.

Step 4: Generate possible courses of action. Dr. Ellis began listing possible courses of action that included the following:

1. Go to the client's office and retrieve the fax.

2. Call the office and ask a receptionist to retrieve and destroy the fax.

3. Contact the client and after describing the dilemma ask what he would like to have done.

4. Wait, do nothing and see what happens.

Step 5: Consider the potential consequences of all options. In reviewing the first two ideas, Dr. Ellis concluded that his very presence and need to introduce himself and explain why retrieving the fax was necessary would in fact be a public disclosure of his client's engagement in therapy. Further, Option Number 4, given the potential for damage to the client's reputation and even work status, was not viable. As such, he chose to track down the client in order to discuss the situation.

Step 6: Evaluate the selected course of action. Upon reflection, Dr. Ellis realized that contacting his client and disclosing what has occurred could at minimum shake the strength of his therapeutic alliance and level of trust and even invite client legal action. However, having worked with the client for more than 8 months, Dr. Ellis felt secure that the relationship was strong enough to weather this situation and thus proceeded to call.

Step 7: Implement the course of action. On contacting the client, Dr. Ellis was relieved to find out that his client was not ill but rather taking a "mental health day" and that the only other person in the office was his personal secretary, whom he had already instructed to look for a fax and to file his insurance claim.

While any damage to the therapeutic relationship had been averted in this situation, the potential damage to future clients and client relationships remained, and as such, Dr. Ellis developed a very clear, specific policy regarding the use of social media, e-mail, and faxing, which he would distribute and discuss to all current and future clients.

Exercise 7.2

Applying a Step-Wise Model

Directions: Exercise 7.1 presented a number of situations that may place a practitioner in an awkward situation and potentially an ethical bind. Your task in this exercise is to select one of these scenarios and employ the steps identified by Forester-Miller and Davis (1996) in order to decide on the action you would ultimately take. It would be useful to share your thinking and your decision with a colleague/classmate to gain their perspective.

Situation: (select one situation presented in Exercise 7.1)

Apply Forester-Miller and Davis Step-Wise Approach

- Step 1: Identify the problem articulating the ethical concern.
- Step 2: Apply the *ACA Code of Ethics* (or employ the code that best reflects your profession).
- Step 3: Determine the nature and dimensions of the dilemma.
- Step 4: Generate possible courses of action.
- Step 5: Consider the potential consequences of all options.
- Step 6: Evaluate the selected course of action.
- Step 7: Implement the course of action.

Values-Based Virtue Approach

Jordan and Meara (1990, 1995) introduced a rather unique perspective on the issue of ethical decision-making. Their virtue ethics model focuses not on what the counselor should DO but rather on HOW as well as on WHO the counselor should be. Advocates of virtue ethics argue that practitioners should not merely seek to conform to codes but should aspire to an ethical ideal. For example, consider the situation in which a therapist approaches a termination session with a Chinese American couple. They have worked together for over a year, and the therapy has helped the couple achieve their goals. At the end of this last session, the couple presented the therapist with an original pen-and-ink drawing of their parents' village back in Mainland

China. The questions that flooded the therapist included, is it appropriate to take the gift? Is something in reciprocation required? Are boundaries being threatened? Would it be disrespectful not to take the gift?

Turning to his code of ethics, the therapist can clearly see that taking a gift as a form of bartering (AAMFT, 2015, Principle 8.5) is something that a therapist should ordinarily avoid. However, when it comes to simple reception of gifts from clients, there is not clear directive as to its appropriateness, and there even seems to be a general reluctance to discuss the issue (Zur, 2007).

While turning to one's code of ethics may help direct the clinician's response, it is, according to this model, important for the therapist to reflect upon his own personal values as they reflect his desire to both respect the persons of the clients and their culture. From this perspective and understanding that the gifts came from a desire to celebrate their success and give thanks for the professional assistance, the therapist decided to gracefully and gratefully accept this gift.

Jordan and Meara's emphasis on the values, the virtues, and the person of the therapist certainly fits with the primary theme of this text, a theme that encourages BEING ethical rather than simply knowing ethics. Jordan and Meara's approach appears to these authors as a valuable addition to any step-wise model of ethical decision-making. Further, with its emphasis on ever-increasing self-awareness and ongoing reflection and development, their model offers valuable direction for each of us as we continue to grow and evolve both personally and professionally.

Integrating Codes, Laws, and Personal-Cultural Values

Tarvydas (2012) offers an integrative approach to decision-making that highlights the need for the practitioner to view all decision-making in light of not just ethical codes and laws but cultural and social values and context. The Tarvydas Integrative Decision-Making Model of Ethical Behavior comprises four stages: (a) interpreting the situation through awareness and fact finding; (b) formulating an ethical decision; (c) weighing competing non-moral values and affirming course of action; and (d) planning and executing the selected course of action. Each of these stages is described below as applied to the following brief scenario (Case Illustration 7.3).

Stage I. Interpreting the Situation Through Awareness and Fact Finding

During this stage, the counselor will reflect upon the client's unique circumstances and characteristics as well as the nature of the specific

---

Case Illustration 7.3

Boundary Violation?

The client's response came as totally unexpected, truly catching the therapist off guard. It was a very productive yet emotionally draining and intense session. Dr. Thwarp helped to facilitate the client's review of a long-standing history of abuse, both emotionally and, in two situations, physically.

While emotionally draining, the session appeared productive. The client gave evidence of feeling empowered, no longer blaming herself as being responsible and even "deserving" of the abuse. This was truly a significant therapeutic breakthrough.

As the session came to an end and Dr. Thwarp stood to walk the client to the door, the client suddenly turned and threw both arms around Dr. Thwarp's neck, holding her tightly for a few seconds and then exiting the office saying, "Thank you for all of your support."

---

concerns and claims of all stakeholders. In addition, the clinician will engage in a fact-finding process that unearths all the facts reflecting the situation and the dimensions of ethical concern. For example, in reviewing the case of Dr. Thwarp (Case Illustration 7.3), she would want to process the event through her knowledge of the content and dynamic of the session; her reflections on her own responses prior to, during, and after the event; as well as the client's unique familial, cultural, and perhaps religious values.

Stage II. Formulating an Ethical Decision

An initial step in the formulation process is to review and clearly identify the various levels or elements of potential ethical concern.

Continuing our brief illustration of the unexpected hug, the therapist in this situation may identify potential concerns around issues of power, transference and countertransference, and most clearly boundary violations. Clearly, the theme of abuse and its implication of power and trust needs to be considered. Each of these concerns would then be viewed through relevant ethical codes, laws, and principles as well as institutional policies and procedures that apply to the situation.

With this clarity of situation, as contrasted to the standards and codes, the therapist would next consider both the positive and negative impacts of various potential courses of action. Perhaps in our scenario, the therapist is considering the following potential courses of action: (a) to immediately contact the client to define boundaries of their relationship; (b) to engage in a dialogue around boundaries at the beginning of the next session; (c) to invite the client to reflect upon her actions and the meaning they may have; (d) to increase her own sensitivity to the potential for such action and to be sure to preempt it in the future with this or any client; or (d) to simply accept the hug as a reflection of a deep sense of appreciation. As directed by the model, she would then consider the positive and negative impacts of each. During this process, it is recommended that a clinician confer with a colleague or supervisor before selecting a course of action.

Stage III. Selecting an Action by Weighing Competing, Non-Moral Values, Personal Blind Spots, or Prejudices

The model reminds us that we all have blind spots and personal prejudices that can impact our decisions, and as such, it is important to engage in reflective recognition and analysis of personal, competing non-moral values and personal biases. Our illustrative therapist would need to be open to the possibility of her own seductive behavior or countertransference. She would want to consider what, if any, impact the lack of an intimate relationship in her own life may have on her feelings and her behaviors around this client and this experience. In addition, she may want to reflect on own personal experience with hugging: Was it always and only in a sexual context or was hugging a common form of social greeting?

In addition to reflecting on personal values and biases, it is important to filter the experience through an awareness of contextual influences, including institutional, cultural, and societal, before determining the best course of action.

Stage IV. Planning and Executing the Selected Course of Action

In the final stage, the clinician identifies a sequence of specific actions to be taken, with awareness of the potential personal and contextual barriers to effective implementation. For example, Dr. Thwarp recognizes that her schedule and the fact that she has a client waiting prevents an immediate reaction or follow-up response to the client. Further, as she reflected on the session in light of the client's history, she believes that any quick, impersonal response to her, like a phone call, may be received as evidence of her rejection and may result in the client's developing feelings of shame. As such, she decided to assess the nature and strength of their relationship at the time of her next session, and if it appeared to be of therapeutic value, she would invite the client to review the hug in light of the previous session and her needs and feelings at that time. Should the nature of the next session be such that review of this incident did not seem productive, Dr. Thwarp would be aware of future attempts of physical contact, at which time she would invite the reflection while establishing a boundary.

With the implementation of a plan of action, the clinician is now invited to evaluate and document the ultimate impact and effectiveness.

Readers interested in seeing a more detailed application of this model as applied to a complex case should go to http://www.counseling.org/docs/default-source/vistas/why-can-t-we-be-friends-maintaining-confidentiality.pdf?sfvrsn=11 and review the presentation by Heather A. Warfield, Stephen D. Kennedy, and Megan Hyland Tajlili, Winners of the 2012–2013 ACA Doctoral Student Ethics Competition.

COMMON ELEMENTS: AN INTEGRATED ● APPROACH TO ETHICAL DECISION-MAKING

The previous section provided brief descriptions of a number of ethical decision-making models. These are but a few of the numerous models suggested throughout the literature. While each of these models provides a unique perspective, a number of common elements seem to run through each and as such have been extracted and presented as the following "Common Elements Integrated Approach."

The common, recurring elements found within the various ethical decision-making models include the following: ***awareness*** of the existence and nature of the dilemma along with personal values and biases; ***grounding*** in both knowledge of the professional codes of practice, laws, and institutional policies and procedures; ***support,*** which is found via consultation with all parties involved and professional colleagues and supervisors; and finally, ***implementation,*** including documentation and evaluation. Each of these elements is described in detail below and applied to the following case scenario (Case Illustration 7.4).

Awareness

As the first step to resolving an ethical dilemma, one must first note the existence and specific nature of the dilemma. An ethical dilemma occurs

Case Illustration 7.4

How Much Do I Share?

John Kelly, PhD, a licensed psychologist, was asked to assess an 8-year-old third-grade student in a local school district because of her parents' concern over her recent withdrawal from social interaction and her failing grades. The parents' explicit concern was in ruling out a possible learning disability and in developing some strategies for returning her to her previous level of academic and social functioning.

The psycho-educational assessment included an extensive clinical interview, a developmental history, as well as the administration of a battery of tests including the following: achievement tests, behavioral observational scales, and cognitive and personality assessments. The data suggested that Tina was functioning within the normal range in achievement and cognitive functioning but did give evidence of general anxiety that appeared to be in response to parental marital discord and the occurrence of parental arguing about an issue of "infidelity."

In his report, Dr. Kelly noted the hypothesized interfering impact of Tina's current anxious state and, in addition to suggesting the family engage in family therapy, provided a number of specific psycho-educational recommendations aimed at increasing her social engagement and academic performance.

A month after his contact with Tina, her school counselor sent a request, with an appropriately signed parental release for any and all information regarding his work with Tina. The request sought not only the psychologist's report but the raw data and any "working notes" the psychologist had made during his meetings with the client and client's family.

when a practitioner is confronted with a situation that offers multiple courses of action, where any one decision is less than perfect and will result in a comprise to some ethical principle. Recognition of the situation as presenting an ethical dilemma may occur as a result of the practitioner's reflection on the experience and the cognitive dissonance it creates when contrasted to his knowledge of the elements of his code of conduct (Johnson, 2012).

In addition to the identification of the principles being compromised, it is important for the practitioner to be aware of personal values and biases that may be operative in this situation. It is possible that one's personal values could run contrary to the ethical standards of her profession. However, as a member of a profession, one has agreed to comply with the standards of that profession as articulated within its code of ethics. As such, it is important to distinguish between personal and professional dimensions and as noted by the Council on Social Work Education (2008), "manage personal values in a way that allows professional values to guide practice" (EPAS 1.1).

In terms of our case illustration, Dr. Kelly was very aware of his discomfort with the request for information that he received. While valuing the school counselor's interest in helping Tina and even appreciating the fact that some of the information he had gathered would be useful in guiding the counselor's work with Tina, he "felt" uncomfortable with releasing all of his data as requested. The discomfort seemed to arise from his awareness that some of the "family" information that might be disclosed focused more on the marital discord without direct translation to education programming or intervention. In addition, he had concerns over releasing raw test data, being unsure of the counselor's qualifications for interpreting such data. He was further concerned about sharing the hypotheses and speculations that may be listed in his working notes, all of which were not fully developed or completely supported by data.

Grounding

When confronted with a "sense" that we are entering or even in dangerous territory, the next step is to find grounding in the ethical codes, organizational policies, and legal standards that should guide our practice. As noted in the *ACA Code of Ethics* (2014, Section I.1.a), "Lack of knowledge or misunderstanding of an ethical responsibility is not a defense against a charge of unethical conduct." Thus, listing the specific codes being called into play along with any policies that may exist or laws established that have relevance to the situation provides the data and the grounding one needs to choose a path forward. Take note of how Dr. Kelly uses his code of ethics.

As a licensed psychologist in private practice, Dr. Kelly was aware of HIPPA regulations that specify patients' access rights to their health and mental health files. While HIPPA provides for the release of psychotherapy notes, it does so only under a special designation in the release or waiver signed by the client. A general request for medical records does not automatically allow for the release of these notes. Further, when it comes to "working notes," their impressionistic nature makes them relatively meaningless other than for the clinician drafting them. It is generally agreed that these should be temporary in nature, taking form in a more formal summary or report and subsequently destroyed. This is not the type of information that should be released to anyone, or maintained as a permanent file.

In reviewing his profession's code of ethics (APA, 2010), Dr. Kelly was struck by the following:

"Psychologists may refrain from releasing test data to protect a client/patient or others from substantial harm or misuse or misrepresentation of the data or the test, recognizing that in many instances release of confidential information under these circumstances is regulated by law (APA 2010, 9.04). He also found that his code directed that disclosure of information should be "only to the extent necessary to achieve the purposes of the consultation" (APA 2010, 4.06).

Support

The very fact that our codes are not always clear and prescriptive to every situation and that they may even be in conflict with existing organizational policies or legal standards calls practitioners to seek out support and consultation when confronted with an ethical dilemma. As noted in the *ACA Code of Ethics* (2014), "Counselors strive to resolve ethical dilemmas with direct and open communication among all parties involved and seek consultation with colleagues and supervisors when necessary" (Sec. I, Introduction). This same code further directs that "when uncertain about whether a particular situation or course of action may be in violation of the *ACA Code of Ethics,* counselors consult with other counselors who are knowledgeable about ethics and the *ACA Code of Ethics*, with colleagues or with appropriate authorities, such as the ACA Ethics and Professional Standards Department" (Sec. I.2.c).

The provision of another perspective can serve to not only bring increased clarity to the situation and the applicability of an existing code but may help to counteract our own bias.

Returning to Case Illustration 7.4, Dr. Kelly's understanding of HIPPA law and of professional code led him to conclude that neither the raw data nor his working notes should be released as per request. However, prior to making that decision he wanted to consult with someone more schooled in and familiar with this type of issue. As such, he called the chair of his state ethics committee, who in turn consulted with the ethics committee.

The response he received supported his decision to be selective in the information released. The committee's response did note, however, that its position was not intended to serve as legal advice and was educational in nature based on members' understanding of the APA code of ethics.

Implementation

Ethical decision-making is not merely an intellectual activity, it is a process that results in action. As is evident from our previous discussion on ethical decision-making models, the implementation stage requires (a) the generation of possible pathways to resolving the dilemma; (b) an assessment of the potential positive and negative consequences for all involved parties for each of the possible pathways; (c) the selection of the path to follow; and (d) documentation and evaluation of the ultimate impact.

So in Case Illustration 7.4, Dr. Kelly considered a number of options ranging from ignoring the request to sending all the data requested. Upon reflection and consultation, he felt that the most prudent and beneficial approach would be to contact his client's parents to inform them of his reception of a request for information and explain to them his plan to respond. In talking with the parents, he explained that while his notes and actual test data were important to his understanding and assessment that these, even though requested, would be of little value to the school counselor. He suggested that it would be more productive if he sent an abbreviated report with specific focus on the educational recommendations that could be implemented within the school setting. Further, he suggested that rather than sending this report directly to the counselor, he would provide the parents with the report, and they in turn could share the information, if they so desired, with the school.

Both parents were appreciative of the suggestion. Both admitted that they had not completely thought through the implications of what was being requested when they signed the release and were very happy that Dr. Kelly was aware of the possible negative effects of releasing all of his data to the school. Also, given the fact that he had previously gone over the entire report and recommendation with them, they both felt comfortable with sharing the sections relevant to the school and the counselor's work with their daughter.

Dr. Kelly invited the parents to come into the office to once again review the recommendations, but neither felt that was necessary. Finally, he asked if they would send him a written request for the release of this "educational report" so that he could have it in his records. He also documented the telephone conversation as well as the suggested and agreed upon plan.

● CONCLUDING CASE ILLUSTRATION

Throughout the past chapters, you have seen Ms. Wicks, our school counselor, experience a number of ethical concerns while engaging with Maria. None of these seem to be as disruptive to the relationship as evidenced by Maria's disclosure regarding her boyfriend having AIDS and the couple being engaged in unprotected sex. Ms. Wicks has concerns about both the legal mandate and ethical concerns that should guide her response to this information. In addition, she now has information that the district "prohibits" her from talking to students about sexual issues, which arouses her concern that she has violated some boundary. The situation is complicated, and the options are not completely clear.

Reflections

1. Has Ms. Wicks given any evidence of employing one of the many models of ethical decision-making described in this chapter?
2. What one specific step discussed within the chapter as contributing to ethical decision-making do you feel Ms. Wicks needs to employ?
3. From your perspective, which of the models discussed within the chapter provides the best guidance for ethical decision-making when applied to this case?

● COOPERATIVE LEARNING EXERCISE

As noted in the beginning of the chapter, it is our responsibility to not only know and embrace our professional code of ethics but also to employ a process that will facilitate our application of these principles within our professional practice. The failure to do so is in and of itself an ethical problem (Welfel, 2010). As such, you are now invited to close this chapter by engaging in the following learning exercise (Exercise 7.3). It is hoped that engaging in this exercise will help your understanding, valuing, and employment of our common elements integrated approach.

Exercise 7.3

Making a Decision

Directions: Read the following case scenario and then respond to questions posed under each of the stages of ethical decision-making listed below. As with each of these cooperative learning exercises, benefit is accrued through personal reflection and the sharing of perspectives among your colleagues.

Dr. Mattison is a retired clinical social worker who had a large private practice for over 35 years. In retirement, she was hired as an adjunct professor to teach one graduate course a semester and also volunteered as an intake worker at the local community mental health center.

The center operated more like a crisis and referral agency seeing clients for a maximum of three sessions and making referrals when additional sessions were necessary. During the month of August, the agency experienced a high number of staff taking vacations. Dr. Mattison was asked to step in to provide direct service to new clients seeking support during the month.

In the week prior to her stepping back into the clinical chair, she remained on the phone as intake worker. The intakes she was completing were on clients whom she would see in the following week.

One caller, Kathy, was clearly very upset, crying to the point where gathering the basic information was difficult. Dr. Mattison gently calmed the caller and identified that the initial source of crisis was the fact that she had just been terminated at her job and gotten into a major argument with her boyfriend. While the caller felt as if the "world was collapsing," Dr. Mattison was able to assess her level of crisis and the possibility of her harming herself or another. Both possibilities were felt to be of very low probability, and the caller had numerous supports in her life, living at home with her family. After setting up the appointment to meet with Kathy, Dr. Mattison did a final assessment to see how she was feeling and what her plans for the night and the days to follow were. Kathy's response provided Dr. Mattison with the data she needed to feel that Kathy was okay and was not at risk.

After hanging up and as she was taking the next call, Dr. Mattison realized that in her focusing on the "crisis" she forgot to get Kathy's last name or address. She felt that she could gather that information at the time of her first session, which was scheduled that coming Monday.

(Continued)

(Continued)

On Monday, as Dr. Mattison enters the office, she becomes aware that the young woman waiting is not only Kathy, her first appointment, but that Kathy is actually a student in her Tuesday night class.

Awareness: Does the case present any possible ethical or legal challenges? If so, what are they?

Grounding: Using your profession's code of ethics, what, if any, principles may be compromised or called into play given this situation?

Support: What do your colleagues or classmates see is operating in this situation? How about your professor or supervisor? Are their perspectives different from yours? If so, what is the impact of multiple perspectives on your own awareness of the situation or your own biases and values?

Implementation: Generate at least three possible paths to follow in response to this situation. Further, identify the potential positive and negative impacts of each? Which would you select to implement? Discuss with your colleagues to gain further perspective as to whether they identified similar paths, impacts, and implementation plans.

● SUMMARY

- As professionals, it is our duty, our responsibility, to not only understand and embrace our codes of ethics but to also engage in self-reflection and the employment of a decision-making process.
- Our professional organizations direct us to employ accepted decision-making models that are most applicable to our situations (e.g., ACA, 2014, I.1.b).
- One approach (Kitchener, 1984) invites practitioners to employ the values of autonomy, nonmaleficence, beneficence, fidelity, and justice as reference points when making ethical decisions.
- A more sequential approach to ethical decision-making was presented by Forester-Miller and Davis (1996) and included seven steps: (a) identifying the problem, (b) applying the code of ethics, (c) determining the nature and dimensions of the dilemma, (d) generating possible courses of action, (e) considering potential consequences of

all options, (f) evaluating the selected course of action, and (g) implementing the course of action.

- Jordan and Meara (1990, 1995) introduced a rather unique perspective on the issue of ethical decision-making. Their virtue ethics model focuses not on what the counselor should DO but rather on HOW as well as on WHO the counselor should be.

- Tarvydas (2012) offers an integrative approach to decision-making that highlights the need for the practitioner to view all decision-making in light of not just ethical codes and laws but cultural and social values and context. The Tarvydas Integrative Decision-Making Model of Ethical Behavior comprises four stages: (a) interpreting the situation through awareness and fact finding; (b) formulating an ethical decision; (c) weighing competing non-moral values and affirming course of action; and (d) planning and executing the selected course of action.

- Identifying recurrent themes or elements found within the various models of ethical decision-making can direct us to a "common elements integrated approach" that includes *awareness* of the existence and nature of the dilemma, along with personal values and biases; *grounding* in both knowledge of the professional codes of practice, laws, and institutional policies and procedures; *support* that is found via consultation with all parties involved and professional colleagues and supervisors; and finally *implementation* including documentation and evaluation.

IMPORTANT TERMS ●

American Counseling Association (ACA)	ethical decision-making
	ethical justification model
American Association for Marriage and Family Therapy (AAMFT)	fidelity
American Psychological Association (APA)	Integrative Decision-Making Model of Ethical Behavior
aspirational ethics	justice
autonomy	mandatory ethics
beneficence	nonmaleficence
common elements approach	step-wise approach
	virtue ethics model

● ADDITIONAL RESOURCES

Print

Hecker, L., & Associates. (2010). *Ethics and professional issues in couple and family therapy*. New York: Taylor Francis.

Pope, K., & Vasquez, M. (2011). *Ethics in psychotherapy and counseling: A practical guide* (4th ed). San Francisco, CA: Jossey Bass.

Sheperis D. S., Henning, S. L., & Kocet, M. M. (2016). *Ethical decision making for the 21st century counselor*. Thousand Oaks, CA: Sage.

Sisti, D. A., Caplan, A. L., Rimon-Greenspan, H. (2013). *Applied ethics in mental health care: An interdisciplinary reader*. Cambridge, MA: MIT Press.

Web-Based

Constable, E. G., Kreider, T. B., Smith, T. F., & Taylor, Z. R. (2011). *The confidentiality of a confession: A counseling intern's ethical dilemma*. Retrieved from http://counselingoutfitters.com/vistas/vistas11/Article_37.pdf

Josephson, M. (2014). *The six pillars of character*. Retrieved from http://josephsoninstitute.org/MED/MED-2sixpillars.html

Markkula Center for Applied Ethics. (2014). The ethical decision making assistant: Making an ethical decision app (Version 1.0) [Mobile application software]. Retrieved from http://www.scu.edu/ethics/ethical-decision/

Velasquez, M., Andre, C., Thomas Shanks, T., & Meyer, M. J. (2014). *Thinking ethically: A framework for moral decision making*. Retrieved from http://www.scu.edu/ethics/practicing/decision/thinking.html

Williams, R. (2007, November). Solutions to ethical problems in schools. *ASCA schoolcounselor*. Retrieved from https://www.schoolcounselor.org/magazine/blogs/november-december-2007/solutions-to-ethical-problems-in-schools

● REFERENCES

American Association for Marriage and Family Therapy. (2015). *Code of ethics*. Retrieved from https://www.aamft.org/iMIS15/AAMFT/Content/Legal_Ethics/Code_of_Ethics.aspx

American Counseling Association. (2012). Ethics committee summary—FY 11. Retrieved from http://counseling.or/Resources/CodeOFEthics/TP/Home/CT2.aspz

American Counseling Association. (2014). *Code of ethics*. Retrieved from http://www.counseling.org/resources/aca-code-of-ethics.pdf

American Psychological Association. (2010). *Ethical principles of psychologists and code of conduct*. Retrieved from: http://www.apa.org/ethics/code/principles.pdf

Anderson, S. K., & Kitchener, K. S. (1998). Nonsexual post-therapy relationships: A conceptual framework to assess ethical risks. *Professional Psychology: Research and Practice, 29*, 91–99.

Council on Social Work Education. (2008). Education policy and accreditation standards (EPAS). Retrieved from http://www.cswe.org/NR/rdonlyres/2A 81732E-1776-4175-AC42-

Forester-Miller, H., & Davis, T. (1996). *A practitioner's guide to ethical decision making.* American Counseling Association. Retrieved from http://www.counseling .org/counselors/practitionersguide.aspx

Johnson, C. E. (2012). *Organizational ethics: A practical approach* (2nd ed.) Thousand Oaks, CA: Sage.

Jordan, A. E., & Meara, N. M. (1990). Ethics and the professional practice of psychologists: The role of virtues and principles. *Professional Psychology: Research and Practice, 21*, 107–114.

Jordan, A. E., & Meara, N. M. (1995). Ethics and the professional practice of psychologists: The role of virtues and principles. In D. N. Bersoff (Eds.), *Ethical conflicts in psychology* (pp. 135–141). Washington, DC: American Psychological Association.

Kitchener, K. S. (1984). Intuition, critical evaluation, and ethical principles: The foundation for ethical decisions in counseling psychology. *The Counseling Psychologist, 12*, 43–55.

Kocet, M. (2006). Ethical challenges in a complex world: Highlights of the 2005 *ACA Code of Ethics. Journal of Counseling & Development, 84*(2), 228–234.

Pope, K. S., Tabachnick, B. G., & Keith-Spiegel, P. (1987). Ethics of practice: The beliefs and behaviors of psychologists as therapists. *American Psychologist, 42*(11), 993–1006.

Sheperis D. S., Henning, S. L., & Kocet, M. M. (2016). *Ethical decision making for the 21st century counselor.* Thousand Oaks, CA: Sage.

Shiles, M. (2009). Discriminatory referrals: Uncovering a potential ethical dilemma facing practitioners. *Ethics & Behavior, 19*(2), 142–155.

Tarvydas, V. M. (2012). Ethics and ethics decision making. In D. R. Maki & V. M. Tarvydas (Eds.), *The professional practice of rehabilitation counseling* (pp. 339–370). New York, NY: Springer.

Urofsky, R. E., Engels, D. W., & Engebretson, K. (2008). Kitchener's principle ethics: Implications for counseling practice and research. *Counseling and Values, 53*(1), 67–78.

Welfel, E. R. (2010). *Ethics in counseling and psychotherapy: Standards, research and emerging issues* (4th ed.). Pacific Grove, CA: Brooks/Cole.

Zur, O. (2007). *Boundaries in psychotherapy: Ethical and clinical explorations.* Washington, DC: APA.

PART III

Applying Ethical Standards

CHAPTER 8

Informed Consent

Ms. Wicks: Hi, Maria, have a seat. I really appreciate you coming down to see me. I need to share some things with you and ask you for a favor.

Maria: A favor?

Ms. Wicks: Well, not really a favor, just your permission to do something.

M s. Wicks is apparently about to speak to Maria about her desire to do something about which she feels Maria should be fully informed. While we are not clear what it is that Ms. Wicks is going to seek permission for, it is clear that she respects Maria's right to be a full participant in those helping decisions that may impact her. Seeking informed consent is an ethical imperative and requires that a helper be fully versed and skilled in establishing the conditions that will allow a client to provide fully informed consent.

OBJECTIVES ●

The chapter will discuss the rationale for seeking clients' informed consent for the implementation of one's helping decisions. Further, the chapter will discuss the conditions under which such informed consent is not required and the conditions that may make obtaining informed consent difficult. Finally, the chapter will review specific issues related to the format and content of informed consent procedures. After reading this chapter you should be able to do the following:

- Define informed consent as applied to a helping relationship.
- Explain the rationale and utility of gaining informed consent while working with a client.
- Identify the essential elements required to ensure informed consent.
- Discuss the special considerations and difficulties incurred while gaining informed consent when working with minor and cognitively impaired clients.

● THE RATIONALE FOR INFORMED CONSENT

Informed consent is a legal and ethical term defined as the consent by a client to a proposed medical or psychotherapeutic procedure or for participation in a research project or clinical study. Informed consent refers to the client's right to agree (and/or disagree) to participate in the various forms of helping and the specific procedures and services to be applied. It is a "process of sharing information with patients that is essential to their ability to make rational choices [for psychotherapy] among multiple options in their perceived best interest" (Beahrs & Gutheil, 2001, p. 4). In order for the consent to be *informed*, the client must first achieve a clear understanding of the relevant facts, risks and benefits, and available alternatives.

The practice of gaining informed consent for treatment has its origins both ethically and legally in the medical profession. Although general medicine began incorporating informed consent in the late 1950s, psychotherapy avoided the widespread use of informed consent until the *Osheroff v. Chestnut Lodge* (1984) legal case during the 1980s. This case raised serious questions about the duty of providers to explain fully the diagnoses and alternative treatments (i.e., risks and benefits) to clients (Beahrs & Gutheil, 2001). While the practice of obtaining patient/client involvement in treatment decisions could be seen as somewhat contemporary, in employment as an ethical practice it has moved beyond that of a "nice" idea to become a more stringent requirement in recent years (Walker, Logan, Clark, & Leukefeld, 2005). Informed consent is a moral, ethical, and legal obligation in medical, psychiatric, and psychological treatment and research (Berg, Appelbaum, Lidz, & Parker, 2001) and is clearly articulated in all of our profession's codes of ethics (See Table 8.1).

Table 8.1 Informed Consent

Professional Ethical Standards	Statement on Confidentiality
National Association of Social Workers (2008)	1.03. Informed consent a. Social workers should provide services to clients only in the context of a professional relationship based, when appropriate, on valid informed consent. Social workers should use clear and understandable language to inform clients of the purpose of the services, risks related to the services, limits to services because of the requirements of a third-party payer, relevant costs, reasonable alternatives, clients' right to refuse or withdraw consent, and the time frame covered by the consent. Social workers should provide clients with an opportunity to ask questions. b. In instances when clients are not literate or have difficulty understanding the primary language used in the practice setting, social workers should take steps to ensure clients' comprehension. This may include providing clients with a detailed verbal explanation or arranging for a qualified interpreter or translator whenever possible. c. In instances when clients lack the capacity to provide informed consent, social workers should protect clients' interests by seeking permission from an appropriate third party, informing clients consistent with the clients' level of understanding. In such instances social workers should seek to ensure that the third party acts in a manner consistent with clients' wishes and interests. Social workers should take reasonable steps to enhance such clients' ability to give informed consent. d. In instances when clients are receiving services involuntarily, social workers should provide information about the nature and extent of services and about the extent of clients' right to refuse service. e. Social workers who provide services via electronic media (such as computer, telephone, radio, and television) should inform recipients of the limitations and risks associated with such services. f. Social workers should obtain clients' informed consent before audiotaping or videotaping clients or permitting observation of services to clients by a third party.

(Continued)

Table 8.1 (Continued)

Professional Ethical Standards	Statement on Confidentiality
American Counseling Association (2014)	Section A. The counseling relationship
	A.2.a. Informed consent
	Clients have the freedom to choose whether to enter into or remain in a counseling relationship and need adequate information about the counseling process and the counselor. Counselors have an obligation to review in writing and verbally with clients the rights and responsibilities of both the counselor and the client. Informed consent is an ongoing part of the counseling process, and counselors appropriately document discussions of informed consent throughout the counseling relationship.
	A.2.b. Types of information needed
	Counselors explicitly explain to clients the nature of all services provided. They inform clients about issues such as, but not limited to, the following: the purposes, goals, techniques, procedures, limitations, potential risks, and benefits of services; the counselor's qualifications, credentials, and relevant experience; continuation of services upon the incapacitation or death of a counselor; and other pertinent information. Counselors take steps to ensure that clients understand the implications of diagnosis, the intended use of tests and reports, fees, and billing arrangements. Clients have the right to confidentiality and to be provided with an explanation of its limitations (including how supervisors and/or treatment team professionals are involved); to obtain clear information about their records; to participate in the ongoing counseling plans; and to refuse any services or modality change and to be advised of the consequences of such refusal.
	Standard of practice 2 (SP-2). Disclosure to clients
	Counselors must adequately inform clients, preferably in writing, regarding the counseling process and counseling relationship at or before the time it begins and throughout the relationship. (See A.3.a)
	Section A. The counseling relationship
	A.2.d. Inability to give consent
	When counseling minors, incapacitated adults, or other persons unable to give voluntary consent, counselors seek the assent of clients to services and include them in decision-making as appropriate. Counselors recognize the need to balance the ethical rights of clients to make choices, their capacity to give consent or assent to receive services, and parental or familial legal rights and responsibilities to protect these clients and make decisions on their behalf.

Professional Ethical Standards	*Statement on Confidentiality*
American Association for Marriage and Family Therapy (2015)	Principle I. Responsibility to clients 1.2. Marriage and family therapists obtain appropriate informed consent to therapy or related procedures and use language that is reasonably understandable to clients. When persons, due to age or mental status, are legally incapable of giving informed consent, marriage and family therapists obtain informed permission from a legally authorized person, if such substitute consent is legally permissible. The content of informed consent may vary depending upon the client and treatment plan; however, informed consent generally necessitates that the client: (a) has the capacity to consent; (b) has been adequately informed of significant information concerning treatment processes and procedures; (c) has been adequately informed of potential risks and benefits of treatments for which generally recognized standards do not yet exist; (d) has freely and without undue influence expressed consent; and (e) has provided consent that is appropriately documented. 1.12. Marriage and family therapists obtain written informed consent from clients before recording any images or audio or permitting third-party observation 2.4. Marriage and family therapists use client and/or clinical materials in teaching, writing, consultation, research, and public presentations only if a written waiver has been obtained in accordance with Standard 2.2, or when appropriate steps have been taken to protect client identity and confidentiality.
American Psychological Association (2010)	3.10 Informed consent a. When psychologists conduct research or provide assessment, therapy, counseling, or consulting services in person or via electronic transmission or other forms of communication, they obtain the informed consent of the individual or individuals using language that is reasonably understandable to that person or persons except when conducting such activities without consent is mandated by law or governmental regulation or as otherwise provided in this Ethics Code. b. For persons who are legally incapable of giving informed consent, psychologists nevertheless (1) provide an appropriate explanation, (2) seek the individual's assent, (3) consider such persons' preferences and best interests, and (4) obtain appropriate permission from a legally authorized person, if such substitute

(Continued)

Table 8.1 (Continued)

Professional Ethical Standards	Statement on Confidentiality
American Psychological Association (2010)	consent is permitted or required by law. When consent by a legally authorized person is not permitted or required by law, psychologists take reasonable steps to protect the individual's rights and welfare. c. When psychological services are court ordered or otherwise mandated, psychologists inform the individual of the nature of the anticipated services, including whether the services are court ordered or mandated and any limits of confidentiality, before proceeding. d. Psychologists appropriately document written or oral consent, permission, and assent.
American School Counselor Association (2016)	A.2 b. Confidentiality [School counselors] inform students of the purposes, goals, techniques, and rules of procedure under which they may receive counseling. Disclosure includes informed consent and clarification of the limits of confidentiality. Informed consent requires competence, voluntariness, and knowledge on the part of students to understand the limits of confidentiality, and therefore can be difficult to obtain from students of certain developmental levels, English-language learners, and special-needs populations. If the student is able to give assent/consent before school counselors share confidential information, school counselors attempt to gain the student's assent/consent. B.1 f. Responsibilities to parents/guardians [School counselors] inform parents/guardians of the confidential nature of the school counseling relationship between the school counselor and student.

Ethically, the concept of informed consent is grounded in the belief in a client's right to self-determination and the right to benefit from treatment. In addition to reflecting ethical obligations, informed consent is generally viewed as good clinical practice. The concept of informed consent reflects the profession's belief that the client has the right to be supported in autonomous decision-making regarding his or her own treatment.

An informed consent discussion not only protects the rights of client autonomy and self-direction, but it is thought also to enhance subsequent participation and responsibility of engaging in psychotherapy. Through informed consent, the client is made a collaborator in the work. Research has shown that when clients experience themselves to be true partners in the therapeutic process, the likelihood of a beneficial outcome increases (Behnke, 2004). The use of proper informed consent procedures has been reported to decrease a client's anxiety, increase client compliance with treatment, and ultimately facilitate a more rapid recovery (Pope & Vasquez, 2011). Further, Sullivan, Martin, and Handelsman (1993) found that clients "may be more favorably disposed to therapists who take the time and effort to provide informed consent information" (p. 162).

INFORMED CONSENT ACROSS THE PROFESSION ●

The mental health professions recognize the importance of informed consent and require practitioners to disclose to clients the various risks, benefits, and alternatives to the proposed treatment. All codes of professional ethics require informed consent process (see Table 8.2), with informed consent being seen as one of the primary ways of protecting both the self-governing and the privacy rights of clients. It is one way in which ethical practitioners give form to their valuing of a client's autonomy and their respect for that client and his or her self-determination. Further, informed consent is seen as helping to maintain a "culture of safety" (Knapp & VandeCreek, 2006, p. 100).

Table 8.2 Areas of Informed Consent

Area of Informed Consent	Description
Nature and Orientation of Helping	It is important to inform the client as to orientation and theory employed by the practitioner. Further, it is important to inform the client of the possible negative experiences one may encounter (e.g., anxiety, depression, etc.) in the process of therapy. Finally, goals and steps anticipated need to be disclosed.
Therapist Credentials	Details regarding the therapist's specific training, education, experience, and unique credentials should be disclosed to the client. Similarly, any anticipated involvement with consultants and supervisors regarding this case needs to be discussed with the client.

(Continued)

Table 8.2 (Continued)

Area of Informed Consent	Description
Fees and Insurance	All costs and fees for service should be discussed at the beginning of the relationship. Procedures and processes involved in seeking insurance reimbursement along with limitations of the specific coverage need to be discussed, along with an agreed upon plan addressing any and all gaps in coverage. Additional points of information may be required and included when the clinician is part of a managed care process. Factors such as any limitations to amount or type of service, disclosure requirements, and any other limitations imposed by the managed care contract should also be discussed.
Record Keeping and Access to Files	Records are kept for the benefit of the client, and clients generally should be provided access as long as the information would not be misleading or detrimental to the client. While the type of information stored as well as the decision to share this information with the client may vary as a function of the setting, the client, and the helper, the nature of a practitioner's records and access policies should be clearly explained to the client.
Limits to Confidentiality	All of the professional codes note the importance of providing the client with the limitations of confidentiality from the outset of the relationship. Further, the helper needs to inform the client about the distinction and application of confidentiality, privileged communication, and privacy of files.
Treatment: Benefits, Risks, and Alternatives	Within the limits of current research on treatment techniques and strategies, it is important to discuss what is known in the research and what has been the experience of the practitioner in terms of effectiveness of specific techniques to be employed, the potential benefits and risks, as well of best practice alternatives.

The provision of information upon which a client can make informed decisions starts with the initial contact. In fact, helpers should begin the informed consent process at the initial intake, almost as a "pre-helping" screening and information session. As suggested by Knapp & VandeCreek (2012), informed consent is a legal and ethical obligation to provide information to clients *before* treatment or services are initiated. During one's initial contact with a client, basic information about the process of helping, the policies and procedures typically employed (e.g., billing, scheduling, and canceling appointments, limits to confidentiality, etc.), helper competency, and the initial client issues and objectives can be identified. But the issue of informed consent is not something restricted to the beginning of the professional contact. Rather than viewing informed consent as a single event where clients sign on the dotted line at the end of a long, detailed document, we view it as dialogue between therapists and clients and as a decision-making process where clients get to make decisions based on discussion and information (Goddard, Murray, & Simpson, 2008). Anytime a significant change in the treatment or procedure being carried out is contemplated, it is imperative to obtain informed consent for the change.

The specific content and the manner of the presentation (e.g., written or oral, early, pre-treatment, etc.) may vary as a function of legal requirements, agency policies, the unique characteristics of the client, and/or the setting in which services are provided. However, the conditions or elements essential to informed consent appear to hold across the professions or clients. Most agree that informed consent requires that the client be competent, have knowledge of what will occur, and engage in treatment voluntarily (Knapp & VandeCreek, 2012). Each of these components is discussed in some detail below.

Competence

Implicit in any discussion of informed consent is the assumption of a client's competency or capacity to make informed decisions that are in his or her own best interests. Competency refers to the client's ability to make decisions for himself or herself. Appelbaum & Grasso (1988) broke the concept of competence down to four components:

- Express and sustain a choice. The client is able to communicate in some fashion their choice regarding the decision at hand and be able to sustain that choice over the course of treatment.
- Understand information that is presented. The client must have a factual understanding of the information presented about the treatment.
- A realistic appreciation of the situation. The client understands the facts and is able to integrate that information into the reasons that information is relevant to him or her at the present time.
- Rational utilization of the information. The client is able to rationally employ the information to come to a logical decision, one seen as being in his or her best interest.

A client judged to be competent to make these judgments is then also viewed as having a right to be fully informed about the nature of the treatment, the alternatives available, possible risks and benefits of each, and the practitioner's competency to provide service.

This sense of competency is not an all-or-none proposition. The identification of competence will fluctuate as a function of the context or the decision criteria defining competence (see Case Illustration 8.1). Clearly, while George lacks the competency to make business decisions, he appears able to understand the nature of the relationship and to consent to the process.

Case Illustration 8.1

A Limited Competence

George is a 43-year-old who has been a successful owner of a mid-sized manufacturing company. Over the course of the past month, George has gone on a spending spree that has not only jeopardized his own financial well-being but has actually placed his company on the brink of bankruptcy.

In addition to purchasing a new foreign sports car and refurbishing his house and office with expensive European furniture, George has recently placed an order for an executive jet plane. The truth is that George's business does not require him to travel nor can his business afford the multimillion-dollar expenditure. In addition to the spending spree, George has not been sleeping, exhibits a general restlessness, and has been developing plans to expand his company to the level of an international conglomerate.

In response to a confrontation by his wife and the chair of his board of directors, George agreed to go for a psychiatric evaluation. Following general introductions, the following exchange occurred:

Dr. Wincock: George, I can understand that you feel that people are overreacting to your recent purchases and behavior, but it does appear that you are not sleeping well and that a number of the decisions, for example, placing a down payment on a company jet, may not reflect the best of your business and personal decisions.

George: Well, it may look like the business can't afford it, but I have plans for that as well. We are going to grow the business significantly! I know I can get the business to be an international concern within the next year and can probably triple our bottom line. I am even thinking about writing up my business plan and publishing it. I think it can revolutionize the way business is done.

Dr. Wincock: Well, perhaps that is something we could talk about. But for the time being, I would like to thank you for coming and explain a little about what I do and what I hope we can do during the session. Would that be okay?

George: I really don't think I need to do this, but if it helps ease the minds of my family and friends, then I am willing to give it a try. Hell, maybe I'll decide to even change my career. This seems to be a pretty cushy job.

Dr. Wincock: Well, as you know, I am a psychiatrist, and in addition to seeing patients here in the professional building, I am also on staff at the hospital and teach in the university. I have been working in the field of psychiatry for over 15 years, and while I am able to and do often prescribe medication to my clients who may benefit from it, I also am trained in a type of therapy called cognitive behavioral therapy.

George: I am little familiar with that type of therapy . . . I mean I read a book by . . .

I can't remember his name . . . it was a little yellow book on depression. . . .

Dr. Wincock: Was the book *Feeling Good* by David Burns?

George: Yeah, I think that was the title. I liked the concept, you know, none of that laying down stuff and talking about your childhood . . . just get to the point. . . .

Dr. Wincock: Well, I'm glad you are somewhat familiar with cognitive therapy. As we go along I would like to explain a little more about the approach and the possible benefit of combining it with some medication.

(Continued)

(Continued)

George: Well, no meds for me, Doc, that stuff slows you down . . . and they are for whackos.

Dr. Wincock: Well, before we talk about the pros and cons of medication in your case, let me explain that I would like to spend the remainder of our time together, which is about 50 minutes, to find out about some of the decisions and plans you've been making as well as how you've been in general.

               Now, I know that you read my little brochure, "Welcome to My Practice," which describes my fees, length of sessions, policies regarding cancellations, insurance, and so forth. Did you have any questions about that information?

George: No, it was real clear. In fact, I'm going to make something like that up for my own business . . . great idea. . . . .

Dr. Wincock: Okay. Now I do know that pamphlet talked about the fact that the information you share with me will be held in confidence, and if you look here on page 3, it points out a number of exceptions to that principle of confidentiality. In general, if you share information with me that seems to suggest that you are jeopardizing your own life or intend to harm someone else, then I may have to share that information as a way of protecting you or anyone you may seek to harm. Do you understand that? Do you have any questions about what I just shared or what is in the brochure?

George: No, I got it, it makes sense . . . no fear I'm not gonna hurt myself or anyone else, unless you consider the fact that my business is going to wipe out my competitors . . . "doing harm to others." Hell, maybe you should warn them! Only kidding, Doc. Actually I've been through this before, so I think I know the routine and I'm okay with it.

> Dr. Wincock: Well, that's good, but if there is any question now or as we proceed about what we are doing or why we are doing it, I really want you to ask. The more you and I work together, the better it will be. You mentioned that you were familiar with this information since you've been through it before. Would you tell me about that?

Competency may also be temporarily impaired as a result of psychological and or physical trauma or could be more permanently impaired as a result of a degenerative disease or irreversible brain damage. When an individual is judged not to be competent enough to understand the nature of the helping relationship or to fully consent to participation in the helping, a legal guardian or parent should be identified and provide consent. Exercise 8.1 invites you to explore some of these times.

Exercise 8.1

Comprehensibility?

Directions: Below you will find descriptions of the form, timing, and language used in providing a client with information needed to gain informed consent. Review the details of each scenario and identify what may be modified to increase the comprehensibility of the information.

Scenario 1: Mrs. Lewis, an elementary school counselor, is sitting with Mrs. Robinson, mother of Tommie, a third grader who recently wrote in his journal: "I wish I died!"

Mrs. Lewis:	Mrs. Robinson, I'm glad you could come right in.
Mrs. Robinson:	Yes, I left work immediately after you called. What's up? It sounded serious.
Mrs. Lewis:	Well, as you are aware we have a policy in the district that requires that we inform parents

(Continued)

(Continued)

anytime we (counselors) wish to work with a child. We feel it is important that parents know that we are counseling their children and understand how we would like to handle issues such as confidentiality.

Mrs. Robinson: (anxiously) Counsel Tommie? Why? What happened?

Mrs. Lewis: Well, Tommie has given some evidence of having suicidal ideation, and I would like to begin working with him immediately.

Mrs. Robinson: WHAT? Suicide?

Scenario 2: R. L. Linquist is a social worker providing community service to a group of migrant farm workers. Juan is a 38-year-old farm worker who came to the community mental health center because of his concern about possibly having a drinking problem. Prior to meeting with Juan, the social worker went to the waiting room and handed Juan a five-page booklet explaining the policies and processes employed at the center. The social worker asked Juan to read the document and to sign before they began their session.

Scenario 3: Rene is a psychiatric nurse assigned to do intake at a residential treatment center. Tony and Harriet Bledshoe brought their 83-year-old father in because, according to the Bledshoes, he seems to be drifting off, has become incommunicative, and has been twice found wandering outside the house without his shoes and/or pants. Rene met with Mr. Bledshoe (the client) and the following dialogue occurred:

Rene: Hello, Mr. Bledshoe, have a seat.

Mr. Bledshoe: Hi, Harriet.

Rene: Mr. Bledshoe, my name is Rene and I am a nurse here at Taylor Manor.

Mr. Bledshoe: Yes, dear. Where is your mother?

Rene: Mr. Bledshoe, this is Taylor Manor and you were brought here by your son and his wife. They are concerned about you.

Mr. Bledshoe:	Is Tony coming to lunch?
Rene:	Mr. Bledshoe, I would like to ask you some questions and then have you meet with our psychiatrist. It may be a good idea for you to stay with us for a while.
Mr. Bledshoe:	Of course . . . anything you say.
Rene:	So you understand and are willing to sign yourself into our hospital?
Mr. Bledshoe:	Of course . . . Harriet. Is Tony going to be here with us for lunch?

Comprehension

In addition to having the general cognitive competency and ability to process information, the client must be able to comprehend the information being presented. The form in which such information is transmitted is truly open to the discretion of the helper and the needs and abilities of the client. Information could be presented in writing, and if one has real concern that such disclosure is documented, acknowledgment of understanding could be documented by way of a client's signature. Regardless of the specific format, the guiding principle is that this information needs to be provided in a clear, comprehensible form and language that is presented at a level that the client can understand. This has special significance when information is provided in written form. Consent forms have become increasingly long and difficult to understand, often using technical language. As such, it is essential that practitioners are sensitive to the client's ability to read and understand such forms (Hochauser, 2004).

It is essential that a helper present information in a way that maximizes the client comprehension of both what is being suggested and the possible impacts of these decisions. The standard is that the practitioner shares the information in a way that a reasonable individual in the client's position would be able to understand and make a reasonably informed decision (Murray, 2012). The information should be provided in simple, declarative sentences that avoid jargon. The ethical helper must be sure that the form of the information (e.g., oral, written) is comprehensible to the client, that the language is one in which the client is fully literate, and that the timing of presentation is sensitive to the client's fatigue, emotional state, or level of distractibility (see Exercise 8.2).

Exercise 8.2

Was the Client Informed?

Directions: After reading the following scenarios, discuss the cases with a colleague and identify whether you feel the duty to inform and gain informed consent was achieved. If not, what else do you feel should have been done?

Scenario 1: An individual is referred by his employer because of what his employer suspected was a drinking problem. At the first meeting, the counselor informed the client that one of the purposes for their coming together was for the counselor to make an assessment of the client for possible alcohol abuse. The counselor informed the client that he was asked by the employer to assess the employee and to determine whether he had an alcohol problem and if so to determine the degree to which it would impair his work performance. The counselor noted that he was expected to give this information in a written report to the employer as a condition of the employee's return to work. The counselor suggested that any specific information gathered in their interview would not be shared with the employer but that his clinical impressions regarding the existence of a possible drinking problem and the degree to which that, should it exist, could impair the employee's work performance would be shared with his employer. The clinician presented in writing the steps he would take and asked the client if he understood and if he would sign the paper as evidence of his informed consent to release that information to his employer.

Scenario 2: Enrique is a 14-year-old freshman who asked to see his school counselor. The counselor met with Enrique and in the process of the initial interview found out the following: Enrique described himself as feeling very sad and lonely, and while he had never entertained thoughts of hurting himself, he just wished his "down feelings" would disappear. Enrique said that he started feeling this way a long time ago. He was very concerned that maybe he is "strange," not like the other boys, and that maybe he's gay. The counselor asked Enrique if he would like to talk again, especially about his feelings of being gay and feeling so sad. Enrique agreed. Following the initial interview the counselor consulted his chairperson and shared the information he received from Enrique. The chair suggested that the counselor call Enrique's parents and inform them of his sexual-orientation concerns. The counselor calls and sets up an appointment to meet with the parents.

As a measure of ensuring comprehension, the ethical helper will ask questions that elicit evidence of the client's comprehension (see Case Illustration 8.2).

Case Illustration 8.2

Ensuring Comprehension

Dr. Federico is a marriage and family therapist in private practice. She was about to meet Anthony and Carol for an initial session. About 10 minutes before the session was scheduled to begin, Dr. Federico went out to greet the couple. She introduced herself and informed the couple that she would be with them in about five minutes. In the meantime, she provided them with a little brochure that described her practice. She invited them to review the brochure prior to their session. She explained that this would help them understand her practice and that it provided answers to some of the typical questions often asked by clients.

At the scheduled time, Dr. Federico came out to invite the couple into the office. After some initial chatting, Dr. Federico asked the couple if they were able to review the brochure and if they had any questions.

Carol: Yes, we both looked at it. It is very clear. We are both a little nervous, because we've never done this kind of thing before.

Dr. Frederico: Well, I am glad you reviewed the brochure, and I can understand how this may be a little anxiety provoking. How about if we just take a few minutes to try to relax and get some general information as well as answer any questions you may have about me or the practice?

Carol: That would be fine, but I don't think we have any questions.

Dr. Frederico: Anthony, I can see you nodding in agreement? As outlined in the brochure, you understand I am certified as a marriage counselor and have been in private

(Continued)

(Continued)

	practice for 9 years. Our session will be 50 minutes and my fee is $110 per session. Do you have any questions about the fee or about the possibility of insurance reimbursement?
Anthony :	Carol and I talked about it before even coming, and we checked with our insurance carrier. They don't cover marriage counseling, but luckily we can afford this, and we both think it is important enough to do even without insurance.
Dr. Frederico:	That's a good start, with both of you valuing yourselves and your marriage enough to commit to counseling. The other issue that some people are often concerned about is whether the information we talk about is going to be private.
Anthony:	We are not ashamed about coming here.
Carol:	We actually have shared with our family we were doing this, and they are thrilled.
Dr. Frederico:	Well, the fact that you come here would be something that would be hard to keep private, given the public nature of the office building. But you certainly have a right to know that what we talk about will be held in confidence, with some of the restrictions that were noted in the information I provided.
Carol:	We actually understand that in order to protect us you may have to disclose information, but we don't see that as a problem (Anthony nodding agreement).
Anthony:	We also saw in your brochure that sometimes with couple counseling, when it ends in some legal action, that often one spouse may have the records subpoenaed by a lawyer. We really have no intention of going to a divorce; we just know we have to work on some things to improve our marriage. But, we also understand that if court ordered, you will release the records.

> Dr. Frederico: Well, you guys certainly did read the information and appear to understand it. But as we proceed, I want to encourage you to ask if something I am doing is unclear or if you have any questions about the process you are experiencing.

In deciding what type of information should be provided, the common position is that as much information is required as would be needed by a "reasonable patient or client" to make this decision.

There has been some discussion around the issue of withholding information that in the clinician's opinion may cause the client excessive stress or anxiety. The legal recognition of therapeutic privilege can be traced to the landmark case of *Canterbury v. Spence* (1972), which recognized that sometimes disclosure could cause emotional distress, that it could complicate or hinder the treatment or even pose psychological damage to the client. In this case, the court allowed for restricted disclosure. The argument for enactment of therapeutic privilege has been that in some circumstances it is a way of promoting patient well-being and respecting the Hippocratic dictum of *primum non nocere* (or first do no harm) (Edwin, 2008). The position taken here echoes that offered by Edwin (2008), which is that such therapeutic privilege should be rarely, if ever, invoked and if done needs to be accompanied with documentation of the rationale and evidence employed to invoke this exception.

Voluntariness

Informed consent is rooted in our respect and valuing of the autonomy of our clients. The right to informed consent reflects respect for individual freedom, autonomy, and dignity, and requires the consent, whenever possible, to be given freely and without undue influence (Pope & Vasquez, 2011).

In cases when clients are seeking treatment on their own initiative, the condition of voluntariness is typically easy to ensure. However, there may be situations in which the client is "sent" to treatment or mandated to participate in assessment or therapy. This might occur as a result of court order or employer mandate or in the case of a school counselor—a student "sent" by a teacher. Under these conditions, consent, without any coercion, undue influence, misrepresentation, fraud, or duress being applied to the person's decision-making may be hard to obtain. However, even though these conditions mitigate against voluntariness, it is still important to foster that sense of autonomy and choice as essential components of informed consent (Case Illustration 8.3). As noted in the *Code of Ethics* for Social Workers (NASW, 2008), "In instances when clients are receiving services involuntarily, social workers should provide information about the nature and extent of services and about the extent of clients' right to refuse service (Principle 1.03.d).

The ethical practitioner will help these "involuntary" clients to understand their rights to withdraw from treatment or evaluation at any time, while explaining the potential consequences of such a decision. This is clearly articulated in the American Counseling Association's *ACA Code of Ethics* that states: "The client may choose to refuse services. In this case, counselors will, to the best of their ability, discuss with the client the potential consequences of refusing counseling services" (ACA, 2014, A.2.e).

Case Illustration 8.3

Compulsory Treatment

Warren was recently arrested for driving while under the influence. As part of the conditions of his sentence, he was required by the judge to attend a 14-week group-counseling program. At an individual session scheduled prior to the first group meeting, Warren met with Linda, the drug and alcohol counselor.

Warren: What do I have to do?

Linda: I'm not sure what you are asking.

Warren: Just tell me what to do and I'll do it.

Linda: Warren, this is a session that we set up for the people who are going to start our group program. We want to explain to you what we are intending to do with the group, let you know that we are required to make an assessment following your participation in the group program, and then provide a written report with recommendations to the court. So, we need to be sure that you understand all of this and agree to it before beginning the process.

Warren: Agree? You gotta be kidding. I have to be here. Look lady, I am here to do what I gotta do.

Linda:	Warren, I am aware that you are here because it was part of your sentencing. But I want you to understand that we really have found that if you understand our program and have a feel for what you can get out of fully participating, that it really can be beneficial. Now, while it may not seem it, you do have options. Even though this was mandated by the judge, you can choose not to come or not to participate. However, you know that decision would result in your incarceration.
Warren:	Yeah, great choice. Do this or go to jail!
Linda:	Well, it is a choice and it is yours. Further, the degree to which you participate in the group or not participate is also your choice. But again, we have found . . . and you will hear from others who have attended, that the more you put into it the more beneficial it is for you. Plus, we will be describing your level of participation in our report to the court.
Warren:	I get it, and yeah, I guess I have choices to make. . . . Let's just see how things unfold.
Linda:	Well, that sounds a little more open, and that's good. After our first group session, I want to meet with you again so that we can evaluate your experience. At that time, maybe we could find other options or choices available to make the program as beneficial as possible for you. How about that?
Warren:	That sounds like a plan . . . thanks.

SPECIAL CHALLENGES TO INFORMING FOR CONSENT ●

Most agree that all information relevant to the understanding of the nature of the treatment process should be provided to the client. However, while providing the client with needed information, it is important not to overwhelm the client with too much information. Finding the balance and the timing of information is an important consideration for all mental health professionals. Further, without full understanding, the process of helping should not proceed. This last point demands that the clinician present the material in a manner that is understandable to the client so that the client's choices are free and non-coerced.

Working With Minors

Competency, as noted above, refers to the ability to make a rational decision. The client must have the cognitive capacity to make a competent decision concerning the proposed relationship and/or the procedure(s) contemplated.

With the exception of emancipated minors, most states recognize that minors generally lack the capacity to give informed consent. When this is the case, the capacity for informed consent goes to the parents or guardian. Emancipation is defined differently in various states, but in general, it refers to an individual living independently and supporting himself or herself (see *Smith v. Seilby*, 1967). However, there are exceptions to this. In some states, minors are allowed to seek birth control counseling and counseling related to venereal disease, pregnancy/abortion, and substance abuse without consent of a legal guardian or parents. Beyond these exceptions, it is important to realize that the ethical practitioner will seek "assent" from clients even when conditions are such that they prevent voluntary consent. This practice of seeking assent has been codified in the *ACA Code of Ethics,* which directs its members to "seek the assent of clients to services and include them in decision making as appropriate. Counselors recognize the need to balance the ethical rights of clients to make choices, their capacity to give consent or assent to receive services, and parental or familial legal rights and responsibilities to protect these clients and make decisions on their behalf" (2014, Principle A.2.d).

Similarly, psychologists by way of their code of ethics are directed to "(1) provide an appropriate explanation, (2) seek the individual's assent, (3) consider such persons' preferences and best interests, and (4) obtain appropriate permission from a legally authorized person, if such substitute consent is permitted or required by law. When consent by a legally authorized person is not permitted or required by law, psychologists take reasonable steps to protect the individual's rights and welfare" (APA, 2012, 3.10.b).

Thus, while it is ethical and good therapeutic practice to ask clients to assent to treatment, it must be remembered that in most cases it is not required and may not be sufficient. It is up to the practitioner to understand the policies and mandates of the organization in which he or she is employed as well as any state or federal laws governing the need for parental consent in working with minors.

Third-Party Involvement

A second area in which the issue of informed consent can be complicated is in the case of third-party referral. A client may be directed to therapy by a third party, which under some situations could have taken place involuntarily or compulsorily (e.g., court ordered, employer mandated). Even in these cases of compulsory treatment, a client has the right to refuse service. However, it is important for the practitioner to fully inform the client of the process and the procedures that will be enacted should he continue and/or terminate the treatment. In court situations or legal proceedings, the client also has the right to know the helper's role in relationship to the court and the current legal proceedings. For example, will the helper disclose information? Testify? And if so, the client needs to know these consequences before accepting treatment.

An interesting variation on the theme of "voluntarism" comes when informed consent is viewed within the context of managed care. Managed care requires the exchange of information and disclosure of information for initial and continued care to be approved. There is a potential problem with maintaining helper-client confidentiality that needs to be understood and agreed upon by the client. This limitation of a helper's ability to retain confidentiality needs to be fully disclosed and consented to before the establishment of a helping relationship.

Working With the Cognitively Impaired or the Elderly

A final population for whom informed consent is sometimes difficult to acquire is the elderly and/or cognitively impaired. A client cannot give informed consent when he or she is mentally impaired, demented, or confused. While the elderly with diminished cognitive capacities may be considered legally competent, he or she may still have difficulty understanding the nuance of treatment. When one questions the ability of the client to fully comprehend the elements of the treatment along with possible consequences, it is important to gain the client's consent to inform and consult with family members so that appropriate treatment can be monitored (see Case Illustration 8.4).

Case Illustration 8.4

Competent Yet Cognitively Impaired

Maryellen is a social worker specializing in gerontology. Maryellen has been asked to work with Louise, a 74-year-old woman who recently lost her husband and who is presenting as depressed. Louise was brought to the session by her daughter, who also accompanied her into the office. Maryellen asked Louise if it would be all right if just she and Maryellen met, without the presence of her daughter. Louise said that would be fine but noted that she has problems with remembering things and that if Maryellen needs some information, her daughter may need to provide it. According to her daughter, Louise has been diagnosed by a neurologist as giving evidence of mild dementia, a condition that in the last month has worsened following the death of her husband.

Maryellen began the interview with Louise and noted that Louise was unable to provide her daughter's address or phone (where she has been living for the past month) or the names of her current physician and neurologist. Throughout the interview, Louise would often drift off and have to ask Maryellen to repeat a question or to tell her again what she just said. While it was clear that Louise had a diminished cognitive ability, when asked where she was and why she was there, Louise was very clear that she came to a counselor because, as she noted, she was having a difficult time feeling okay after her husband's death. Because she understood both the need and nature of the reason she was with Maryellen, Maryellen decided to explain the process and policies she would be using. In the course of describing how she would like to proceed, Maryellen asked Louise for permission to contact her neurologist. Louise said, "That would be fine . . . I can't remember who he is, you should ask my daughter, she'll know." Maryellen thanked her and said that at the end of the session she would invite Louise's daughter in and ask her for some information, like her home address, phone number, and doctor's names, if that would be okay. Louise responded positively, stating, "Actually, I appreciate you letting my daughter give you the information. It sometimes gets me upset when I can't remember."

BEYOND PROFESSIONAL STANDARDS: ●
A PERSONAL MORAL RESPONSE

Gaining client informed consent is clearly an ethical and legal mandate. However, gaining informed consent is more than a process of practice. It is a reflection of the nature of the helping relationship that is respectful of the client's autonomy and valuing of a client's full participation. Moving from the mandates of law and ethical codes to this type of relationship is the hallmark of the ethical practitioner. It demonstrates that for this practitioner, informed consent has moved from an ethical principle to a personal moral value and response in relationship with the client.

Moving beyond professional standards to a personal moral response may take a conscious effort on the part of the practitioner. The following checklist is a list of reminders for the ethical helper. The information presented has been adapted from materials presented by Wheeler and Bertram (1994) in their workshop "Legal Aspects of Counseling: Avoiding Lawsuits and Legal Problems." These items are useful both in developing informed written consent procedures and more importantly, in reinforcing the basic trust and fundamental valuing of the client that characterizes ethical helping. They are presented here as a mechanism to be used by a practitioner with each client and in so doing will facilitate elevation of informed consent to a personal value and a moral response.

- Voluntary participation: Assist clients to commit to treatment voluntarily with knowledge that termination can occur at any time without penalty.
- Client involvement: Identify the level and type of involvement expected and desired from the client.
- Helper involvement: Describe the level and type of involvement to be given by the helper, along with information regarding the hows and whys for contacting the helper, especially in the case of emergencies.
- Model and approach: Describe the helper's particular model and/or orientation and how this will affect treatment.
- Risks and benefits associated with helping: Identify potential beneficial outcomes as well as possible risks, if any, associated with a particular approach to helping.

- Confidentiality, privilege, and limitations: Specify how confidentiality will be handled and maintained along with the conditions under which confidential and privileged information will be released.
- Helper credentials: Disclose training and experience relevant to this case along with special credentials, certifications, and licenses held.
- Fees and reimbursements: Identify all fees and charges and describe how these are collected and what involvement the helper will take in terms of insurance and insurance filings.
- Cancellations: Inform client as to cancellation policies and whether a fee is charged.
- Consultation and suspension: Describe any required supervisory or consultative relationships in which the helper is engaged, along with the specific impact of such a relationship on the current client-helper relationship.
- Disputes and complaints: Inform the client of the address and phone number of state credentialing departments (certification, licensing) should complaints about fee or service result.

● CONCLUDING CASE ILLUSTRATION

We began the chapter with a brief dialogue between Ms. Wicks and Maria. As you read the continuation of the dialogue, which is presented below, observe Ms. Wicks's behavior as it reflects or fails to reflect the principles discussed within this chapter. Further, a number of brief questions for your reflection are offered following the case to stimulate your application of your knowledge on informed consent.

Ms. Wicks: Hi, Maria. Have a seat. I really appreciate you coming down to see me. I need to share some things with you and ask you for a favor.

Maria: A favor?

Ms. Wicks: Well, not really a favor, just your permission to do something.

Maria: I don't understand.

Ms. Wicks: Well, after we met last time, I was very concerned about the possibility that you may be engaging in dangerous behavior, something that could harm you. So I went to Mr. Harolds, the chairperson for the counseling department, to ask him for some advice.

Maria: Wait, what are you saying? You're blabbing everything I tell you to other people?

Ms. Wicks: No, that's not what happened and in fact, that's what I wanted to talk with you about. In speaking with Mr. Harolds, I didn't let him know who the student was, and I was careful not to disclose any information with which he could identify you. But I asked him if I needed to contact anyone or call your mom about the risk you are running by having unprotected sex with a boy who has AIDS.

Maria: Okay, so you didn't call my mom or anything, right? And Mr. Harolds doesn't know you are talking about me?

Ms. Wicks: That's correct. But the truth is I don't feel real comfortable with what you are doing. I care about you and I feel you are really endangering yourself by having unprotected sex with a person with AIDS. Maria, I would like to share some information about this situation with Ms. Armstrong. I will not tell her who you are by name and I will try not to share any identifying information. But I want her permission to refer you to a clinic for some blood work as well as some information on safe sex. I would be willing even to go with you, if you would like . . . but I need Ms. Armstrong's permission to give that type of information out.

Maria: I think you are overreacting, but I would be willing to go to some clinic if you would come with me.

Ms. Wicks: I will, if it is permitted as part of my work here. But for that, I need to talk to Ms. Armstrong. I outlined the type of information I would like to share with Ms. Armstrong as a way of convincing her of the importance of allowing me to do this. Let's go over this list so that I can explain each item and make sure it is okay with you. Okay?

Maria: Okay!

Reflections

1. Do you feel this discussion was even necessary, or could/should Ms. Wicks simply have discussed this issue with Ms. Armstrong, the principal?
2. Ms. Wicks spoke with Mr. Harolds without receiving Maria's informed consent. Did she violate confidentiality? Did she need Maria's consent?
3. Ms. Wicks is going to discuss a list of points that she wishes to convey to Ms. Armstrong. Is there anything in addition to that which you feel she should do?
4. Should Ms. Wicks have Maria sign a formal consent form?
5. What is the rule in your state for providing information to a minor regarding family planning, safe sex, and venereal disease?

● COOPERATIVE LEARNING EXERCISE

The purpose of this chapter was to introduce you to the concept of informed consent, along with the elements involved in obtaining such consent. As noted throughout the chapter, gaining client informed consent is not always necessary or even possible in some situations. Working with a colleague or classmate, contact a person working as a (a) school counselor, (b) drug and alcohol counselor, (c) court-appointed mental health practitioner, and (d) marriage counselor and ask each of the following questions. Share your information with other colleagues and/or classmates looking for common areas of practice and or concern.

- Do you gain informed consent from all of your clients? If not, why not and how is that decision determined? If so, when and where within the helping process do you seek informed consent?
- When you seek informed consent, how do you ensure (a) capacity/competency, (b) comprehension, and (c) voluntarism?
- How do you document that you have gained informed consent?
- What value, if any, do you find in gaining informed consent?

● SUMMARY

- The doctrine of informed consent involves the right of the client to both consent to and to refuse the procedure(s) that are contemplated. Ethically, the concept of informed consent is grounded in the belief of a client's right to self-determination and right to benefit from treatment.
- Most agree that informed consent requires that the client be competent, have knowledge of what will occur, and engage in treatment voluntarily.
- The identification of competence will fluctuate as a function of context or decision criteria defining competence.
- In ensuring comprehension, the practitioner needs to share the information in a way that a reasonable individual in the client's position would be able to understand and make a reasonably informed decision.
- Consent is to be given and solicited freely and without undue influence.
- Working with minors presents a challenge to the principle of competency. With the exception of emancipated minors, most states

recognize that minors generally lack the capacity to give informed consent. When this is the case, the capacity for informed consent goes to the parents or guardian.

- In some states, minors are allowed to seek birth control counseling, and counseling related to venereal disease, pregnancy/abortion, and substance abuse without consent of a legal guardian or parents.
- The issue of voluntary consent is potentially compromised when a client may be directed to therapy by a third party, which can take place involuntarily or compulsorily (e.g., court ordered). Even in these cases of compulsory treatment, a client has the right to refuse service.
- Comprehension can be challenged in situations in which a practitioner is working with a client with diminished cognitive capacities. It is possible that the client may be considered legally competent but still has difficulty understanding the nuances of treatment. Often it is important to gain consent to inform and consult with family members so that appropriate treatment can be monitored.

IMPORTANT TERMS ●

client compliance	informed consent
competency	legal guardian
comprehension	nondisclosure
context power	pre-helping screening
decision criteria	self-determination
emancipated minors	third party
impaired	voluntariness

ADDITIONAL RESOURCES ●

Print

Appelbaum, P., & Guthell, T. (2007). *Clinical handbook of psychiatry & the law*. Philadelphia, PA: Lippincott Williams & Wilkins.

Bridges, N. (2010). Clinical writing about clients: Seeking consent and negotiating the impact on clients and their treatments. *Counseling and Values, 54*(2), 103–116.

Parekh, S. A. (2007). Child consent and the law: An insight and discussion into the law relating to consent and competence. *Health and Development, 33*(1), 78–82.

Simon, R., & Shuman, D. (2007). *Clinical manual of psychiatry & law*. Washington, DC: American Psychiatric Publishing.

Web-Based

American Counseling Association. (n.d.). *Implementing informed consent*. Retrieved from http://www.counseling.org/docs/private-practice pointers/implementing_informed_consent.pdf?sfvrsn=2

The Center for Ethical Practice (n.d.). *Selected ethical standards about informed consent: Counselors* (from *ACA Code of Ethics*). Retrieved from http://www.centerforethicalpractice.org/ethical-legal-resources/ethical-information/ethical-obligations-informed-consent/selected-ethical-standards-counselors-from-aca-code-of-ethics/

Fisher, C. B., & Oransky, M. (n.d.). *Informed consent to psychotherapy and the American Psychological Association's Ethics Code*. Retrieved from http://www.e-psychologist.org/index.iml?mdl=exam/show_article.mdl&Material_ID=79

Pope, K. (n.d.). *Informed consent in psychotherapy and counseling: Forms, standards & guidelines, & references*. Retrieved from http://kspope.com/consent/#forms

Stone, C. (2014, September). *Informed consent: Is it attainable with students in schools? ASCA Schoolcounselor*. Retrieved from https://www.schoolcounselor.org/magazine/blogs/september-october-2014/informed-consent-is-it-attainable-with-students-i

● REFERENCES

American Association for Marriage and Family Therapy. (2015). *Code of ethics*. Retrieved from http://www.aamft.org/iMIS15/AAMFT/Content/Legal_Ethics/Code_of_Ethics.aspx

American Counseling Association. (2014). *Code of ethics*. Retrieved from http://www.counseling.org/resources/aca-code-of-ethics.pdf

American Psychological Association. (2010). *Ethical principles of psychologists and code of conduct*. Retrieved from http://www.apa.org/ethics/code/principles.pdf

American School Counselor Association. (2016). ASCA *ethical standards for school counselors*. Retrieved from https://www.schoolcounselor.org/school-counselors-members/legal-ethical

Appelbaum, P. S., & Grasso, T. (1988). Assessing patients' capacities to consent to treatment. *The New England Journal of Medicine, 319*(25), 1635–1638.

Beahrs, J. O., Gutheil, T. G. (2001). Informed consent in psychotherapy. *American Journal of Psychiatry, 158*, 4–10.

Behnke, S. (2004). Informed consent and APA's new ethics code: Enhancing client autonomy, improving client care. *Monitor on Psychology, 35*(6), 80.

Berg, J. W., Appelbaum, P. S., Lidz, C. W., & Parker, L. S. (2001). *Informed consent: Legal theory and clinical practice.* New York, NY: Oxford University Press.

Canterbury v. Spence, 464 F 2d 772, 789 (DC Cir, 1972).

Edwin, A. (2008). Don't lie but don't tell the whole truth: The therapeutic privilege— Is it ever justified? *Ghana Medical Journal, 42*(4), 156-161.

Goddard, A., Murray, C. D., & Simpson, J. (2008). Informed consent and psychotherapy: An interpretative phenomenological analysis of therapists' views. *Psychology and Psychotherapy—Theory, Research and Practice, 81*(2), 177-191.

Hochauser, M. (2004). Informed consent: Reading and understanding are not the same: Subjects may read consent forms, but they don't always understand them. *Applied Clinical Trials.* Retrieved from http://www.appliedclinical trialsonline.com/informed-consent-reading-and-understanding-are-not-same? id=&pageID=1&sk=&date=

Knapp, S. J., & VandeCreek, L. (2006). *Practical ethics for psychologists: A positive approach.* Washington, DC: American Psychological Association.

Murray, B. (2012). Informed Consent: What must a physician disclose to a patient? *AMA Journal of Ethics, 14*(7), 563-566.

National Association of Social Workers (2008). *Code of ethics* (Rev. ed.). Retrieved from http://www.socialworkers.org/pubs/code/code.asp

Osheroff v. Chestnut Lodge, Inc., 301 Md. 189, 191-192, 482 A.2d 873, 874-877 (1984).

Pope, K. S., & Vasquez, M. J. T. (2011). *Ethics in psychotherapy & counseling: A practical guide* (4th ed.). San Francisco, CA: Jossey-Bass/John Wiley.

Smith v. Seilby, 72 Wash.2d 16 (1967).

Sullivan, T., Martin, W., & Handelsman, M. (1993). Practical benefits of an informed-consent procedure: An empirical investigation. *Professional Psychology: Research and Practice, 24*, 160-163.

Walker, R., Logan, T. K., Clark, J. J., & Leukefeld, C. (2005). Informed consent to undergo treatment for substance abuse: A recommended approach. *Journal of Substance Abuse Treatment, 29*, 241-251.

Wheeler, N., & Bertram, B. (1994). *Legal aspects of counseling: Avoiding lawsuits and legal problems,* (Workshop Material and Video Seminar) Alexandria, VA: American Counseling Association.

CHAPTER **9**

Confidentiality

Maria: It's okay. You can talk to Ms. Armstrong as long as you don't tell her who I am. I don't want anyone knowing what I told you. Besides, I thought talking to you was like talking to a priest in confession . . . you know, a major secret?

Maria understands the fundamental nature of the helping relationship. It is one in which the individual's right to privacy is respected. However, as with most things in this profession, the issue of privacy or confidentiality is not simply yes or no.

While confidentiality is a value held and practiced by all ethical practitioners, the extent of such confidentiality can and will vary as a result of the context, client characteristics, and the nature of the information shared (see for example Chapter 13). The concept and ethical principal of confidentiality, along with those conditions that define the extent and limits of confidentiality, will serve as the focus for the current chapter.

OBJECTIVES ●

After reading this chapter you should be able to do the following:

- Describe what is meant by the terms *confidentiality* and *privilege*.
- Identify the conditions under which confidentiality and privilege should be breached.

- Discuss the conditions that need to exist for *duty to warn* to be implemented.
- Describe the special challenges facing practitioners working with both minors and those with HIV/AIDS in regard to confidentiality.
- Describe challenges of the technological era, including distance counseling, social media, texting, and corresponding by fax machine and e-mail.

● CONFIDENTIALITY: WHAT AND WHEN WARRANTED?

Privacy and the right to decide for oneself the time and circumstances under which to disclose personal beliefs, behaviors, and opinions is a cornerstone to our individual rights under the Constitution of the United States. It is this constitutional right to privacy that serves as the legal basis of privileged communication and the professional concept of confidentiality (Kurpius, 1997). Confidentiality is a central factor underlying the public trust in mental health practitioners.

● CONFIDENTIALITY IS NOT PRIVILEGED

Confidentiality refers to the ethical principal that conveys that the information discussed within the context of the professional relationship will not be disclosed without a client's informed consent. Confidentiality is truly the client's right (Sheperis, Henning, & Kocet, 2016) and is essential to the nature of a helping relationship. Research suggests that people are more apt to self-disclose in therapy when their privacy is protected and their confidentiality assured (Evans-Marsh, 2003). Clients who cannot trust professionals to treat information as confidential may withhold information that is important to the assessment and treatment. The helping relationship requires a client to place his or her trust in the helper, knowing that the information will remain confidential.

Confidentiality should not be equated with privileged communication. Privileged communication is a legal term describing situations in which the client is legally protected in a court of law from having personal, confidential information disclosed by the therapist. Whereas therapists are directed under their code of ethics to maintain client privacy or confidentiality with privilege, that protection is ensured by the law, such that client information will be protected from disclosure even in legal proceedings (Corey, Corey, Corey, & Callahan, 2015).

Confidentiality is the broader concept that includes the expectation that material will not be divulged, whereas privileged communications carry a strong admonition that material will not and may not be divulged even in court. While confidential material covers most of what transpires between the client and the practitioner, privilege belongs only to certain defined *protected relationships*, such as physician and patient; lawyer and client; and psychologist, social worker, and psychiatrist and their clients. The privilege brings with it the necessity to receive permission from the client, the holder of the privilege, prior to disclosure (see Case Illustration 9.1).

Case Illustration 9.1

Release Only With Consent

Dr. Ramerez is a licensed psychiatrist. Dr. Ramerez is currently working with Alfred, who has been diagnosed as having post-traumatic stress disorder (PTSD) as a result of a serious car accident in which 13 people were killed. Alfred was the only one of four people within his car that survived. The accident, which involved an oil truck and seven cars, was caused by an oil-tank truck driver falling asleep at the wheel. An insurance company representing one of the other victims in the crash in a lawsuit against the oil company subpoenaed Dr. Ramerez's records on his diagnosis and treatment of Alfred.

Dr. Ramerez, respectfully declined to honor the subpoena, claiming the information to be privileged and stating that he would release this information only when his client would consent to its release. The lawyer representing the complainant in the lawsuit against the truck company explained that the only purpose of the request was to demonstrate the "potential" psychological impact that his client could experience well after her physical wounds had healed, and he wanted to use Alfred's case as an illustration of PTSD. Dr. Ramerez explained the request to Alfred, who wanted to sign a consent form to release the information. Dr. Ramerez still felt that releasing the information was neither required nor desired. However, Dr. Ramerez understood that privilege belonged to the client and not to the therapist; since Alfred consented to release the information, he did.

For communication to be privileged, the standard that has been historically held is that the communication must satisfy specific criteria. The requirements of this privilege are (a) the communications must be confidential, (b) the therapist must be a licensed psychotherapist, and (c) the communications must occur in the course of diagnosis or treatment (*Jaffee v. Redmond*, 1996).

With these criteria as backdrop, it would appear that the legal concept of privileged communication does not apply in group situations or even couple therapy, since the presence of the third person makes ensuring the origination of confidence difficult to enforce. Clearly, when working with groups, couples, or other situations in which the disclosures fail to meet criteria of privilege, practitioners have an ethical responsibility to maintain confidentiality while explaining the limitations to both confidentiality and privilege communications. Further questions regarding who can claim the privilege, what type of information is privileged, and what the limitations to privilege are can vary extensively state to state. Not all states, for example, grant privilege to all psychotherapists. It is federal law that provides and supports privilege for medical doctors and psychologists (Remley and Herlihy, 2014). It is important for each practitioner to know the answers to these questions as defined within the state in which they practice. Exercise 9.1 is provided to assist in this process.

Exercise 9.1

A Question of Privilege?

Directions: As suggested in the text, the nature of privileged communication can vary state by state. Contact either your state professional organization or the state board of professional affairs and gather information to answer the following questions:

- Who can claim privileged communication, or under what conditions can privilege be claimed?
- What types of communications are covered by privilege?
- Which professions and professionals have privilege?
- What are the limitations to privilege?
- What constitutes a waiver of privilege?

● CONFIDENTIALITY ACROSS THE PROFESSIONS

The provision of confidentiality is common throughout human service professions and is widely held as a therapeutic necessity. All professional organizations address the issue of confidentiality (see Table 9.1). While the specific wording varies, the principle of confidentiality articulated by the various professional organizations all reflect the fundamental values underlying ethical

Table 9.1 Confidentiality

Professional Ethical Standards	Statement on Confidentiality
American Psychological Association (2010)	4.01. Psychologists have a primary obligation and take reasonable precautions to protect confidential information obtained through or stored in any medium, recognizing that the extent and limits of confidentiality may be regulated by law or established by institutional rules or professional or scientific relationship.
National Association of Social Workers (2008)	1.07. Privacy and confidentiality c. Social workers should protect the confidentiality of all information obtained in the course of professional service, except for compelling professional reasons. The general expectation that social workers will keep information confidential does not apply when disclosure is necessary to prevent serious, foreseeable, and imminent harm to a client or other identifiable person. In all instances, social workers should disclose the least amount of confidential information necessary to achieve the desired purpose; only information that is directly relevant to the purpose for which the disclosure is made should be revealed.
American Counseling Association (2014)	B.1.b. Respecting client rights Counselors respect the privacy of prospective and current clients. Counselors request private information from clients only when it is beneficial to the counseling process. B.1.c. Respect for confidentiality Counselors protect the confidential information of prospective and current clients. Counselors disclose information only with appropriate consent or with sound legal or ethical justification.
American Association for Marriage and Family Therapy (2015)	Section 2. Confidentiality Marriage and family therapists have unique confidentiality concerns because the client in a therapeutic relationship may be more than one person. Therapists respect and guard the confidences of each individual client.

practice. With the primary purpose of confidentiality being the protection of client privacy and the placing of control over shared information in their hands, our adherence to confidentiality shows our genuine valuing of client autonomy, right of self-determination, and our commitment to beneficence.

Neither confidentiality nor privilege is an absolute. Since both are in place in support of the protection of the client, not the helper, both can be waived by the client. Beyond client waiver, conditions exists that limit the degree to which communications can be maintained as confidential. Conditions such as those dictated by local laws and organizational regulations as well as situations in which a client or an identifiable person might be harmed should confidentiality be maintained necessitate the breaching of confidentiality and privilege. These conditions and other complicating factors are discussed in the next section.

● LIMITS AND SPECIAL CHALLENGES TO CONFIDENTIALITY

Since confidentiality is not an absolute, in addition to respecting the confidentiality of the client's information, the ethical professional is directed by standards of practice to inform the client, when appropriate, of the limits of confidentiality. The *Code of Ethics* for Social Workers (2008), for example, states, "Social workers should inform clients, to the extent possible, about the disclosure of confidential information and the potential consequences, when feasible before the disclosure is made" (NASW, 2008, 1.07.d).

It is essential that the professional helper explicate the restrictions on confidentiality and assist the client to understand the unique conditions under which information may be shared in the course of providing service. The American Psychological Association's (APA) code of ethics states that disclosure of the limits of confidentiality should occur at the outset of a professional relationship: "Unless it is not feasible or is contraindicated, the discussion of confidentiality occurs at the outset of the relationship and thereafter as new circumstances may warrant" (APA, 2010, Standard 4.02.b).

Beyond the client's consent to waive privilege or disclose confidential material, the courts and the various professions have identified a number of conditions under which disclosure of this information may be required. These conditions include sharing for professional support when a client is a danger to self or others, in child abuse situations, and when court ordered.

Since breach of confidentiality may be mandated in these and other circumstances, clients should be adequately informed about the limitations of confidentiality early within the relationship (see Chapter 8). Once informed, it becomes the client's responsibility to share such personal information, knowing that confidence may not be maintained.

The ethical professional will maintain that breach of confidentiality is such a strong issue that the basis needs to be strong and justifiable. Further, because a breach of confidentiality that is outside of these conditions may make the professional susceptible to legal and ethical sanctions, ranging from sanctioning by the professional organization to a malpractice suit, it is essential for the practitioner to be fully versed in the laws and ethical standards existing for his or her profession and in his or her state of practice.

Professional Support

It is generally accepted that confidential material may be shared with colleagues and supervisors for professional purposes. However, only that material essential to the consultation or supervision should be disclosed. Additionally, the conditions under which the information is shared needs to reflect the respect for client privacy and the attempt to maintain maximum confidentiality. Case Illustration 9.2 demonstrates how in our day-to-day professional interactions we may become somewhat insensitive to the conditions under which we share confidential information.

Case Illustration 9.2

Faculty Room Chatter

Allison is a secondary-school counselor. She has been working with Ricky, a twelfth-grade student who has been speaking with Allison about his concern and anxiety over his sexual orientation. Ricky has started to accept the fact that he is gay and has been working with the school counselor to determine ways in which he can disclose this information to his parents. Because of the anxiety he has been feeling and the amount of psychic energy he has been giving to this concern, Ricky's academic performance has fallen off quite dramatically.

Ricky is very concerned that his two honors teachers may feel that he has simply stopped caring about their courses, and he would like them to write him letters of recommendation. Thus he asks Allison if she will talk to the teachers about his personal struggle, so that they will better understand his falling grades. Ricky gives permission to disclose the information they have discussed, including his own coming out.

Allison sets up a meeting with Mr. Hansen and Ms. Wallace, the two honors teachers. She explains that she has been working with

(Continued)

(Continued)

Ricky and would like to share some information that may better help them understand his current academic difficulty. Both teachers express concern for Ricky and are glad to have the meeting. The three meet at a table in the faculty lounge, where Allison begins to share the information with both teachers with the intent of having them more fully understand Ricky's change in performance. While Allison is fully aware that other teachers are in the room, she feels that if they speak in a conversational tone that no one else will either overhear or care to listen.

Client as Danger to Self or Others

While it may be obvious that the ethical practitioner concerned for the well-being of his or her client will break confidence if doing so can protect a client from self-inflicted harm, what may not be as obvious is that a break in confidence may be required as a way of taking reasonable care to protect others who may be in jeopardy of harm at the hands of a client. The professional obligation to warn a third party of a potential danger has been widely discussed, starting with the now famous case of *Tarasoff v. The Regents of the University of California* (1976). In this case, the California Supreme Court found a duty to warn and to protect an identifiable and foreseeable victim. The case focused on Posenjit Poddar, the defendant charged with the 1969 killing of Tatiana Tarasoff. Tarasoff's parents alleged that two months prior to the murder, Poddar confided his intention to kill Tatiana to a psychologist employed by the Cowell Memorial Hospital at the University of California at Berkeley. The psychologist had Poddar detained by the campus police, but Poddar was later released. No one warned Tarasoff of the possible peril to her life. Following the appeal, the court ruled that a duty to warn existed, stating,

> When a therapist determines, or pursuant to the standards of his profession should determine, that his [client] presents a serious danger of violence to another he incurs an obligation to use reasonable care to protect the intended victim against such danger. The discharge of this duty may require the therapist to take one or more of various steps, depending upon the nature of the case. Thus it may call for him to warn the intended victim or others likely to apprise the victim of the danger, to notify the police, or to take whatever other steps are reasonably necessary under the circumstances. (*Tarasoff*, 1976)

The courts in this situation concluded the following:

> Public policy favoring protection of the confidential character of [client], psychotherapist communication must yield to the extent to which disclosure is essential to avert dangers to others. The protective privilege ends where the public peril begins. (*Tarasoff*)

This case has served as the foundation for the concept of duty to warn, making mental health professionals responsible for assessing the risk of danger that their clients may present to others and assessing the need to breach confidentiality and to warn. Legal extensions of the *Tarasoff* case are presented later within this chapter. One special arena in which *Tarasoff* continues to be debated is in working with clients with HIV/AIDS. For example, the American Counseling Association (ACA) notes, "The general requirement that counselors keep information confidential does not apply when disclosure is required to protect clients or identified others from serious and foreseeable harm or when legal requirements demand that confidential information validity of an exception" (ACA, 2014, B.2.a). Further, "when clients disclose they have a disease commonly known to be communicable and life threatening, counselors may be justified in disclosing information to identifiable third parties" (ACA, 2014, B.2.C).

Persons With AIDS

Traditional approaches to client confidentiality have certainly been challenged by the introduction of the issue of AIDS and at-risk behaviors. Thanks to advances in medical care, HIV infection has become a chronic life-threatening condition, as opposed to the more rapidly fatal illness at the outset of the AIDS epidemic. However, it remains a very serious medical condition, and many state laws have been enacted to protect both the confidentiality of HIV-infected individuals and the safety of their sexual partners (Koocher & Keith-Spiegel, 2013). It is important for practitioners to remain current regarding medical data, treatments, transmission risks, interventions, and state laws regarding professional interactions with HIV patients.

Given the discrimination that individuals with HIV have faced, confidentiality is an extremely important issue. Individuals with HIV may be hesitant to seek needed treatment without the assurance of confidentiality (Koocher & Keith-Spiegel, 2013). However, individuals with HIV who engage in unsafe sexual practices or IV drug use and are unwilling to disclose that information to their partners or use safe practices place the practitioner within the ethical dilemma of if and when to break confidence in response to a duty to protect (Alghazo, Upton, & Cioe, 2011). The APA (2000), as outlined in a recommendation made by the HIV/AIDS Office for Psychology Education, supports the presumption that "confidentiality on behalf of the client shall be maintained except in extraordinary circumstances wherein individuals are unwilling or incapable of reducing the risk of infection to sexual or needle-sharing partners."

While there have been attempts at apply the *Tarasoff* decision to HIV-related cases, Webber (1999) found that approximately half of the rulings provided support for maintaining confidentiality, whereas the other half provided support for limited disclosure.

It appears that the application of *Tarasoff* principles to HIV cases is variable at best. The extent to which *Tarasoff* is extended to situations involving HIV appears to depend on statutory and case law, which varies by jurisdiction. Given this variability in statutory and state law, it is essential for the ethical practitioner to become familiar with the laws applicable to his or her state and place of employment and thus to refer to legal precedent, state statutes, and professional codes of ethics when attempting to resolve the HIV disclosure dilemma (see Exercise 9.2).

Exercise 9.2

The Duty to Warn and Clients With AIDS

Directions: The application of *Tarasoff* to situations involving clients with AIDS has not been clarified within the courts.

Part 1: Contact a professional in practice within your local community. Pose the following questions to the professional and share your findings with your classmates/colleagues.

- Are you familiar with the *Tarasoff* case?

- If you had a client who expressed an intention to seriously harm an identifiable victim, what would you do? Has this ever happened in your practice?

- What would you do if your client, who had AIDS, was actively engaged in unprotected sex with an identifiable partner? Has this ever happened in your practice?

Part 2: Contact your state professional organization and ask for the latest position on applying *Tarasoff* and the duty to warn in situations involving a client who has AIDS or is HIV positive.

The issue of disclosure and the duty to warn when in relation to working with an HIV/AIDS client are not at all clear-cut. The professional's response certainly is a decision that needs to reflect the current position of her or his profession and the directives of the local and federal courts. Exercise 9.3 is presented to give you a "practitioner's view" of this difficult area of professional decision-making.

Exercise 9.3

To Disclose or Not to Disclose?

Directions: Given the lack of clarity and directions regarding the issue of disclosure and duty to warn in cases of working with clients with HIV/AIDS, individual decisions and standards of colleagues are important reference points for the practitioner attempting to make an ethical decision. Contact at least two professionals currently working in your particular professional arena and pose to them the questions in the following scenario. Record their responses and share your findings with a colleague or a classmate in an attempt to identify the standard of practice currently enacted within your locale.

Scenario: Assume you are working with a client who has admitted having AIDS and engaging in unprotected sex. Further assume that the client refused to give you consent to disclose this information.

- Would you warn the client's spouse/partner?

- Would you warn the client's current, live-in lover (assuming the client was not married)?

- Would you warn individuals whom your client identified as recent sexual partners?

- Would you warn individuals whom your client identified as having sex with over the past 5 years?

- Would you continue to work with the client, if he or she refused to begin to practice safe sex?

Mandated Reporting

The Child Abuse Prevention and Treatment Act (CAPTA) of 1974 defined child abuse and neglect and set the standards for state mandatory reporting laws. Amended in 2010 by the CAPTA Reauthorization Act, the existing definition of child abuse and neglect was retained to include at a minimum, "any recent act or failure to act on the part of a parent or caretaker which results in death, serious physical or emotional harm, sexual abuse or exploitation; or an act or failure to act, which presents an imminent risk of serious harm." Most states recognize four major types of maltreatment: neglect, physical abuse, psychological maltreatment, and sexual abuse. Although any of the forms of child maltreatment may be found separately, they can occur in combination (U.S. Department of Health and Human Services, Administration for Children and Families, Administration on Children, Youth and Families, Children's Bureau, 2016). Under these conditions, disclosure is mandated. And even though our codes of ethics direct us to value clients' autonomy and respect for their decision-making, laws governing mandated reporting override this value of autonomy, especially when applied to minors who are in danger of harm by others, to others, or to self (Sheperis, Henning, & Kocet, 2016). In fact, while professional standards direct the practitioner to protect the information disclosed within the helping process, breaking the law by not complying with a legal mandate to report is in itself unethical. The APA code of ethics (2010), for example, states that "psychologists disclose confidential information without the consent of the individual only as mandated by law, or where permitted by law for a valid purpose" (Standard 4.05.b). The tension and conflict between professional values and standards with legal requirements are not easy to resolve. But, as with any ethical dilemma, addressing the issue of mandated reporting can be approached by the employment of a solid decision-making model (see Chapter 7) and by consulting with a colleague about the situation. The use of consultation and ethical decision-making models for the purpose of mandating reporting is recommended in several ethical codes (Henderson, 2013).

Records: Court Ordered

All professional codes of conduct provide for the maintenance and utilization of records as well as the maintenance of privacy of these records (see Chapter 12). Records should be maintained in a secure manner in order to protect the client's confidentiality. Failure to maintain adequate records may be seen as a breach of the standard of care and thus serve as a basis for a malpractice suit (Anderson, 1996).

In the case of educational records, confidentiality is protected under federal law, the Family Educational Rights and Privacy Act (FERPA) (1974). This law applies to any educational agency (public or private) receiving federal funds. It specifies that parents have access to student education records and that any release of educational records requires parental or student (if over 18) written consent. Without consent, only "directory information," limited to name, address, telephone, date of birth, major, and date of attendance, is released. This is not an open-file policy. Some records, such as those maintained by a physician, psychiatrist, psychologist, or other recognized professional or paraprofessional acting in his or her professional and paraprofessional capacity, are made, maintained, or used only in connection with the provision of treatment to the student. These are not available to anyone other than persons providing such treatment (20 U.S.C., sec. 1232[a][4][B]).

While records, including educational records, may be requested by various agencies or legal professionals, the only request to which the practitioner must respond without client consent is one issued in the form of a court order. Often records are requested by insurance companies or others in legal proceedings, often in the form of a subpoena. And while it is important for a mental health specialist to respond to a subpoena, the response can be in the form of a request. Rather than disclosing the information requested, a helper can request that the agency or individual seeking the information obtain a signed release of information from the client. However, if a practitioner is issued a *duces tecum* subpoena—a court order—then the practitioner must appear in court and bring the client's records. Under this condition, a claim of privilege could be offered at the court and would require the court to either honor the privilege or demand a breach.

Another condition in which a breach of confidentiality and privilege may occur is when a client files a lawsuit or ethical grievance against the practitioner. Under these conditions, the practitioner has a right to reveal relevant information about the client in his or her own defense. One final area in which release of information may invite a breach of confidentiality is in the case of providing information for insurance claims. Clients need to be informed that information released to insurance companies for the purpose of third-party payment may remain within their records. Typically, the information required includes the client's name, services provided, dates of services, and a diagnosis. The importance of this fact is that once these data are conveyed to the insurance company, the practitioner will no longer have control over access to these records and thus cannot restrict to whom they are given or how the information is used.

Confidentiality and Working With Minors

Although children and adolescents increasingly have been granted rights to free choice, informed consent and privileged communication in counseling these issues remain complex in practice and often confusing to practitioners. Behnke & Warner (2002) noted that, while minors cannot consent to treatment, a parent or guardian consents on the minor's behalf. However, there are some exceptions. These authors noted that certain states allow minors whom the law deems especially mature, such as those who are married or in the armed services, to consent to treatment, and sometimes minors may consent to treatment for substance abuse or sexually transmitted diseases. However, it is important to note that these exceptions are few and that generally one must be 18 years or older to be considered sufficiently mature to provide informed consent and with it the benefits of engaging in a confidential therapeutic relationship. Even with this proviso regarding the restrictions on confidentiality when working with minors, the ethical practitioner will do well in gaining informed "assent" from minors prior to the release of information.

The *ACA Code of Ethics* (2014) directs its members to inform clients (including minor clients) consistent "with their level of understanding and take culturally appropriate measures to safeguard client confidentiality" (Principle B.5.c). Further, the ACA codes (2014) direct counselors "When counseling minor clients or adult clients who lack the capacity to give voluntary, informed consent, counselors protect the confidentiality of information received in the counseling relationship as specified by federal and state laws, written policies and applicable ethical standards (ACA, 2014, Principle B.5.a).

For those working with minors in a school setting, the minors' rights to confidentiality are protected by the Family Educational Rights and Privacy Act (2015). While this act provides for access by parents to student records, it also exempts counselor notes, assuming that they are not considered part of the official school record. Because this final designation of "official school record" is open to the interpretation of each school district, counselors should be aware of their own districts' policies regarding counselor notes and minor confidentiality.

All states have laws that permit minors to consent to treatment for some conditions, such as alcohol and drug abuse, venereal disease, pregnancy, and sexual health. While some states prohibit disclosure to parents, some leave this to the practitioner's discretion, and others require disclosure under certain circumstances. The Center for Adolescent Health and the Law published a compendium of state laws that address confidentiality and consent (English & Kenney, 2003). The rationale is such that right to privacy and freedom to choose increases the likelihood that children and adolescents needing counseling will seek it. Because of the variation from state to state and the ever-shifting legal landscape, it is important for all practitioners to check with their state professional organizations to align with local practice regulations.

Confidentiality in the Technological Era

In an age when people may use digital technology to communicate more than face-to-face interactions, practitioners need to be cognizant of the use of such items as e-mail, texting, and fax machines and possible breaches in confidentiality. Many professional codes of ethics have started to include use of technology in their codes. The *ACA Code of Ethics* has an entire section devoted to distance counseling, technology, and social media (2014). The section cites the client as having the "freedom to choose whether to use distance counseling, social media and/or technology within the counseling process" (ACA, 2014, H.2.a). In addition, issues are addressed in which the practitioner is aware of and discusses "limitations of maintaining confidentiality of electronic records and transmissions" with the client (ACA, 2014, H.2.b; H.2.c).

LEGAL DECISIONS: CONFIDENTIALITY AND ●
PRIVILEGED COMMUNICATIONS

Professionals With Privilege

Psychotherapist-client privilege has been supported by a Supreme Court decision. The case involved the ability of a clinical social worker licensed in Illinois to assert privilege for communications between herself and her client in a lawsuit. The client, Mary Lu Redmon, was a police officer who killed Ricky Allen Sr. The officer responded to a reported fight and found Mr. Allen allegedly poised to stab another individual. The lawsuit brought against Officer Redmond, the City of Hoffman Estates, and its police department by Carrie Jaffee, the administrator of the Allen estate, alleged that excessive force had been used. In the course of the legal proceedings, the family petitioned to obtain notes made by the therapist in counseling sessions with Officer Redmond after the incident. Redmond refused to provide consent, and the therapist refused to respond by providing notes. The judge in that case informed the jury to assume that the notes were unfavorable, and the jury found for the plaintiff. On appeal in the U.S. Court of Appeals for the 7th Circuit, the jury verdict was thrown out and the case was remanded for a new trial with the court opinion stating the trial court had erred by not protecting the confidentiality of the records. Jaffee appealed this decision to the U.S. Supreme Court, which in a ruling in *Jaffee v. Redmond* (1996) upheld a strict standard of privileged communication. This decision upheld the ability of licensed psychotherapists to maintain the confidences of their clients in federal court cases.

While the *Jaffee v. Redmond* ruling directly applies only within the federal court system, it does extend psychotherapist privilege to another group of licensed professionals, clinical social workers. Many believe that opens the door to the extension of that privilege to other mental health professionals. Each state has laws that govern the conditions and the relationships under which a communication is considered privileged. As such, each practitioner should check on the specific laws and court rulings defining the conditions of privilege for practitioners within their state of employment.

Extending the Duty to Protect

While the release of educational records under the conditions set forth in the FERPA generally require the informed consent of the parent or the student, if over 18, the need to breach confidence appears to extend to situations involving school counseling when the client appears to be in danger of harming himself or herself. In a court case, *Eisel v. Board of Education of Montgomery County* (1991), the Maryland Court of Appeals applied the duty to violate confidentiality to school counselors if a client is judged to be at risk for self-harm. In this case, a child threatened suicide in the presence of schoolmates. These schoolmates told both the parents of the child and the school counselor. The counselor interviewed the child, who denied the threat. The counselor did not follow up or notify the parents or school administration. The father sued the counselors and the school following the child's suicide, alleging breach of duty to intervene to prevent the suicide, and the court found in favor of the plaintiff (Anderson, 1996).

Extending *Tarasoff*

There have been many court cases that have used the *Tarasoff* ruling to find a "duty to warn." These court cases have attempted to further clarify the elements of *foreseeable danger* and *identifiable victim*. While the specifics of what defines foreseeable danger are still being debated, the courts have generally upheld that such foreseeable danger is present when there is a readily identifiable victim and the prediction of danger is based on professional standards, such as the existence of death threats, possession of a weapon, and the individual's having a clear plan of action. In *Emerich v. Philadelphia Center for Human Development* (1996), the Pennsylvania

Supreme Court held that, based upon the special relationship between a mental health professional and his or her patient, when the patient has communicated to the professional a specific and immediate threat of serious bodily injury against a specifically identified or readily identifiable third party, and the professional determines that his or her patient presents a serious danger of violence to the third party, then that professional bears a duty to exercise reasonable care to protect by warning the third party against such a danger (Tepper & Knapp, 1999). Several subsequent court decisions have expanded and clarified the duty to warn and protect from dangerous clients. For example, victims who are not specifically identified by the client but who could be considered foreseeable, likely targets of client violence (such as individuals in close proximity to an identifiable victim) should be warned according the ruling of *Hedlund v. Superior Court of Orange County* (1983) and *Jablonski Pahls v. United States* (1983).

Other court cases have extended this duty to warn even when the victim is not clearly identifiable. In *Lipari v. Sears, Roebuck & Co.* (1980), the court ruled that the therapist failed in the duty to protect others by not detaining a potentially violent client who had purchased a gun, even though no identifiable victim was named. And in a Vermont Supreme Court ruling in 1985 (*Peck v. Counseling Services of Addison County*), the *Tarasoff* duty to warn was extended to cases involving property—and not just personal-injury. In this case, the client was viewed as posing a serious risk of danger in that the client's intent of arson represented a "lethal threat to human beings who may be in the vicinity of the conflagration" (*Peck v. Counseling Services of Addison County*, 1985).

Keeping client rights in the forefront while considering the safety of third parties who may potentially be harmed, counselors need to consider how they will warn or protect within the confines of sound clinical judgment (Buckner & Firestone, 2000). Making use of consultations and second opinions when threats of violence occur as well as implementing an increase of therapy sessions are strategies to be considered when there are threats of violence (Buckner & Firestone, 2000).

Protecting the Practitioner

Violations of confidentiality and privilege are determined by statutes, court decisions, and professional codes of ethics. These violations may be responded to with criminal action, civil action, and/or professional sanctioning. However, because of the increasing court support for breach of confidentiality in the protection of others (identified or not), many confidentiality and privilege violations have legislation protecting mental health professionals from civil liability if they issue warnings in attempts to protect others from potential harm. The protection rests in the fact that such reporting is often mandated by the state. Moving the breach of confidentiality from permissive to mandatory protects the therapist from both civil and criminal liability, if they act in good faith (National Conference of State Legislatures, 2015). Because laws vary across the states, it is essential for the ethical helper to understand the laws existing in his or her state of employment that govern such disclosures and such protection.

● BEYOND PROFESSIONAL STANDARDS: A PERSONAL MORAL RESPONSE

As noted, confidentiality is essential to the nature of a helping relationship. Clients need to feel safe within the helping relationship and trust that their disclosures will be held in confidence. The ethical principle of confidentiality is founded on the fundamental respect for a client's privacy and the helper's concern for maintaining client welfare. This underlying respect for privacy and the valuing of the welfare of the client need to be more than simply the rationale for the ethical principle of confidentiality. Both need to be personal values.

The ethical professional, who values client privacy and welfare, will maintain that the breach of confidentiality is such a strong issue that the basis needs to be strong and justifiable. However, even with this as a personal value, balancing client need, professional ethics, and legal mandate is not always easy or clear. Thus it is essential for each ethical practitioner to keep current on the profession's stance and application of ethical principles and the laws governing practice and practice decisions. Specifically, each practitioner should commit to

- Knowing state laws mandating reporting or breaching of confidence
- Understanding thresholds and criteria for breach of confidence
- Providing disclosure to clients regarding the limitations to confidentiality
- Keeping thorough and detailed records
- Seeking consultation before disclosure
- Maintaining current knowledge of legal and ethical decisions guiding the disclosure of information
- Seeking ongoing education on the issue of confidentiality and its limits

Finally, fear of litigation or concerns about adhering to legal mandates can serve as the motivation for committing to each of the above. However, the ethical professional, one who has assimilated the ethical principle as personal value, will hold client well-being and welfare as the motive for such a commitment. A similar concern for the client's welfare can serve as the guiding light for all practice decisions regarding disclosure.

CONCLUDING CASE ILLUSTRATION ●

We began the chapter with Maria, the client in our ongoing case, giving Ms. Wicks, the counselor, permission to talk with Ms. Armstrong about her case. As you read the continuation of the dialogue, review Ms. Wicks's behavior as it reflects or fails to reflect the principles discussed within this chapter. Further, a number of brief questions are presented as a stimulus for the application of your knowledge regarding principles guiding confidentiality and its limitations.

Maria: It's okay. You can talk to Ms. Armstrong as long as you don't tell her who I am. I don't want anyone knowing what I told you. Besides, I thought talking to you was like talking to a priest in confession . . . you know, a major secret?

Ms. Wicks: Thank you for the permission to speak with Ms. Armstrong. Maria, I certainly don't want to break your confidence or reveal private conversations we may have had, but your welfare and your well-being are my primary concern, and I want to do all that I can do to keep you safe.

Maria: But you gotta promise me you ain't gonna tell her who I am.

Ms. Wicks: Remember the first day we met? I know you were angry and really didn't want to speak with me. But after a while you seemed to relax, and you started to share some of your story. Well, when we had that meeting, I told you that things we spoke about would be kept private. In fact, I said I wouldn't share information without your permission.

Maria: Yeah, I remember that . . . that's what I mean . . . you can't tell no one. . . .

Ms. Wicks: I'm glad you remember that. Maybe you also remember me saying that, while I will respect your privacy, some things just can't be private or confidential. I said if you are thinking about hurting yourself. . . .

Maria: I am not going to hurt myself . . . I know you said that, but it was no big deal, since I knew I wasn't planning on hurting myself. . . .

Ms. Wicks: Again, I am glad you remember that and I'm happy that you aren't thinking that you would like to hurt yourself. But, I also said that if you were thinking about hurting someone else that I may have to inform that person so that they could be protected and you would be safe, as well. Do you remember that?

Maria: Yeah . . . but, I'm not sure what this has to do with anything, now?

Ms. Wicks: Well, even though you are telling me that you have no intention of hurting yourself, I am very concerned that having unprotected sex with your boyfriend, who has AIDS, is endangering your life. And the truth is, I am not sure what I am supposed to do with this information. You know I want you to stop, 'cause I care about you. I'm just not sure if I have to tell someone else for legal reasons.

Maria: Legal reasons . . . it's my life. . . .

Reflections

1. Does Ms. Wicks give evidence of providing Maria with the limits to confidentiality early within the sessions?
2. In addition to discussing with a colleague and the principal, what else would you suggest Ms. Wicks do?
3. What would you do? Do Maria's actions constitute a basis for breaching confidence?
4. If Maria refuses to refrain from engaging in unprotected sex with her boyfriend, should Ms. Wicks continue to work with her? Would you?

● COOPERATIVE LEARNING EXERCISE

The purpose of this chapter was not only to introduce you to concepts of confidentiality and privileged communications but also to introduce you to the many elements complicating decisions to maintain or breach confidentiality. Translating theory to practice is not always an easy process.

Directions: Contact two professionals operating in one of the following roles and ask them the questions that are listed below. Discuss your findings with a supervisor, colleague, or classmate, looking for common approaches shared across professions:

- School counselor
- Licensed marriage and family therapist in private practice
- A mental health counselor
- A clinical social worker currently employed with a county agency
- A therapist who does custody evaluations in divorce cases

Questions:

1. When meeting with a new client, do you explain the concept of confidentiality? If so, do you also describe the limits to confidentiality or the conditions under which confidentiality may be breached? How do you present these issues?
2. Have you ever had your records subpoenaed? How did you respond?
3. Have you ever had a situation in which you believe a duty to warn existed? If so, what did you do? If not, what do you think you would do?
4. If you work with minors, how do you address the issue of confidentiality with them? With their parents?
5. In your professional role, do you have privilege? If so, have you ever called on privilege as a basis for not disclosing client information?

SUMMARY ●

- Confidentiality is the general standard of professional conduct that obligates a professional not to discuss information about the client with anyone.
- Privileged communication is a legal term that describes the quality of certain specific types of relationships that prevent information acquired from such relationships from being disclosed in court or other legal proceedings.
- Questions about who can claim the privilege, what type of information is privileged, and the limitations to privileges can vary extensively from state to state.
- Most human service professionals believe that without compelling reasons to breach it, confidentiality must be protected. Compelling

reasons for breaching confidence include preventing serious, foreseeable, and imminent harm to a client or other identifiable person, and when laws or regulations require disclosure without a client's consent.

- The *Jaffee v. Redmond* (1996) ruling extends psychotherapist privilege to another group of licensed professionals: clinical social workers. Many believe that this opens the door to the extension of that privilege to other mental health professionals.
- In *Eisel v. Board of Education of Montgomery County* (1991), the Maryland Court of Appeals applied the duty to violate confidentiality to school counselors if a client is judged to be at risk for self-harm.
- Several subsequent court decisions have expanded and clarified the duty to warn and protect from dangerous clients (see *Hedlund v. Superior Court,* 1983; *Jablonski Pahls v. United States,* 1983; *Lipari v. Sears, Roebuck & Co.,* 1980).
- *Peck v. Counseling Services of Addison County* (1985) expanded on *Tarasoff* to include the duty to warn in cases involving threat to property and not just personal injury.
- The ethical principle of confidentiality is founded on the fundamental respect of a client's privacy and the helper's concern for maintaining client welfare. It is essential for each ethical practitioner to embrace a value of client welfare and keep current on the profession's stance on and application of ethical principles and the laws governing practice and practice decisions.

● IMPORTANT TERMS

breach	Family Educational Rights and Privacy Act (FERPA)
Child Abuse Prevention and Treatment Act of 1974	foreseeable danger
client waiver	identifiable victim
confidentiality	imminent danger
constitutional	privileged communications
court order	protected relationships
duces tecum subpoena	right to privacy
duty to warn	*Tarasoff*

ADDITIONAL RESOURCES ●

Print

Kaplan, D., & Martz, E. (2014). New concepts in the *ACA code of ethics:* Distance counseling, technology and social media. *Counseling Today, 57*, 22-24.

U.S. Department of Health and Human Services. (2014). *Mandated reporters of child abuse and neglect.* Retrieved from https:www.childwelfare.gov/systemwide/laws_policies/statues/manda.pdf

VandeCreek, L., & Knapp, S. (2001). Tarasoff *and beyond: Legal and clinical considerations in the treatment of life-endangering patients.* Sarasota, FL, Professional Resource Press.

Wheeler, A. M. N., & Bertram, B. (2012). *The counselor and the law: A guide to legal and ethical practice* (6th ed.). Alexandria, VA: American Counseling Association.

Web-Based

Author. (n.d.). Risk management. ACA. Retrieved from http://www.counseling.org/knowledge-center/ethics/risk-management

Koocher, G. P., & Keith-Spiegel, P. (2013). "What should I do?"—39 ethical dilemmas involving confidentiality. [Continuing Ed Courses on the Internet]. Retrieved from http://www.continuingedcourses.net/active/courses/course049.php

Ostrowski, J. (2014). HIPPA compliance: What you need to know about the new HIPAA-HITECH rules. Retrieved from http://www.nbcc.org/assets/HIPPAA_Compliance.pdf

REFERENCES ●

Alghazo, R., Upton, T. D., & Cioe, N. (2011). Duty to warn versus duty to protect confidentiality: Ethical and legal considerations relative to individuals with AIDS/HIV. *Journal of Applied Rehabilitation Counseling, 42*, 43–49.

American Association for Marriage and Family Therapy. (2015). *Code of ethics.* Retrieved from http://www.aamft.org/iMIS15/AAMFT/Content/Legal_Ethics/Code_of_Ethics.aspx

American Counseling Association. (2014). *Code of ethics.* Alexandria, VA: Author.

American Psychological Association. (2000). *Duty to warn.* HIV/AIDS Office for Psychology Education (HOPE). Washington, DC: Author. Retrieved from http://www.apa.org.proxy- wcupa.klnpa.org/pi/aids/hope.html

American Psychological Association. (2010). *Ethical principles of psychologists and code of conduct.* Retrieved from: http://www.apa.org/ethics/code/principles .pdf

Anderson, B. S. (1996). *The counselor and the law* (4th ed.). Alexander, VA: American Counseling Association.

Behnke, S. H., & Warner, E. (2002). Confidentiality in the treatment of Adolescents. *Monitor on Psychology, 33*(3), 44. Retrieved from http://www.apa.org/monitor/ mar02/confidentiality.aspx

Buckner, F., & Firestone, M. (2000). "Where the public peril begins": 25 years after *TARASOFF. The Journal of Legal Medicine, 21*(2).

Child Abuse Prevention and Treatment Act (CAPTA) P. L. 93-247 (1974).

Child Abuse Prevention and Treatment (CAPTA) Reauthorization Act P. L. 111-320 (2010).

Corey, G., Corey, M., Corey, C., & Callahan, P. (2015). *Issues and ethics in the helping professions.* Pacific Grove, CA: Brooks/Cole.

Eisel v. Board of Education of Montgomery County, 68, 130,135 (1991).

Emerich v. Philadelphia Center for Human Development. Slip Opinion #J-253-96 (Pa. Sup. Ct., Dec 11, 1996).

English, A., & Kenney, K. E. (2003). *State minor consent laws: A Summary* (2nd ed.). Chapel Hill, NC: Center for Adolescent Health and the Law.

Evans-Marsh, J. (2003). Empirical support for the United States Supreme Court's protection of the psychotherapist–patient privilege. *Ethics & Behavior, 13*(4), 385–400.

The Family Educational Rights and Privacy Act (FERPA), 20 U.S.C. § 1232g; 34 CFR Part 99 (1974).

Haas, L. J., & Malouf, J. L. (2002). *Keeping up the good work: A practitioner's guide to mental health ethics* (2nd ed.). Sarasota, FL: Professional Resource Press.

Hedlund v. Superior Court of Orange County, 669, P.2d41,191 Cal. Rptr. 805 (1983).

Henderson, K. L. (2013). Mandated reporting of child abuse: Considerations and guidelines for mental health counselors. *Journal of Mental Health Counseling, 35*(4), 296–309.

Jablonski Pahls v. United States, 712 F. 2d 391 (1983).

Jaffee v. Redmond, 518 U.S. 1, 15 (U.S. 1996).

Koocher, G. P., & Keith-Spiegel, P. (2013). "What should I do?"—39 ethical dilemmas involving confidentiality. [Continuing Ed Courses on the Internet]. Retrieved from http://www.continuingedcourses.net/active/courses/course049.php

Kurpius, D. J. (1997). *Current ethical issues in the practice of psychology.* The Hartherleigh Guide Series (Vol. 10, pp. 1-16). New York: Hatherleigh Press.

Lipari v Sears, Roebuck & Co., 497 F. Supp. 185 (D. Neb. 1980).

National Association of Social Workers. (2008). *Code of ethics* (Rev. ed.). Retrieved from http://www.socialworkers.org/pubs/code/code.asp

National Conference of State Legislatures. (2015). Mental Health Professionals' Duty to Warn. Retrieved from http://www.ncsl.org/research/health/mental-health-professionals-duty-to- warn.aspx

Peck v. Counseling Services of Addison County, 499 A.2d422 (Vt., 1985).

Remley, T. P., & Herlihy, B. (2014). *Ethical, legal and professional issues in counseling* (4th ed.). Upper Saddle River, NJ: Pearson/Merrill Prentice Hall.

Sheperis, D. S., Henning, S. L., & Kocet, M. M. (2016). *Ethical decision making for the 21st century counselor*. Thousand Oaks, CA: Sage.

Tarasoff v. The Regents of the University of California, 551 P.2d 334 (Cal. Sup. Ct., 1976).

Tepper, A. M., & Knapp, S. (1999). Pennsylvania recognizes an affirmative duty to warn third party victims. *The Pennsylvania Psychologist Quarterly, 8,* 29.

U.S. Department of Education. (2015). *Family Educational Rights and Privacy Act (FERPA)*. http://www2.ed.gov/policy/gen/guid/fpco/ferpa/index.html

U.S. Department of Health and Human Services, Administration for Children and Families, Administration on Children, Youth and Families, Children's Bureau. (2016). *Child maltreatment 2014*. Retrieved from http://www.acfhhs.gov/programs/cb/stats_research/index.htm#can

Webber, D. W. (1999). *AIDS and the law: 1999 cumulative supplement* (3rd ed.). New York: Panel.

CHAPTER **10**

Boundaries and the Ethical Use of Power

Ms. Wicks: But Maria. I do care about you. I am worried you are placing yourself in harm's way. If it would be easier for you, I would be willing to let you stay with me for a while.

Certainly Ms. Wicks is a very caring and concerned counselor. Ms. Wicks has consistently demonstrated a real care and concern as well as a desire to help. However, it appears that her level of concern and her felt sense of urgency about the situation may be clouding her professional judgment. Knowing the boundaries of a professional relationship and being able to operate within those boundaries while expressing professional care and concern is not always an easy process. The power of the helping relationship can be quite awesome and often times seductive. When such power is not restricted by the boundaries of the professional relationship, it invites misuse and abuse of the client.

OBJECTIVES ●

The chapter will introduce you to the concept of professional boundaries and the conditions under which boundary crossing and violation may occur. After reading this chapter, you should be able to do the following:

- Describe what is meant by the concept of professional boundaries.
- Describe the difference between boundary violation and boundary crossing.
- Explain how simple identification and transference can interfere with the maintenance of professional boundaries.
- Describe what is meant by "dual" or "multiple" relationships.
- List questions for reflection that can guide a practitioner's decisions regarding the ethics of dual relationship.
- Explain why sexual intimacy with a client is clearly a boundary violation.

● SETTING AND MAINTAINING PROFESSIONAL BOUNDARIES

A professional relationship is a special entity. The professional relationship is definable and does require unique dynamic and role definition. However, the intensity of the emotions shared, the isolation provided, and the level of intimacy sometimes experienced can challenge the boundaries of a professional relationship. Under these conditions, it is possible for ethical problems to occur as the helper blends professional role and relationship with more personal involvement. The concepts of boundaries and boundary violations have received increased attention as a result of the increasing litigation and ethics committee hearings related to violation of boundaries (Parsons & Zhang, 2014). Setting and maintaining professional boundaries are essential steps in preventing such personal involvement and the maintenance of an ethical relationship. But the issues involved with the setting and maintaining of professional boundaries is neither clear-cut nor black and white. For example, the American Counseling Association's *Code of Ethics* (2014) does not strictly prohibit extending the nature of the boundaries between counselor and client but rather directs its members to: "consider the risks and benefits of extending current counseling relationships beyond conventional parameters" (ACA, 2014, Principle A.6.b). While there are numerous terms used to discuss the issue of boundaries and boundary extensions in professional practice, two terms, *boundary violations* and *boundary crossing*, appear to dominate the literature.

Fasasi & Olowu (2013) suggest a distinction between boundary violations and boundary crossing. While both involve a counselor's deviation from strict adherence to a professional role, boundary violations typically result in the exploitation of a client. Boundary violations, such as what occurs when helpers become sexually involved with clients, are almost always harmful; however, nonsexual boundary transgressions may be just as harmful.

When the practitioner's needs are given primacy at the client's expense, it is unethical. Whether it is something as subtle as the rearrangement of furniture or seating arrangement in order to bring the helper into closer physical proximity to an attractive client or a pause in the conversation that may be inferred as having sexual innuendo, decisions by practitioners that are directed to satisfy their professional needs at the expense of the client are violations of professional boundaries and need to be avoided (see Case Illustration 10.1).

Case Illustration 10.1

Changing Seats: Moving Closer

Allison, a 32-year-old recent divorcee, has been working with Dr. Manel for the past 5 weeks. Their sessions have been focusing on Allison's sense of grief and her anxiety about establishing or reestablishing herself as a single woman.

For each of the past five sessions, Allison sat on the sofa with Dr. Manel directly across from her in a large overstuffed chair. Allison has, in each of the previous sessions, disclosed fears that she is not attractive and would often break down in tears when she considered the possibility of being alone. At these times, Dr. Manel would allow Allison to cry and, when appropriate, would challenge her conclusions that she would forever be alone.

Allison entered the current session more upset than she had been in the previous three or four. Allison sat and shared with Dr. Manel that she had just received divorce papers and that she wanted to die. Allison began to sob and stated, "I can't stand this! He doesn't love me. No one could ever love me. . . ."

At this point, Dr. Manel moved from his chair and took up a seat on the couch next to Allison. As soon as he sat down, Allison flung her arms about his neck, placing her head on his shoulder. Dr. Manel, wiping her tears, stated, "I think you are lovable."

In reviewing the case of Allison and Dr. Manel (Case Illustration 10.1), one must wonder whether Dr. Manel's change in seating and verbal comment were meant simply to support a client in crisis or were in response to his own interest in physical contact.

While such crossing of professional boundaries is clearly unethical, the extension of boundaries in the form of boundary crossing is less clear in its ethical implications. Boundary crossing places the helper outside of a strict professional role; however, it does not occur with the intent of client exploitation (Parsons & Zhang, 2014).

Boundary crossing occurs when the helper finds herself simultaneously operating from both a professional and nonprofessional role. This might be the case when a school counselor receives and accepts an invitation to attend her client's graduation party or even when unexpectedly she finds herself at a social gathering with a client. In these situations, what was once a professional helper-client relationship may now have moved to a casual social encounter.

It is important that as professional helpers we monitor the nature of the relationship we have with our clients and take steps to ensure that the boundaries are those that reflect our standard of ethics and clearly serve to uphold the welfare and dignity of our clients (Kitchener & Anderson, 2011). Accepting gifts from clients, participating in social activities or events provided by the client, engaging in investment activities or bartering professional services for goods or client service all blur the boundaries of a professional practice. Throughout these situations, it is essential we reflect on the question of "whose needs are being met?" Clearly, placing the personal needs of the helper above that of the client invites unethical practice. Identifying whose needs are being met by the decisions and actions of the helpers will help to identify the potential for boundary violation. It is essential that our primary goal is to do that which is in the best interest of the client (Gutheil & Brodksy, 2008) and remember "that in choosing our profession we made a decision to serve others and have our needs met by those whom we do not we serve; we will fulfill our professional obligations" (Gottlieb & Younggren, 2009, p. 570). All of our professional codes of ethics highlight the need to attend to the issue of boundaries and the need to assure that we protect against the creation of an exploitative relationship and eventual harm to our clients (see Table 10.1.)

Table 10.1 Boundaries and Mixing of Multiple Relationships

Professional Ethical Standards	Statement on Multiple Relationships
American Counseling Association (2014)	A.6.b. Extending counseling boundaries Counselors consider the risks and benefits of extending current counseling relationships beyond conventional parameters. Examples include attending a client's formal ceremony (e.g., a wedding/commitment ceremony or graduation), purchasing a service or product provided by a client (excepting unrestricted bartering), and visiting a client's ill family member in the hospital. In extending these boundaries, counselors take appropriate professional precautions such as informed consent, consultation, supervision, and documentation to ensure that judgement is not impaired and no harm occurs.

Professional Ethical Standards	Statement on Multiple Relationships
	A.5.d. Friends or family members Counselors are prohibited from engaging in counseling relationships with friends or family members with whom they have an inability to remain objective. A.5.b. Counselors are prohibited from engaging in counseling relationships with persons with whom they have had a previous sexual and/or romantic relationship. A.5.e. Counselors are prohibited from engaging in a personal virtual relationship with individuals with whom they have a current counseling relationship (e.g., through social and other media).
American Association for Marriage and Family Therapy (2015)	1.3. Marriage and family therapists are aware of their influential positions with respect to clients, and they avoid exploiting the trust and dependency of such persons. Therapists, therefore, make every effort to avoid conditions and multiple relationships with clients that could impair professional judgment or increase the risk of exploitation. Such relationships include but are not limited to business or close personal relationships with a client or the client's immediate family. When the risk of impairment or exploitation exists due to conditions or multiple roles, therapists document the appropriate precautions taken.
American Psychological Association (2010)	3.05 Multiple relationships a. A multiple relationship occurs when a psychologists is in a professional role with a person and (1) at the same time is in another role with the same person, (2) at the same time is in a relationship with a person closely associated with or related to the person with whom the psychologist has the professional relationship, or (3) promises to enter into another relationship in the future with the person or a person closely associated with or related to the person. A psychologist refrains from entering into a multiple relationship if the multiple relationship could reasonably be expected to impair the psychologist, or otherwise risks exploitation or harm to the person with whom the professional relationship exists. Multiple relationships that would not reasonably be expected to cause impairment or risk exploitation or harm are not unethical.

(Continued)

Table 10.1   (Continued)

Professional Ethical Standards	Statement on Multiple Relationships
	b. If psychologist finds that, due to unforeseen factors, a potentially harmful multiple relationship has arisen, the psychologist takes reasonable steps to resolve it with due regard for the best interests of the affected person and maximal compliance with the Ethics Code.
	c. When psychologists are required by law, institutional policy, or extraordinary circumstances to serve in more than one role in judicial or administrative proceedings, at the outset they clarify role expectations and the extent of confidentiality and thereafter as changes occur.

● PROFESSIONAL OBJECTIVITY: ESSENTIAL TO PROFESSIONAL BOUNDARIES

The effective, ethical helper places the concerns and needs of the client as top priority. Placing the client's concerns as a priority (i.e., altruism) rather than the concerns of the helper (i.e., narcissism) requires the helper to distinguish his or her personal issues and emotional needs from those presented by the client. The ability to be empathic, while emotionally objective, may be difficult to maintain. However, if the helper's objectivity becomes compromised, the professional nature of the relationship may be threatened. The ethical helper must be aware of the various situations that can compromise professional objectivity and know when referral to another helper, who can maintain objectivity, is indicated.

Professional objectivity can be compromised by a number of situations (see Exercise 10.1). While some, such as simple identification and transference, reflect a distortion of reality on the part of the helper, a more common form stems from the development of a dual relationship with the client involving both a professional and personal tone. Each of these conditions is discussed in some detail.

Simple Identification

A subtle form of loss of emotional objectivity is simple identification. Simple identification occurs when the helper identifies himself or herself

Exercise 10.1

Threats to Emotional Objectivity

Directions: After considering each of the following, share your response with your colleagues or classmates in order to identify ways of preventing such loss of objectivity.

1. Identify one person with whom you have a personal relationship and discuss how that relationship could block your emotional objectivity and thus interfere with you being an effective helper.

2. How might your own social roles (e.g., son, daughter, mother, father, ex-boyfriend, girlfriend, struggling student, etc.) be the source of interference and loss of objectivity when working with some clients or specific types of problems?

3. Identify a number of themes or issues that arouse an emotional response in you (e.g., themes of emotional dependency, victimization, authority, power, etc.) and which might prove too close to your own emotional experience for you to remain objective while working with a client presenting similar concerns.

with the client. It typically occurs when some element or characteristic of the client or the client's experience and story, causes the helper to relate to the client's experience as his or her own. Under these conditions, that helper can begin to view the client as himself or herself (see Case Illustration 10.2) and thus fails to discern the important difference between his or her experience and that of the client.

Case Illustration 10.2

Mr. Watkins: A Case of Simple Identification

Mr. Watkins was an elementary school counselor. One student with whom he had special concern was Jamal. He felt Jamal needed his help because the other fifth-grade boys "always teased Jamal and pushed him and took his things." According to Mr. Watkins, the other boys were always mean to Jamal. Mr. Watkins was absolutely sure that Jamal

(Continued)

(Continued)

was devastated by all of this. Well, the reality was that Jamal was fine. In fact, Jamal went to Dr. Thomas, the director of counseling, and asked that Mr. Watkins stop calling him down to the office. Jamal felt it was embarrassing, and he didn't understand why Mr. Watkins kept telling him that he "could protect me from the bullies in school." Apparently, while the boys certainly did tease Jamal, he teased the other boys as much as they teased him, and the fifth graders generally liked Jamal and included him in their activities.

Mr. Watkins's (Case Illustration 10.2) objectivity was certainly compromised, and his pursuit of Jamal was a violation of his professional boundaries. The problem was that Mr. Watkins was not "seeing" Jamal as he was but rather was seeing himself in Jamal's experience. Jamal looked like Mr. Watkins. He was small and somewhat frail looking. He wore thick glasses and appeared nonathletic. Because Mr. Watkins "identified" with Jamal on the basis of physical similarity, his emotional objectivity was destroyed, and he assumed that what happened to him as a fifth grader was most likely happening to Jamal.

Clearly, such loss of emotional objectivity needs to be identified and confronted if one is to be an effective, ethical helper. Exercise 10.2 provides you with an opportunity to anticipate the conditions under which you may fall prey to simple identification.

Exercise 10.2

Condition Eliciting Helper Identification

Directions: As noted, simple identification occurs when the helper identifies himself or herself with the client. It typically occurs when some element or characteristic of the client or the client's experience and story causes the helper to relate to the client's experience as his or her own. Below you will find a number of descriptors of client characteristics or client issues. Place a check mark next to those characteristics or elements with which you have some personal experience or history. Next, identify how your identification with that element may influence your objectivity.

Element or Characteristics	Helper Experience or Characteristics	Impact on Helper Objectivity
(Example): Client is a freshman in college. His father wants him to be an engineer and join his firm. The client wants to be a music major but is afraid to upset his dad. He is thinking that he could double major, recognizing that he does like engineering and may be able to use the music as a performance option.	Helper was a star athlete in high school. His father has always prepped him to play in college, even though he did not want to play in college. The helper still resents the fact that he went to the college his dad wanted him to and played football there though he truly did not enjoy it.	The helper is extremely confrontational with the client. The helper suggests that compromising and doing a double major is a failure of mature assertiveness. The helper keeps pushing the client to confront his father and simply say NO, it is my time to define my life.
1. Client experiencing a personal loss (via divorce or death or breakup)		
2. A client who has been teased for being overweight, underweight, an early developer, or a late developer		
3. A client who is in an unhappy relationship or work situation		
4. A client who is the one in the family to whom every one turns when there is a problem		

(Continued)

(Continued)

Element or Characteristics	Helper Experience or Characteristics	Impact on Helper Objectivity
5. A person who is currently having sexual difficulties (impotence, premature ejaculation, low libido, limited opportunity, etc.)		
6. A person whose beliefs (religious, political, sexual) have brought a sense of isolation		
7. Identify a significant experience in your life, and in the space to the right identify a type of client or client condition with which you may identify.		

Transference

A more complex distortion occurs with transference. In this case, the helper forces the story of the client to fit some aspect of his or her own life. This is a major distortion of reality and occurs below the conscious level of the person distorting. It often results in the person, in this case the helper, using the context of the helping relationship and presence of the client to express feelings, beliefs, or desires that the helper has buried in his or her unconscious and rightfully should address to some other significant person in his or her life. The ability to be sensitive to the possibility of transference is essential to effective, ethical helping.

While the loss of objectivity as a result of distorting the client's reality, as in the case with simple identification and transference, may be infrequent, any helpers are at the risk of losing emotional objectivity if engaged in direct personal involvement with clients. The possibility of engaging with the client in a relationship outside of the boundaries of helping is a topic that has received a lot of attention within the professional literature. The ethics of such dual relationships with clients has been and continues to be debated. It is clear, however, whichever side of the debate one finds himself or herself on, dual relationships may serve as a condition in which one's professional objectivity can be compromised.

Dual Relationships: Crossing and/or Mixing Boundaries

A dual relationship is one in which the helper has two (or more) overlapping roles with the client. It is important to consider dual relationships and to reflect on the possible impact they may have on the counseling relationship (Exercise 10.3).

Loss of professional objectivity and boundary violations are possible anytime a professional is engaged in multiple relationships with his or her client. This may also occur when professional helpers are engaged in personal friendships, family or business relationships, or social activities with their clients (see Case Illustration 10.3).

Case Illustration 10.3

Tom and Elaine: Direct Personal Involvement

Tom is a master's level counselor working in a college career center. Elaine asked Tom to help her with a decision about joining the Peace Corps. Elaine, who is also Tom's girlfriend, explained that she really is unsure if she should move away from their hometown to spend four years in the Peace Corps or stay at home and continue in graduate school.

Tom suggested that Elaine employ an actuarial technique in which she would generate all of the costs and benefits to be accrued to both Elaine AND the significant people in her life if she stays or goes into the Peace Corps. This was a technique Tom had found successful with other clients. Typically, he would provide an initial example and then ask clients to complete the process on their own as a "homework." He would then review their matrixes at the next session. With Elaine, however, Tom suggested that they do it together. He felt that he could help identify the possible benefits and costs to both Elaine AND, certainly, to the others in her life.

While Tom (Case Illustration 10.3) may truly want to assist Elaine in making the best decision (for her), he may have difficulty keeping his own strong desire to keep her close to him and at home out of the equation. Thus, his suggestions may be aimed more at meeting his needs for a personal relationship than at Elaine's need to make the best vocational choice. Under this situation, the dual nature of their relationship (i.e., love relationship and helping relationship) is contaminating the helping process.

It appears that while all professional codes of conduct warn about the risk of dual relationships (see Table 10.2), not all within the professions are as clear-cut about the evils of dual relationships or if sanctions should be applied. For example, Zur (2015) has suggested that engaging in limited personal connections can be helpful as an integral part of a treatment plan. For example, consider the value of giving a supportive hug to a grieving client, accepting a small termination gift from a client whose culture dictates such gift giving, or even flying in an airplane with a patient who suffers from a fear of flying. Clearly, it is essential for the professional helper to monitor all engagement in boundary modifications and extensions to ensure that the needs of the clients are being served as the primary outcome.

Table 10.2   Codes Restricting Nonsexual Dual Relationships

Professional Ethical Standards	Statement Regarding Dual Relationship
American Psychological Association (2010)	3.06. Conflict of interest Psychologists refrain from taking on a professional role when personal, scientific, professional, legal, financial, or other interests or relationships could reasonably be expected to (1) impair their objectivity, competence, or effectiveness in performing their functions as psychologists or (2) expose the person or organization with whom the professional relationship exists to harm or exploitation.
National Association of Social Workers (2008)	1.06. Conflicts of interest c. Social workers should not engage in dual or multiple relationships with clients or former clients in which there is a risk of exploitation or potential harm to the client. In instances when dual or multiple relationships are unavoidable, social workers should take steps to protect clients and are responsible for setting clear, appropriate, and culturally sensitive boundaries. (Dual or multiple relationships occur when social workers relate to clients in more than one relationship, whether professional, social, or business. Dual or multiple relationships can occur simultaneously or consecutively.)

Professional Ethical Standards	Statement Regarding Dual Relationship
American Counseling Association (2014)	A.6.e. Nonprofessional interactions or relationships Counselors avoid entering into non-professional relationships with former clients, their romantic partners, or their family members when the interaction is potentially harmful to the client. This applies to both in-person and electronic interactions or relationships.
American Association for Marriage and Family Therapy (2015)	1.3. Therapists, therefore, make every effort to avoid conditions and multiple relationships with clients that could impair professional judgment or increase the risk of exploitation.

While caution is advised, it is clear that there is no one directive to which practitioners can turn for guidance in terms of boundary extension and the engagement in dual relationships. Exercise 10.3 is provided to assist you in gaining the perspective of your local professional community in regard to the ethics of dual relationships.

Exercise 10.3

The Ethics of Dual Relationships

Directions: Using the questions listed below, assess the perception of the professionals in your area in regard to the ethics of dual relationships. If possible, contact a representative from each of the following professions and share your findings with a colleague or classmate. The professions include school counselor, marriage counselor, clinical social worker, licensed psychologist, and psychiatrist.

Questions:

1. Have you ever had a professional helping relationship with a friend? A relative? A close professional associate?

2. What are you feelings about the ethics or ethical challenges confronting a professional helper when working with a friend, relative, or colleague?

3. Would you ever engage in a business venture or investment with an active client?

(Continued)

(Continued)

4. What are your feelings about professional helpers who engage in sexual intimacies with a client while still in a helping relationship with that client?

5. What would you do if you were aware that a professional helper, in your locale, was engaged in a sexual relationship with a client?

6. What length of time, if any, needs to pass between the end of a helping relationship and the freedom to date and become emotionally and physically intimate with a previous client?

Once again it is important to highlight that the position taken here is that it is not the existence of duality that is the problem but the possibility that such duality will invite exploitation of the client. As such, each case should arouse concern and vigilance on the part of the ethical helper in order to ensure that exploitation does not occur. It is incumbent on the ethical practitioner to consult with colleagues, supervisors, and even the research whenever experiencing boundary extension and to employ a consistent model for ethical decision-making (see Chapter 7).

Kitchener and Anderson (2011), while echoing many of the steps found in multiple ethical decision-making models, offers the following as fundamental considerations to be taken prior to engaging in any form of professional boundary extension. These considerations or direction include the following:

- Taking a moment of reflection: Consider the benefits of such a boundary extension. To what degree is the relationship improved and the possibility of service to the client increased?
- Facts: What are the specific facts directing the desire to extend the boundaries? Would these have directed the clinician to do the same with other clients?
- Options: In exploring costs and benefits, what other options are available and potentially less costly?
- Include the client in the review of costs and benefits and the decisions to be made.
- Identify the ethical codes and legal issues involved or implicated.
- Document the process and outcome of the decision-making.
- Review and reassess the outcome or impact of decisions, making adjustments in service of ethical helping.

Sexual Intimacy: A Clear Violation of Professional Boundaries

The depth of intimacy and the conditions surrounding the interaction found in a helping relationship may stimulate feelings of attraction between the helper and client. For helpers, acting on this attraction is a serious ethical violation. Sexual relationships of any kind are unethical in the helping setting/context. All professional organizations are very clear about prohibition of sexual intimacy between a helper and a client (see Table 10.3).

The inappropriateness of a sexual relationship between helper and client rests in the fact that the helping relationship is unbalanced in power and dependency issues. Thus, the reciprocal natural characteristics of a healthy intimate relationship are not possible. When sexual contact becomes part of a therapeutic relationship, the expectation of trust that is fundamental to the process of therapy is violated.

Table 10.3 Intimate Relationships With Clients

Professional Ethical Standards	*Statement on Intimate Relationships*
American Counseling Association (2014)	A 5.a. Sexual and/or romantic relationships prohibited
	Sexual and/or romantic counselor-client relationships with current clients, their romantic partners, or their family members are prohibited. This prohibition applies to both in person and electronic interactions or relationships.
	A.5.c. Sexual and/or romantic relationships with former clients
	Sexual and/or romantic counselor client interactions or relationships with former clients, their romantic partners, or their family members are prohibited for a period of 5 years following the last professional contact. This prohibition applies to both in person and electronic interactions or relationships. Counselors, before engaging in sexual and/or romantic interactions or relationships with former clients, their romantic partners, or their family members, demonstrate forethought and document (in written form) whether the interaction or relationship can be viewed as exploitive in any way and/or whether there is still potential to harm the former client; in cases of potential exploitation and/or harm, the counselor avoids entering into such an interaction or relationship.

(Continued)

Table 10.3   (Continued)

Professional Ethical Standards	Statement on Intimate Relationships
American Psychological Association (2010)	3.08. Exploitative relationships a. Psychologists do not exploit persons over whom they have supervisory, evaluative, or other authority such as clients/patients, students, supervisees, research participants, and employees. (See also Standards 3.05 multiple relationships; 6.04 fees and financial arrangements; 6.05 barter with clients/patients; 7.07 sexual intimacies with students and supervisees; 10.05 sexual intimacies with current therapy clients/patients; 10.06 sexual intimacies with relatives or significant others of current therapy clients/patients; 10.07 therapy with former sexual partners; and 10.08 sexual intimacies with former therapy clients/patients.) 7.07 Sexual relationships with students and supervisees Psychologists do not engage in sexual relationships with students or supervisees who are in their department, agency, or training center or over whom psychologists have or are likely to have evaluative authority. 10.06. Sexual intimacies with relatives or significant others of current therapy clients/patients Psychologists do not engage in sexual intimacies with individuals they know to be close relatives, guardians, or significant others of current clients/patients. Psychologists do not terminate therapy to circumvent this standard. 10.07. Therapy with former sexual partners Psychologists do not accept as therapy clients/patients persons with whom they have engaged in sexual intimacies. 10.08. Sexual intimacies with former therapy clients/patients a. Psychologists do not engage in sexual intimacies with former clients/patients for at least two years after cessation or termination of therapy. b. Psychologists do not engage in sexual intimacies with former clients/patients even after two-year interval except in the most unusual circumstances. Psychologists who engage in such activity after the two years following cessation or termination of therapy and of having no sexual contact with the former client/ patient bear the burden of demonstrating that there has been no exploitation, in light of all relevant factors, including

Professional Ethical Standards	Statement on Intimate Relationships
	(1) the amount of time that has passed since therapy terminated; (2) the nature, duration, and intensity of the therapy; (3) the circumstances of termination; (4) the client's/patient's personal history; (5) the client's /patient's current mental status; (6) the likelihood of adverse impact on the client/patient; and (7) any statements or actions made by the therapist during the course of therapy suggesting or inviting the possibility of a posttermination sexual or romantic relationship with the client/patient.
American Association for Marriage and Family Therapy (2015)	1.4. Sexual intimacy with current clients or with known members of the client's family system is prohibited. 1.5. Sexual intimacy with former clients or with known members of the client's family system is prohibited.
National Association of Social Workers (2008)	1.09.a. Social workers should, under no circumstances, engage in sexual activities or sexual contact with current clients, whether such contact is consensual or forced.

In addition to barring intimate sexual contact within a helping context, most codes of behavior also speak to the restriction of sexual behavior between a helper and client after the helping relationship has ended. Some, for example, the APA (2010), suggest that a period of 2 years pass before a personal relationship may be entered, or the ACA (2014) suggests a period of 5 years.

While it should be obvious that sexual contact with one's client is unethical, it is also important for all clinicians to be mindful of the danger that can result from "innocent" comments about a client's appearance, manner of dress, or physique. The power of sexual or physical attraction of client to counselor or counselor to client can be both subtle and compelling. When it comes to a feeling of attraction to one's client, it is essential that the helper engage in consultation, supervision, or even personal therapy. It is possible that a simple comment, such as "that is a wonderful looking blouse," can lead down a slippery slope to boundary violations (Sheperis, Henning, & Kocet, 2016).

LEGAL DECISIONS ●

Arguments for the unethical nature of dual relationships usually highlight the fact that a helping relationship is one in which there is a power imbalance and one in which the client may be extremely vulnerable (*Norberg v. Wynrib*, 1992). The unethical nature of dual relationships reflects the courts' view that the helping relationships (i.e., physician-patient, psychiatrist-patient, and social worker-client) are of a fiduciary nature (*McInerney v. MacDonald*, 1992), fiduciary meaning that the professional has a duty to act to the benefit of the other individual in any matters related to an undertaking between them (Black, 1991). Since a fiduciary relationship has been defined as occurring when an individual places his or her trust in a party who has the potential to influence his or her actions (Black, 1991), it could be reasonably argued that all professional helping relationships have this fiduciary potential. The courts, however, have not made de facto rulings on the fiduciary nature of each professional relationship. Rather, rulings have suggested that it is the specific nature of each relationship that determines the existence of a fiduciary responsibility (*Hodgkinson v. Simms*, 1994; *M. (K.) v. M. (H.)*, 1992; *McInerney v. MacDonald*, 1992).

If the fiduciary obligation exists, it could be argued that the practitioner is obliged

- to act with good faith and loyalty toward a client (*McInerney v. MacDonald*, 1992);
- to not abuse the power imbalance by exploiting the client (*Norberg v. Wynrib*, 1992); and
- to act in the best interest of the client (*Hodgkinson v. Simms*, 1994; *M. (K.) v. M. (H.).*, 1992).

Given the conditions of a fiduciary relationship, it is clear that any sexual contact between a helper and a client is in violation of these conditions. Such sexual contact is also subject to civil law as a tort (i.e., offenders may be sued for malpractice), and some states have criminalized the offense. At least 23 states criminalize sexual contact between psychotherapists and clients, and nearly all of these states classify the violations as felony offenses. Further, in these states, the power differential and possible vulnerability of the client to influence makes consent by the client viewed as no defense.

● BEYOND PROFESSIONAL STANDARDS: A PERSONAL MORAL RESPONSE

Sexual misconducts, while being one of the most serious ethical issues, continue to occur (Gottlieb & Younggren, 2009). Thus, while ethical standards are in place that address professional boundaries and ethical use of power, enactment of these standards within the client-helper relationship is less than perfect.

It is clear that more than simply having an awareness of the ethical codes of conduct is needed. Practitioners need to embrace this standard as a personal moral response. As with each of the ethical principles, respect and valuing of the client and client well-being serve as the preventive base for most ethical abuses. Keeping client needs as primary in the relationship can prove invaluable for maintaining appropriate boundaries and use of power within the helping relationship.

In addition to understanding codes of ethics governing the creation and maintenance of professional boundaries, the ethical practitioner needs to continually appraise his or her own personal needs and to monitor how these may impact the nature of his or her helping relationships. For example, in addressing sexual misconduct, Stake and Oliver (1991) recommended a multifaceted approach highlighting the importance of sensitizing and training therapists to their own sexuality and the power of the helping relationship.

In addition to increasing a clinician's awareness of personal needs and the power that comes from the helping relationship, it is also essential to move from an ethics of avoiding misconduct to positive ethics (Handelsman, Knapp, & Gottlieb, 2002). This directs the practitioner to that which is truly reflecting their value of care and concern for the welfare of the client. A focus on embracing such "positive ethics" brings a "shift of emphasis from avoiding professional misconduct to a more balanced and integrative approach that includes encouraging [the helper] to aspire to their highest ethical potential" (Handelsman et al., p.731).

The need to be aware of self and relationships is essential in order to create and maintain appropriate professional boundaries. Ethical practitioners will be aware of their decisions to depart from what is typical and be able to explain the therapeutic reasons for such departures. The question that needs to be answered, especially at times of departure from typical or model procedures is "Whose need is being served?" It is this type of self-questioning, if assimilated into the practitioner's approach to all clients, that will help move issues of boundaries and power from ethical guidelines to a personal, moral response.

CONCLUDING CASE ILLUSTRATION ●

At the beginning of the chapter, we see Ms. Wicks expressing her concern for Maria. The question one needs to ask is, is this level of concern and type of behavior well within the boundaries of a professional counseling relationship?

As you read the continuation of the dialogue, ask yourself, whose needs are being met? Further, after reading the presentation, use the reflections to begin to conceptualize how you would respond in a situation such as this.

Ms.Wicks: But Maria, I do care about you. I am worried you are placing yourself in harm's way. If it would be easier for you, I would be willing to let you stay with me for a while.

Maria: Stay with you?

Ms. Wicks: Well, I mean, sometimes it is easier to get away from a guy like Carlos, when you can get out of the area.

Maria: I don't need to get away from Carlos, I love him.

Ms. Wicks: Sometimes, Maria, we romanticize our relationships, and we feel like it is love. It is just our way of justifying having sex with somebody. I know . . . I almost ruined my life by quitting school and running away with a high school sweetheart just because I lost my virginity to him. It's real easy to think you love someone when it is only lust.

Maria: Well, I'm not sure what you are talking about. I love Carlos and he loves me. I don't need to run away from him.

Ms. Wicks: I know it seems like love, but trust me, Maria, if you could step back and get away for just a little while, you would see it differently.

Maria: Ms. Wicks . . . I like you, but . . . you are wrong here. Anyway . . . how did we get talking about this? I thought we were talking about you telling Ms. Armstrong about me having sex or something?

Reflections

1. What is your feeling about Ms. Wicks's invitation to come and live with her for a while? Why?
2. Do you feel it is appropriate for Ms. Wicks to share her own high school story of romance? Why? Why not?
3. Is Ms. Wicks exhibiting the effects of simple identification or simply demonstrating her real personal understanding of Maria's situation?

COOPERATIVE LEARNING EXERCISE •

As suggested within this chapter, while the need to create and maintain professional boundaries is essential to an ethical helping relationship, boundary violations do occur. Often boundaries are crossed and inappropriate helper behavior is manifested as a result of the helper's loss of emotional objectivity.

Part 1: Review each of the following scenarios and along with a classmate or colleague, identify where the loss of emotional objectivity may exist and how boundary violations may be manifested.

> Helper 1: A marriage counselor currently going through her own very painful divorce

> Helper 2: A young, attractive school counselor working with senior high school honors students

> Helper 3: A drug and alcohol counselor who himself has been an addict and who has recently returned to drinking

Part II: Interview three professional helpers, asking the following questions:

1. During your professional career, have you experienced any major life crises (e.g., death of a loved one, loss of a job, divorce)?
2. (For those who have experienced such life crises) during that time, what adjustments to your professional work did you make, if any?
3. (For those who have not experienced such a crisis) if you were to experience one of these life crises, would you adjust your approach to your professional work during the time of the crisis. If so, how and why? If not, why not?

Share your findings with a colleague and discuss the implications of the responses in light of the content of this chapter.

SUMMARY •

- All professional codes of ethics attend to the issue of boundaries and the need to assure nonexploitation of the client through boundary crossing and the mixing of multiple relationships.
- All boundary crossings (i.e., departure from commonly accepted professional roles and practices) can become problematic and need to be

avoided. Any boundary violation in which the practitioner's needs are given primacy at the client's expense is unethical.

- The effective, ethical helper places the concerns and needs of the client as top priority. Placing the client's concerns as a priority (i.e., altruism) rather than the concerns of the helper (i.e., narcissism) requires the helper to distinguish his or her personal issues and emotional needs from those presented by the client.
- Professional objectivity can be compromised by a number of situations. While some, such as simple identification and transferences, reflect a distortion of reality on the part of the helper, a more common form stems from the development of a dual relationship with the client, involving both a professional and personal tone.
- A dual relationship is one in which the helper has two (or more) overlapping roles with the client. While all professional codes of conduct warn about the risk of dual relationships, not all codes are as clear-cut about the evils of dual relationships or about the sanctions that should be applied.
- It is not the existence of duality that is the problem but the possibility that such duality will invite exploitation of the client. As such, each case should arouse concern and vigilance on the part of the ethical helper in order to ensure that exploitation does not occur.
- Sexual relationships of any kind are unethical in the helping setting/ context. All professional organizations are very clear about prohibition of sexual intimacy between a helper and a client.
- The inappropriateness of a sexual relationship between helper and client rests in the fact that the helping relationship is unbalanced in power and dependency issues. As such, the reciprocal nature of a healthy intimate relationship is not possible. When sexual contact becomes part of a therapeutic relationship, the expectation of trust that is fundamental to the process of therapy is violated.
- The unethical nature of dual relationships reflects the courts' view that the helping relationships (i.e., physician-patient, psychiatrist-patient, and social worker-client) are of a fiduciary nature, meaning that the professional has a duty to act to the benefit of the other individual in any matters related to an undertaking between them.
- If the fiduciary obligation exists, it could be argued that the practitioner is obliged to act in the best interest of and in good faith and with loyalty toward the client and not abuse the power imbalance by exploiting the client.
- Keeping client needs as primary in the relationship can prove invaluable for maintaining appropriate boundaries and use of power within the helping relationship.

● The need to be aware of self and relationships is essential in order to create and maintain appropriate professional boundaries. Ethical practitioners will be aware of their decisions to depart from what is typical and be able to explain the therapeutic reasons for such departure. The question that needs to be answered, especially at times of departure from typical or model procedures is, whose need is being served?

IMPORTANT TERMS ●

altruism	multiple relationship
boundaries	narcissism
boundary crossing	professional objectivity
boundary violations	professional relationship
dual relationships	sexual identification
exploitation	sexual intimacy
fiduciary obligation	transference
fiduciary relationship	

ADDITIONAL RESOURCES ●

Print

Calmes, S. A., Piazza, N. J., & Laux, J. M. (2013). The use of touch in counseling: An ethical decision-making model. *Counseling & Values, 58*(1), 59–68.

Herlihy, B., & Corey, G. (2014). *Boundary issues in counseling: Multiple roles and Responsibilities*. Alexandria, VA: American Counseling Association.

Pope, K. S., & Vasquez, M. J. (2005). *How to survive and thrive as a therapist: Information, ideas, and resources for psychologists in practice*. Washington, DC: American Psychological Association.

Syme, G. (2003). *Dual relationships in counselling and psychotherapy: Exploring the limits*. Thousand Oaks, CA: Sage.

Zur, O. (2007). *Boundaries in psychotherapy: Ethical and clinical explorations*. Washington, DC: American Psychological Association.

Zur, O. (2015). *Therapeutic boundaries and dual relationships in psychotherapy*. Retrieved from http://www.zurinstitute.com/boundariesbrochure.pdf

Web-Based

Bleiberg, J. R., & Baron, J. (2004). Entanglement in dual relationships in a university counseling center. *Journal of College Student Psychotherapy, 19*(1), 21–34.

Pope, K. S. (n.d.). Dual relationships, multiple relationships, & boundary decisions. Retrieved from http://www.kspope.com/dual/

Pope, K. S., & Keith-Spiegel, P. (n.d.). A practical approach to boundaries in psychotherapy: Making decisions, bypassing blunders, and mending fences. Retrieved from http://kspope.com/ethics/boundary.php

Reamer, F. G. (2003). Boundary issues in social work: Managing dual relationships. *Social Work, 48*(1), 121–133.

● REFERENCES

American Association for Marriage and Family Therapy. (2015). *Code of ethics.* Retrieved from http://www.aamft.org/iMIS15/AAMFT/Content/Legal_Ethics/Code_of_Ethics.aspx

American Counseling Association. (2014). *Code of ethics.* Retrieved from http://www.counseling.org/resources/aca-code-of-ethics.pdf

American Psychological Association. (2010). *Ethical principles of psychologists and code of conduct.* Retrieved from http://www.apa.org/ethics/code/principles.pdf

Black, H. C. (1991). *Black's law dictionary* (Abridged, 6th ed.). St. Paul, MN: West Publishing.

Fasasi, M. I., & Olowu, A. A. (2013). Boundary transgressions: An issue in psychotherapeutic encounter. *IFE Psychologia, 21*(3S), 139–151.

Gottlieb, M. C., & Younggren, J. N. (2009). Is there a slippery slope? Considerations regarding multiple relationships and risk management. *Professional Psychology: Research and Practice, 40*(6), 564–571.

Gutheil, T., & Brodsky, A. (2008). *Preventing boundary violations in clinical practice.* New York: Guilford.

Handelsman, M. M., Knapp, S. J., & Gottlieb, M. C. (2002). Positive ethics. In C. R. Snyder & S. J. Lopez (Eds.), *Handbook of positive psychology* (pp. 731–744). New York: Oxford University Press.

Hodgkinson v. Simms, 3 S.C.R. 377 (1994).

Kitchener, K. S., & Anderson, S. (2011). Foundations of ethical practice, research, and teaching in psychology and counseling (2nd ed.). New York: Routledge.

McInerney v. MacDonald, 2 S.C.R. 138 (1992).

M. (K.) v. M. (H.), 96 DLR (4th) 289, (1992).

National Association of Social Workers. (2008). *Code of ethics.* Retrieved from http://socialworkers.org/pubs/code/default.asp

Norberg v. Wynrib, 2 S.C.R. 226 (1992).

Parsons, R. D., & Zhang, N. (2014). *Becoming a skilled counselor.* Thousand Oaks, CA: Sage.

Sheperis, D. S., Henning, S. L., & Kocet, M. M. (2016). *Ethical decision making for the 21st century counselor*. Thousand Oaks, CA: Sage.

Stake, J. E., & Oliver, J. (1991). Sexual contact and touching between therapist and client. A survey of psychologists' attitudes and behaviors. *Professional Psychology: Research and Practice, 22*(4), 297–307.

Zur, O. (2015). Therapeutic boundaries and dual relationships in psychotherapy. Retrieved from http://www.zurinstitute.com/boundariesbrochure.pdf

CHAPTER 11

Efficacy of Treatment

Michelle: Hi, Lynn. Do you have a minute?

Lynn: Sure, Michelle. What's up?

Michelle: I've been working with this girl, Maria, and we have a real good working relationship, but I just don't feel like I have a true grasp of what is going on or that I am approaching this situation the best way. I explained this to Maria, and she has given me written permission to speak with you about the case. I know you are really busy, but I was hoping that you could provide some supervision around this case to see if you feel like I'm on the right track and using the best approach.

While our counselor, Ms. Wicks (Michelle), is certainly skilled and trained professionally, her real interest and concern for her client and her own self-awareness of the limits of her expertise have led her to seek consultation from a colleague. Approaching helping with the essential training and experience is an ethical must. However, beyond this initial training, ongoing professional development, consultation, and supervision are the hallmark of the ethical professional.

The ethical responsibility to be competent extends beyond the basic credentialing of a helper and includes the helper's ability to employ treatment strategies that are efficacious. It is these issues of treatment efficacy and helper competency that serve as the focus for the current chapter.

● OBJECTIVES

The chapter will review the ethics and legality surrounding the issue of competent practice and efficacy of treatment. The value of professional training, action research, and referral as elements of competent practice will be highlighted.

After reading this chapter you should be able to do the following:

- Describe what is meant by the term competence.
- Discuss the role of continuing education, ongoing supervision, and consultation in the continuous development of professional competence.
- Describe the value of approaching practice from a reflective, action research orientation.
- Discuss the conditions under which referral would appear to be the most efficacious treatment decision.
- Describe legal considerations and concerns in relation to the issue of helper competence, standard of care, and treatment efficacy.

● PRACTICING WITHIN THE REALM OF COMPETENCE

The ethical professional is called upon to accept responsibilities and employment on the basis of competence and professional qualification. Table 11.1 provides the position taken by a select group of professional associations on the issue of professional practice and competency. What should be evident by reviewing Table 11.1 is that each of these organizations supports the notion that one should not engage in practices that require skills beyond those possessed. To be ethical as a helper requires that competency be developed and maintained and that the helper's competence level be represented accurately to clients, employers, and the general public.

Competence

Being competent means that the helper has the knowledge, skills, and abilities needed to perform those tasks relevant to that profession. To suggest one is competent implies that the individual is capable of performing a minimum quality of service that is within the limits of his or her training, experience, and practice, as defined in professional standards or regulatory statutes.

Table 11.1 Ethical Codes Addressing Helper Competence

Professional Organization	*Ethical Principle/Standards*
American Counseling Association (2014)	C.2.a. Boundaries of competence Counselors practice only within the boundaries of their competence, based on their education, training, supervised experience, state and national professional credentials, and appropriate professional experience. Whereas multicultural counseling competency is required across all counseling specialties, counselors gain knowledge, personal awareness, sensitivity, dispositions, and skills pertinent to being a culturally competent counselor in working with a diverse client population.
American Psychological Association (2010)	2.01. Boundaries of competence a. Psychologists provide services, teach, and conduct research with populations and in areas only within the boundaries of their competence, based on their education, training, supervised experience, consultation, study, or professional experience.
American Association for Marriage and Family Therapy (2015)	3.10. Marriage and family therapists do not diagnose, treat, or advise on problems outside the recognized boundaries of their competencies.
National Association of Social Workers (2008)	4.01. Competence c. Social workers should base practice on recognized knowledge, including empirically based knowledge, relevant to social work and social work ethics. Ethical principle: Social workers practice within their areas of competence and develop and enhance their professional expertise. Social workers continually strive to increase their professional knowledge and skills and to apply them in practice. Social workers should aspire to contribute to the knowledge base of the profession. 1.04. Competence a. Social workers should provide services and represent themselves as competent only within the boundaries of their education, training, license, certification, consultation received, supervised experience, or other relevant professional experience. b. Social workers should provide services in substantive areas or use intervention techniques or approaches that are new to them only after engaging in appropriate study, training, consultation, and supervision from people who are competent in those interventions or techniques.

Competence is defined in relative terms; that is, rather than having one clear, objective standard against which to judge a professional's level of performance as competent or incompetent, competence is most often defined using the conduct of others within the profession as the comparative standard. Thus, one might ask, what would a reasonable person do in a similar situation?

● PROFESSIONAL DEVELOPMENT: KNOWING THE STATE OF THE PROFESSION

Competence can be developed from formal training as might be found in graduate training or training for certification and licensure. Further, one's own ongoing continuing education, professional reflective practice, and supervision may serve as additional resources for developing and maintaining competence.

Formal Training

Formal training occurs both at the undergraduate and graduate levels of study. Foundations of general knowledge of helping theory and skills along with research supporting intervention strategies may be acquired through undergraduate and graduate course work. However, in addition to these cognates, the competent practitioner must have guided practice in the application of this knowledge. In many disciplines (e.g., psychology), the doctorate along with supervised field and intern experiences is considered essential to competent independent practice.

For most of the helping professions, professional organizations and/or certifying and licensing bodies have identified both aspirational levels and mandatory levels of training as a way of defining competence. Each of these levels of governance monitor the development and application of professional practice. Colleges and universities often offer programs of training that have been shaped by the professional standards under the review of professional accrediting organizations. Professional accrediting bodies (e.g., American Psychological Association, Council for the Accreditation of Counseling and Related Educational Programs [CACREP]) qualify educational programs as meeting standards beyond those demanded for colleges or universities to offer degrees and certify that these programs meet high professional standards, thus establishing the foundation for ethical practice. Beyond these school-based programs, professional organizations (e.g., American School Counseling Association, American Rehabilitation Counseling Association, Academy of Certified Social Workers) often develop aspirational codes of ethics, which while not having any internal mandatory enforcement mechanism, call their members to perform at the highest level of professional practice.

Beyond the professional organization level, the professional regulatory bodies at the state and national level promulgate and enforce standards of practice through the establishment of certification and licensure standards. Often these requirements exceed those demanded for entrance into the profession, requiring additional post degree experience and supervision. The definition of minimum professional training for entry-level helpers as well as the mandate to remain up-to-date on the state of the profession through continuing education varies from state to state. It is essential for the ethical helper to be knowledgeable about these standards (see Exercise 11.1).

Being an ethical, competent practitioner requires not only a basic level of initial training but also the development and maintenance of this knowledge and these skills via continuous professional growth. The ethical helper continually strives for increased competence. The ethical helper strives to increase his or her competence by continuing to develop his or her skills and understanding of the helping process.

Exercise 11.1

Licensing and Certification Requirements

Directions: Since the requirements defining minimum requirements for competent practice vary from profession to profession and in many instances from state to state, it is helpful for you to be aware of the specific requirements for entrance into your particular field of practice.

Step 1: Identify two arenas for professional practice (e.g., school counselor, psychologist, marriage counselor, clinical social worker, etc.).

Step 2: Identify two states, one in which you intend to practice and a neighboring state.

Step 3: Contact each state's department or bureau of professional license and practice.

Step 4: Complete the following grid.

(Continued)

(Continued)

State	Practice Specialty 1		Practice Specialty 2	
	Home State	Neighboring State	Home State	Neighboring State
Minimum Education (bachelor's, master's, master's + doctorate)				
Supervised Experience (internship, practice, etc.)				
Post Degree Requirements (course work, field experience, etc.)				
Other Requirements				

Continuing Education

All the codes of conduct call for practitioners to be current with emerging knowledge relevant to their professions (see Table 11.2). It is incumbent upon the ethical practitioner to upgrade knowledge and skill by participating in continuing education experiences. Continuing education may be in the form of trainings through a professional conference or additional course work at the local university or courses taught through qualified associations and organizations.

While the call for ongoing education and professional development is clear, the specifics are still lacking. Does this suggest a certain number of courses? Credits? Hours of supervision? Many organizations and state licensing and certifying bodies require that a number of continuing education hours be completed within a number of years. For example, in Pennsylvania, all licensed marriage and family therapists seeking renewal of their licenses are directed to gain 30 hours of continuing education every

Table 11.2 Maintaining Professional Development

Professional Ethical Standards	Statement on Professional Development
American Association for Marriage and Family Therapy (2015)	3.1. Marriage and family therapists pursue knowledge of new developments and maintain their competence in marriage and family therapy through education, training, and/or supervised experience.
American Counseling Association (2014)	C.2.f. Counselors recognize the need for continuing education to acquire and maintain a reasonable level of awareness of current scientific and professional information in their fields of activity. Counselors maintain their competence in the skills they use, are open to new procedures, and remain informed regarding best practices for working with diverse populations.
American Psychological Association (2010)	2.03. Maintaining competence psychologists undertake ongoing efforts to develop and maintain their competence.
National Association of Social Workers (2008)	4.0.l.b. Social workers should strive to become and remain proficient in professional practice and the performance of professional functions. Social workers should critically examine, and keep current with, emerging knowledge relevant to social work. Social workers should routinely review the professional literature and participate in continuing education relevant to social work practice and social work ethics.

two years (http://pamft.com/for-professionals/licensure/faq/). Similarly, the State Board of Licensing for Psychologists in Pennsylvania requires psychologists to complete 30 hours of approved continuing education every two years in order to maintain and/or renew their licenses. While the specific requirements vary across professions (e.g., marriage counselor, school psychologists, clinical social worker) and from state to state, similar demand for maintaining competence is built into all certification and licensing requirements. It is important for each practitioner to be aware of the standards set by his or her own professional organization or those required for relicensing or recertification within the state where they intend to practice.

Supervision and Consultation

Practicing within the realm of competence starts with a practitioner operating within the scope of practice. Practitioners are ethically bound to restrict their professional activities to the professions and specialties for which they have been trained and supervised. When required, they must possess the appropriate certification and licensure. Practicing within the realm of competence also means knowing when it is essential to consult and/or refer to another professional who has more experience and training with this particular type of client and or problem.

The use of peer consultation, in which specific concerns can be shared with an experienced colleague, is a valuable means for maintaining competence. Peer consultation may be useful in enhancing the clinical care of the client as well as acting as a risk management tool for the helper by providing trusted resources (Gottlieb & Younggren, 2009). Peer consultation can provide mutual support for problematic cases. However, when consulting with colleagues regarding a client, the ethical practitioner needs to balance the need for his or her own continued support with the client's right to maintain confidentiality. The American Psychological Association's (APA) ethical standards, for example, state:

> When consulting with colleagues, (1) psychologists do not disclose confidential information that reasonably could lead to the identification of a client/patient, research participant, or other person or organization with whom they have a confidential relationship unless they have obtained the prior consent of the person or organization or the disclosure cannot be avoided, and (2) they disclose information only to the extent necessary to achieve the purposes of consultation. (APA, 2010, 4.06)

Even with this sensitivity to the requirements of confidentiality, the ethical helper can employ a peer consult to formulate the problem, review the decisions made, and tap a different point of view on the process. Often a colleague with more experience can provide some clarity about the helping process and may even assist the practitioner to develop additional insights or adjustments in the treatment process.

Consulting with a professional peer not only provides the helper a valuable resource for expanding his or her knowledge and skill but also can also serve as a valuable check and balance for the helper when the boundaries of competence may be exceeded. This is especially true when the helper's own objectivity may be blurred (see Chapter 10). Under these conditions, the peer consultation can provide a mechanism for examining the ethical and professional issues involved (Gottlieb & Younggren, 2009).

For those working within certain clinical settings, formal peer review may be incorporated as a way of maintaining professional competence and standards of care. For those serving in an independent practice, it would be valuable to develop a network of colleagues who can continue to serve as peer consultants.

THE STANDARD OF CARE: APPROPRIATE TREATMENT ●

Most malpractice cases turn on the question of negligence (Bennett, Bryant, VandenBos, & Greenwood, 1990). Negligence implies that the practitioner failed to meet the relevant standard of care. According to Bennett and colleagues (1990), the question of negligence will be determined by the debate over the clinical connectedness and efficacy of the treatment that was given, along with the practitioner's judgment in choosing it (p. 33).

While there is no single prescribed way to conduct "helping," ethical guidelines establish some standards of care that must be followed. For example, sexual intimacies with clients are prohibited. Further, innovative therapy involving physical contact with clients can be the basis for malpractice suits, particularly when the contact is extreme (e.g., hitting, choking). While these are extreme examples that most mental health providers will not encounter, failure to properly administer and interpret tests and inventories, failure to warn to take appropriate steps in the face of homicide and suicide, and failure to employ appropriate methods and forms of treatment may be areas in which helpers are more likely to fall short of recognized standards of care, failing to provide appropriate treatment.

Defining an Appropriate Treatment

Standards of practice have not specifically been identified. There are no preordained directives for what must be done under each condition of helping. The standard of care and the definition of appropriate treatment are typically determined by comparing the practitioner's performance with that of other professionals in the same community with comparable training and experience.

There is an evolving sense of what should prevail, and it is the standard of what a reasonable and prudent practitioner may do in situations like this that sets the standard of care (see Exercise 11.2).

Exercise 11.2

Standard of Care: A Reasonable, Prudent Response

Directions: Below you will find two clinical scenarios. Read each situation and contact two mental health providers in your local community and ask them what they would do in this situation.

Situation 1: You are treating an individual diagnosed with AIDS. This individual has informed you that he is in and has been in a long-term relationship. The client also has informed you of the name of his partner, with whom he lives. In your most recent session, your client informs you that not only is he engaging in unprotected sex with his lover but that he has not informed his lover that he has AIDS. What do you do? Do you inform the lover?

Situation 2: You have been seeing a couple for marriage counseling. You receive a subpoena for your records on the case from one partner's lawyer. What do you do? Do you respond to the subpoena? How?

Reflections:

- Did the two practitioners essentially agree on the steps to be taken?

- Did their responses seem to be in line with what you have read about confidentiality, duty to warn, informed consent, and so forth?

- Share your findings with a classmate/colleague who may have performed the exercise. Does there seem to be consistency in practitioner response that could be interpreted as a definition of standard of care?

Share your findings with your classmates or colleagues.

Employing Effective Treatments

Beyond a generic standard of what a reasonable and prudent practitioner may do, attention has been drawn to the importance of employing tried-and-true techniques and strategies of intervention. A number of professionals and professional organizations have called for use of effective treatments, as have consumer groups. The *ACA Code of Ethics*, for example, notes, "Counselors have a responsibility to the public to engage in counseling practices that are based on rigorous research methodologies" (ACA, 2014,

Introduction Section C). Or even more specifically, "When providing services, counselors use techniques/procedures/modalities that are grounded in theory and/or have an empirical or scientific foundation" (ACA, 2014, Principle C.7.a). A similar directive is found within in the National Association of Social Workers' (NASW) *Code of Ethics*, which notes, "Social workers should base practice on recognized knowledge, including empirically based knowledge, relevant to social work and social work ethics" (NASW, 2008. Principle 4.01.c). Thus, it is firmly rooted in our codes of ethics that counselors use techniques that are empirically based. It is clear that the ethical helper needs to be aware of the current research on treatment effectiveness and employ these strategies when and where appropriate.

Defining Efficacious

Providing the most effective treatment available requires professionals to keep current on the research on treatment effectiveness for their particular client populations. In line with this need to identify and employ effective treatment strategies, the Task Force on Promotion and Dissemination of Psychological Procedures (1995) from the division of clinical psychology within the APA, developed criteria for determining whether a treatment should be considered empirically valid. The task force also established a list of interventions that have been "well established" and a list that are "probably efficacious," citing the literature that supports this claim (Chambless et al. 1998).

A review of those treatments that prove effective suggest that they share the following characteristics: These interventions are targeted to specific problems, incorporate continuous monitoring and assessment, involve client skill development, and are generally brief, requiring 20 or fewer sessions (O'Donohue, Buchanan, & Fisher, 2000).

As the professions and the research identify specific strategies with demonstrated effectiveness, these interventions become the standard of care. As such, it is essential for the ethical practitioner to not only be aware of this research and these techniques but to develop the competency required for the ethical application of these strategies.

Managed Care: Compounding the Standard of Care Issue

The issue of treatment efficacy is of special consideration when a practitioner is operating within a managed care situation (Cohen, Marecek, & Gillham, 2006). With managed care pushing for brief, more cost-effective forms of treatment, the ethical practitioner must be able to identify for whom these services are appropriate and which form of service is required. Discerning for whom brief therapy is appropriate and advocating for those clients for whom such an approach may not be appropriate becomes an essential role of the ethical, competent practitioner operating within a managed care environment. Further, competence to perform short-term models of treatment, when appropriate, requires that the practitioner be prepared and able to focus on achievable, specific treatment goals and to be active and more directive in conducting the treatment. Short-term models are not simply long-term therapy models condensed in time. Utilization of these short-term models requires the ethical practitioner to possess unique understanding and skills. Thus, the ethical practitioner will not only know for whom such treatment is appropriate but will also have been trained in this approach. If the practitioner is not trained in the area that is specified, it is the responsibility of the practitioner to receive the appropriate training, at times before accepting an offer for employment (Daniels, 2001).

● EMPLOYING AN ACTION RESEARCH APPROACH TO PRACTICE

In areas for which there is not solid research to direct best practice or in which the standard of the profession is not clearly articulated, service needs to be predicated on theoretical and technical ideas that are held by a substantial portion of the profession. Thus, knowing the recognized models, theories, and schools of thought is as essential as having the ability to assess the validity and reliability of a particular strategy for one's own practice. In speaking of psychology, for example, Chambless and colleagues (1996) noted:

> Psychology is a science. Seeking to help those in need, clinical psychology draws its strength and uniqueness from the ethic of scientific validation. Whatever interventions that mysticism, authority, commercialism, politics, custom, convenience, or carelessness might dictate, clinical psychologists focus on what works. They bear a fundamental ethical responsibility to use, where possible, interventions that work *and to subject any intervention they use to scientific scrutiny* [emphasis added]. (p. 10)

This last point suggests subjecting any intervention to scientific scrutiny is a directive to all ethical practitioners and not just those interested in performing large empirical research. The ethical helper will approach his or her practice as a reflective professional, integrating research and practice.

In order to be effective in their practice, human service providers must blend the method and findings of research with the realities of their professional practice. As practitioner-researchers, they will need not only to interact in the moment but also to reflect, inquire, and critique their own interactions. Further, for their observations to provide meaningful data and useful guidance, they must be systematic and valid. Action research methodology provides practitioners with the means of acquiring these valid, useful data and results in the development of effective strategies of professional practice.

Action Research Defined

As presented here, action research is applied research in which the researcher-investigator is also the practitioner (e.g., a counselor, psychotherapist, social worker) attempting to use research as a methodology for identifying the "what" they do and for making decisions on doing it better. Action research provides practitioners with the method for viewing their professional decisions systematically and deciding on them rationally. It is the opportunity to blend theory with practice, becoming true practitioner-researchers. Action research has a circular nature (plan-act-observe-reflect and then start all over again), which supports a reflective practitioner and guides increased awareness of effectiveness.

Action Research: An Ethical Consideration

Viewed as a frame of mind, action research calls us to a continued interest in serving our constituencies better and providing increased accountability for our service. As such, action research is not simply a good idea, rather it becomes an ethical responsibility for monitoring the effectiveness of our practice and increasing the competency of our service. No one professional can guarantee success in each and every encounter or situation. However, ethical practitioners need to assess the degree to which their practices are both valid and effective. Action research provides a mechanism for monitoring the efficacy and adequacy of practice decisions and methods.

Table 11.3 provides a brief review of one model of action research that has application to the mental health professional. While presented as a linear set of steps to be taken, in practice it is a recurring, recycling process that continually takes shape in and gives shape to practice.

Table 11.3 Steps in the Action Research Process

Step	Description
1. Identification of the research question	Three types of questions seem to emerge. First, what are our practice decisions? Second, what specifically about our practice is effective? And finally, what can we do to enhance our effectiveness as practitioners?
2. Problem relevance, problem significance	The goal is to be able to answer questions such as, why study it? What do I expect will happen as a result of this investigation? How is the problem and the study significant to my practice?
3. Definitions	The practitioner–action researcher needs to begin to more concretely identify and define the concepts, the constructs, the variables involved. When and where possible, the action researcher needs to define these by his or her actions or operations performed (i.e., operational definitions).
4. Review of related literature	Reviewing the professional literature for evidence of similar investigation may prove a valuable step to intervention planning.
5. Developing hypotheses	With action research, it should be remembered that these are truly "working hypotheses." As data is collected and decisions are made, the hypotheses may be reshaped. In fact, true to the qualitative nature of the action research, new hypotheses can emerge from the data as the study progresses.
6. Outcome measures	If the action researcher seeks to increase his or her understanding of the operations of his or her professional practice or the impact of specific practice decisions, then measurement of those decisions and their impacts needs to take place. One should employ outcome assessment that measures change from multiple perspectives (i.e., the subject/client, the practitioner-researcher, and others) and through multiple approaches.
7. Methods: creating a design	As with any study, for our conclusions to be valid we must consider the use of an approach or a design that provides validity of data collection and interpretation.
8. Data collection	The types of data collected and the method of collection will clearly be situation, researcher, and problem specific. But the information gathered needs to be as detailed and as informative as possible so that as an action researcher, you will know what is happening in ways that you previously did not know. The action researcher needs to remember that he or she is a practitioner as well as a researcher and that he or she has a professional responsibility for those involved. There are ethical considerations, especially those regarding informed consent, that need to be considered.

Step	Description
9. Data analysis	At a minimum the data needs to be organized and grouped by themes, with trends and characteristics noted. When appropriate, visual presentation and descriptive and inferential statistics should also be employed.
10. Interpretation	In reviewing the data, the action researcher needs to balance research significance with practical relevance. Having answered the question what happens if, the researcher now needs to answer questions such as these: What does knowing what happens if mean for my clients, my students, and for those whom I service? To me? To my professional decision-making? To my current practice decisions?

THE USE OF REFERRAL ●

The ethical helper provides only those services for which he or she is trained, experienced, and credentialed (e.g., certified or licensed). Competence refers not only to the degree to which the professional possesses the knowledge, skills, and abilities required to perform the various tasks and procedures relevant to that profession but also to the ability to discern when it is appropriate to provide the services and when it is desirable to refer.

In the private confines of a helper's office, however, where a practitioner is free from direct supervision or teacher scrutiny, it may be all too easy to be seduced into engaging in problem solving in areas for which one is ill prepared. Consider the following case of Mrs. Robinson (see Case Illustration 11.1).

Even if we assume the best intent on the part of Dr. Hansen, the truth of the matter is that he lacks the training and appropriate experience to work with Mrs. Robinson's clinical depression. Further, his lack of experience and training is more evidenced by his willingness to serve as both Mrs. Robinson's therapist and marital counselor.

If one were to assume that Dr. Hansen was qualified to work with a depressed client, it might be easy to believe the transition from working with the distraught Mrs. Robinson to couple-marriage counseling was a logical extension of the helping contract. However, suppose Dr. Hansen has not had the specialized training that may be required.

The American Association for Marriage and Family Therapy highlights the unique training necessary to be a clinical member, training that includes specific graduate training in marriage and family therapy and two years of supervised practice. Given the special training necessary, assuming expertise and competence with a couple, even when competent working with individuals,

---

Case Illustration 11.1

Moving From Individual to Couple Counseling

Dr. Hansen received a call from Mrs. Alice Robinson, who described herself as "a little down" and unclear about the direction she wanted to go with her career. Dr. Hansen, a certified vocational counselor, scheduled to meet with Mrs. Robinson to begin the process of a vocational career assessment.

Following the initial intake, Dr. Hansen concluded that Mrs. Robinson, while interested in vocational and career counseling, was doing this in reaction to what she "perceived to be a failing marriage." Dr. Hansen saw Mrs. Robinson three more times with the intent of more clearly identifying Mrs. Robinson's goals for counseling. Through these three sessions, Dr. Hansen came to realize that Mrs. Robinson was seriously depressed. She revealed a long-standing history of depression and self-medicating alcohol consumption. She also described considering committing suicide on more than three occasions in the past month. Further, Mrs. Robinson noted that she is unable to eat, has lost approximately 20 pounds in a one-month period, and is having difficulty sleeping. The root of this depression, according to Mrs. Robinson, is the fact that "she cannot communicate" with her husband, and she knows unless something is done, they will get a divorce. And according to Mrs. Robinson, she simply "would not, could not live without him!"

Mrs. Robinson described how long she has been wanting to seek counseling for herself (her depression) and for she and her husband. But according to Mrs. Robinson, she just didn't feel comfortable seeking help since there are so many "wacko doctors" out there. Mrs. Robinson expressed her comfort and trust with Dr. Hansen and asked if he would help her and her marriage.

Dr. Hansen, while being trained and supervised in career/vocational counseling, agreed to work both individually with Mrs. Robinson in order to assist her with her depression and also to set up an arrangement to see her and her husband as a couple to start "communications training."

---

invites unethical behavior and a failure to provide appropriate standard of care. Thus, Dr. Hansen needs to reflect not only on his own training (formal and informal) and supervised experience working with clinically depressed individuals but also on the extent of his preparation in systemic-relational treatment before proceeding to treat if the couple. This would be essential for ethical, competent practice.

Helpers, regardless of their knowledge and skill, cannot provide every service needed by every client. Ethically, therefore, a helper needs to know not just the when and how of applying helping skills but also when the situation is beyond his or her capabilities or when the boundaries of his or her competence have been exceeded.

Knowing When to Refer

Knowing when to refer is not always easy. At a minimum, the ethical helper will refer anytime it is determined that she or he is unable to provide the professional, competent services required. The ethical, competent helper needs to be aware of his or her areas of expertise, the kinds of support and supervision available, and an accurate sense of his or her own time, energy, and availability to take on a particular case. When any of these areas are in question, referral should be considered.

If Dr. Hansen (see Case Illustration 11.1) reflected on his own decision-making, he might have concluded that a trained, experienced marriage relational counselor might more competently provide the services that Mrs. Robinson and her husband currently need. As such, he would have made a referral rather than attempted to provide those services himself.

Each practitioner can provide competent service, but no one practitioner can be a master of all the knowledge and skills required to competently address the myriad of situations and clients presented. As each profession develops its knowledge base and refines the skills required, it will become increasingly incumbent on the practitioner to recognize the limits of his or her own competency and the richness of resources available through the use of referral.

Knowing Where to Refer

In making a competent referral, the practitioner needs to understand the nature of the specific support and services requested. As such, the ethical, competent helper will have a cadre of available referral sources whose character and capacities are known (Zhang & Parsons, 2016). Building a referral system, branching through the surrounding geographic area, is essential. This referral network should include a variety of professional and indigenous helpers, including psychologists, psychiatrists, social workers, ministers, physicians, clinics, social service agencies, hospitals, and so on.

Being fully versed on the resources available not only enables the ethical helper to select the service(s) that most effectively meet the client's needs but also allows the helper to explain the reason for and the process of referral to the client. Being familiar with the services available allows the helper the opportunity to highlight the unique qualifications of the person or program to which the client is being referred, along with other information needed to make for a smooth and comfortable referral and transition for the client.

While a listing of various human services agencies and providers may be obtained by contacting the local county government or mental health/ (mental retardation) intellectual disability agencies listed in your phone book or on a webpage, more personalized knowledge is required for adequate referral. Exercise 11.3 is offered as a guide for developing this personalized, referral network.

Exercise 11.3

Developing a Referral Network

Directions: You can begin developing a referral network by contacting local agencies and human service providers by phone, letter, or e-mail and gathering the following information:

Name: _____

Address: _____

Phone: _____

1. What is the purpose or mission of your professional service or practice?

2. What population (age, gender, socioeconomic position, ethnicity, etc.) is best served by your service?

3. What type of difficulty, problem, or concern is most often addressed by you/your service?

4. What resources are available (e.g., 24-hour hotlines, medical facilities, educational materials, housing, job placement, etc.)?

5. What is the procedure or process for gaining access, making an appointment, or seeking assistance?

6. What is the general therapeutic theory or model employed?

7. What are the training levels of the helpers who provide these services?

8. Are there fees? How much? Payment plans? Sliding scales? Insurance? Other?

9. Who is the contact person?

10. Is there a waiting list?

11. Other information (e.g., special services, general impressions, etc.).

Making the Referral

Recognizing the need or value of referral is only the first step. In addition to recognizing the need and having available resources to whom to refer, the competent helper will also have the skill to assist the client to accept and embrace this referral. It is not unusual for a client to interpret the suggestion of a referral as a sign of rejection or as evidence of the hopeless nature of his or her condition.

The competent, ethical helper will present the idea of referral in a way that it is seen as a continuing, productive step in the helping process that, far from being evidence of rejection, it is evidence of the helper's concern. And rather than evidence of the hopelessness of the situation, it is evidence of the clarity of the nature of the problem and the reality of the existence of a resource with a record of success in these situations. Consider the dialogue presented in Case Illustration 11.2.

Case Illustration 11.2

Preparing Margaret for Referral

Linda is a master's-level mental health counselor working for an Employee Assistance Program (EAP). Her training is in counseling psychology, and she has experience working with individual, solution-focused approaches to counseling. As a counselor in an EAP, she is contracted to provide a maximum of six sessions of direct service, while overseeing and case managing all clients whom she refers for

(Continued)

(Continued)

ongoing assistance. Margaret, her client, has come to her because her husband "kicked her out" of their house and is filing for divorce. Margaret, in addition to being depressed about the situation with her marriage, is in crisis over her current living conditions. The exchange occurs near the end of the first session.

Linda: Margaret, you have certainly been open and honest with me. And I know that speaking about the marriage and your relationship with Tom has at times been very upsetting.

Margaret: It has been easier than I thought. You are a very kind person and a good listener.

Linda: Thank you. But as we've talked, it has become clear to me that of the things you are concerned about, the one thing that seems to need immediate attention, is helping you with your housing problem.

Margaret: Yeah, I don't have any money to go and get a new apartment right now and last night I slept in the car. I know I have enough money to go to a motel for a night or two, but I don't know what I can do (starts to cry). Where can I go?

Linda: You are correct in saying that you can't continue to sleep in the car, and finding an answer to your question of, where can you go? should be our primary concern. Do you agree?

Margaret: Yes (crying).

Linda: Housing or social service support for displaced women is not something that we provide here at the EAP or that I am very experienced with.

Margaret: (interrupting): Oh, NO! You have to help me . . .

Linda: It is going to be all right. I am going to help. Even though I do not work with these types of situations, I know someone who can really help us, who has a lot more experience in these situations. So what I would like to do is call Ms. Anderson over at the Women's Center and see if she has the time to talk with us and see you today. The Women's Center is right around the corner from here and it provides ongoing counseling for women who are in situations just like yours.

They also have resources for temporary housing and even help women find low-cost housing. Plus, once they help you get settled, they can help you with some of the job training we started discussing.

Margaret: But how about you . . . ? I like you . . .

Linda: And I like you. In fact, I really want you to get the best help you can get and I think the Women's Center is the answer. But I can still help, by talking with Ms. Anderson and telling her some of things you have shared with me, especially things about your current concerns and some of your goals. I could also work with you and Ms. Anderson, if that makes sense after talking with her. And if you want to come back to talk with me, or if we want to look into another referral source, we could do that as well. So how do you feel about me calling and seeing if we can set up an appointment for you?

Margaret: Okay . . . but I can still call you if I need to?

Linda: Absolutely, and I will call you to see how things are going after you have had a chance to work with the Women's Center.

As evident in the exchange (see Case Illustration 11.2), presenting the client with a referral needs to be done as a hopeful, positive step in the helping process. The helper needs to convey to the client that this is not an abandonment but an extension and refinement of the helping process. In making a referral the helper should

- Be clear and direct about the goal and expectation for seeking referral
- Confront what referral is NOT, that is, it is not a rejection or a statement of hopelessness
- Share information about the referral source, nature of service, costs, location, and so forth
- Discuss the client's feelings and concerns
- Answer all client questions regarding the referral
- Reassure the client about the value of the referral
- Assist the client in making the initial contact
- Establish a mechanism for follow-up with each other. Encourage the client to let the helper know how the initial visit went

If you are requesting special services for a client from a colleague, it is important to provide the colleague with the information about the case that is necessary to support the goals of the referral. Needless to say, it is essential to gain the client's consent for such collaboration prior to speaking with the professional to whom you are referring. Once the referral contract has been established, it is important for the referring helper to back off from case involvement unless specifically requested by the attending professional.

● RECENT LEGAL DECISIONS

Malpractice or professional liability lawsuits are quite often based on the issue of therapist negligence. A client, who in legal proceedings is the plaintiff, would assert that the helper has breached the standard of care. A simple way of looking at negligence is to think of it as the failure to do something that a reasonable person in ordinary circumstances would do or something a reasonable person in ordinary circumstances would not do. When viewed through the lens of the professional helper, negligence would be a failure to do that which the typical clinician would do or not do in that same situation. While malpractice requires a demonstrating of injury even when such proof of injury is absent, complaints to professional ethics committee or regulatory agencies (e.g., licensing boards) can result in sanctions.

The legal concept of negligence is based on the premise that all members of society owe to one another the duty to exercise a certain inherent standard of care. In most cases, the courts will look to the profession itself to define which standard should be used. The standard of care has been described as the qualities and conditions that prevail, or should prevail, in a particular mental health service, and that a reasonable and prudent practitioner follows (Zur, 2007). The standard is based on community and professional standards and, as such, professionals are held to the same standard as others of the same profession or discipline with comparable qualification in similar localities.

Case law on the standard of care question varies around the country. Some courts will put the emphasis on "accepted" practice, others on what is "customary." In this latter case, an attorney will develop evidence to define the customary standard applied by others in the field, with "field" defined in the most specific sense possible. For example, when a clinical psychologist who has been trained in cognitive techniques offers this orientation explicitly to his or her clients, when he comes to the courtroom, the standard for his or her performance is predefined. The cognitive school is recognized by the community of psychologists as a distinct and viable orientation, with well-defined standards for training and clinical guidelines. Should this psychologist be operating without the appropriate training or outside the customary procedures for a cognitive therapist, he or she may be vulnerable to negligence and malpractice. Therefore, not only do helpers need to legally perform within their scope of training, but they also must perform in ways that are typically or customarily associated with that form of service. Helpers who develop or subscribe to innovative therapies might find themselves having to prove that a "respectable minority" in their profession concurs in their techniques or treatment strategies.

An alternative approach to negligence, malpractice, and the issue of standard of care is that derived not from one's own training but from the clinical imperatives of the client's condition. In *Hammer v. Rosen* (1960) the court ruled that a therapist's (psychiatrist) decision to beat his patient as part of therapy was a prima facie case of malpractice. The court noted that some acts are so obviously unacceptable that expert testimony is not needed to justify the conclusion of malpractice. If a nontraditional therapy is employed, documentation of the reasons for its choice rather than a more traditional approach, along with expert testimony showing the efficacy of the therapy in a similar situation and/or its theoretical and scientific bases, may be needed should a malpractice action be filed (Dickson, 1998). It could be assumed that the same logic may be applied to the situation in which a practitioner used a traditional but less than effective strategy of intervention. The theoretical and empirical base for that decision may be essential should a malpractice action be filed.

BEYOND PROFESSIONAL STANDARDS: ● A PERSONAL MORAL RESPONSE

While the threat of malpractice can certainly motivate one to perform within the boundaries of his or her training, it is not insurance in and of itself that such ethical, competent performance of duty will occur. As with all of the ethical standards and practice guidelines, directives to provide competently within the standard of care are or can be a mere statement of expectation rather than an operative schema guiding practice decisions.

As ethical practitioners, we need to move the concepts and principles discussed within this chapter from levels of comprehension to incorporation as personal values and moral imperatives. Once assimilated as a personal value and moral response, acting competently will be a simple consequence of being competent in the broadest sense of the term. The final exercise (Exercise 11.4) is provided to assist you in adding the affective, personal component to this theoretical, conceptual discussion.

Exercise 11.4

Personalizing the Importance of Competence

Part 1: Below you will find a list of presenting concerns. As you read the list, place a check mark under the column indicating whether you would work with the person and provide service or refer the person to another helper. If you are currently in a formal degree/ training program, answer the question as if you had just completed that training.

Presenting Concerns	Provide Service	Refer to Another Helper
A person with anxiety about making a career decision		
A person grieving the recent death of her parent		
A person thinking about leaving his partner		
A person concerned about the possibility of having a drinking problem		
A person who has questions about her sexual orientation		
A person having academic difficulties in college		
A person who feels extremely depressed		
A person who is experiencing headaches and muscle tensions as a result of job-related stress		
A person who is concerned about his explosive temper		
A person who is having conflict with her adolescent child, which at times has exploded into physical confrontations		

Part 2: Now for each of the above, reconsider your decision. This time assume that the client was viewed by you with the same level of care and concern as you would have for someone very close to you (e.g., family member, spouse, best friend, etc.). Once you personalized the level of concern for the client, did you adjust your original decisions? What might this say about your customary standard of care? Consider steps you can take to approach all clients with the same depth of concern and provision of quality, competent service.

Part 3: For those situations in which the decision was to refer, begin to establish referral resources that you would feel comfortable referring all clients to, including a person who was personally very close to you.

CONCLUDING CASE ILLUSTRATION ●

The scenario that opened this chapter not only revealed Ms. Wicks's (Michelle's) deep concern for her client, Maria, but her personal awareness of the possible limitations to her own competence and ability to assist Maria. With these two conditions in place, Michelle sought out a peer for consultation and possible referral.

Michelle: Hi, Lynn. Do you have a minute?

Lynn: Sure, Michelle, what's up?

Michelle: I've been working with this girl, Maria, and we have a real good working relationship, but I don't feel like I have a huge grasp of what is going on or that I am approaching this situation the best way that I might. I explained this to Maria, and she has given me written permission to speak with you about the case. I know you are really busy, but I was hoping that you could provide some supervision around this case to see if you feel like I'm on track and using the best approach.

Following a discussion of case details, their conversation continued.

Lynn: It really does appear that you have gained Maria's trust and given her recent experience and background, that was not an easy task.

Michelle: Oh, thanks . . . you are right, it wasn't the easiest, but that's why I want to do the best for her.

Lynn: Well, your specific solution-focused approach really does appear to be effective, especially in helping her with the "life crisis" of finding a place to live, support herself, and essentially stay safe. So, I would suggest you continue to strategize with her the way you have been and identify additional resources that she can use . . .

Michelle: I will, but as I said, I feel there is much more here than the immediate crisis.

Lynn: I agree . . . It is very clear that Maria has some real issues with her family, especially her father, and I think one of the goals you could try to work on would be to get her to feel safe and crisis-free so that she might be willing to work with her family in some family therapy.

Michelle: We touched on that a couple of times, but she was resistant. But as you were speaking, I remembered that her resistance did seem to be diminishing. It appears the more she feels comfortable with me and what we are planning, the more she may be willing to risk some family sessions! But I am really not trained in family work. I mean, I've had a course, but that's not something I've done. So if she agrees, I would like to refer her. I really respect you and the work you do with families, and I have heard great things about Dr. Hemingway and his work with families. Would it be okay if when we get to that point, I give her your name along with Dr. Hemingway's?

Reflections

1. In reviewing the case, can you see evidence of the helper (Ms. Wicks) placing the client's welfare above her own image and ego?
2. Identify two specific things done by Ms. Wicks that reflect her awareness of the need to provide competent and efficacious service.
3. In addition to having a course in family-systems therapy, what would you suggest is minimally required before one engage in such an intervention?
4. What might you suggest Ms. Wicks do prior to including Dr. Hemingway on a referral list?
5. What might you suggest Ms. Wicks do to prepare Maria for referral? What role could Ms. Wicks continue to play?

COOPERATIVE LEARNING EXERCISE ●

As with all of the previous cooperative learning exercises, the current exercise is designed to help you personalize the material and begin to move your understanding to professional practice. Therefore, before proceeding to the next chapter, read and respond to each of the following. Working with colleagues, classmates, or supervisors, share your insights and develop the comprehensive plan for developing increased levels of competency.

Goal Identification: Briefly share your vision or goal in terms of the type of work you would like to do as a practitioner—that is, the type of client you envision working with, the nature/scope of problems, and the setting in which you wish to work.

Legal Requirements: Identify the professional standards and minimal requirements necessary to perform the tasks described in the question above. What are the specific licensing and certification requirements in your state that apply to the practice you envision performing?

Contact: Contact one professional currently practicing in an area similar to the one that you have identified as your professional goal. Identify the level of training, experience, and model this practitioner employs. Identify clients or presenting complaints that this professional feels are outside the boundaries of his or her competence and gather two resources to which he or she refers.

Contract: Finally, in discussion with your colleague, classmate, or supervisor, compare your current level of training and experience to the standards established within your state and the level of expertise identified by the professional you contacted. What specific gaps exist and what is your plan to fill those gaps in competency?

SUMMARY ●

- Being competent means that the helper has the knowledge, skills, and abilities needed to perform those tasks relevant to that profession. Competence is defined in relative terms, most typically using the conduct of others within the profession as the comparative standard.
- Competence can be developed from formal training, as might be found in graduate training or training for certification and licensure.

Further, all the codes of conduct call for practitioners to be current with emerging knowledge relevant to their profession. It is incumbent upon the ethical practitioner to upgrade his or her knowledge and skill through participating in continuing education experiences and peer consultation.

- Most malpractice cases turn on the question of negligence, which suggests that the practitioner failed to meet the relevant standard of care. The question of negligence will be determined by the debate over the clinical correctness and efficacy of the treatment that was given, along with the practitioner's judgment in choosing it.

- Malpractice or professional liability lawsuits are based on negligence theory. That is, a client would assert that the helper has breached the standard of care. A review of recent court decisions could lead to the assumption that where a practitioner used a traditional but less than effective strategy of intervention, the theoretical and empirical base for that decision may be essential should a malpractice action be filed.

- The standard of care and the definition of appropriate treatment are typically determined by comparing the practitioner's performance with that of other professionals in the same community with comparable training and experience. However, as the professions and the research identify specific strategies with demonstrated effectiveness, these interventions become the standard of care.

- Practitioners bear a fundamental ethical responsibility to use, when possible, interventions that work and to subject any intervention they use to scientific scrutiny.

- In order to be effective in their practice, human service providers must blend the method and findings of research with the realities of their professional practice. As practitioner-researchers, they will need not only to interact in the moment but also to reflect on and critique their own interactions. Action research methodology provides practitioners with the means of acquiring these valid, useful data and results in the development of effective strategies of professional practice.

- Knowing when to refer is not always easy, and there are no simple or clear answers.

- At a minimum, the ethical helper will refer anytime it is determined that he or she is unable to provide the professional, competent services required. In addition to recognizing the need and having available resources to whom to refer, the competent helper will also have the skills to assist the client to accept and embrace this referral.

IMPORTANT TERMS ●

action research	malpractice
best practice	managed care
brief therapy	negligence
certification	peer consultation
competence	professional development
continuing education	referral
customary	referral network
efficacy of the treatment	regulatory bodies
formal training	standard of care licensing

ADDITIONAL RESOURCES ●

Print

Bean, R. A., Davis, S. D., & Davey, M. P. (2014). *Clinical supervision activities for increasing competence and self-awareness.* Hoboken, NJ: John Wiley & Sons

O'Hagan, K. (2007). *Competence in social work practice: A practice guide for students and professionals* (2nd ed.). Philadelphia, PA: Jessica Kingsley Publishers.

Shelton, C. F., & James, E. L. (2005). *Best practices for effective secondary school counselors.* Thousand Oaks, CA: Corwin Press.

Web-Based

American School Counselor Association. (n.d.). ASCA school counselor competencies. Retrieved from http://schoolcounselor.org/asca/media/asca/home/SCCompetencies.pdf

Caudill Jr., B. (n.d.). Malpractice & licensing pitfalls for therapists: A defense attorney's list. Retrieved from http://kspope.com/ethics/malpractice.php

Fairburn, C. G., & Cooper, Z. (2011). Therapist competence, therapy quality, and therapist training. *Behaviour Research and Therapy, 49*(6-7), 373–378.

Martz, E., & Kaplan, D. (2014, October). New responsibilities when making referrals. *New Concepts in the ACA Code of Ethics.* Retrieved from http://www.counseling.org/docs/default-source/ethics/ethics_ocober-2014.pdf?sfvrsn=2

● REFERENCES

American Association for Marriage and Family Therapy. (2015). *Code of ethics.* Retrieved from http://www.aamft.org/iMIS15/AAMFT/Content/Legal_Ethics/Code_of_Ethics.aspx

American Counseling Association. (2014). *Code of ethics and standards of practice.* Alexandria, VA: Author.

American Psychological Association. (2010). *American Psychological Association's ethical principles of psychologists and code of conduct.* Retrieved from http://www.apa.org/ethics/code/principles.pdf

Bennett, B. E., Bryant, B. K., VandenBos, G. R., & Greenwood, A. (1990). *Professional liability and risk management.* Washington, DC: American Psychological Association.

Chambless, D. L., Baker, M. J., Baucom, D. H., Beutler, L. E., Calhoun, K. S., Crits-Christoph, P., . . . Woody, S. R. (1998). Update on empirically validated therapies, II. *The Clinical Psychologist, 51*(1), 3-16.

Cohen, J., Marecek, J., & Gillham, J. (2006). Is three a crowd? Clients, clinicians, and managed care. *American Journal of Orthopsychiatry, 76*(2), 251-259.

Daniels, J. (2001). Managed care, ethics, and counseling. *Journal of Counseling & Development, 79*(1), 119-122.

Dickson, D. (1998). *Confidentiality and privacy in social work: A guide to the law for practitioners and students.* New York: The Free Press.

Gottlieb, M. C., & Younggren, J. N. (2009). Is there a slippery slope? Considerations regarding multiple relationships and risk management. *Professional Psychology: Research and Practice, 40*(6), 564-571.

Hammer v. Rosen, 165 N.E. 2d 756 (1960).

National Association of Social Workers. (2008). *Code of ethics.* Retrieved from https://www.socialworkers.org/pubs/code/code.asp

O'Donohue, W., Buchanan, J. A., & Fisher, J. E. (2000). Characteristics of empirically supported treatments. *The Journal of Psychotherapy Practice and Research, 9*(2), 69-74. Retrieved from http://www.ncbi.nlm.nih.gov/pmc/articles/PMC3330591/

Task Force on Promotion and Dissemination of Psychological Procedures. (1995). Training in and dissemination of empirically validated treatments: Report and recommendations. *The Clinical Psychologist, 48*(1), 3-23.

Zhang, N., & Parsons, R. D. (2016). *Field experience: Transitioning from student to professional.* Thousand Oaks, CA: Sage.

Zur, O. (2007). *Boundaries in psychotherapy: Ethical and clinical explorations.* Washington, DC: American Psychological Association.

CHAPTER **12**

Evaluation and Accountability

Dr. Flournoy: Hello, Ms. Wicks?

Ms. Wicks: Yes.

Dr. Flournoy: I am Dr. Flournoy from Children and Youth Services.

Ms. Wicks: Hello.

Dr. Flournoy: The Ramerez family has been referred to our service, and I understand that you have been working with Maria, here at school. I have requested that your counseling records be subpoenaed, and I simply wanted to let you know ahead of time, so that you could begin to get them in order.

Counseling records? Subpoenas? For some mental health practitioners the idea of maintaining records may be an anathema to the nature of the helping process. Further, the invitation to disclose these records as a result of a simple request, subpoena, or court order can arouse debilitating anxiety.

The need and ethical responsibility of keeping and maintaining records along with the inherent conflict that may exist when disclosure of these records is requested serves as the focus for the current chapter.

● OBJECTIVES

The chapter will introduce you to the importance of maintaining records as both a measure of professional accountability and an essential step toward demonstrating ethical practice. After reading this chapter you should be able to do the following:

- Describe the benefits of utilizing a system of evaluation within one's practice
- Define the terms formative and summative evaluation
- Describe one approach to measuring outcome and goal achievement
- Identify the minimal records necessary for demonstrating competent, ethical practice

While it is true that no one professional can guarantee success in each and every encounter, the ethical practitioner will monitor services and adjust as required. Such a monitoring—or evaluation—be it through the informal collection of data or more formal forms, can offer direction and serve to demonstrate accountability. However, for some helpers, the concept of evaluation may be viewed as superfluous or tangential to the primary function of helping. While there is abundant evidence of the need for all mental health professionals to be able to demonstrate client progress and treatment effectiveness to the stakeholders they serve (Astramovich & Coker, 2007), the use of a well-developed system of practice assessment simply makes good practical sense. Such a system of assessment and accountability not only highlights the reality of the *terminal nature* of the professional relationship and provides a reference point for knowing when the process has achieved its desired end (i.e., summative evaluation), but it also provides markers to guide the process (i.e., formative evaluation) and thus ensure it remains on target for goal achievement. When viewed through the lens of accountability, to the client and the profession, an evaluation system becomes an essential ethical practice (see Table 12.1).

● MONITORING AND EVALUATING INTERVENTION EFFECTS

Evaluation is often thought of as something that is done at the end of a process. As suggested above, for evaluation to be prescriptive it needs to be ongoing and *formative* as well as *summative* in form.

Table 12.1 Ethical Positions on Record Keeping

Professional Organization	*Position on Record Keeping*
American Counseling Association (2014)	B.6. Records and documentation a. Creating and maintaining records and documentation Counselors create and maintain records and documentation necessary for rendering professional services. b. Respect for confidentiality Counselors protect the confidential information of prospective and current clients. Counselors disclose information only with appropriate consent or with sound legal or ethical justification.
American Psychological Association (2010)	6.01. Documentation of professional and scientific work and maintenance of records Psychologists create, and to the extent the records are under control, maintain, disseminate, store, retain, and dispose of records and data relating to their professional and scientific work in order to (1) facilitate provision of services later by them or by other professionals, (2) allow for replication of research design and analysis, (3) meet institutional requirements, (4) ensure accuracy of billing and payments, and (5) ensure compliance with law. 6.04. Maintenance, dissemination, and disposal of confidential records of professional and scientific work a. Psychologists maintain confidentiality in creating, storing, accessing, transferring, and disposing of records under their control, whether these are written, automated, or in any other medium. b. If confidential information concerning recipients of psychological services is entered into databases or systems of records available to persons whose access has not be consented to by the recipient, psychologists use coding or other techniques to avoid the inclusion of personal identifiers. c. Psychologists make plans in advance to facilitate the appropriate transfer and to protect the confidentiality of records and data in the event of psychologists' withdrawal from positions or practice.
American Association for Marriage and Family Therapy (2015)	2.5. Marriage and family therapists store, safeguard, and dispose of client records in ways that maintain confidentiality and in accord with applicable laws and professional standards.

(Continued)

Table 12.1 (Continued)

Professional Organization	Position on Record Keeping
National Association of Social Workers (2008)	3.04. a. Social workers should take reasonable steps to ensure that documentation in records are accurate and reflective of services provided. b. Social workers should include sufficient and timely documentation in records to facilitate the delivery of services and to ensure continuity of service provided to clients in the future. c. Social workers' documentation should protect clients' privacy to the extent that is possible and appropriate and should include only information that is directly relevant to the delivery of services. d. Social workers should store records following the termination of services to ensure reasonable future access. Records should be maintained for the number of years required by state statues or relevant contracts.

Formative Evaluation

Formative evaluation is evaluation that occurs as an ongoing process throughout the helping encounter. It is the gathering of feedback and data used to expedite decision-making about the current process and the upcoming steps and procedures to be employed. It provides data that give form to the ongoing process. The means of collecting formative data can range in degree of formality. For example, a practitioner may choose to use a structured survey or questionnaire at various points in the helping encounter. Or more informally, the practitioner may simply set time aside to solicit feedback from the client about his or her experience in the relationship with the helper and the procedures employed up to this particular point (see Case Illustration 12.1).

Case Illustration 12.1

Formative Evaluation

Dr. Brown: First let me tell you how much I appreciate your openness and willingness to share with me some of your concerns about your social relationships and your desire

---

to become more assertive in these. I feel very comfortable working with you and feel that the things we have talked about in this first session have really helped us to clarify your goal and even begin developing a strategy for getting there. I think it may be helpful if we took a moment to share our perceptions on this session as a way of making future sessions more productive. I would be very interested in receiving your feedback about our session today.

Jim: To be honest, I was very nervous when I made the appointment. However, I am really surprised how much I shared. I really feel like I can trust you. I feel very comfortable speaking with you, and that is not my style, usually.

Dr. Brown: Well, that is very nice to hear, and I know from what you told me that you tend to be a private person. Jim, as you are aware, we will probably want to talk more about your family background and previous relationships as our sessions go on. How do you feel about that? (Dr. Brown checks Jim's understanding of the helping process.)

Jim: I know that probably needs to be done. It makes me a little anxious, but as I said, I do feel comfortable with you and trust you, especially how you explained the idea of confidentiality, I just may need to go slow.

Dr. Brown: That's good feedback for me. The pace of the sessions really will be the one that feels right for you. So if we need to go slow, we will. If you want to dive into something and it seems right to me, we will. I think as long as we continue to "process" how we are doing, we can make sure we stay on track at a pace which is both productive and comfortable. (Dr. Brown checks Jim's comfort level and takes direction.)

Jim: Yeah, me too.

Dr. Brown: So, while overall you are hoping to get some help with developing assertiveness skills, our immediate goal is for you to take notes on two incidents: one in which you felt you were assertive and one in which you felt

(Continued)

(Continued)

| | very unassertive. Are these the goals we agreed on? (Dr. Brown checks agreement on goals.) |
| Jim: | Yes, that's exactly what I want to do . . . get more assertive! And I like the idea of doing some "research work" for our next session. |

For this evaluation to truly form and give shape to the decision-making processes, it should begin with the first session. As evident in Case Illustration 12.1, the helper engaged in formative evaluation within the first session. The approach taken by this helper provided insight into the client's level of comfort with the interaction and his ability to engage collaboratively in the helping process. This evaluation also served as a check on the accuracy of the helper's understanding regarding the desired goals and outcome for the helping process. The use of such a formative evaluation not only provides for helper accountability but also provides the data for monitoring and increasing efficacy of treatment.

Summative Evaluation

Summative evaluation is the type of evaluation most typically thought of when considering goal or outcome assessment. The specific purpose of summative evaluation is to demonstrate that the action plan has reached its original objective. Summative evaluation provides the helper and the client data to determine (a) if the original goals were achieved, (b) the factors that contributed to this goal attainment, and (c) maybe even the value of this strategy versus some alternative. The articulation of clear treatment goals and the employment of summative evaluation strategies serve as invaluable sources for demonstrating treatment efficacy and helper accountability.

The presence of clearly articulated goals or outcomes is essential for both formative and summative forms of evaluation. Without a clear, shared vision of where the helping process is going, it will be hard to know if it is on track or even if it has arrived. Thus, the establishment of treatment goals and objectives, the identification of outcome measures, and the maintenance of appropriate responsible records serve as keystones to ethical and efficient practice.

Setting Treatment Goals and Objectives

While it may seem obvious that the counseling relationship and process is neither totally open ended nor aimless, as a professional encounter, our helping is both intentional and directional. To be effective, it is essential that the helper, along with the client, identifies and clarifies client needs and desired goals. Research (e.g., Seijts, Latham, Tasa, & Latham, 2004) has demonstrated that the articulation of goals is essential to the problem-solving process. However, to be effective, these goals cannot be vague, overly generalized, or unrealistic. As such, it is suggested that the effective, ethical practitioner will help the client to set goals that are specific, measureable, attainable, relevant, and time bound (Parsons & Zhang, 2014). Such goals may be identified with the acronym SMART goals. Taking these into consideration for one's own practice, the questions posed in Table 12.2 will be helpful in the development of these goals.

Table 12.2   Developing SMART Goals

Goal Characteristics	Questions to Guide Goal Setting
Specific	Does the goal outline exactly what you are trying to achieve?
Measurable	How will you know if progress is being made?
	How will others know if progress is being made?
	Is the progress quantifiable?
Attainable	What resources do you need to achieve this goal?
	Can the goal be achieved independently?
	Is the goal too big? If so, can the goal be broken down into smaller SMART goals?
	What factors or forces exist that could interfere with the achievement of the goal?
	What is the plan to remove or navigate these forces?
Relevant	How important to you is this goal?
	What are the positive consequences of achieving this goal?
	How will achieving this goal affect your personal and professional life?
Time Bound	Have you set a target date?
	Can you establish benchmarks along the way to use as evidence of progress?
	Is the timeline reasonable? Flexible?

Source: Adapted from Zhang & Parsons (2016). *Field experience: Transitioning from student to professional.* SAGE Publications, Thousand Oaks: CA.

Measuring Outcome and Goal Achievement

The selection of appropriate outcome measures is far from easy. Clinicians recognize that the helping process, when effective, can reveal itself in many ways—even beyond the achievement of the terminal goal. For example, while attempting to help a client cope with his social anxiety it may not be unusual to find that the client exits the relationship with a better sense of his own vocational calling or insight into his current relationships or even a desire to pursue additional growth-oriented counseling. Using more than one outcome and outcome measure increases the probability of accurately depicting the entirety of the experience. At the most fundamental level, the practitioner can assume that one outcome reflects the nature of the presenting concern. For example, if a clinician is interested in ameliorating a presenting complaint, the nature of that complaint (e.g., test anxiety, marital dissatisfaction, depression, etc.) provides direction to the outcomes desired. After targeting the general area in which the helper expects to demonstrate impact (i.e., reduce test anxiety, increase achievement level, etc.), that particular area needs to be clearly and concretely defined. It is important to realize that while there will be a primary focus for the assessing outcome (e.g., reduce the amount of client depression or increase student attention, etc.), these targets may be manifested in a number of different ways and occur within a unique context. The more perspectives we take on the outcome and the more measures we employ, the greater the chance we have of understanding the nature and depth of impact our practice may have produced. Consider the approach taken by the helper illustrated in the following case (Case Illustration 12.2).

Case Illustration 12.2

Assessing Outcomes of Treatment With Depressed Client

Alicia came to therapy because of a "constant" feeling of sadness and an inability to get motivated about anything in her life. At the initial meeting with Alicia, Dr. Warrick attempted to identify the various ways in which her feelings of sadness were experienced and were impacting her life.

Dr. Warrick: Alicia, you have mentioned that you are not "doing anything" and you can't get motivated. Could you tell me more about that?

Alicia: Well, I have a lot of school work that should be done, and each time I sit down to do it I think, why bother,

	nothing is going to come out, and then I walk away from the computer and get something to eat or go to bed.
Dr. Warrick:	So it seems that you not only feel sad, at times, but you also have this belief that "nothing is going to work"?
Alicia:	That's right! And it is not just with school stuff. If I get a call from a friend I typically go out with, I think, why bother going out, it is not going to help. And I stay home.
Dr. Warrick:	So one of the things that we may watch as we work together isn't just your feelings of sadness but also the frequency of this, why bother, it's hopeless thinking?
Alicia:	I don't want to feel sad anymore, but I also understand what you mean about the thinking.
Dr. Warrick:	You also seem to suggest that when you are feeling this way, you avoid your friends and avoid engaging in activities (like school work)?
Alicia:	Yeah, I have not seen my friends in weeks. I'm sure they are annoyed. And I don't even do housework anymore. My place is a mess.
Dr. Warrick:	Well, Alicia, I appreciate how open you have been with me today, and I truly feel we have taken a good step toward helping you to feel and behave the way you want to. As we continue working together, we will not only keep our eyes on your feelings of sadness with the intent of gaining some relief, but we will see if there is an increase in the frequency with which you go out with your friends or do house chores and school work. Further, we will hopefully also see a change in your thinking. Rather than thinking why bother thoughts, we will see more productive thoughts. How does that sound?
Alicia:	It sounds like a lot and I'm not sure that we can do this. Wow, there is that why bother thought again!

(Continued)

> (Continued)
>
> But, if I would start feeling and thinking and acting differently, then I would not need to be here.
>
> Dr. Warrick: That's good! I like the way you already attacked that thought of yours!

While most individuals recognize depression to be a mood, an affect, or a feeling, depression also manifests itself in a person's behavior, thought processes, and interpersonal interactions. A helper, like Dr. Warrick (see Case Illustration 12.2), who may be attempting to assess the effectiveness of a particular medication or treatment approach on depression, should assess changes not only in the client's mood but also in the client's behavior (e.g., doing school work), thought processes (e.g., having less frequent thoughts of suicide or thoughts of why bother), and interpersonal interactions (e.g., beginning to reengage with family and friends), along with gathering information about how the client feels about these changes.

Table 12.3 provides one useful way for conceptualizing the various domains in which interventions may impact the client. It is useful to consider gathering data in many, if not all, of these domains in an attempt to accurately evaluate the impact of practice decisions. The listing presented is an adaptation of the work of Arnold Lazarus (1989). The essence of this model is the belief that a person's functioning or dysfunctioning is manifested along seven modalities: behavior, affect, sensation, images, cognition, interpersonal relationships, and biology/physiology. Lazarus represented these seven domains with the acronym BASIC ID. Using each of these components as a reference point, the helper can conceptualize the impacts of his or her practice more broadly.

Table 12.3 presents three dimensions for consideration when identifying outcomes to action research. First, modality refers to the specific arena in which this construct may be manifested (i.e., BASIC ID). The second dimension, manifestation, is the place where the practitioner identifies the manner or form in which this particular target of the investigation appears. The final column, data collection techniques, identifies the types of techniques that can be useful when assessing that domain. It should be noted that while a specific method of data collection has been identified in Table 12.3, other methods may work as well.

Exercise 12.1 provides an opportunity to employ to this approach with a problem of your choosing.

Table 12.3 Classification Scheme for Outcome Measures: Using an Example of a Client

Experiencing Anxiety in Social Settings		
Modality	*Manifestation*	*Sample Methods of Data Collection*
Behavior	Withdraws from social contact	Observation
Affect	Anxious	Survey (anxiety checklist)
Sensation	Muscle tension	Self-report (journal)
Imagery	Dreams about being abandoned	Self-report (journal)
Cognition	Believes he has no right to say no	Assertiveness questionnaire
Interpersonal	Withdraws and fails to maintain eye contact	Observation, interview peers
Drugs/Biology	Stomach upset/blood pressure high	Self-report and blood pressure recordings

Exercise 12.1

Identifying Personal Outcomes

Directions: Below are a number of general statements about personal improvement and growth. Select one that may be of interest to you and using the table below, identify the various manifestations of this goal achievement along with techniques for assessment.

- Become a better student

- Become more social

- Become more spiritual

- Improve general health

Modality	*Definition*	*Sample Methods of Data Collection*
Behavior		
Affect		

(Continued)

(Continued)

Modality	Definition	Sample Methods of Data Collection
Sensations		
Imagery		
Cognition		
Interpersonal		
Drugs		

Record Keeping

Record keeping is important not just to document service but also to guide and direct the practitioner in his or her practice decisions. Accurate, complete records can, for example, allow a practitioner to review the therapeutic process and thus foster self-monitoring on the part of the practitioner. Thus, implicit within the discussion of evaluation and outcome measurement is the understanding that data will be collected and recorded for later analysis. These data can be of various forms, including test scores, clinician observations, and notations. In whatever form they are, these data constitute a client's record and must be handled with sensitivity.

Maintaining thorough records and clinical notes is essential to the planning and monitoring of services as well as to providing data, should the interaction ever be questioned as in the case of a lawsuit. Keeping good and accurate records provides a strong foundation for counselors in the event of claims regarding legal issues and ethics violations (Mitchell, 2007). Thus, even with concern about possible requirements to disclose, experiences of inconvenience, or a practitioner's belief in the power of his or her memory, the ethical practitioner will collect and maintain useful professional records. In fact, all of the professional organizations (see Table 12.1) call for the ethical collection, maintenance, and dissemination of client information.

Nature and Extent of Records

Records should document the nature, delivery, and progress of services provided. Additional information may be required by state statute and/or contract, as when services are provided as part of a managed care organization. While the specifics of what may be required as part of a client's record varies from state to state, generally it is important to maintain a legible record that includes at a minimum the following: identifying data; dates of services; types of services; fees; any assessment, plan for intervention, consultation, and/or summary reports as may be appropriate; and any release of information obtained. One example of the types of records one should maintain was developed by the Committee on Professional Practice and Standards of the APA. While the model is somewhat dated it remains a useful guide for practitioners. This committee adopted a set of guidelines (see Canter, Bennett, Jones, & Nagy, 1994), which suggests that at a minimum records should contain the following:

- Intake sheet, including client identifying information
- Documentation of a mental status assessment
- Signed informed consent
- Treatment plans
- Psychological tests
- Documentation of referrals
- Types of services provided
- Appointment dates and times
- Release of information
- Discharge summary

While the above provides some minimal guidelines for identifying the nature and type of records to be collected and maintained, the specific form of each of the above or the nature and content and style of clinical notes and records will be determined by the specific regulations of the setting in which the services are provided, state laws, or helper preferences (see Exercise 12.2).

Exercise 12.2

Nature of Records to be Kept

Directions: Using the questions listed below, interview two professional helpers in each of the following professions:

- Private practitioner
- School counselor
- Criminal justice worker/counselor

(Continued)

(Continued)

- Drug and alcohol counselor

- Marriage therapist

Ask each helper if he or she keeps client files and if not, why not. If yes, ask him or her

- What type of information do you keep in your files?

- How long do you maintain your files?

- Does your client have access to these files?

- Have you had your records subpoenaed? If so, what was your response?

Compare and contrast the helpers' responses. Was there commonality within the specific helping profession? What similarities or differences existed across professional groups?

Regardless of the types of data collected, clarity and utility should guide the process. The notes are meant to assist in the treatment (utility), and since records belong to the client and copies could be requested, they should be clearly written in a manner that is honest and non-demeaning.

Storage and Access

The collection and maintenance of such sensitive information can conflict with a client's right to personal privacy if not handled professionally and ethically. For example, the American Psychological Association's ethical code (2010), Principle 6.02 (a) states, "Psychologists maintain confidentiality in creating, storing, accessing, transferring and disposing of records under their control, whether these are written, automated, or in any other medium."

There is, however, no one set of standards that concretely and universally applies across professions and settings. It is incumbent for each professional to understand the ethical principles articulated within his or her profession. In addition to these standards, the practitioner needs to be aware of the legal statutes and practice principles governing the acquisition, storage, and maintenance of records in his or her own particular setting. For example, practitioners working within a school setting that receives federal funding will be governed by the Family Educational Rights and Privacy Act (FERPA) (U.S. Department of Education. 2015). This act provides rights of access to educational records to students and their parents and defines educational record as any record kept by employees of the educational institution. Since broad access of records is not required of practitioners working within a non-federally funded setting, it is clear that the decisions regarding the nature of records collected and the forms of storage can vary setting to setting.

In what is now a significant event in the history of educational record keeping, the Russell Sage Foundation convened a conference in 1969 of representatives from educational and legal institutions as well as experts in related fields to address the issue of collecting, maintaining, and disseminating records within the schools. The members concluded that "current practices of schools and school personnel relating to the collection, maintenance, use and dissemination of information about pupils threaten a desirable balance between the individual's right to privacy and the school's stated 'need to know'" (Russell Sage Foundation, 1970). The outcome of this conference was the production of a proposed set of guidelines that, while targeted to pupil records, has value for all practitioners, regardless of the setting and the population with whom they work. A number of points gleaned from the historic conference are presented in and serve as a reference point for Exercise 12.3.

Table 12.4 Summary of Russell Sage Conference

Collection of Data	*Consent*	*No information should be collected without prior informed consent.*
		The client should be informed as fully as possible, consonant with the practitioner's professional responsibility and the capacity of the client to understand.
		Even when data is collected under conditions of anonymity, the obligation to obtain consent remains.
Maintenance of Data	Levels: Category A	Data included here reflect the minimum personal data necessary (e.g., name, address, date of birth, academic background, etc.).
		For schools, these data should be maintained in perpetuity.

(Continued)

Table 12.4 (Continued)

Collection of Data	Consent	No information should be collected without prior informed consent.
	Category B	Data are of clear importance but not absolutely necessary for helping the client or protecting others over time (e.g., scores on standardized testing, family background data, observations and rating scales).
		These data (in regard to school settings) should be eliminated as unnecessary at periodic intervals (e.g., transition points, such as moving from elementary to junior high).
	Category C	This is useful information needed for the immediate present (e.g., legal or clinical findings).
		Data should be reviewed at least once a year (in school settings) and destroyed as soon as their usefulness is ended. If usefulness continues and validity of information has been verified, they may be transferred to Category B.
	Confidential, personal files	Any and all data that are considered personal property of the professional should be guarded by the rules given above and dictated by professional ethics, terms of employment, and any special agreements made between the professional and the client.
Dissemination	Releasing without consent	In school setting, category A and B data may be released to other school officials including teachers who have a legitimate educational interest in pupil records.
	With consent/ judicial order	School may not divulge any information to anyone outside of the legitimate school personnel without written consent or compliance with judicial order.
	Non-release	Under no conditions, except court order, should school release information in Category C.

Source: Adapted from *Guidelines for the Collection, Maintenance and Dissemination of Pupil Records. Report of a Conference on the Ethical and Legal Aspects of School Record Keeping* (1969). © Russell Sage Foundation, 112 East 64th Street, New York, NY 10065. Reprinted with Permission.

Database and Computer Storage

The issue of storage and access takes on special significance when considered within the advances of this technological era and the use of

---

Exercise 12.3

Assessing School Record Keeping

Directions:

Step 1: Contact your high school or a local high school. Inquire what their policy is regarding the gathering, maintenance, access, and disposal of the following types of records:

- Student attendance

- Student course grades

- Student discipline record

- Student health records

- Student standardized test scores

- Student counseling records (if any)

- Student Individualized Education Plan (IEPs) or specialized academic program plans

- Teacher, counselor, administrator anecdotal notes on students

Step 2: Using the category breakdown listed in Table 12.4 (Russell Sage Foundation, 1970), evaluate the degree to which this school is following the Russell Sage guidelines.

---

computers for database storage. For example, the American Psychological Association's ethical code describes the situation: "If confidential information concerning recipients of psychological services is to be entered into databases or systems of records available to persons whose access has not been consented to by the recipient, psychologists use coding or other techniques to avoid the inclusion of personal identifiers" (APA, 2010, 6.02 [b]).

RECENT LEGAL DECISIONS ●

One area of professional practice that has recently been impacted by court decisions is in regard to a client's right to access psychiatric records. The federal Freedom of Information Act of 1966 and various state patients' rights laws often specify client right to access certain personal records. While mental health records have previously been exempted from this policy, the trend appears to be reversing in favor of client access.

For example, it was initially successfully argued that such free access could result in harm to a client, that sharing technical information with clients who are not equipped to understand or deal with this information may prove counterproductive and/or harmful. This argument found support in the case of *Godkin v. Miller* (1975). Janet Godkin had been a voluntary patient at three different New York hospitals. Later, she and her husband decided to write about the experience and requested access to her records. Her requests were denied. In her lawsuit against the New York State Commissioner of Mental Hygiene and the directors of the hospital, the court ruled that the refusal was warranted in light of the fact that the hospitals stated a preference to release the information to another professional. There are a number of points in the process of record acquisition, storage, maintenance, access, and disposition in which a practitioner may be confronted with ethical and or legal questions. However, the courts have not provided a clear directive covering all of these aspects. Without clear legal direction, it is important for practitioners to adhere to commonly held and customary practices and those reflecting their specific codes of ethics. As such it is important to keep the following in mind when keeping records:

1. Ensure that all records and documentation be kept in secure locations where unauthorized access is denied (e.g., ACA, 2014, Principle B.6.b).

2. Write notes in nontechnical, clear, and objective statements with behavioral descriptions. Subjective or evaluative statements involving professional judgments should be designated as such and written in a separate section clearly set aside from factual content. Many practitioners use the S.O.A.P. (subjective, objective, assessment, and plan) format for note taking (Cameron, & Turtle-Song, 2002).

3. All client records should be written with the understanding that they might be seen by the client, a court, or some other authorized person, who may refer to the notes for continuity of care (e.g., see APA, 2010, Principle 6.01).

4. Realizing the purposes for which we maintain records, only information that is necessary for documenting that which was done and directing that which should be or will be done, should be recorded. The American Counseling Association, for example, is clear in stating that its members "include sufficient and timely documentation to facilitate the delivery and continuity of services" and "ensure that documentation accurately reflects client progress and services provided" (ACA, 2014, Principle A1.b).

CONCLUDING CASE ILLUSTRATION ●

The scenario that opened this chapter highlighted the importance of record keeping and the potential that such records may be requested. As we continue the scene, however, we will see that it also raises a number of issues regarding (a) the types of information one collects; (b) the way that records are maintained, and (c) the questions of access to records.

Dr. Flournoy: Hello, Ms. Wicks?

Ms. Wicks: Yes?

Dr. Flournoy: I am Dr. Flournoy from Children and Youth Services.

Ms. Wicks: Hello.

Dr. Flournoy: The Ramerez family has been referred to our service, and I understand that you have been working with Maria, here at school. I have requested that your counseling records be subpoenaed, and I simply wanted to let you know ahead of time, so that you could begin to get them in order.

Ms. Wicks: I appreciate your notification. Even though we utilize computerized intake forms, inventories, and counseling notes, it is always nice to have some lead time to get them together. As I am sure you are aware, I will need a copy of the Release of Information and I would like one from Maria, in addition to her parents.

Dr. Flournoy: I understand that you would like a release, and actually I brought copies of both a parent release and the client's signed release. You can keep them for your records. You mentioned that you have intake forms, inventories, and client notes with computer access.

Ms. Wicks: Yes.

Dr. Flournoy: Well, I'm going to ask for all the notes, including your professional observations and anecdotal notes.

Ms. Wicks: Well, Dr. Flournoy, the school's policy is that counselor records include

- Intake sheet, including client identifying information
- Signed informed consent
- Documentation of referrals
- Types of services provided

- Standardized test scores and/or inventories employed
- Appointment record
- Release of information
- Summary of contact

So I will be happy to provide these to you.

Dr. Flournoy: Thank you. But I know as a counselor you probably kept personal notes. I would like to see those as well.

Ms. Wicks: The notes that we have are those identified by school policy. I've already listed those and I will be glad to provide them. But first, I do want to speak with Maria, and even though she signed the release, I would like her to know exactly what we will be releasing.

Reflections

1. What do you think about Ms. Wicks's request for a release of information from both the parents and Maria? Was it legally required? Ethically required?
2. Ms. Wicks outlined the type of information that the school directed counselors to maintain. How adequate do these records appear to be? Is there anything you feel is missing?
3. What concerns would you have with having this data in computer storage?
4. What is your reaction to Ms. Wicks's response in regard to personal, anecdotal notes?
5. Ms. Wicks noted that she wanted to explain to Maria the types of material to be released. Was that necessary? Required? What are your feelings regarding that decision?

● COOPERATIVE LEARNING EXERCISE

As with all of the previous cooperative learning exercises, the current exercise is designed to help you personalize the material and begin to move your understanding to professional practice. Working with a colleague and/or classmate, identify the types of client information that you feel are needed in the course of your professional practice and that will be retained within a client record. Next, complete the following:

- Design samples of the specific forms or data collection tools you will employ.
- Contact three individuals currently working in the area of professional practice that you envision doing and request copies of their data collection tools and instruments.
- Finally, contact your state association and inquire about the length of time you will be responsible for maintaining these records.

SUMMARY ●

- Evaluation of the helping process needs to be ongoing and formative as well as summative in form. Formative evaluation is evaluation that occurs as an ongoing process throughout the helping encounter. Summative evaluation is the type of evaluation most typically thought of when considering goal or outcome assessment.
- Because of the potential to influence the client and the client's ability to formulate his or her own goals and objectives, it is important for the practitioner to be sure to engage the client in terminal goal formulation.
- When articulating treatment goals, the more perspectives we take on the outcome and the more measures we employ, the greater the chance we have of understanding the nature and depth of impact our practice may have produced.
- Record keeping is important not just as a documentation of service but also to guide and direct the practitioner in his or her practice decisions.
- Maintaining thorough records and clinical notes is essential to the planning and monitoring of services as well as to providing data should the interaction ever be questioned, as in the case of a lawsuit.
- Records should document the nature, delivery, and progress of services provided. The collection and maintenance of such sensitive information can conflict with a client's right to personal privacy if not handled professionally and ethically.

● IMPORTANT TERMS

accountability	modality
data collection techniques	outcome measures
evaluation	record keeping
Family Educational and Privacy Act (FERPA)	Russell Sage guidelines
	summative
formative	terminal goal

● ADDITIONAL RESOURCES

Print

American Psychological Association. (2007). Record keeping guidelines. *American Psychologist, 62*(9), 993–1004.

Christiansen, R. (2012*). Zig zag principle: The goal setting strategy that will revolutionize your business and life*. New York, NY: McGraw-Hill.

Hatch, T. (2014). *The use of data in school counseling: Hatching results for students, programs, and the profession*. Thousand Oaks, CA: Corwin.

Luepker, E. T. (2012). *Record keeping in psychotherapy and counseling: Protecting confidentiality and the professional relationship*. New York, NY: Taylor & Francis.

Wed-Based

Johnson, V. (2010, February 16). *Jim Rohn setting goals part 1* [Video file]. Retrieved from www.youtube.com/watch?v=YuObJcgfSQA

Stone, C. (2013, July 1). FERPA: The ever-changing federal statue. *ASCA school-counselor*. Retrieved from http://www.schoolcounselor.org/magazine/blogs/july-august-2013/ferpa-the-ever-changing-federal-statute-(1)

Wehrman, J. D., Williams, R., Field, J., & Schroeder, S. D. (2010). Accountability through documentation: What are best practices for school counselors? *Journal of School Counseling, 8*(38), 1–23.

REFERENCES ●

American Association for Marriage and Family Therapy. (2015). *Code of ethics.* Retrieved from https://www.aamft.org/iMIS15/AAMFT/Content/Legal_Ethics/ Code_of_Ethics.aspx

American Counseling Association. (2014). *ACA code of ethics.* Alexandria, VA: Author.

American Psychological Association. (2010). *American Psychological Association's ethical principles of psychologists and code of conduct.* Retrieved from http:// www.apa.org/ethics/code/principles.pdf

Astramovich, R. L., & Coker, J. K. (2007). Program evaluation: The accountability bridge model for counselors. *Journal of Counseling & Development, 85*(2), 162-172.

Cameron, S., & Turtle-Song, I. (2002). Learning to write case notes using the SOAP format. *Journal of Counseling and Development, 80,* 286-292.

Canter, M. B., Bennett, B. E., Jones, S. E., & Nagy, T. F. (1994). *Ethics for psychologists: A commentary on the APA ethics code.* Washington, DC: American Psychological Association.

Godkin v. Miller, 379 F. Supp. 859 (ED N.Y. 1974). Aff'd. 514 F 2d 123 (2d Cir. 1975).

Lazarus, A. (1989). *The practice of multimodal therapy* (2nd ed). Baltimore: John Hopkins University Press.

Mitchell, R. W. (2007). *Documentation in counseling records: An overview of ethical, legal, and clinical issues* (3rd ed.). Alexandria, VA: American Counseling Association.

National Association of Social Workers (2008). *Code of ethics of the National Association of Social Workers.* Retrieved from https://www.socialworkers.org/ pubs/code/code.asp

Parsons, R. D., & Zhang, N. (2014). *Becoming a skilled counselor.* Thousand Oaks, CA: Sage.

Russell Sage Foundation. (1970). *Guidelines for the collection maintenance and dissemination of pupil records.* Hartford, CN: Russell Sage Foundation.

Seijts, G. H., Latham, G. P., Tasa, K., & Latham, B. W. (2004). Goal setting and goal orientation: An integration of two different yet related literatures. *Academy of Management Journal, 47,* 227-239.

U.S. Department of Education. (2015). *Family Educational Rights and Privacy Act (FERPA).* Retrieved from http://www2.ed.gov/policy/gen/guid/fpco/ferpa/ index.html

Zhang, N., & Parsons, R. D. (2015). *Field experience: Transitioning from student to professional.* Thousand Oaks, CA: Sage.

CHAPTER 13

Ethical Challenges Working With Groups, Couples, and Families

I am starting to panic . . . I am running a therapy group and realize that while I can ensure confidentiality, at least from my end, I can't control what the other group members do with what they hear. Am I responsible if they break the group's confidence?

Maintaining confidentiality when working with a group, a family, or even a couple is a lot more difficult and complicated than when working with a single client one-on-one. Challenges to ethical practice when working with multiple participants is not limited to the maintenance of confidentiality. While there are many subtle challenges that will be encountered by any human service provider working with groups, families, and couples, the current chapter will address the dilemmas that may surface in relationship to (a) practitioner competency, (b) identification of the "client," (c) informed consent, (d) confidentiality, (e) boundaries, and (f) client welfare.

● OBJECTIVES

- Describe the competencies required for one to ethically engage in professional practice with couples, families, and groups.
- Explain the challenge encountered when defining who is the client when working with couples, families, and groups.
- Describe the challenges encountered and the steps to be taken to ensure informed consent when working with couples, families, and groups.
- Describe the challenges encountered to the maintenance of professional boundaries when working with couples, families, and groups.

● COMPETENCY TO PRACTICE

As noted previously (see Chapter 3), a core ethical responsibility of every human service provider is to do "good" on the client's behalf (i.e., beneficence). While this value is evident throughout our codes of ethics, it starts with the practitioner's competence to provide the service rendered. It would be easy for one who has been trained in providing direct service in a one-on-one context to assume that the same principles of therapeutic relationship, intervention, and ethics would transfer to their work with couples, families, or even groups. This is NOT the case. When professionally providing counseling to couples, families, and/or groups, specific, specialty training is a must.

Jacobs, Masson, Harvill, & Schimmel, 2012), for example, assert that the most frequent unethical practice in-group facilitation is when untrained leaders lead groups. Without specific training and the development of those competencies identified as fundamental to effectively working with couples or families or groups, one risks violating the core ethical principle of our duty to care, to do good (i.e., beneficence) and avoid doing harm (i.e., maleficence).

Practicing within the limits of one's competency is clearly articulated in our ethical codes; for example, the American Counseling Association's (ACA) code of ethics states: "Counselors practice only within the boundaries of their competence, based on their education, training, supervised experience, state and national professional credentials, and appropriate professional experience" (ACA, 2014, Principle C.2.a). Similar calls to function within one's level of knowledge, skill, training, and experience have been made by other professional organizations including the American Psychological Association (APA, 2010, Principle 2.01), the American Association for

Marriage and Family Therapy (AAMFT, 2015, Principle 3.10), the American Mental Health Counselors Association (AMHCA, 2010, Principle 1.b), and the International Association for Group Psychotherapy and Group Processes (IAGP, 2009, Principle 6).

Beyond a general directive to practice within one's level of knowledge and skill as formed in education and training and supported through supervision, professional codes of ethics and conduct caution professionals against engaging in specialty areas without specific training and experience in those areas. For example, counselors are ethically mandated to receive appropriate supervision when working with a population or employing a technique in which they have had no special training: Counselors practice in specialty areas new to them only after appropriate education, training, and supervised experience (ACA, 2014, Principle C.2.b) and similarly, school counselors are directed to "practice within their competence level and develop professional competence through training and supervision" (ASCA, 2016, A.7.h).

With this emphasis on competency as fundamental to ethical practice, we invite you to consider Exercise 13.1, which not only asks you to assess your levels of competency but also invites you to begin to develop a preliminary plan for advancing that competency.

Exercise 13.1

Assessing Competency

Directions: Read the following case scenario and with a colleague, faculty member, or supervisor discuss the questions posed at the end.

The Case: I Don't Want Or Need to Come. . . .

The call was, at first, one like he had received literally hundreds of times. A mother, clearly concerned, opened the conversation with, "Dr. Alonzo, I was referred to you by the school counselor. My son, who is a senior, was just busted with marijuana and our family is in turmoil." Dr. Alonzo provided support for the distraught mother and asked if she had discussed the possibility of coming in for family counseling with her son. Mrs. Gage responded by informing Dr. Alonzo that when they met with the counselor, it was she, her husband, and her only child, Michael. They discussed the situations regarding falling grades, his new group of friends, his verbalized disinterest in going to college, the

(Continued)

(Continued)

current "drug bust," and the tension at home. He agreed to the idea of connecting with a family counselor.

Following this brief explanation, a time for the intake session was established. Thus went the initial contact.

Two days later and 4 days prior to the scheduled appointment, Dr. Alonzo received a phone call from Michael. After introducing himself and noting that he was 18 years old, Michael proceeded to say that he did not want to attend and that the only reason he even suggested agreement in the counselor's office was that his parents threatened to take his car away. He was calling to tell Dr. Alonzo, "I don't want to appear rude or waste your time, but I do not want to come, and if I do it is only because they are threatening me with the car." He ended the conversation with, "I don't want you to tell my parents that I called."

Needless to say, the phone call was both informative and challenging. Dr. Alonzo was confronted with numerous questions about how to proceed.

Reflection

How would you respond to each of Dr. Alonzo's concerns?

- Do I proceed with the scheduled session?

- Do I address the issue of "freedom" to participate at the risk of revealing Michael's call and concern?

- Do I see the family as the client or is each member a client, and accordingly, how do I attend to the concern and support Michael's welfare?

- Do I keep Michael's phone call in confidence?

- If in session with the family all members agree to continue in the counseling, can I trust that Michael will be honest and provide true consent?

- Do I schedule separate individual sessions, and what possible ethical can of worms might I be opening, especially in terms of encouraging more private disclosure or appearing to have "identified" the problem client or even being seduced into an alliance with one member or another?

IDENTIFYING THE "CLIENT" ●

For clinicians who typically provide service to individual children, teens, or adults, identifying the client is relatively simple and clear. In these situations, the client is typically the individual sitting before the clinician and the one who is seeking help. For those who work with couples, families, or groups, this process of identifying the client is not so clear-cut.

When working with multiple participants, a clinician needs to decide on who is the client—be that each individual in the couple, the family, the group, or the collective as a whole—but also be clear about the implications that definitions have for ethical practice. The importance of identifying and clarifying the nature of the relationship of therapist to individual participants and to the collective as a whole is significant because various participants engaged with the collective in this helping process can and often do have conflicting needs (Glick, Berman, Clarkin, & Rait, 2000). And as noted by Corey, Corey, & Corey (2010), it is important, when defining the client, to be careful not to make things better for one member while simultaneously making things worse for another.

The ethical directive is clear. The identification of the client is an essential first step to the ethical provision of service when multiple participants are involved. Psychologists who work with couples in relationship therapy are, for example, advised to "take reasonable steps to clarify at the outset (1) which of the individuals are clients/patients and (2) the relationship the psychologist will have with each person" (APA, 2010, Principle 10.02.a). Similarly, when working with groups, psychologists are directed in this way: "When psychologists provide services to several persons in a group setting, they describe at the outset the roles and responsibilities of all parties" (APA, 2010, Principle 10.03). Along the same line, counselors are directed to clearly define who is considered the client when working with couples and families and unless otherwise specified in writing, consider the client to be the couple or family (ACA, 2014, Principle B.4.b). Perhaps the clearest, most explicit statement on the ethics of defining the client comes from the International Association of Marriage and Family Counselors (Hendricks, Bradley, Southern, & Birdsall, 2011), which notes: "Marriage and family counselors have an obligation to determine and inform counseling participants who is identified as the primary client . . . and . . . should make clear when there are obligations to an individual, couple, family, third party or institution" (Section A:7, p.218).

The options defining who is the client are many, and thus what is important is the presentation of clarity around the issue of who is the client. For example, some couple therapists will define the couple and the actual relationship as the client, with the goal focused on improving that relationship.

Whereas others, recognizing that the relationship is composed of two individuals with unique needs, will target each individual as contributing to and benefitting from the relationship (Epstein & Baucom, 2002). This issue isn't fixed, nor is direction given. What's important is that the definition, the explanation, and the nature of the focus of the therapy be provided at the outset.

The way we define or conceptualize the client, be that each individual with which we engage or the collective of the couple, the family, or even the group, has significant impact on how a clinician addresses issues such as informed consent, confidentiality, record keeping, and maintenance of boundaries. The standard ethical practice employed by those serving individual clients may not be readily transferrable to situations in which there are multiple participants. In fact, maintaining ethical practice when working with families, couples, or groups can be multitiered and complex.

While the various codes (e.g., APA, 2010) imply that the choice of defining the client as each individual or the group is up to the discretion of the clinician, it should be noted that when working with families, the law typically sees the *individuals* as the client and/or at least having rights (Remley & Herlihy, 2014). The way one defines the client is not only an ethical concern but also one having clear legal ramifications. As such, clinicians need to be aware not only of their governing code of ethics and conduct but also the laws and regulations governing their practice with specific populations and with specific modes of delivery.

● INFORMED CONSENT

Informed consent is a legal and ethical term defined as the consent by a client to engage in a specific process or procedure, including a proposed psychotherapeutic process. The practitioner's ethical concern for achieving informed consent is a reflection of his valuing of the client's autonomy and human dignity.

In order for the consent to be *informed*, the client must first achieve a clear understanding of the relevant facts, risks and benefits, and available alternatives involved. Specific principles reflecting the valuing of informed consent can be found in almost all professional organizations' codes of ethics. However, when it comes to the *why*, the *what*, and the *how* of gaining informed consent, the discussion most typically addresses those clinical situations in which the interaction is dyadic, as that is where it involves a counselor and a single client. When working with couples, families, and/or groups, the value of gaining informed consent remains; however, the specifics of what and how can vary.

Consistency is needed when it comes to providing the essential information required for gaining informed consent. For example, the AMHCA posits the ethical requirement that therapists "clarify at the outset the nature of the relationship they will have with each involved person" (2010, B.2.a) and "gain informed consent from all involved in counseling" (2010, B.3.b). This additional step of clarifying roles and relationships is also cited by the American Psychological Association, whose code of ethics directs psychologists, when working with several persons who have a relationship (i.e., spouses, families), that in addition to the general components of informed consent psychologists should take "reasonable steps to clarify at the outset (1) which of the individuals are clients/patients and (2) the relationship the psychologist will have with each person" (APA, 2010, Principle 10.02) or when working with groups that "they describe at the outset the roles and responsibilities of all parties and the limits of confidentiality" (APA, 2010, Principle 10.03).

General Components

Gaining informed consent, regardless of whether it is in the context of a single client or multiple participants, involves three general components. First, all participants should be given information regarding the nature, risks, and benefits of the treatment processes to be employed. This would include things such as the limits of confidentiality, the conditions governing the release of information, the types of records to be kept and the process and limits of accessing those records, payment schedule, and so forth. The second general component to be addressed while gaining informed consent, in any practice, would be to evaluate whether or not the participant(s) has (have) the capacity to understand the information shared and is (are) competent to provide informed consent. Finally, all practitioners will then gain some form of documentation or client acknowledgment that shows that they have been informed and provide competent consent. While this appears relatively clear-cut, when applied to work with couples, families, and groups, numerous challenges will be encountered.

Working With Couples, Families, and Groups

While the previously identified general components of informed consent apply to all practices, additional concerns and challenges emerge for those working with couples, families, or groups. The challenge can emerge even at the point of initial contact. Consider an issue that is often overlooked

Table 13.1   Informed Consent—Group Work

- **Goals** of the group along with expectations of what can be accomplished

- **Risks** unique to group experiences, including group pressure, scapegoating, and lack of guarantee of confidentiality

- **Roles** of all participants, including leader (and any relationships with individual participants), and the role of each member in the group and their responsibilities to the group as a whole and to one another

- **Rules**—including members' respect for privacy (i.e., confidentiality, even after the group ends), procedures for leaving the group, and the responsibilities to other members, and participants' rules for outside contact/disclosures/discussions

relating to the initial call or request for service. When working with an individual outside of mandated or coerced conditions, it is usually fair to assume that the individual who is calling is the one who is "freely" seeking service. However, can that assumption automatically be made for a couple where one spouse makes the call or a family where a parent arranges for an appointment?

When considering the nature and composition of these multiple member configurations, it becomes clear that sometimes individuals within the grouping have different levels of power and opportunity to influence the decisions and direction the collective takes. In these situations, the possibility of "social coercion" and influence imposed on any one member, at the cost to their autonomy, may exist (Ramisch, 2010). Consider the illustration presented in Table 13.1.

This recognition of the possibility of coercion and influence and the ethical directive to take steps to ensure against such means of limiting informed consent is highlighted in the *AAMFT Code of Ethics,* which states that family therapists will ensure that all participants have "freely and without undue influence expressed consent" and (e) "provided consent that is appropriately documented" (2015, Standard 1.2).

While the directive is clear, meeting the ethical standards governing informed consent can be fraught with challenges. What should a clinician do, for example, if it is clear that one member, perhaps a child, has been forced/coerced into attending therapy and truly does not want to participate? Or what if an adult member of a couple is in attendance simply as a way of placating the other member?

The need to inform and gain consent or assent (depending on legal age) from all involved prior to engaging in service is essential. However, it is not a one-time only process, and procedures need to be enacted that ensure the ongoing acquisition of that consent from ALL participants. Such a process is essential to ethical practice.

This point has been highlighted, for example, by the AMHCA, who notes the ethical requirement to "clarify at the outset, the nature of the relationship they will have with each involved person" (AMHCA, 2010, B.2.a) and "gain informed consent from all involved in the counselling" (AMHCA, 2010, B.3.b). This additional step of clarifying roles and relationships is also cited by the APA, whose code of ethics directs psychologists, when working with several persons who have a relationship (i.e. spouses, families), that in addition to the general components of informed consent psychologists should take "reasonable steps to clarify at the outset (1) which of the individuals are clients/patients and (2) the relationship the psychologist will have with each person" (APA, 2010, Principle 10.02); or when working with groups, "they describe at the outset the roles and responsibilities of all parties and the limits of confidentiality" *(APA, 2010, Principle 10.03).*

Because of the uniqueness of the conditions presented when working with couples, families, or groups, therapists who work with these populations may consider providing an addendum to the normal information shared in a consent form, to include those elements unique to these modalities. For example, Bass and Quimby (2006) suggest that couples therapists should develop an addendum to their informed consent document that outlines their policy regarding privacy and the sharing of individual secrets. While highlighting the value and purpose of meeting with the partners individually, this addendum would explain how the therapist would handle any secret information shared in these meetings along with the therapeutic rationale for that policy. Similarly, the Association for Specialists in Group Work, a division of the ACA, highlights the additional information to be shared when gaining informed consent. In their *Best Practice Guidelines* (2007), the Association for Specialists in Group Work direct group workers to do the following:

> Provide in oral and written form to prospective members (when appropriate to group type): the professional disclosure statement; group purpose and goals; group participation expectations including voluntary and involuntary membership; role expectations of members and leader(s); policies related to entering and exiting the group; policies governing substance use; policies and procedures governing mandated groups (where relevant); documentation requirements; disclosure of information to others; implications of out-of-group contact or involvement among members; procedures for consultation

between group leader(s) and group member(s); fees and time parameters; and potential impacts of group participation. (Thomas & Pender, 2007)

● CONFIDENTIALITY

The ability to speak openly and with emotional honesty is supported by a trusting relationship that ensures a respect for privacy. The clinician's commitment to maintaining confidentiality is a sign of his respect for the client's right to decide what and to whom she will disclose. Confidentiality, which is reflective of a practitioner's valuing of client autonomy as well as his own commitment to fidelity to the client, serves as a foundation of a therapeutic alliance.

When working with a single client in a one-to-one therapeutic relationship, the maintenance of confidence is within the control of the clinician. The ethical practitioners, working in concert with prevailing laws, codes of ethics, and their organizational regulations, will inform the client of limits of confidentiality and will then work to maintain the confidence of all material falling within those limits.

When working with multiple people in one room, as will be the case for those working with couples, families, or groups, the challenges to confidentiality are compounded and yet the ethical standards to protect the privacy and confidence of each participant remains. For example, The AAMFT notes, "Marriage and family therapists have unique confidentiality concerns because the client in a therapeutic relationship may be more than one person. Therapists respect and guard the confidences of each individual client" (2015, Standard II).

Secrets as Confidential?

A question that must be considered by those working with multiple participants is, how do standard practices of confidentiality translate from the traditional dyadic client-therapist relationship to a therapeutic relationship that includes a spouse, other family members, or "strangers" in a group? Consider a situation in which a therapist is working with a couple experiencing marital conflict and as part of the treatment, meets with each member privately for one session. During the session with one spouse, that member discloses having an affair. If the therapist believes the affair is contributing to the couple's difficulties, should the therapist reveal that information during the couple's joint sessions? What if the individual specifically asks that it not be revealed? Exercise 13.2 provides you with a scenario experienced by one marriage counselor. Reviewing

---

Exercise 13.2

In a Bind

Directions: Review the following case illustration and then, along with a colleague or a supervisor, discuss your position on each of the questions posed.

The Case

As part of her marriage and family practice, Dr. Martin schedules individual sessions with the individual members of the couple. In her session with Mrs. Francisco, she discovered that Mrs. Francisco, while attending the sessions, was truly not invested in saving the marriage. In fact, Mrs. Francisco shared that she had begun developing an emotionally intimate relationship with a colleague, who has directed her to a divorce attorney. In the individual session, Dr. Martin was able to convince Mrs. Francisco of the benefit of sharing, in the couple session, her interest in ending the marriage. Although she agreed in the individual session with Dr. Martin, when it came to the joint session, Mrs. Francisco hedged, stating, "I am not sure if this will work—I mean, I'll come, but I'm not real hopeful . . . I just don't know."

When Dr. Martin asked if she could elaborate on her feelings and what it is that she felt was contributing to lack of hope, Mrs. Francisco became somewhat agitated and defensive and stated that she wasn't sure and that she would give it some thought for future sessions.

Given the information previously shared with Dr. Martin in the individual session, this response seemed less than honest and forthcoming. However, Mr. Francisco seemed accepting and encouraged that his wife would continue to think about it and come to sessions. Dr. Martin felt like he was in a bind.

For Reflection

How would you respond if you were in Dr. Martin's position, and specifically, how would you respond to each of the following?

(Continued)

(Continued)

- Should the therapist push the client to more fully and more honestly disclose?

- Would disclosure at this time be what was best for each individual or for the couple as an entity?

- Should the therapist meet with Mrs. Francisco again to confront her failure to disclose honestly and to discuss the value of a full disclosure?

- What "rules" would you have established and shared as part of gaining informed consent prior to holding individual sessions?

- Would doing or saying nothing be ethical?

the case will allow you to reflect upon the ethical challenges encountered when working in this modality.

The issue of handling private or "secret" disclosures, as encountered by Dr. Martin (see Exercise 13.2) is complicated and something a practitioner working with couples, families, and/or groups needs to consider prior to engaging with clients. The challenge of course is finding ways to balance the individual's right to privacy with the relationship's need for safety, which requires more transparency.

It is generally recognized that individual disclosures should be held in confidence only if doing so DOES NOT contribute to maintaining unhealthy family dynamics. The IAMFC, for example, notes, "Couple and family counselors do not maintain family secrets, collude with some family members against others, or otherwise contribute to dysfunctional family system dynamics" (2011, Section B., p. 219). Likewise, the AAMFT takes the following position:

> When providing couple, family or group treatment, the therapist does not disclose information outside the treatment context without a written authorization from each individual competent to execute a waiver. In the context of couple, family or group treatment, the therapist may not reveal any individual's confidences to others in the client unit without the prior written permission of that individual." (2015, Standard 2.2)

While there is no one single position on the above, those engaged in family, group, or couple work may find the first step in addressing the sharing of "secrets" to rest in their position on whether they treat members as individual clients and maintain private communication or see the couple, family, or group as client. It can be argued that treating each member as an individual client can encourage privacy and triangulation. The alternative position would be to allow all members, by way of informed consent, to understand private communication would not be encouraged and would not be held in confidence. In either case, a "safe" position for all practitioners would be to inform all participants of the therapist's stance and practice regarding the maintenance of confidential information.

Limits to Ensuring Confidentiality

The importance of providing participants this information has been emphasized by our professional organizations. Psychologists who provide services in a group setting, for example, are directed to describe "at the outset the roles and responsibilities of all parties and the limits of confidentiality" (APA, 2010. Standard 10.03). The ACA not only supports a similar position but also directs counselors to "discuss expectations and limitations of confidentiality" and "seek agreement and document in writing such agreement among all involved parties regarding the confidentiality" (2014, Principle B.4.b). The *AAMFT Code of Ethics* directs therapists to be upfront with the family from the beginning of treatment to inform them of their right to confidentiality and let them know that a therapist may not disclose to other family members any information an individual family member might share in private (2015, Principle 2.1).

For individuals working in a group therapy context, the IAGP directs its members to not only respect the participants' privacy and keep information about participants in confidence (2009, Principle 3.1) but also inform participants "of the limits of confidentiality" (2009, Principle 3.4). It has been suggested that group leaders have members of a group complete a confidentiality agreement, an agreement that explains that comembers have no confidentiality privilege, along with the need to avoid socializing outside of the group (MacKenzie, 1997).

Concerns about maintenance and limitations to confidentiality extend to the creation and maintenance of session notes. Would, for example, one family member or one member of the couple have the right to request and utilize family session notes in a lawsuit against one of the other family members? The IAMFC directs practitioners to share that which is unique and personal to the individual requesting notes "in situations involving multiple clients, couple and family counselors provide individual clients with parts of records related directly to them, protecting confidential information related to other clients who have not authorized release" (Hendricks, Bradley, Southern, Oliver, & Birdsall, 2011), a point that is supported legally by the HIPAA standards, which requires that each individual have his or her own records, notes, consent, and other individual data.

Maintaining Confidentiality

For those who work with couples and families, there can be no absolute guarantee of confidentiality, since unlike the therapist, other participants are NOT bound by a professional ethic directing confidentiality. Encouraging members to respect the privacy of all involved and uphold the spirit of confidentiality does not automatically equate to members' actions. Because of this, some have suggested enforcing confidentiality with the possibility of termination from the therapy. While this is not feasible in couples or marriage therapy, the International Association for Group Psychotherapy and Group Processes (IAGP) directs its members "to take steps to intervene with group members who violate the confidentiality of another in order to restore a sense of safety to the group" (2009, Principle 3.8). It has even been suggested that therapists take a position of enacting expulsion from the group as a possible consequence in the violation of confidentiality (Brabender, 2002).

It is our position that, prior to adopting such a position, it is important to understand the ethical principles guiding "termination" along with a consideration given to the potential impact that such a termination may have on the individual and the remaining members of the group (See Table 13.2).

Table 13.2 Ethical Directives Guiding Termination

Professional Organization	Principle or Standard
American Association for Marriage and Family Therapy, (2015)	1.11. Non-Abandonment Marriage and family therapists do not abandon or neglect clients in treatment without making reasonable arrangements for the continuation of treatment.
American Counseling Association, (2014)	A.11.a. Abandonment prohibited Counselors do not abandon or neglect clients in counseling. Counselors assist in making appropriate arrangements for the continuation of treatment, when necessary, during interruptions such as vacations, illness, and following termination.

Professional Organization	Principle or Standard
American Psychological Association (2010)	10.10. Terminating therapy c. Except where precluded by the actions of clients/patients or third-party payors, prior to termination psychologists provide pre-termination counseling and suggest alternative service providers as appropriate.
National Association of Social Workers (2008)	1.16. b. Social workers should take reasonable steps to avoid abandoning clients who are still in need of services. Social workers should withdraw services precipitously only under unusual circumstances, giving careful consideration to all factors in the situation and taking care to minimize possible adverse effects. Social workers should assist in making appropriate arrangements for continuation of services when necessary. e. Social workers who anticipate the termination or interruption of services to clients should notify clients promptly and seek the transfer, referral, or continuation of services in relation to the clients' needs and preferences.

BOUNDARIES ●

Boundaries and the ethics of a clinician engaging in nonprofessional roles and relationships with clients is an issue that has received a lot of attention across the spectrum of human services. Distinctions have been made between what has been termed boundary violations and boundary crossings (see Chapter 10).

Boundary violations by therapists are by definition exploitive and harmful to patients and thus unethical. A typical prohibition from such exploitation can be found in the IAGP code of ethics that clearly states "psychotherapists shall not exploit their patients sexually or financially, nor should they use information gained during the course of treatment for their own benefit" (2009, Standard 4.1). While all clinicians have been directed to avoid exploitative relationships that result from boundary violations, these same codes of ethics do NOT prohibit boundary crossings. In fact, some forms of boundary crossing have been posited as serving a purposeful, therapeutic value and can be an integral part of a well-formulated treatment plan (Zur, 2015). Exercise 13.3 invites you to review a number of extra-therapeutic encounters and along with a colleague or supervisor, discuss the potential risks and benefits afforded by each.

Exercise 13.3

Extra Therapeutic Encounters

Directions: Complete the table for each of the following "extra-therapeutic encounters." It is suggested you discuss your reflections with a colleague or supervisor.

Activity	Boundary Violation or Crossing	Potential Benefits	Potential Risks	Ethical (yes/no)
• Client lost job as a union carpenter • No longer has ability to pay for marriage counseling • Wishes to barter				
• Couple being treated for grief following the loss of their newborn infant • Mother, in exiting the session, reaches out to hug the therapist				
• Family invites a school counselor to their son's graduation party as a "thank you" for working with the family through a number of developmental crises				

Activity	Boundary Violation or Crossing	Potential Benefits	Potential Risks	Ethical (yes/no)
• Couple invites their marriage counselor to the celebration of their renewing of their vows				
• Group therapist goes on a private plane owned and operated by a member of his group • The member invited the therapist and two other members who had disclosed in group their fear of flying (i.e., aviophobia)				

Discerning the ethics of boundary crossing requires one to identify the benefits and helpful therapeutic value afforded by the crossing. Since that which constitutes a "helpful" boundary crossing is not always clear-cut, most ethical codes direct practitioners to either avoid such dual or multiple relationships or to proceed with caution. For example, The International Association of Marriage and Family Counselor's (IAMFC) code of ethics encourages family counselors to "avoid whenever possible multiple relationships, such as business, social, or sexual contacts with any current clients or family members" (2011, Section A9, p. 218). A similar directive is found within the *AAMFT's Code of Ethics*, which gives the following direction: "Marriage and family therapists are aware of their influential positions with respect to clients, and they avoid exploiting the trust and dependency of such persons. Therapists, therefore, make every effort to avoid conditions and multiple relationships with clients that could impair professional judgment or increase the risk of exploitation" (2015, Standard 1.3). The strength of this directive to avoid, when possible, dual relationships and maintain professional boundaries and distance, while found in all professional codes of conduct and ethics (e.g., APA, 2010, Standard 3.05; NASW, 2008, Standard 1.06.c), is most clearly articulated by the IAGP in its statement that "during ongoing group psychotherapy any other form of relationship with the patient should be avoided and professional contact outside therapy should be kept to a minimum. . . . " (2009, Standard 4.3).

● RESPONSIBILITY: CLIENT WELFARE

As we end the chapter, it is important to remind ourselves that the primary directive guiding all of our practice decisions should be to promote the welfare of our clients (see ACA, 2014, A.1.a). This is the ethical provider's primary responsibility regardless if he or she is working with a single client or multiple participants as in the case of couple, family, or group counseling.

However, those engaged with couples, families, or groups understand that attending to the welfare of all participants requires some additional steps and considerations. The dilemma with multiple clients is that in some situations an intervention that serves one person's best interests may be counter-therapeutic to another. Consider the marriage counselor who is working with a couple where one member is seeking a "peaceful and amicable divorce," whereas the other party's goal is to maintain the relationship. How is the welfare of the "client" protected?

Also as noted early in the chapter, even the initial session may reveal a conflict of participant needs, such as when one member has been coerced to attend. How does such attendance, under the force of coercion, jeopardize the primary directive of caring for the welfare of each participant?

For the professional working with couples, families, or groups, it is important to establish the fact that all parties freely engage in the service and that all parties are aware of and embrace the goals of the therapeutic encounter. While fundamental, such a focus is an expression of the provider's commitment to supporting the welfare of each participant. In addition to these steps, the ethical practitioner needs to ensure that the actual modality of treatment is appropriate for all participants. The IAGP, for example, directs its members to "recommend group treatment only for patients for whom it is indicated, making sure that the group is appropriate to the individual's treatment plan and that other essential psychiatric and psychological services are also provided" (2009, Standard 2.1). Similarly, the *AMHCA Code of Ethics* highlights the need to match individual to group needs and goals stating, "When working in groups, mental health counselors screen prospective group counseling/therapy participants. Every effort is made to select members whose needs and goals are compatible with goals of the group, who will not impede the group process, and whose well-being will not be jeopardized by the group experience" (2010, B.3.e).

An interesting "challenge" highlighted in the AMHCA (2010, B.3.e) position is that counselors need not only to screen participants to match needs and goals with those of the groups but also to ensure that the selected participants "will not impede the group process." While this latter directive may be clear, the application is not always so. Consider the case and questions presented in Exercise 13.4, as they clearly offer a unique challenge to the group therapist working with this group.

Exercise 13.4

Boundaries: Extending the Group . . . Work?

Directions: Review the following case illustration and then, along with a colleague or a supervisor, discuss your position on each of the questions posed.

The Case

The group, which is voluntary and provided as a "benefit" to employees of Company X, focused on mindfulness and stress reduction. Members of the group were screened prior to inclusion. At the time of screening, members were informed of the length of each session and number of the sessions, the focus of the group, the general goals for the sessions, and the fact that disclosures within the group would be held in confidence by the therapist. The therapist explained that she was ethically bound to confidence but also that the norm and expectation for group members would be that they too would respect the privacy of these disclosures. Four weeks into the group, Mary, a group member, contacted the therapist to say that Rob and Amelia (coworkers from different departments) were using the evening group meetings as an excuse for having an extramarital affair. She stated that her disclosures were meant to be confidential but that she was "concerned" the spouses may realize what is happening and that could cause problems for Rob and Amelia not only domestically but careerwise, as well.

(Continued)

(Continued)

    Dr. Delassandra was concerned that this this extra-group interaction would expose her to a malpractice suit based on negligent group psychotherapy, should Rob and Amelia's spouses discover the affair.

For Reflection

- Does the information shared by Mary matter for therapist confidence?

- Would this "extra-group" interaction expose the therapist to malpractice suit?

- What, if any, ethical concerns and considerations come into play given the apparent post-group meetings?

    The concern for the welfare of all members of the group directs those working in that modality to not only match the individual goals to those of the group and ensure that members have the personal and social resources to engage and benefit from the group dynamic but also to ensure that they do not present with needs or behaviors that would place other members in harm's way or prove to be destructive to group progress. Simply put, a client should be excluded from group work when it is clear that she cannot engage and benefit from the primary activities of the group (Yalom & Leszcz, 2005) and/or when their presence can prove destructive or impeding to the benefits to be experienced by the other participants.

● CONCLUDING CASE ILLUSTRATION

Well, it is clear that working with Maria has certainly been a professional challenge for Ms. Wicks. While her concern was on Maria's well-being, Ms. Wicks began to realize that the decision-making exhibited by Maria was not unique to her. Other students were similarly engaged in unprotected sex and were equating becoming impregnated with evidence of being "loved." Because of the potential for an expanding client base, Ms. Wicks began to consider the potential preventive value of offering a "women's group" in the school. The idea, while having preventive potential, also brought with it a number of ethical considerations. Because of the system's apparent prohibition regarding the counselor's engagement in discussion about sex-ual practices or anything that also may hint at "values" counseling, Michelle once again turned to her supervisor, Mr. Harolds.

Ms. Wicks:	Good morning, Tom.
Mr. Harolds:	Good morning, Michelle. Hmmm . . . I think I recognize that expression. What's up?
Ms. Wicks:	I've been thinking. My work with Maria has really got me thinking.
Mr. Harolds:	I know you have been very concerned with her, and her situa-tion has certainly occupied a lot of your time.
Ms. Wicks:	Actually it is the complexity of the situation and the amount of time that it requires that got me to think about some approaches that may be preventative.
Mr. Harolds:	Preventative?
Ms. Wicks:	Well, I know from listening to other students that this attitude about being protected from disease and pregnancy simply because "we" are in love is not unique to Maria. It seems that many of our students are engaged in unprotected sex, and many hold the opinion that if they do get pregnant, it's a sign that this "true love."
Mr. Harolds:	Michelle, we talked about this. Talking about sex or values is a no, no.
Ms. Wicks:	I know. But I was thinking, how about a group on "women's issues" or "women's empowerment"?
Mr. Harolds:	But are you just playing with words? Trying to sneak in the back door?
Ms. Wicks:	That is not my intent. I just think our female students might benefit from discussing issues of power, discrimination, self-esteem, and how to make decisions that are healthy for them, as individuals.
Mr. Harolds:	I don't know . . . not sure this will fly with Ms. Armstrong (the principal), but if you want to work up the description, goals, and so forth, go for it.

Reflections

1. Knowing the district and the principal's position on counseling students about sexual issues or confronting cultural values, is Ms. Wicks violating her ethics to serve the mission of her school?
2. Assuming that Ms. Wicks gets permission to move forward with a group, what issues does she need to consider in terms of screening, goals, informed consent, and confidentiality?
3. Should Ms. Wicks include Maria in the group, and if so, what challenges (e.g., boundaries) might this present?

● COOPERATIVE LEARNING EXERCISE

Groups as a mode of service delivery are used in a variety of settings with a variety of populations and goals. Working with a colleague, identify two specific groups providing service in your community.

Connect with the group leader(s) and gather data about the following questions. It would then be helpful to share your information with others engaged with this exercise as a way of connecting ethical principles and theory of group to the lived experience of those in the field.

- What specific training/experience do you feel is essential to be ethical and effective with this type of group?
- The group is clearly meeting the needs of those engaged; how did you identify the need for the specific type of group?
- Were members screened in any way? If so, what criteria did you employ, and what if any alternative was there for those for whom the group was inappropriate?
- As you lead the group, what specific ethical challenges (e.g., confidentiality, boundaries, etc.) have been encountered?

After collecting your data, share your information with others who similarly engaged with this exercise. What insights have you gained about the ethical practices and challenges encountered by those engaged in leading groups?

● SUMMARY

- Without specific training and the development of those competencies identified as fundamental to effectively working with couples, families, or groups, one risks violating the core ethical principle of duty to care.

- The way we define or conceptualize the client, be that each individual we engage or the collective of the couple, the family, or even the group has significant impact on how a clinician addresses issues of informed consent, confidentiality, record keeping, and maintenance of boundaries.
- The need to not only inform of the need to gain consent or assent from all involved but to employ procedures that ensure the ongoing acquisition of that consent from ALL participants is essential to ethical practice and difficult in situations such as family counseling, where subtle coercion to participate can exist.
- Because of the uniqueness of the conditions, those working with couples, families, or groups can provide an addendum to the typical information shared in a consent form to include those elements unique to these modalities.
- When working with multiple people in one room, as will be the case for those working with couples, families, or groups, the challenges to confidentiality are compounded, and yet the ethical standards to protect the privacy and confidence of each participant remain.
- When considering maintaining a private communication of an individual member of a couple, family, or group in confidence, it is generally recognized that individual disclosures should be held in confidence only if doing so DOES NOT contribute to maintaining unhealthy family dynamics.
- While all clinicians have been directed to avoid exploitative relationships that result from boundary violations, these same codes of ethics do NOT prohibit boundary crossings. In fact, some forms of boundary crossing have been posited as serving a purposeful therapeutic value and can be an integral part of a well-formulated treatment plan (Zur, 2015).
- Attending to client welfare can be a challenge when working with couples, families, or groups, since in some situations an intervention that serves one person's best interests may be counter therapeutic to another.

ADDITIONAL RESOURCES ●

Print

American Group Psychotherapy Association. (2007). *Practice guidelines for group psychotherapy*. New York: American Group Psychotherapy Association. Retrieved from http://www.agpa.org/home/practice-resources/practice-guidelines-for-group-psychotherapy

Hecker, L. (Ed.). (2010). *Ethics and professional issues in couple and family therapy*. New York: Routledge.

Shaw, E. (2014). Relational ethics and moral blindness: Startling incongruities in couple and family life. *Australian & New Zealand Journal of Family Therapy, 35*(4), 493–509. doi:10.1002/anzf.108.

Wilcoxon, S. A., Remley, T. P., Gladding, S. T., & Huber, C. H. (2007). *Ethical, legal, and professional issues in the practice of marriage and family therapy*. Columbus, OH: Pearson/Merrill/Prentice-Hall.

Web-Based

The Association for Specialists in Group Work. http://www.asgw.org/

Group Work for School Counselors. http://www.schoolcounselor.org/asca/media/asca/PositionStatements/PS_Group-Counseling.pdf

Shaw, E. (2011). *Ethics and the practice of couple and family therapy*. Retrieved from http://www.psychology.org.au/publications/inpsych/2011/feb/shaw/

● REFERENCES

American Association for Marriage and Family Therapy. (2015). *Code of ethics*. https://www.aamft.org/iMIS15/AAMFT/Content/Legal_Ethics/code_of_ethics.aspx

American Counseling Association. (2014). *ACA code of ethics*. Alexandria, VA: Author.

American Mental Health Counselors Association. (2010). *AMHCA code of ethics*. Alexandria, VA: Author:

American Psychological Association. (2010). *Ethical principles of psychologists and code of conduct*. Washington, DC: Author.

Bass, B. A., & Quimby, J. L. (2006). Addressing secrets in couples counseling: An alternative approach to informed consent. *The Family Journal: Counseling and Therapy for Couples and Families, 14*(1), 77–80.

Brabender, V. (2002). *The ethical practice of group therapy*, New York: Wiley.

Corey, M. S., Corey, G., & Corey, C. (2010). *Groups: Process and practice* (8th ed.). Belmont, CA: Brooks/Cole.

Epstein, N. B., & Baucom, D. H. (2002). *Enhanced cognitive-behavioral therapy for couples: A contextual approach*. Washington, DC: American Psychological Association.

Glick, I. D., Berman, E. M., Clarkin, J. F., & Rait, D. S. (2000). *Marital and family therapy* (4th ed.). Washington, DC: American Psychiatric Press.

Hendricks, B. E., Bradley, L. J., Southern, S., Oliver, M., & Birdsall, B. (2011). Ethical code for the International Association of Marriage and Family Counselors. *The Family Journal, 19*, 217–224. doi: 10.1177/1066480711400814

International Association for Group Psychotherapy and Group Processes. (2009). Retrieved from http://www.iagp.com/about/ethicalguidelines.htm

Jacobs, E. E., Masson, R. L., Harvill, R. L., & Schimmel, C. J. (2012). *Group counseling: Strategies and skills* (7th ed.). Belmont, CA: Brooks/Cole.

MacKenzie, K. R. (1997). Clinical application of group development ideas. *Group Dynamics: Theory, Research, and Practice, 1*, 275–287.

National Association of Social Workers. (2008). *Code of ethics*. Retrieved from http://www.naswdc.org/pubs/code/code.asp

Ramisch, J. (2010). Ethical issues in clinical practice. In L. Hecker (Ed.), *Ethics and professional issues in couple and family therapy* (pp. 203–224). New York: Routledge.

Remley, T. P., & Herlihy, B. (2014). *Ethical, legal, and professional issues in counseling* (4th ed.). Upper Saddle River, NJ: Pearson/Merrill Prentice Hall.

Thomas, R. V., & Pender, D. A. (2007). Association for Specialists in Group Work: Best practice guidelines 2007 revisions. Retrieved from http://www.asgw.org/pdf/best_practices.pdf

Yalom, I., & Leszcz, M. (2005). *The theory and practice of group psychotherapy* (5th ed.). New York: Basic Books.

Zur, O. (2015). *Therapeutic boundaries and dual relationships in psychotherapy and counseling*. Retrieved from http://www.zurinstitute.com/boundaries brochure.pdf

CHAPTER 14

Competence and the Ethics of Self-Care

I don't know if it is I'm just overworked or whatever. I'm having trouble sleeping, don't want to do anything or go out with friends, and truthfully, I look at my appointment schedule and start hoping clients cancel. I'm not sure what's up, but I sometimes wonder if it's time to simply get out of this profession?

The experience being described by the human service provider who opened this chapter is sadly neither unique to this profession nor that unusual. For all who work as human service providers, the mental fatigue and emotional exhaustion that accompany the intense work we do can be destructive to our health, mental well-being, and ability to provide ethical and effective service to our clients.

Table 14.1 highlights the fact that our professional codes of ethics are clear in their mandating of professional competence as a primary ethical requisite to providing service.

As suggested in the codes posted (see Table 14.1), the primary focus rests on competence as defined by one's knowledge, skill, and experience. While these are clearly essential to effective, ethical practice, they are not the only considerations that should be made when assessing one's ability or one's competency to perform professional service.

Table 14.1 Addressing Competency

Professional Organization	Principle
American Counseling Association (2014)	C.2.a. Counselors practice only within the boundaries of their competence, based on their education, training, supervised experience, state and national professional credentials, and appropriate professional experience.
American Psychological Association (2010)	2.01.a. Psychologists provide services, teach, and conduct research with populations and in areas only within the boundaries of their competence, based on their education, training, supervised experience, consultation, study, or professional experience.
American Association for Marriage and Family Therapy (2015)	Standard III. Marriage and family therapists maintain high standards of professional competence and integrity.
International Association for Group Psychotherapy and Group Processes (2009)	Principle 3. Group psychotherapists who are members of the IAGP should have either completed formal education in group psychotherapy or be presently receiving supervision in an ongoing educational program by an established training organization that meets specific requirements.
National Association of Social Workers (2008)	1.04. a. Social workers should provide services and represent themselves as competent only within the boundaries of their education, training, license, certification, consultation received, supervised experience, or other relevant professional experience.

The current chapter reviews the ethical principles of provider competence with special emphasis on the threats to competency emanating from the experience of burnout and compassion fatigue.

● OBJECTIVES

As such, the current chapter will help you to

- Describe what is meant by burnout and compassion fatigue
- Explain the difference between burnout and compassion fatigue
- Describe the ethical challenges burnout and compassion fatigue present for the human service provider

- Identify ways a human service provider can reduce the possibility of burnout and compassion fatigue
- Articulate a personal wellness plan

COMPETENCY: MORE THAN KNOWLEDGE AND SKILL •

In their book, *Field Experience: Transitioning From Student to Professional*, Zhang and Parsons (2016) introduced the concept of self-care with an Anton Wildgans's (1881–1932) quote, which has been made famous by Viktor Frankl, the author of *Man's Search for Meaning* (1963): "What is to give light must endure burning." While Wildgans's quote is clearly reflective of his own experience as a provider of care and support to self and others during the Holocaust, the simple quote speaks volumes for all human service providers who have been engaged in providing care and support to others.

Perhaps, you are just starting your training in the field or are coming to the end of your training. In either case, it is likely you have already experience the awesome gift and responsibility of serving in the role of human service provider. Being invited to journey with another, especially during a time of turmoil and challenge, demands knowledge and skill of the helping process, awareness of that which constitutes "best practice," and the physical and emotional energy to engage in a dynamic and challenging therapeutic relationship. They are responsibilities that provide light, while at the same time opening the provider to the possibility of emotional "burning."

Helping: Being With, Not Doing To

Unique to the role and function of a human service provider is the fact that we are required to "walk with" our clients and not simply do for them. Our clients are not cogs on a conveyor belt needing to be assembled, nor are we simply information providers to those requesting direction. Our clients are those navigating through a challenging time in their lives, for whom support, emotional, social and physical, is required.

As human service providers, we are engaged in a service that requires our personal, emotional engagement with the client (Bakker, Van der Zee, Lewig, & Dollard, 2006). The very process of engaging with others who are suffering can pose a threat to the human service provider (O'Brien, 2011). The work we do is fertile ground for stress. The fact that we work in situations of physical and social isolation, where we often encounter unexpected and unpredictable schedules and demands and by definition immerse ourselves in intense personal interactions, provides the conditions to make this work stressful and emotionally demanding (Bakker et al., 2006). The stress of taking on the responsibility for assisting one in crisis, especially when work conditions are such as to add to that stress or, conversely, fail to provide the essential support necessary for providing ethical, effective service, can accumulate and will negatively impact the provider's ability to perform competently. Research would suggest that those engaged in the helping professions are vulnerable to effects of enduring stress (Lee et al., 2007).

Given the nature of our work it is not unexpected to find that many find it difficult to maintain their own health and well-being. According to a study by the American Counseling Association (ACA, 2010), of those surveyed, over 63 percent reported knowing a colleague whom they would consider impaired. The magnitude of the finding moved the ACA to develop a task force for the sole purpose of decreasing impairment and enhancing wellness among its members.

The impact of enduring stress and the toll it can take on both the professional and the clients whom they serve makes it a clear ethical concern. While the impact of enduring stress can take many forms, two—burnout and compassion fatigue—are the focus of the remainder of this chapter.

● BURNOUT

Burnout has been described as the "gradually intensifying pattern of physical, psychological and behavioral responses to a continual flow of stressors" (Gladding, 2011, p. 24). Burnout is experienced as emotional exhaustion and often manifests in form of apathy, negative job attitude, and perhaps most concerning from an ethical perspective of competence, a loss of concern and feeling for the client (Gladding, 2011).

For some practitioners experiencing burnout, the impact is evident in their tendency to withdraw from social contact, become defensive and aggressive in relationships, and when it comes to clients, exhibit a dehumanizing attitude (Lambie, 2002). That dehumanization often reveals itself in the provider's identification of clients by a diagnostic label such as "my borderline" or in personal characteristics, for example, the "divorcee," and serves to distance and detach the counselor from the person of the client and thus his or her suffering (Maslach, Schaufeli & Leiter, 2001). Consider the case of Dr. L., one practitioner for whom burnout clearly impacted her ability to provide effective, ethical service (Case Illustration 14.1).

Case Illustration 14.1

Dr. L.: A Case of Burnout

Dr. L. is a 48-year-old clinical psychologist working in a community mental health center. She has worked as a clinician for over 19 years and has been employed within this center over the past 8 years. Over the course of the past 8 years, she has experienced a decline in both professional and support staff, while at the same time an increase in both the number of clients seen and the level of severity of the issues being presented. The pressure from external funding sources as well as internal administration placed emphasis on a mandate to see more clients and produce results with fewer sessions. The increased workload resulted in her working late hours, often 10 hour days, and twice a month being required to work a sixth day, Saturday, to increase her "productivity" figures.

The physical exhaustion of the increased workload, the reduction of physical and emotional support, and a general dissatisfaction and discomfort with what she saw as her inability to provide "adequate" service began to take its toll. As one who considered her work more than a job, a true vocation, the situation left her feeling professionally inadequate.

While these changes developed slowly, it became obvious that Dr. L. was experiencing a deep sadness and a lack of interest in engaging in previously enjoyable activities (e.g., racquet ball, golf, etc.). She was finding it difficult to make decisions within her practice, even to the point of failing to develop meaningful treatment plans for her clients. Dr. L. reported a concern that her ability to attend to her clients seemed diminished and that she had on occasion experienced moments when her memory went "blank." She reported entering sessions in which she brought the wrong case file and even had three occasions where she either could not remember the client's name or referred to the client by using another client's name.

She found the experience to be such that she "dreaded" going to work and hoped that clients would cancel. In addition, she began calling out and taking sick days, often canceling appointments at the last moment. While her colleagues privately expressed concern, no one reached out to Dr. L. Fortunately, her diminishing level of professional

(Continued)

(Continued)

effectiveness along with her increased reliance on alcohol as a means of self-soothing led Dr. L to ask for, and receive, medical leave.

While her break from work was brief, only two weeks, it was a time when, with reflection and discussion with a supervisor, Dr. L gained insight into what she was experiencing and the steps she needed to take to engage in her own healing. After this break, during which time she returned to a regimen of healthy eating, regular exercise, engagement with friends, and getting 7 to 8 hours of sleep each night, her symptoms diminished and she found not only a desire to return to her clients but also an energy and enthusiasm to advocate organizational changes in order to bring their services in line with that expected of an ethical, effective center.

As is evident in our case illustration, the experience of burnout is multidimensional. In addition to somatic and cognitive symptoms, burnout can affect a professional's emotional stability, resulting in conditions ranging from annoyance and frustration to more severe presentations, such as depression and anxiety (Maslach, Schaufeli, & Leiter, 2001). For others, burnout results in apathy, fatigue, anger, and conflict (Gladding, 2011). In any presentation, it becomes clear that burnout will impair one's ability to provide ethical care and service (Maslach, 1993).

● COMPASSION FATIGUE

A hallmark of the both the helping relationship and the role of the human service provider is our ability to enter into the other's phenomenological field, experiencing their world as they do, sharing their feelings, and better understanding their world and self-views. This ability to experience deep empathy is both a gift and a potential risk. Sharing in the pain, the anxiety, the sadness, or the sense of hopelessness often presented by our clients can challenge our ability to balance professional objectivity and distance while at the same time truly walking with our client. For clinicians lost in the lived experience of their clients, the result can be quite destructive, leading to increased stress and an inability to continue to feel and convey the compassion so characteristic of the helping professions.

Compassion fatigue has been defined as a "state of exhaustion and dysfunction—biologically, psychologically, and socially—as a result of prolonged exposure to compassion stress (Figley, 1995, p. 253). Compassion fatigue differs from burnout in that it occurs suddenly, rather than gradually as is the case with burnout, and presents often with symptoms that mirror post-traumatic disorders (Trippany, Wilcoxon, & Satcher, 2003). As such, it is often referred to as secondary post-traumatic stress disorder.

The impact of compassion fatigue is both broad and deep. Compassion fatigue can result in mental fatigue and an inability to concentrate, a deterioration of one's ability to work effectively, a change in a person's fundamental values and beliefs, and an increase in feelings of sadness, anxiety, and guilt (Zhang & Parsons, 2016). In addition, for some, compassion fatigue results in excessive emotional numbing and, like those with post-traumatic stress syndrome, the experience of intrusive images and thoughts of their client's traumatic material. This experience can reduce the clinician's ability to empathically engage with a client and thus presents a very real threat to one's ability to provide competent, ethical service.

THE ETHICAL CHALLENGE ●

Burnout and compassion fatigue must be recognized and accepted as real threats to ethical practice. Consider the following case (Case Illustration 14.2) as reflecting the unethical decisions and behavior that result from compassion fatigue.

Case Illustration 14.2

Compassion Fatigue: Undermining Ethical Behavior

While serving as a middle school counselor for 18 years, Mr. E. had spent the last 2 years working in the capacity of *crisis interventionist*. In that role, he engaged with students who were physically and sexually abused, those exhibiting suicidal ideation and behavior, and others with depression and debilitating anxieties. Now, halfway through the academic year, he began experiencing a reduction of energy and a loss of enthusiasm for his job. He began to exhibit attitudes and behaviors that could best be described as atypical for him and clearly unprofessional.

(Continued)

(Continued)

Whereas students historically sought out his service and support and parents spoke highly of his effectiveness and real care for the students, it was clear by student complaints about his lack of availability and tendency to be sarcastic when interacting with them that something was changing. Even faculty began to report on the apparent changes in his demeanor and professional behavior, noting that something was negatively impacting his ability to function in his role as crisis intervention counselor.

Faculty reported experiencing his increased venting and complaining about the students he was seeing. They noted that he often referred to the students and their life conditions as hopeless and that he, as one person, was impotent in "rescuing" them from the "hands they were dealt." While concerned about the apparent heavy heart he exhibited when speaking of some of the students, the faculty were equally concerned by what appeared to be his angry, dismissive, and devaluing attitude toward other students. Faculty reported hearing him use inappropriate terms, such as referring to some students as "diagnosable" or others as falling into the category of "P.I.T.A." (pains in the ass). The dismissiveness and depersonalization was even experienced by teachers seeking consultation who were told to "do their own damn jobs."

While certainly unprofessional, the language and labeling was so out of character for Mr. E., a person who had previously been a model of caring and professionalism, that faculty went to the district supervisor to report their concerns.

It would be easy to dismiss both compassion fatigue and burnout as things that happen to those who have worked "too long" in the field. However, failing to embrace the reality of burnout and compassion fatigue as real possibilities for ourselves, regardless of our tenure within the profession, positions us to engage in unethical behavior (Everall & Paulson, 2004). These conditions not only attack the professional's physical stamina but also as detailed above result in psychological exhaustion, emotional distress, and potential exploitation of clients (Norcross, 2000), and they can occur at any stage of our professional life.

A Challenge to Core Values

A review of the core values that serve as the foundation of our codes of ethics, values such as autonomy, beneficence, nonmaleficence, and justice

(See Chapter 3), illuminates the ethical challenge presented when a practitioner is experiencing burnout and/or compassion fatigue.

As ethical providers, we are directed to respect and attend to the welfare of our clients. Respecting the integrity of those with whom we work, committing to serving their welfare, and engaging in competent best practice are principles found across our professional codes of ethics. For example, the American Psychological Association (APA, 2010) notes that psychologists, embodying the values of beneficence and nonmaleficence "strive to benefit those with whom they work and take care to do no harm. In their professional actions, psychologists seek to safeguard the welfare and rights of those with whom they interact professionally" (Principle A). Consider this standard in light of the two previous case illustrations (i.e., Case Illustrations 14.1, 14.2). Certainly, meeting this ethical standard and the similar standards expressed by the other professional human service organization is difficult, if not impossible, when one is experiencing burnout and/or compassion fatigue.

A Challenge to Developing and Maintaining an Ethical Therapeutic Relationship

As noted by Everall & Paulson (2004), a counselor who is having difficulty meeting her personal needs appropriately may violate boundaries and become more deeply enmeshed with her clients. The physical, psychological, and emotional exhaustion that accompanies burnout and compassion fatigue can result in the human service provider disengaging from the client to a point of negating the client as person and not only demonstrating the inability to maintain a sense of empathy but even a basic respect for the client. Since responsible caring requires professionals to actively demonstrate a concern for the welfare of individuals, the practitioner's diminished ability to function as a result of burnout or compassion fatigue may constitute a serious violation of a fundamental principle of ethical practice. Further, with a personal sense of exhaustion, a human service provider not only runs the risk of failing to engage and maintain a therapeutic alliance but also runs the risk of aligning with a client's feelings of frustration, anger, and hopelessness to the point of conveying a doubt in the effectiveness of their service. Under these conditions, the practitioner risks exploiting the client through boundary violations or role reversal in order to meet personal needs.

Disengagement from one's client or using clients to meet personal needs clearly violates the primary directive to respect the dignity and promote the welfare of our clients (e.g., ACA, 2015, Principal A.1.a;

AMHCA, 2010, Principle I.A.1.a). The inability to care and respect truly undermines one's competence to engage in effective therapeutic relationships and as such is a violation of our ethical principles. For those experiencing the inability to perform competently because of burnout and/or compassion fatigue, the directive, as noted the APA, is to "refrain from initiating an activity when they know or should know that there is a substantial likelihood that their personal problems will prevent them from performing their work-related activities in a competent manner" (2010, Principle, 2.06).

A Challenge to Enacting Ethical, Effective Treatment Plans

Engaging in ethical, effective treatment is a keystone of professional practice. For example, the ACA directs its members to devise treatment plans that offer reasonable promise of success (2014, Principle A.1.c). In support of this principle, other organizations have directed practitioners to continue to seek out on-going training and supervision as a means of maintaining and upgrading competence. For example, social workers are directed as follows:

> [to] strive to become and remain proficient in professional practice and the performance of professional functions. Social workers should critically examine and keep current with emerging knowledge relevant to social work. Social workers should routinely review the professional literature and participate in continuing education relevant to social work practice and social work ethics. (NASW, 2008, Principle 4.01)

Similarly, psychologists are ethically mandated to maintain competence by undertaking "ongoing efforts to develop and maintain their competence" (APA, 2010, Principle 2.03).

While it is notable that our professional organizations recognize the need for the maintenance of a practitioner's knowledge and skill as foundational to competent service, it is equally important that we recognize the fundamental need and value of maintaining a practitioner's physical and psycho-emotional well-being as equally foundational to competent service. For example, the ACA not only calls for its members to maintain knowledge of best practice and to devise treatment plans that offer a reasonable promise of success but calls for its members to do so in concert with their clients (ACA, 2014, Principle A.1.c). One may question how such collaboration is developed and maintained when the practitioner has disengaged and devalued the client as a result of his or her experience of burnout and compassion fatigue. Clearly, the disengagement and devaluing of the client that often accompanies burnout and compassion fatigue diminishes a practitioner's interest and ability to effectively engage with a client to devise, implement, and maintain an effective treatment plan.

The reality of this challenge of enacting ethical effective treatment plans has been noted across the profession and has been clearly articulated by the ACA:

> Counselors monitor themselves for signs of impairment from their own physical, mental, or emotional problems and refrain from offering or providing professional services when impaired. They seek assistance for problems that reach the level of professional impairment, and, if necessary, they limit, suspend, or terminate their professional responsibilities until it is determined that they may safely resume their work. (2014, Principle, C.2.g)

It is evident that effective, ethical practice is threatened when the practitioner is experiencing burnout or compassion fatigue. As we close this section of the chapter, we invite you to review Exercise 14.1. In the exercise you are asked to reflect upon and perhaps discuss with a colleague, guiding principles of ethical practice and how these may be impacted by the experience of burnout and/or compassion fatigue.

Exercise 14.1

Undermining Ethical Practice

Directions: Below you will find a listing of ethical principles found across the spectrum of human service professions. Consider the multidimensional impact that conditions such as burnout and compassion fatigue can have on a human service provider's ability to engage in ethical practice and identify the specific threat these conditions pose to the specific ethical principle listed. Share your reflections with a colleague or supervisor.

(Continued)

(Continued)		
Principle	*Burnout*	*Empathy Fatigue*
Promoting well-being/welfare of the client		
Establishing, maintaining professional boundaries		
Respecting client autonomy		
Respecting client privacy		
Providing competence service		
Termination of service		

● ETHICAL RESPONSE

The possibility of encountering burnout and/or compassion fatigue in one's professional life presents the human service provider with two immediate ethical challenges. The first one is understanding how one should respond to the experience of either of these conditions, be that a personal experience or that of a colleague. Secondly and perhaps more importantly, the human service provider is to be clear about what one should do to prevent the experience of either of these conditions. Ignoring and/or denying the possibility of a personal encounter with burnout and/or compassion fatigue is neither practical nor ethical.

Preventative Measures: An Ethical Response to Self-Care

In the best of all worlds, the human service provider will be insulated from the possibility of burnout and/or compassion fatigue. However, human service is by definition a form of one-way giving, therefore in the absence of the practitioner's emotional replenishment, he or she will soon run dry (Skovholt, 2001).

Thus, while absolute protection and insulation from these conditions is not possible, measures can be taken that will reduce the risk. Understanding and implementing preventative measures as counteraction to the possibilities of burnout and compassion fatigue is not only a rational response to self-care but also truly an ethical one. As noted by Parsons & Zhang (2014), "One cannot foster health and well-being in another if such is lacking in oneself" (p. 284).

Self-care is essential to ethical, competent practice. The ethics of self-care have been made clear by a number of our professional organizations. The ACA, for example, directs counselors to "engage in self-care activities to maintain and promote their own emotional, physical, mental, and spiritual well-being to best meet their professional responsibilities" (2014, Introduction, Section C). Further, a review of the literature (e.g., Trippany, White Kress, & Wilcoxon, 2004; Rupert & Kent, 2007; Ulman, 2008) highlights the importance of human service providers engaging in a program of self-care, as protection from burnout and compassion fatigue. While there are many ways one can care for self, those that have been identified as effective for intervening and preventing burnout and compassion fatigue involve cognitive, emotional, and behavioral self-care strategies (Baird, 2008).

Exercise 14.2 lists a number of self-care strategies and invites you to engage in a self-assessment. The hope is that engaging in this self-assessment will result in your further commitment to your own self-care as a way of strengthening your ability to engage in competent, ethical service.

Exercise 14.2

Self-Care Worksheet

Directions: Below is a list of activities that can contribute to one's general state of health and wellness and could prove valuable in lowering one's risk of compassion fatigue. Your task is to engage in an honest self-assessment and plan for a commitment to a healthier lifestyle. Identify at least one of the items of self-care that you feel you have been lax in performing and commit to increasing your engagement in that form of self-care starting immediately. It is suggested that you repeat this process monthly as a way of promoting your own health and wellness.

(Continued)

(Continued)

Domain	Specific	I am committed to . . .
Physical Health	Eating 4 to 6 meals a day	
	Eating well-balanced meals including fruits and vegetables	
	Reducing sugar intake	
	Monitoring caffeine intake	
	Exercise: some form of exercise, 30 min at least three times a week	
	Dental care 2x annually	
	Consistent, sufficient sleep	
	Engage in enjoyable physical activities: dance, swim, golf, bowl, etc.	
	Other (your ideas)	
Social Connections	Go out with friends	
	Talk with friends and family	
	Visit family member/friend	
	Smile and say "hi" to those you encounter in the course of your typical day	
	Disengage from thoughts of clients when in non-work social settings	
	Attend a group educational or recreational experience (lecture, concert, sporting event)	
	Connect with colleagues around professional issues/questions and concerns	
	Connect with colleagues around nonprofessional issues/activities	

Domain	Specific	*I am committed to . . .*
	Other (your choice)	
Psychological Domain	Engage in self-reflection	
	Read for recreation	
	Contract for personal counseling, coaching, or spiritual direction	
	Increase awareness of personal baggage and issues as well as ways of managing them	
	Engage in stress-reduction activities	
	Employ anxiety-reduction techniques	
	Seek out opportunities to learn and expand skill and knowledge outside the professional realm (e.g., learn foreign language or to play an instrument)	
	Give permission and take the opportunity to "zone" out as a way of decompressing (e.g., watching television, playing a video game, etc.)	
Affective Domain	Engage in activities that make you laugh	
	Find opportunities to celebrate "life" with others (e.g., birthday, holidays, anniversaries)	
	Provide self with affirmation and praise	
	Freely express feelings of sadness or loneliness (freedom to cry)	
	Reconnect via review of old pictures or tapping memories of loved ones and loving experiences	

(Continued)

(Continued)

Domain	Specific	I am committed to . . .
	Appropriately disclose feelings of anger, frustration (rather than repressing or displacing)	
	Sing like you can . . .	
	Dance like you wish . . .	
	Grant yourself permission to do or attempt to do those activities you always wished you could do	
	Other	
Inner Life	Engage in meditational readings	
	Engage in personal reflection	
	Meditate	
	Commune with nature	
	Participate in structured spiritual activity (church service, prayer group, retreat, etc.)	
	Engage with spiritual director or mentor	
	Find opportunities for expressing gratitude	
	Celebrate your gifts of life	
	Read about another's spiritual journey	
	Seek a moment, an opportunity to be in awe	
	Other	
Professional Domain	Set realistic daily task demands	

Domain	Specific	I am committed to . . .
	Identity those tasks/activities that are exciting and life giving and integrate those with those activities that tend to be more draining	
	Move away from the desk by way of a simple break, a quick visit with a colleague, or a short walk	
	Close your door to allow for quiet, uninterrupted time to complete a task	
	Say no to an invitation to do more when you already have enough	
	Leave work issues and concerns within the office	
	Engage in peer support around client and case issues as well as around personal questions and concerns	
	Engage with a supervisor or mentor	
	Establish your work space so that it feels both comfortable and comforting	
	Set boundaries with colleagues, especially when their interactions are intrusions on your limited time or when their requests are overburdening	
	Take a moment to review your day while identifying one aspect that was professionally satisfying	
	Other	

Source: Zhang, N. & Parsons, R. D. (2016). *Field experience: Transitioning student to professional*. Thousand Oaks, CA: Sage. Reproduced with permission of the authors.

Intervening in the Face of Burnout and Compassion Fatigue

Even our best-laid plans will often fall short, and this is true for our efforts to foster wellness. As such, it is possible that any one of us may experience the effects of burnout or compassion fatigue somewhere in the course of our professional life. When prevention is not possible, steps to intervention will be key to our returning to effective practice. The steps necessary are targeted not only to returning the professional to health and well-being but also to protecting those with whom he works.

Awareness and Self-Care

As an initial step, it is our responsibility as professionals not only to broaden our understanding of the impact that burnout and compassion fatigue have on one's ability to perform ethically and effectively but to monitor our own health for signs of impairment. Norcross (2000) reported on surveys of program directors and psychologists in which "self-awareness/ self-monitoring" was identified as the top-ranked contributor to optimal functioning among psychologists. Such monitoring is not simply a "good" idea but is truly an ethical mandate.

A useful tool for the monitoring of both burnout and compassion fatigue is the Professional Quality of Life Scale (ProQOL) (Stamm, 2012). The scale has been included in the section below, identified as "Cooperative Exercise." It is provided as both a reference tool that can be used throughout your career and an exercise in which you are invited to take a snapshot of your current state of well-being. Whether one is a student or engaged in a career, monitoring oneself for signs of impairment is an ethical responsibility. The ACA, for example, directs both students and supervisees to do the following:

> Monitor themselves for signs of impairment from their own physical, mental, or emotional problems and refrain from offering or providing professional services when such impairment is likely to harm a client or others. They notify their faculty and/or supervisors and seek assistance for problems that reach the level of professional impairment, and, if necessary, they limit, suspend, or terminate their professional

responsibilities until it is determined that they may safely resume their work. (2014, Principle F.5)

Responding to Impairment

Our professional codes of ethics are clear in directing us to cease and desist our engagement with clients once we become aware that we are compromised as professionals. The AMHCA, for example, directs its members to do the following:

> Recognize that their effectiveness is dependent on their own mental and physical health. Should their involvement in any activity, or any mental, emotional, or physical health problem, compromise sound professional judgment and competency, they seek capable professional assistance to determine whether to limit, suspend, or terminate services to their clients. (2010, Principal C.1.h)

Similarly, counselors are directed by the ACA to "monitor themselves for signs of impairment from their own physical, mental, or emotional problems and refrain from offering or providing professional services when impaired." (2014, Principle C.2.g.)

Beyond refraining from practice, impaired human service providers should, as noted by the AAMFT (2015), seek appropriate professional assistance for issues that may impair work performance or clinical judgment (2015, Principle 3.3). A point echoed by other professional organizations (See Table 14.2)

Seeking and employing professional support is an essential ingredient to the maintenance of the human service provider's health and ability to perform ethically and effectively (Everall & Paulson, 2004) and as such should apply to all human service providers and not just those who are challenged with burnout and/or compassion fatigue.

Collegial Corrective Response

In addition to self-monitoring and supervision, the human service provider has a professional and ethical responsibility to address concerns that

Table 14.2 Mandate for Professional Support and Assistance

Professional Organization	Statement on Ethical Principles Regarding Objectivity
American Counseling Association (2014)	Principle C.2.g. Counselors monitor themselves for signs of impairment from their own physical, mental, or emotional problems and refrain from offering or providing professional services when impaired. They seek assistance for problems that reach the level of professional impairment, and if necessary, they limit, suspend, or terminate their professional responsibilities until it is determined that they may safely resume their work.
American Psychological Association (2010)	Principle 2.06.b. When psychologists become aware of personal problems that may interfere with their performing work-related duties adequately, they take appropriate measures, such as obtaining professional consultation or assistance, and determine whether they should limit, suspend, or terminate their work-related duties.
American Association for Marriage and Family Therapy (2015)	Principle 3.3 Marriage and family therapists seek appropriate professional assistance for issues that may impair work performance or clinical judgment.
International Association for Group Psychotherapy and Group Processes (2009)	Principle 2.7 Group psychotherapists shall ensure that their own physical and mental health allows them to undertake their professional responsibilities competently. They shall seek appropriate assistance or professional treatment should they suffer ill health or compromised mental health that interferes with their professional duties.
National Association of Social Workers (2009)	Principle 4.05.b. Social workers whose personal problems, psychosocial distress, legal problems, substance abuse, or mental health difficulties interfere with their professional judgment and performance should immediately seek consultation and take appropriate remedial action by seeking professional help, making adjustments in workload, terminating practice, or taking any other steps necessary to protect clients and others.

arise when observing colleagues who are demonstrating signs of impairment (Everall & Paulson, 2004). Clearly a colleague who exhibits signs of fatigue, loss of interest in his work, and an abrasive, dismissive attitude toward his clients is giving evidence of impairment and may be providing less than ethical and effective service.

As ethical human service providers, we are directed to protect all clients as well as the image and reputation of our professions. It is our ethical responsibility to confront impaired colleagues by offering support and providing collegial corrective feedback. Counselors, for example, are directed to "assist colleagues or supervisors in recognizing their own professional impairment and provide consultation and assistance when warranted with colleagues or supervisors showing signs of impairment and intervene as appropriate to prevent imminent harm to clients." (ACA, 2014, Principle C.2.g). A similar directive is given to social workers who are advised to not only "consult with that colleague when feasible and assist the colleague in taking remedial action" (NASW, 2008, Principle 2.09.a) but even "take action through appropriate channels established by employers, agencies, NASW, licensing and regulatory bodies, and other professional organizations" (NASW, 2008, Principle 2.09.b) when an impaired colleague, once confronted, fails to take steps to address the impairment.

While it may be uncomfortable to confront a colleague exhibiting clear signs of impairment, it is our ethical responsibility. We are directed to initially attempt to provide support and increase awareness by bringing our concerns to the impaired professionals. However, if such an informal resolution fails to bring an ethical resolution, then it is essential for us to take further action appropriate to the situation, including reporting to employer, state boards and licensing agencies, or even national committees when national certification is at risk.

CONCLUDING CASE ILLUSTRATION ●

While the focus of our ongoing case has been on Ms. Wicks and her interaction with Maria, the following exchange between Ms. Wicks and her supervisor, Mr. Harolds, suggests that Ms. Wicks may be struggling to maintain her ability to provide effective, ethical service to her students. As you read the exchange, be aware of any indications that Ms. Wicks may be experiencing either burnout and/or compassion fatigue and may have either violated an ethical principle or is close to doing so. Finally, after reading and reflecting upon the interaction consider the points raised in the section entitled Reflections.

Mr. Harolds: Hi, Michelle, thanks for coming down.

Ms. Wicks: Not a problem . . . a little rushed since I have tons of kids to see. I was kind of surprised to get your invite. Is something up?

Mr. Harolds: No, I just wanted to check in and see how things were going with Maria and the year so far.

Ms. Wicks: Maria, yikes! I'll tell you Tom, I can't get her off my mind. This kid is carrying such a heavy load. It's just not fair. And truth be told, there are so many others this year that are in the same situation.

Mr. Harolds: It sounds like she has really gotten you concerned.

Ms. Wicks: This is so different than other years. Besides Maria, I am seeing at least four others who are being abused or had been abused. . . .

Mr. Harolds: Michelle, are you saying you have evidence of abuse? Why haven't you told me before now? We need to report it.

Ms. Wicks: Well, it's not abuse in the legal sense. It's just life has dealt these kids unfair demands, and it's just not fair (starts to tear up). I mean, I feel like I should take them all home and keep them safe and . . .

Mr. Harolds: Michelle, I can see you are concerned and this upsetting, but I hope you really don't mean what you are saying about taking them home.

Ms. Wicks: I know, and truthfully . . . I go between wanting to hug them and protect them to wanting to grab them by the collar and start pounding some sense in their heads. Their view of sex, babies, being "what their man" wants. . . . I just want to yell "damn girl, what's wrong with you!"

Mr. Harolds: Michelle, this doesn't sound like you. It feels like you are getting a little worn down?

Ms. Wicks: Tom, this year has been hell. The entire class seems to be dealing with such heavy stuff. It just seems so unfair (starts to tear up again and is visibly upset). I'm sorry, Tom. I know this is totally inappropriate, but it is mind boggling what these kids are dealing with, and I guess I'm realizing that I am totally impotent in helping them. I look at what is going on and I vacillate from wanting to wrap my arms around them—take them home with me, and keep them all safe— to literally giving up and telling them all to deal with it on their own. I know it's not professional, but sometimes I get so angry that . . . that . . . I don't know, maybe the semester break coming up is all I need. Just a little time away from this place and the job.

Mr. Harolds: Michelle, I know we have talked about this before . . . but you do give your all . . . I mean you are here early before school and usually the last to leave. Also, I don't think you ever miss a student activity if you can help, plus all the support you give to parents and faculty. . . . You know maybe you need to cut back a bit.

Ms. Wicks: Cut back . . . really? Tom, there is so much these kids need (again, starts to tear up). I mean, I spent all day Saturday visiting some of them, bringing some clothes, makeup, and a little treat to the girls in Lincoln apartments.

Mr. Harolds: Michelle that truly concerns me. While I am sure that the girls had fun and appreciated you bringing things, that's not your role, and while it is a nice gesture, it really isn't necessary or even appropriate. I am worried that you are taking more on and emotionally extending yourself in ways that are not healthy for you and, honestly, can put you at risk.

Reflections

1. What type of "risk" do you feel Mr. Harolds was referring to? Physical? Emotional? Professional? Legal?
2. Is there any evidence that might suggest that Michelle is beginning to experience burnout? Compassion fatigue? Or is she setting herself up for such an experience?
3. What ethical principles has Michelle violated? Are there any that she is coming close to violating?

COOPERATIVE LEARNING EXERCISE ●

Introduction: Below you will find the Compassion Satisfaction and Compassion Fatigue (PROQOL), Version 5 scale. We invite you to not only make a copy of this scale and refer to it frequently throughout your career but also take time now to take a snapshot of your current state of well-being. We suggest you work through the scale with your colleague and/or supervisor, discussing your responses.

Exercise 14.3

Monitoring Burnout and Compassion Fatigue

Directions:

COMPASSION SATISFACTION AND COMPASSION FATIGUE (PROQOL) VERSION 5 (2009)

When you [help] people, you have direct contact with their lives. As you may have found, your compassion for those you [help] can affect you in positive and negative ways. Below are some questions about your experiences, both positive and negative, as a [helper]. Consider each of the following questions about you and your current work situation. Select the number that honestly reflects how frequently you experienced these things in the last 30 days.

1 = Never	2 = Rarely	3 = Sometimes	4 = Often	5 = Very Often

_____ 1. I am happy.

_____ 2. I am preoccupied with more than one person I [help].

_____ 3. I get satisfaction from being able to [help] people.

_____ 4. I feel connected to others.

_____ 5. I jump or am startled by unexpected sounds.

_____ 6. I feel invigorated after working with those I [help].

_____ 7. I find it difficult to separate my personal life from my life as a [helper].

_____ 8. I am not as productive at work because I am losing sleep over traumatic experiences of a person I [help].

_____ 9. I think that I might have been affected by the traumatic stress of those I [help].

_____ 10. I feel trapped by my job as a [helper].

_____ 11. Because of my [helping], I have felt "on edge" about various things.

_____ 12. I like my work as a [helper].

_____ 13. I feel depressed because of the traumatic experiences of the people I [help].

_____ 14. I feel as though I am experiencing the trauma of someone I have [helped].

_____ 15. I have beliefs that sustain me.

_____ 16. I am pleased with how I am able to keep up with [helping] techniques and protocols.

_____ 17. I am the person I always wanted to be.

_____ 18. My work makes me feel satisfied.

_____ 19. I feel worn out because of my work as a [helper].

_____ 20. I have happy thoughts and feelings about those I [help] and how I could help them.

_____ 21. I feel overwhelmed because my case [work] load seems endless.

_____ 22. I believe I can make a difference through my work.

_____ 23. I avoid certain activities or situations because they remind me of frightening experiences of the people I [help].

_____ 24. I am proud of what I can do to [help].

_____ 25. As a result of my [helping], I have intrusive, frightening thoughts.

_____ 26. I feel "bogged down" by the system.

_____ 27. I have thoughts that I am a "success" as a [helper].

_____ 28. I can't recall important parts of my work with trauma victims.

_____ 29. I am a very caring person.

_____ 30. I am happy that I chose to do this work.

Based on your responses, place your personal scores below. If you have any concerns, you should discuss them with a physical or mental health care professional.

(Continued)

(Continued)

Compassion Satisfaction

Compassion satisfaction is about the pleasure you derive from being able to do your work well. For example, you may feel like it is a pleasure to help others through your work. You may feel positively about your colleagues or your ability to contribute to the work setting or even the greater good of society. Higher scores on this scale represent a greater satisfaction related to your ability to be an effective caregiver in your job.

The average score is 50 (SD 10; alpha scale reliability .88). About 25 percent of people score higher than 57 and about 25 percent of people score below 43. If you are in the higher range, you probably derive a good deal of professional satisfaction from your position. If your scores are below 40, you may either find problems with your job, or there may be some other reason—for example, you might derive your satisfaction from activities other than your job.

Burnout

Most people have an intuitive idea of what burnout is. From the research perspective, burnout is one of the elements of compassion fatigue. It is associated with feelings of hopelessness and difficulties in dealing with work or in doing your job effectively. These negative feelings usually have a gradual onset. They can reflect the feeling that your efforts make no difference, or they can be associated with a very high workload or a non-supportive work environment. Higher scores on this scale mean that you are at higher risk for burnout.

The average score on the burnout scale is 50 (SD 10; alpha scale reliability .75). About 25 percent of people score above 57 and about 25 percent of people score below 43. If your score is below 43, this probably reflects positive feelings about your ability to be effective in your work. If you score above 57 you may wish to think about what at work makes you feel like you are not effective in your position. Your score may reflect your mood; perhaps you were having a "bad day" or are in need of some time off. If the high score persists or if it is reflective of other worries, it may be a cause for concern.

Secondary Traumatic Stress

The second component of compassion fatigue is *secondary traumatic stress* (STS). It is about your work-related, secondary exposure to extremely or traumatically stressful events. Developing problems because of exposure to other's trauma is somewhat rare but does happen to many people who care for those who have experienced extremely or traumatically stressful events. For example, you may repeatedly hear stories about the traumatic things that happen to other people, commonly called *vicarious traumatization*. If your work puts you directly in the path of danger, for example, fieldwork in a war or area of civil violence, this is not secondary exposure; your exposure is primary. However, if you are exposed to others' traumatic events as a result of your work—for example, as a therapist or an emergency worker—this is secondary exposure. The symptoms of STS are usually rapid in onset and associated with a particular event. They may include being afraid, having difficulty sleeping, having images of the upsetting event pop into your mind, or avoiding things that remind you of the event.

The average score on this scale is 50 (SD 10; alpha scale reliability .81). About 25 percent of people score below 43 and about 25 percent of people score above 57. If your score is above 57, you may want to take some time to think about what at work may be frightening to you or if there is some other reason for the elevated score. While higher scores do not mean that you do have a problem, they are an indication that you may want to examine how you feel about your work and your work environment. You may wish to discuss this with your supervisor, a colleague, or a health care professional.

Source: B. Hundall Stamm, 2009–2012. Professional Quality of Life: Compassion Satisfaction and Fatigue Version 5 (ProQOL).

WHAT IS MY SCORE AND WHAT DOES IT MEAN?

In this section, you will score your test so you understand the interpretation for you. To find your score on **each section**, total the questions listed on the left and then find your score in the table on the right of the section.

Compassion Satisfaction Scale

Copy your rating on each of these questions on to this table and add them up. When you have added them up you can find your score on the table to the right.

3. _____
6. _____
12. _____
16. _____
18. _____
20. _____
22. _____
24. _____
27. _____
30. _____
Total: _____

The Sum of My Compassion Satisfaction Questions Is	So My Score Equals	And My Compassion Satisfaction Level Is
22 or less	43 or less	Low
Between 23 and 41	Around 50	Average
42 or more	57 or more	High

Burnout Scale

On the burnout scale you will need to take an extra step. Starred items are "reverse scored." If you scored the item 1, write a 5 beside it. The reason we ask you to reverse the scores is because scientifically the measure works better when these questions are asked in a positive way though they can tell us more about their negative form. For example, question 1. "I am happy" tells us more about the effects of helping when you are not happy so you reverse the score.

*1. _____ = _____
*4. _____ = _____
8. _____
10. _____
*15. _____ = _____
*17. _____ = _____
19. _____
21. _____
26. _____
*29. _____ = _____
Total: _____

The Sum of My Burnout Questions Is	So My Score Equals	And My Burnout Level Is
22 or less	43 or less	Low
Between 23 and 41	Around 50	Average
42 or more	57 or more	High

You Wrote	Change to
	5
2	4
3	3
4	2
5	1

Secondary Traumatic Stress Scale

Just like you did on Compassion Satisfaction, copy your rating on each of these questions on to this table and add them up. When you have added them up you can find your score on the table to the right.

2. _____
5. _____
7. _____
9. _____
11. _____
13. _____
14. _____
23. _____
25. _____
28. _____
Total: _____

The Sum of My Secondary Trauma Questions Is	So My Score Equals	And My Secondary Traumatic Stress Level Is
22 or less	43 or less	Low
Between 23 and 41	Around 50	Average
42 or more	57 or more	High

Source: B. Hudnall Stamm 2009–2012. *Professional quality of life: Compassion satisfaction and fatigue version 5 (ProQOL).* www.proqol.org. This test freely copied as long as (a) author is credited, (b) no changes are made, and (c) it is not sold. Those interested in using the test should visit www.proqol.org to verify that the copy they are using is the most current version of the test.

SUMMARY

- The stress of taking on the responsibility for assisting one in crisis, especially when work conditions are such as to add to that stress or, conversely, fail to provide the essential support necessary for providing ethical, effective service, can accumulate and will negatively impact the provider's ability to perform competently.
- Burnout is experienced as emotional exhaustion and often manifests in form of apathy, negative job attitude, and perhaps most concerning from an ethical perspective of competence, a loss of concern and feeling for the client.
- Compassion fatigue has been defined as a "state of exhaustion and dysfunction—biologically, psychologically and socially—as a result of prolonged exposure to compassion stress (Figley, 1995, p. 253).
- Compassion fatigue differs from burnout out in that it occurs suddenly rather than gradually, as is the case with burnout, and presents often with symptoms that mirror post-traumatic disorders (Trippany, Wilcoxon, & Satcher, 2003). As such it is often referred to as secondary post-traumatic stress disorder.
- Both burnout and compassion fatigue can impair one's ability to provide ethical care and service.
- The disengagement and devaluing of the client that often accompanies burnout and compassion fatigue diminishes a practitioner's

interest and ability to effectively engage with a client to devise, implement, and maintain an effective treatment plan.

- Self-care is essential to ethical, competent practice. The ethics of self-care have been made clear by a number of our professional organizations.
- Our professional codes of ethics are clear in directing us to cease and desist our engagement with a client once we become aware that we are compromised as professionals.
- Beyond refraining from practice, impaired human service providers should seek appropriate professional assistance for issues that may impair work performance or clinical judgment.
- It is our ethical responsibility to confront impaired colleagues by offering support and providing collegial corrective feedback.

● IMPORTANT TERMS

beneficence	nonmaleficence
burnout	self-awareness
collegial correction	self-care
compassion fatigue	self-monitoring
dehumanization	wellness
enduring stress	

● ADDITIONAL RESOURCES

Print

Baker, E. K. (2003). *Caring for ourselves: A therapist's guide to personal and professional well-being.* Washington, DC: American Psychological Association.

Kottler, J. A. (2012). *The therapist's workbook: Self-assessment, self-care and self-improvement exercises for mental health professionals* (2nd ed.). Hoboken, NJ: John Wiley & Sons.

Ladany, N. (2010). *Counselor supervision.* New York: Routledge

Skovholt, T. M., & Trotter-Mathison, M. (2011). *The resilient practitioner: Burnout prevention and self-care strategies for therapists, counselors, teachers and health professionals* (2nd ed.). New York: Routledge.

Web-Based

ACA's Taskforce on Counselor Wellness and Impairment. Retrieved from www
.counseling.org/wellness_taskforce/index.htm

ProQOL.org. (n.d.). ProQOL 5. Retrieved from http://proqol.org/ProQol_Test.html

PTSD Support Services. (n.d.). Compassion fatigue self-test. Retrieved from http://
www.ptsdsupport.net/compassion_fatigue-selftest.html

REFERENCES ●

American Association for Marriage and Family Therapy. (2015). *Code of ethics.*
Retrieved from https://www.aamft.org/iMIS15/AAMFT/Content/Legal_Ethics/
code_of_ethics.aspx

American Counseling Association. (2014). *Code of ethics,* Washington, DC: Author.

American Counseling Association's Task force on Counseling Wellness and Impairment.
(2010). Retrieved from http://www.counseling.org/wellness_taskforce/index
.htm

American Mental Health Counselors Association. (2010). American Mental Health
Counselors Association (AMHCA) *Code of ethics.* Retrieved from http://www
.amhca.org/assets/content/AMHCA_Code_of_Ethics_11_30_09b1.pdf

American Psychological Association. (2010). *Ethical principles of psychologists and
code of conduct.* Retrieved from http://www.apa.org/ethics/code/principles
.pdf

Baird, B. N. (2008). *The internship, practicum, and field placement handbook:
A guide for the helping professions* (5th ed). Upper Saddle River, NJ: Pearson/
Prentice Hall.

Bakker, A. B., Van der Zee, K. I., Lewig, K. A., & Dollard, M. F. (2006). The relationship between the big five personality factors and burnout: A study among volun-
teer counselors. *The Journal of Social Psychology, 126,* 31–50.

Everall, R. D., & Paulson, B. L. (2004). Burnout and secondary traumatic stress:
Impact on ethical behaviour. *Canadian Journal of Counselling, 38*(1), 25–33.

Figley, C. R. (Ed.). (1995). *Compassion fatigue: Coping with secondary traumatic
stress disorder in those who treat the traumatized.* New York: Brunner/Mazel.

Frankl, V. (1963). *Man's search for meaning.* New York: Simon and Shuster.

Gladding, S. T. (2011). *The counseling dictionary: Concise definitions of frequently
used terms.* Upper Saddle River, NJ: Pearson Education.

International Association for Group Psychotherapy and Group Processes. (2009).
Retrieved from http://www.iagp.com/about/ethicalguidelines.htm

Lambie, G. W. (2002). The contribution of ego development level to degree of
burnout in school counselors (Doctoral dissertation, The College of William &
Mary, 2002). *Dissertation Abstracts International, 63,* 508.

Lee, S. M., Baker, C. R., Cho, S. H., Heckathorn, D. E., Holland, M. W., Newgent, R. A., & Yu, K. (2007). Development and initial psychometrics of the Counselor Burnout Inventory. *Measurement and Evaluation in Counseling and Development, 40,* 142–154.

Maslach, C. (1993). Burnout: A multidimensional perspective. In W. B. Schaufeli, C. Maslach, & T. Marek (Eds.), *Professional burnout: Recent developments in theory and research* (pp. 19–32). Philadelphia, PA: Taylor & Francis.

Maslach, C., Schaufeli, W. B., & Leiter, M. P. (2001). Job burnout. *Annual Review of Psychology, 52,* 397–422.

National Association of Social Workers. (2008). *Code of ethics of the National Association of Social Workers* (NASW). Retrieved from http://www.socialworkers .org/pubs/code/code.asp

Norcross, J. C. (2000). Psychotherapist self-care: Practitioner-tested, research-informed strategies. *Professional Psychology: Research and Practice, 31,* 710–713.

O'Brien, J. M. (2011). Wounded healer: Psychotherapist's grief over a client's death. *Professional Psychology Research and Practice, 42,* 236–243.

Parsons, R. D., & Zhang, N. (2014). *Becoming a skilled counselor.* Thousand Oaks, CA: Sage.

Rupert, P. A., & Kent, J. S. (2007). Gender and work setting differences in career-sustaining behaviors and burnout among professional psychologists. *Professional Psychology: Research and Practice, 38,* 88–96.

Skovholt, T. M. (2001). *The resilient practitioner: Burnout prevention and self-care strategies for counselors, therapists, teachers, and health professionals.* Boston: Allyn & Bacon.

Stamm, B. H. (2012). The Professional Quality of Life Scale (ProQOL 5). Retrieved from http://proqol.org/ProQol_Test.html

Trippany, R. L., White Kress, V. E., & Wilcoxon, S. A. (2004). Preventing vicarious trauma: What counselors should know when working with trauma survivors. *Journal of Counseling & Development, 82,* 31–37.

Trippany, R. L., Wilcoxon, S. A., & Satcher, J. F. (2003). Factors influencing vicarious trauma for therapists of survivors of sexual victimization. *Journal of Trauma Practice, 2,* 47–60.

Ulman, K. H. (2008). Helping the helpless. *Group, 32*(3), 209–221.

Wildans, A. (n.d.). BrainyQuote.com. Retrieved June 23, 2016, from BrainyQuote.com Web site: http://www.brainyquote.com/quotes/authors/a/anton_wildgans.htm

Zhang, N., & Parsons, R. D. (2016). *Field experience: Transitioning from student to professional.* Thousand Oaks, CA: Sage.

APPENDIX A

Professional Organizations

American Association for Marriage and Family Therapy. 112 South Alfred Street Alexandria, VA 22314-3061. https://www.aamft.org/iMIS15/AAMFT/

American Counseling Association. 6101 Stevenson Avenue, Alexandria, VA 22304. https://www.counseling.org

American Mental Health Counselors Association. 675 North Washington Street, Suite 470, Alexandria, VA 22314. http://www.amhca.org

American Psychological Association. 750 First Street, N.E., Washington, DC 20002-4242. http://www.apa.org

American School Counselor Association. 1101 King Street, Suite 310, Alexandria VA 22314. https://www.schoolcounselor.org

International Association for Group Psychotherapy and Group Processes. Besmerstrasse 27, 8280 Kreuzlingen, Switzerland. http://www.iagp.com

International Association of Marriage and Family Counselors. 6101 Stevenson Avenue, Alexandria, VA 22304. http://www.iamfconline.org

National Association of Social Workers. 750 First Street, NE, Suite 800, Washington, DC 20002. https://www.socialworkers.org

APPENDIX B

Codes of Ethics and Standards of Professional Practice

American Association for Marriage and Family Therapy. (2015). *Code of ethics.* Retrieved from https://www.aamft.org/iMIS15/AAMFT/Content/Legal_Ethics/Code_of_Ethics.aspx

American Counseling Association. (2014). *Code of ethics.* Retrieved from http://www.counseling.org/resources/aca-code-of-ethics.pdf

American Mental Health Counselors Association. (2010). *American Mental Health Counselors Association code of ethics.* Retrieved from http://www.amhca.org/assets/content/AMHCA_Code_of_Ethics_11_30_09b1.pdf

American Psychological Association. (2010). *Ethical principles of psychologists and code of conduct.* Retrieved from http://www.apa.org/ethics/code/principles.pdf

American School Counselors Association. (2016). ACA *ethical standards for school counselors.* Retrieved from http://www.schoolcounselor.org/school-counselors-members/legal-ethical

International Association for Group Psychotherapy and Group Processes. (IAGP) (2009). Retrieved from http://www.iagp.com/about/ethicalguidelines.htm

International Association of Marriage and Family Counselors. (2005). *IAMFC code of ethics.* Alexandria, VA: Author.

National Association of Social Workers. (2008). *Code of ethics of the National Association of Social Workers.* Retrieved from https://www.socialworkers.org/pubs/code/code.asp

INDEX